D1037887

**Presented
to**

_____

by

_____

on

_____

The New Testament

IN MODERN SPEECH

RICHARD FRANCIS WEYMOUTH
M.A., D. Lit. (London)

KENNETH
COPELAND
PUBLICATIONS

Unless otherwise indicated, all Scripture quotations are taken from the *King James Version* of the Bibl

The New Testament in Modern Speech
ISBN 1-57562-025-1   21-1003

10 09 08 07 06 05 04 03 02   10 9 8 7 6 5 4 3 2

Kenneth Copeland Publications
Fort Worth, Texas 76192-0001

For more information about Kenneth Copeland Ministries call
1-800-600-7395 or visit www.kcm.org.

LXX. Throughout the Weymouth translation, you will see references to the *Septuagint,* the oldest and most celebrated Greek translation of the Hebrew scriptures. Commonly designated LXX, the name refers to the seventy translators reputed to have translated the Hebrew scriptures into Greek during the time of Ptolemy Philadelphus, 285-247 B.C. This version of the scriptures, widely used in the Greek-speaking culture of Jesus' day, is the source of many of the Old Testament passages quoted by New Testament writers.

[ ] Throughout the text, you will see definitions in brackets following certain words. These have been added by Kenneth Copeland Publications to clarify uncommon or unfamiliar terms.

KENNETH
COPELAND
PUBLICATIONS

Contents

The New Testament

Richard Francis Weymouth

1822-1902

Richard Francis Weymouth, noted linguist and New Testament scholar, was born at Devonport, near Plymouth in southwestern England, on October 26, 1822. The only son of Commander Richard Weymouth, R.N., and his wife, Ann Sprague, Weymouth was educated at a private school. After two years in France, he enrolled, in 1843, at University College, London, where he majored in classics, receiving his B.A. in 1846 and his M.A. in 1849.

Career as an Educator

After graduation from college, Weymouth began a career as an educator, first acting as assistant to educational expert Joseph Payne at the Mansion House School, Leatherhead, and then conducting a successful private school—Portland Grammar School at Plymouth. In 1868, he was the first recipient of the degree of doctor of literature at London University, after a severe examination in Anglo-Saxon, Icelandic, French and English language and literature. The requirements for this degree were so difficult that the degree was not conferred again until 1879.

In 1869, Weymouth, who had been elected fellow of University College, London, was appointed headmaster of Mill Hill School. Mill Hill had been founded by nonconformists and was now reorganized as a public school. A zealous Baptist, Weymouth was long a deacon of the George Street Baptist Chapel, Plymouth, and was subsequently a member of the committee of the Essex Baptist Union.

At Mill Hill, Weymouth proved to be a successful teacher and organizer as well as a strict disciplinarian, and the enrollment of the school increased under his leadership. Among his assistants was Sir James A. H. Murray, editor of *The New English Dictionary [The Oxford English Dictionary]*. Weymouth retired with a pension in July 1886.

Study of Linguistics

During his years as an educator, Weymouth made a number of contributions to the study of linguistics. He joined the Philological Society in 1851, and published many papers in its *Transactions*. Among these were a paper on "Early English Pronunciation, with Especial Reference to Chaucer" (1874), which is now generally accepted by scholars as definitive. He edited the society's edition of Bishop Grosseteste's "Castell of Loue" [Castle of Love] (1864), and translated Cynewulf's "Elene" into modern English (1888).

Weymouth also published papers in the *Journal of Classical and Sacred Philology* and the *Cambridge Journal of Philology*. In 1885, as president of the Devonshire Association, he read an address on "The Devonshire Dialect: A Study in Comparative Grammar," an early attempt to treat English dialect in the light of modern philology [linguistics].

Biblical Study

After his retirement from Mill Hill School, Weymouth devoted himself chiefly to biblical study. He had already spent many years on textual criticism of the Greek Testament, and in 1886, he published *The Resultant Greek Testament,* which exhibited the text representing the greatest measure of agreement among the leading nineteenth century editors. This book is still a useful edition of the Greek Testament.

Weymouth then turned to translating the Greek text into modern English and produced *The New Testament in Modern Speech*. He died before it could be published, and it was edited and seen through the press by Ernest Hampden-Cook, a Congregational minister who was also a biblical translator. It was published in 1903 and was frequently reprinted. In 1924, it was thoroughly revised by Professor James Alexander Robertson of Aberdeen.

As a translator, Weymouth's only intention was to render the New Testament into dignified modern English with no theological or ecclesiastical bias. While he had no desire that his version would take the place of the *King James Version* or the *Revised Version*, he did hope that *The New Testament in Modern Speech* might point the way one day to a new English translation of the Bible which would replace both these versions.

Weymouth was married twice. In 1852, he married Louisa Sarah Marten, daughter of Robert Marten, secretary of the Vauxhall Bridge Company of Denmark Hill. They had six children, three sons and three daughters. After her death in 1891, he married Louisa Salter of Watford, who survived him.

Weymouth died on December 27, 1902, and is buried at Brentwood, England. A portrait of him hangs in the hall of Mill Hill School, and a memorial window is in the chapel.

THE GOSPEL ACCORDING TO ST. MATTHEW

1 The genealogy of Jesus Christ, the son of David, the son of Abraham. 1

Abraham was the father of Isaac; Isaac of Jacob; Jacob 2 of Judah and his brothers. Judah was the father (by Tamar) 3 of Perez and Zerah; Perez of Hezron; Hezron of Ram; Ram of 4 Amminadab; Amminadab of Nahshon; Nahshon of Salmon; Salmon (by Rahab) of Boaz; Boaz (by Ruth) of Obed; Obed of 5 Jesse; Jesse of David—the king. 6

David (by Uriah's widow) was the father of Solomon; Solomon of Rehoboam; Rehoboam of Abijah; Abijah of Asa; 7 Asa of Jehoshaphat; Jehoshaphat of Jehoram; Jehoram of 8 Uzziah; Uzziah of Jotham; Jotham of Ahaz; Ahaz of Hezekiah; 9 Hezekiah of Manasseh; Manasseh of Amon; Amon of Josiah; 10 Josiah of Jeconiah and his brothers at the period of the 11 removal to Babylon.

After the removal to Babylon Jeconiah had a son Shealtiel; 12 Shealtiel was the father of Zerubbabel; Zerubbabel of Abiud; 13 Abiud of Eliakim; Eliakim of Azor; Azor of Zadok; Zadok of 14 Achim; Achim of Eliud; Eliud of Eleazar; Eleazar of Matthan; 15 Matthan of Jacob; and Jacob of Joseph the husband of Mary, 16 who was the mother of JESUS who is called CHRIST.

There are therefore, in all, fourteen generations from 17 Abraham to David; fourteen from David to the removal to Babylon; and fourteen from the removal to Babylon to the Christ.

The circumstances of the birth of Jesus Christ were these. 18 After his mother Mary was betrothed to Joseph, before they were united in marriage, she was found to be with child

through the Holy Spirit. Now Joseph her husband, being a 19
just man and unwilling publicly to disgrace her, determined
to release her privately from the betrothal. But while he was 20
contemplating this step, an angel of the Lord appeared to
him in a dream and said,

"Joseph, son of David, do not be afraid to bring home your
wife Mary, for she is with child through the Holy Spirit. She 21
will give birth to a Son, and you shall call Him JESUS, for He
shall save His People from their sins."

All this took place in fulfillment of what the Lord had spo- 22
ken through the prophet,

"MARK! [look/take note] THE MAIDEN WILL BE WITH 23
CHILD AND WILL GIVE BIRTH TO A SON,
AND THEY WILL GIVE HIM THE NAME IMMANUEL"
(Isaiah 7:14)—a word which signifies "GOD WITH US"
(Isaiah 8:8, 10).

When Joseph awoke, he did as the angel of the Lord had 24
commanded, and brought home his wife, but did not live 25
with her as a husband until she had given birth to a son; and
he called the child JESUS.

2 Now after the birth of Jesus, which took place at 1
Bethlehem in Judaea in the reign of King Herod, there
came to Jerusalem certain Magi from the east, inquiring, 2

"Where is the newly born king of the Jews? For we saw his
star when it rose, and have come here to do him homage."

Reports of this soon reached the king, and greatly agitated 3
not only him but all the people of Jerusalem. So he assem- 4
bled all the high priests and scribes of the people, and anxiously asked them where the Christ was to be born.

"At Bethlehem in Judaea," they replied; "for so it stands 5
written in the words of the prophet,

"'AND THOU, BETHLEHEM IN THE LAND OF JUDAH,   6
BY NO MEANS THE LEAST HONORABLE ART THOU
AMONG PRINCELY PLACES IN JUDAH!
FOR FROM THEE SHALL COME A PRINCE—
ONE WHO SHALL BE THE SHEPHERD OF MY PEOPLE
ISRAEL'" (Micah 5:2).

Thereupon Herod sent privately for the Magi and ascer-   7
tained from them the exact time of the star's appearing. He   8
then directed them to go to Bethlehem, adding,

"Go and make careful inquiry about the child, and when
you have found him, bring me word, that I too may come
and do him homage."

After hearing what the king said, they went away, while,   9
strange to say, the star they had seen when it rose led them
on until it reached and stood over the place where the babe
was. When they saw the star, the sight filled them with   10
intense joy. So they entered the house; and when they saw   11
the babe with His mother Mary, they prostrated themselves
and did Him homage, and opening their treasure-chests
offered gifts to Him—gold, frankincense, and myrrh. And   12
then, being forbidden by God in a dream to return to Herod,
they went back to their own country by a different route.

When they were gone, an angel of the Lord appeared to   13
Joseph in a dream and said,

"Rise: take the babe and His mother and escape to Egypt,
and remain there till I bring you word. For Herod is about to
make search for the child in order to destroy Him."

And Joseph awoke and took the babe and His mother by   14
night and departed into Egypt. There he remained till Herod's   15
death, that what the Lord had said through the prophet
might be fulfilled,

"OUT OF EGYPT I CALLED MY SON" (Hosea 11:1).

Then Herod, finding that the Magi had trifled with him,   16 was furious, and sent and massacred all the boys under two years of age in Bethlehem and all its neighborhood, having in view the date he had so carefully ascertained from the Magi. Then were these words, spoken by the prophet 17 Jeremiah, fulfilled,

"A CRY WAS HEARD IN RAMAH, 18
WAILING AND BITTER LAMENTATION:
IT WAS RACHEL BEWAILING HER CHILDREN,
AND SHE REFUSED TO BE COMFORTED, BECAUSE THEY WERE NO MORE" (Jeremiah 31:15).

But after Herod's death an angel of the Lord appeared in a 19 dream to Joseph in Egypt, and said to him, 20

"Rise, and take the child and His mother, and go to the land of Israel, for those who were seeking the child's life are dead."

And he awoke and took the child and His mother and came 21 to the land of Israel. But hearing that Archelaus had succeeded 22 his father Herod on the throne of Judaea, he was afraid to go there; and being instructed by God in a dream he withdrew into Galilee, and settled in a town called Nazareth, in order that 23 these words spoken through the prophets might be fulfilled,

"HE SHALL BE CALLED A NAZARENE."

3 About this time John the Baptist made his appearance, 1 preaching in the desert of Judaea. "Repent," he said, "for 2 the Kingdom of heaven is now close at hand."

He it is who was spoken of through the prophet Isaiah 3 when he said,

"THE VOICE OF ONE CRYING ALOUD:
'IN THE DESERT PREPARE A ROAD FOR THE LORD:
MAKE HIS HIGHWAYS STRAIGHT'" (Isaiah 40:3).

This man John wore clothing of camel's hair, and a leather 4 girdle; and he lived upon locusts and wild honey.

Large numbers of people at that time went out to him— 5 people from Jerusalem and from all Judaea, and from the whole of the Jordan valley—and were baptized by him in the 6 Jordan, making open confession of their sins.

But when he saw many of the Pharisees and Sadducees 7 coming for his baptism, he exclaimed,

"O brood of vipers, who has warned you to flee from the coming wrath? Let your lives then prove your change of 8 heart; and do not imagine that you can say to yourselves, 9 'We have Abraham as our forefather,' for I tell you that God can raise up descendants for Abraham from these stones. And already the ax is lying at the root of the trees, so that 10 every tree which does not yield good fruit is hewn down and thrown into the fire. I indeed am baptizing you in water for 11 repentance; but He who is coming after me is mightier than I: His sandals I am not worthy to carry; He will baptize you in the Holy Spirit and in fire. His winnowing-shovel is in 12 His hand, and He will make a thorough clearance of His threshing-floor, gathering His wheat into the barn, but burning up the chaff in unquenchable fire."

Just at that time Jesus, coming from Galilee to the Jordan, 13 presents Himself to John to be baptized by him. John protested. 14

"It is I," he said, "who have need to be baptized by you, and do you come to me?"

"Let it be so on this occasion," Jesus replied; "for so we 15 ought to fulfill every religious duty."

Then he consented; and Jesus was baptized, and immedi- 16 ately went up from the water. At that moment the heavens opened, and He saw the Spirit of God descending like a dove and alighting upon Him, while a voice came from 17 heaven, saying,

"This is My Son, the Beloved, in whom is My delight."

4 At that time Jesus was led up by the Spirit into the desert 1
in order to be tempted by the devil. And He fasted for 2
forty days and nights; and after that He suffered from hunger.

So the Tempter came and said to Him: 3

"If you are the Son of God, command these stones to turn
into loaves."

"It is written," replied Jesus, "'IT IS NOT ON BREAD ALONE 4
THAT A MAN SHALL LIVE, BUT ON EVERY WORD THAT PRO-
CEEDS FROM THE MOUTH OF GOD'" (Deuteronomy 8:3).

Then the devil took Him to the holy city and set Him on 5
the summit of the Temple, and said, 6

"If you are God's Son, throw yourself down; for it is written,
"'TO HIS ANGELS HE WILL GIVE ORDERS CONCERN-
ING THEE,
AND ON THEIR HANDS THEY SHALL BEAR THEE UP,
LEST AT ANY MOMENT THOU SHOULDST STRIKE THY
FOOT AGAINST A STONE'" (Psalm 91:11-12).

"Again it is written," replied Jesus, "'THOU SHALT NOT PUT 7
THE LORD THY GOD TO THE PROOF'" (Deuteronomy 6:16).

Then the devil took Him to the top of an exceedingly high 8
mountain, from which he showed Him all the kingdoms of
the world and their splendor, and said to Him, 9

"All this I will give you, if you will kneel down and do
me homage."

"Be gone, Satan!" Jesus replied; "for it is written, 'TO 10
THE LORD THY GOD THOU SHALT DO HOMAGE, AND
TO HIM ALONE SHALT THOU RENDER WORSHIP'"
(Deuteronomy 6:13).

Thereupon the devil left Him, and angels came and minis- 11
tered to Him.

Now when Jesus heard that John was thrown into prison, 12
He withdrew to Galilee, and leaving Nazareth He went and 13
settled in Capernaum, a town by the lake on the frontiers of

Zebulun and Naphtali, in order that these words, spoken 14
through the prophet Isaiah, might be fulfilled,

"ZEBULUN'S LAND AND NAPHTALI'S LAND, 15
THE ROAD OF THE LAKE, THE COUNTRY BEYOND
THE JORDAN;
GALILEE OF THE NATIONS!
THE PEOPLE WHO WERE DWELLING IN DARKNESS 16
HAVE SEEN A BRILLIANT LIGHT;
AND ON THOSE WHO WERE DWELLING IN THE
REGION OF THE SHADOW OF DEATH
LIGHT HAS DAWNED" (Isaiah 9:1-2).

From that time Jesus began to preach. 17

"Repent," He said, "for the Kingdom of heaven is close
at hand."

And walking along the shore of the lake of Galilee He saw 18
two brothers—Simon called Peter and his brother Andrew—
throwing a drag-net into the lake; for they were fishers. And 19
He said to them,

"Come and follow me, and I will make you fishers of men."

So they immediately left their nets and followed Him. As 20
He went farther on, He saw two other brothers, James the 21
son of Zebedee and his brother John, in their boat with their
father Zebedee mending their nets; and He called them. And 22
they at once left the boat and their father, and followed Him.

Then Jesus traveled through all Galilee, teaching in their 23
synagogues and proclaiming the gospel of the Kingdom, and
curing every kind of disease and infirmity among the people.
So His fame spread through all Syria; and they brought all 24
sick persons to Him, who were suffering from various diseases and pains—demoniacs, epileptics, paralytics; and He
cured them. And great crowds followed Him, coming from 25
Galilee, from the Ten Towns, from Jerusalem, from Judaea,
and from beyond the Jordan.

5 Seeing the multitude of people, Jesus went up the hill. 1
There He seated Himself, and when His disciples came
to Him, He proceeded to teach them, and said: 2

"Blessed are the poor in spirit, for to them belongs the 3
Kingdom of heaven.

"Blessed are the mourners, for they shall be comforted. 4

"Blessed are the meek, for they shall inherit the earth. 5

"Blessed are those who hunger and thirst for righteous- 6
ness, for they shall be completely satisfied.

"Blessed are the compassionate, for they shall receive 7
compassion.

"Blessed are the pure in heart, for they shall see God. 8

"Blessed are the peacemakers, for they shall be acknowl- 9
edged as sons of God.

"Blessed are those who have borne persecution in the 10
cause of righteousness, for to them belongs the Kingdom
of heaven.

"Blessed are you when they have insulted and persecuted 11
you, and have said every cruel thing about you falsely for my
sake. Be joyful and triumphant, because your reward is great 12
in heaven; for so were the prophets before you persecuted.

"You are the salt of the earth; but if salt has become taste- 13
less, in what way can it regain its saltiness? It is no longer
good for anything but to be thrown away and trodden on by
the passers by. You are the light of the world; a town cannot 14
be hid if built on a hill-top. Nor is a lamp lighted to be put 15
under the bushel measure, but on the lampstand; and then
it gives light to all in the house. Just so let your light shine 16
before all men, in order that they may see your good deeds
and may give glory to your Father who is in heaven.

"Do not for a moment suppose that I have come to annul 17
the Law or the prophets: I have not come to annul them but
to give them their completion. In truth I tell you that until 18

heaven and earth pass away, not the smallest letter, not a particle shall pass away from the Law until all has taken place. Whoever therefore breaks one of the smallest of these 19 commandments and teaches others to do so, will be called the least in the Kingdom of heaven; but whoever practices them and teaches them, will be acknowledged as great in the Kingdom of heaven. For I assure you that unless your right- 20 eousness greatly surpasses that of the scribes and the Pharisees, you will certainly not find entrance into the Kingdom of heaven.

"You have heard that it was said to the ancients, 'THOU 21 SHALT NOT COMMIT MURDER' (Exodus 20:13), and who- ever commits murder shall be answerable to the magistrate. But I say to you that every one who gets angry with his 22 brother shall be answerable to the magistrate; that whoever says to his brother 'Raca' shall be answerable to the Sanhedrin; and that whoever says, 'You fool!' shall be liable to the Gehenna of fire. If therefore, when you are offering your 23 gift upon the altar, you remember that your brother has a grievance against you, leave your gift there before the altar, 24 and go and make friends with your brother first, and then return and proceed to offer your gift. Come to terms without 25 delay with your opponent while you are yet with him on the way to the court; for fear he should hand you over to the magistrate, and the magistrate should give you in custody to the officer and you be thrown into prison. I solemnly tell you 26 that you will certainly not be released till you have paid the very last farthing.

"You have heard that it was said, 'THOU SHALT NOT 27 COMMIT ADULTERY' (Exodus 20:14). But I tell you that 28 whoever looks at a woman and cherishes lustful thoughts has already in his heart committed adultery with her. If 29 therefore your right eye is to cause your fall, tear it out and away with it; it is better for you that one member should be destroyed rather than that your whole body should be thrown into Gehenna. And if your right hand is to cause your fall, cut it off and away with it; it is better for you that one member should be destroyed rather than that your whole body should go into Gehenna. 30

"It was also said, 'IF ANY MAN PUTS AWAY HIS WIFE, LET HIM GIVE HER A WRITTEN NOTICE OF DIVORCE' (Deuteronomy 24:1). But I tell you that every man who puts away his wife, except on the ground of unchastity, causes her to commit adultery, and whoever marries her when so divorced commits adultery. 31 32

"Again, you have heard that it was said to the ancients, 'THOU SHALT NOT SWEAR FALSELY (Exodus 20:7), BUT SHALT PERFORM THY VOWS TO THE LORD' (Numbers 30:2; Deuteronomy 23:21). But I tell you not to swear at all; either by heaven, for it is God's throne; or by the earth, for it is the footstool under His feet; or by Jerusalem, for it is the city of the great King. And do not swear by your head, for you cannot make one hair white or black. But let your language be, 'Yes, yes,' or 'No, no.' Anything in excess of this comes from the Evil One. 33 34 35 36 37

"You have heard that it was said, 'EYE FOR EYE, TOOTH FOR TOOTH' (Exodus 21:24). But I tell you not to resist a wicked man: if any one strikes you on the right cheek, turn the other to him as well. If any one wishes to go to law with you and to deprive you of your under-garment, let him take your outer one also. And if any one compels you to convey a burden one mile, go with him two. To him who asks, give: from him who would borrow, turn not away. 38 39 40 41 42

"You have heard that it was said, 'THOU SHALT LOVE THY NEIGHBOR (Leviticus 19:18) and hate thine enemy.' But I tell you to love your enemies, and pray for your persecutors; 43 44

that so you may become sons of your Father in heaven; for 45
He causes His sun to rise on the wicked as well as the good,
and sends rain upon those who do right and those who do
wrong. For if you love only those who love you, what reward 46
have you earned? Do not even the tax-gatherers do that? And 47
if you salute only your brethren, are you doing anything
remarkable? Do not even the heathen do the same? You, 48
however, are to be perfect, as your heavenly Father
is perfect.

6 "Beware of doing your good actions in the sight of men, 1
to attract their gaze; if you do, there is no reward for you
with your Father who is in heaven.

"When you give in charity, do not blow a trumpet before 2
you as the hypocrites do in the synagogues and streets in
order that their praises may be sung by men. I solemnly tell
you that they have received in full their reward. But when you 3
are giving in charity, let not your left hand perceive what your
right hand is doing, that your charities may be in secret; and 4
your Father—He who sees in secret—will recompense you.

"And when praying, you must not be like the hypocrites. 5
They are fond of standing and praying in the synagogues
or at the corners of the wider streets, in order that men may
see them. I solemnly tell you that they have received in full
their reward. But you, whenever you pray, go into your 6
own room and shut the door: then pray to your Father who
is in secret, and your Father—He who sees in secret—will
recompense you.

"And when praying, do not use needless repetitions as the 7
heathen do, for they expect to be listened to because of their
multitude of words. Do not, then, imitate them; for your 8
Father knows what things you need before ever you ask Him.

"In this manner therefore pray: 'Our Father in heaven, may 9
Thy name be kept holy; let Thy Kingdom come; let Thy will be 10
done, as in heaven so on earth; give us to-day our bread for the 11
day; and forgive us our shortcomings, as we also have forgiven 12
those who have failed in their duty towards us; and bring us 13
not into temptation, but rescue us from the Evil One.'

"For if you forgive others their offenses, your heavenly 14
Father will forgive you also; but if you do not forgive others 15
their offenses, neither will your Father forgive yours.

"When you fast, do not assume gloomy looks as the hypo- 16
crites do; for they disfigure their faces that it may be evident
to men that they are fasting. I tell you in truth that they have
received in full their reward. But, whenever you fast, pour 17
perfume on your hair and wash your face, that it may not be 18
apparent to men that you are fasting, but to your Father who
is in secret; and your Father—He who sees in secret—will
recompense you.

"Do not lay up stores of wealth for yourselves on earth, 19
where the moth and wear-and-tear destroy, and where
thieves break in and steal. But lay up wealth for yourselves in 20
heaven, where neither the moth nor wear-and-tear destroys,
and where thieves do not break in and steal. For where your 21
wealth is, there also will your heart be.

"The eye is the lamp of the body. If then your eye is sound, 22
your whole body will be lighted up; but if your eye is dis- 23
eased, your whole body will be dark. If then the very light
within you is darkness, how dense must the darkness be!

"No man can serve two masters; for either he will hate one 24
and love the other, or he will attach himself to one and think
lightly of the other. You cannot be servants both of God and
of money. For this reason I say to you do not be anxious 25
about your lives, as to what you are to eat or what to drink,
nor about your bodies, as to what clothes you are to put on.

Is not life more precious than food, and the body than clothing? Look at the birds which fly in the air: they do not sow or 26
reap or store up in barns, but your heavenly Father feeds
them: are not you of much greater value than they? Which of 27
you is able by anxious thought to add a single foot to his
height? And why be anxious about clothing? Observe well 28
the wild lilies, how they grow. They neither toil nor spin, and 29
yet I tell you that not even Solomon in all his magnificence
was arrayed like one of these. And if God so clothes the veg- 30
etation in the fields that blooms to-day and to-morrow is
feeding the oven, will He not much more clothe you, you
men of little faith? Do not be anxious, therefore, asking 31
'What shall we eat?' or 'What shall we drink?' or 'What shall
we wear?' For the Gentiles seek all these things; your heav- 32
enly Father knows that you need them all. But seek first His 33
Kingdom and righteousness, and these things shall all be
given you in addition. Do not be anxious, therefore, about 34
to-morrow, for to-morrow will bring its own anxieties.
Enough for each day is its own trouble.

7 "Judge not, that you may not be judged; for your 1
own judgment will be dealt—and your own measure 2
accorded—to yourselves. And why look at the splinter in 3
your brother's eye, and not notice the beam of timber which
is in your own eye? Or how say to your brother, 'Allow me to 4
take the splinter out of your eye,' while the beam is in your
own eye? Hypocrite, first take the beam out of your own eye, 5
and then you will see clearly how to remove the splinter from
your brother's eye.

"Give not that which is holy to the dogs, nor throw your 6
pearls to the swine; otherwise the swine will trample them
under their feet and the dogs turn and maul you.

"Ask, and it shall be given to you; seek, and you shall find; 7
knock, and the door shall be opened to you. For every one 8
who asks receives, he who seeks finds, and he who knocks
has the door opened to him. What man is there among you, 9
who if his son shall ask him for bread will offer him a stone?
Or if he shall ask him for a fish will offer him a snake? If you 10
then, imperfect as you are, know how to give good gifts to 11
your children, how much more will your Father in heaven
give good things to those who ask Him! Whatever, therefore, 12
you would have men do to you, do you also to them; for in
this the Law and the prophets are summed up.

"Enter by the narrow gate; for wide is the gate and broad 13
the road which leads to ruin, and many there are who enter
by it; because narrow is the gate and contracted the road 14
which leads to life, and few are those who find it.

"Beware of the false teachers—men who come to you in 15
sheep's fleeces, but beneath that disguise they are ravenous
wolves. By their fruits you will recognize them. Are grapes 16
gathered from thorns or figs from thistles? Every good tree 17
produces good fruit, but a worthless tree produces bad fruit.
A good tree cannot bear bad fruit, nor a worthless tree good 18
fruit. Every tree which does not yield good fruit is hewn 19
down and thrown into the fire. So by their fruits you will rec- 20
ognize them.

"Not every one who says to me, 'Lord, Lord,' will enter the 21
Kingdom of heaven, but only those who are obedient to my
Father who is in heaven. Many will say to me on that day, 22

"'Lord, Lord, have we not prophesied in Thy name, and in
Thy name expelled demons, and in Thy name performed
many mighty works?'

"And then I will tell them plainly, 23

"'I never knew you: be gone from me, you doers of
wickedness.'

14

"Every one who hears these my teachings and acts upon 24
them shall be likened to a wise man who built his house
upon rock; and the rain fell, the swollen torrents came, the 25
winds blew and beat against the house; yet it did not fall, for
its foundation was on rock. And every one who hears these 26
my teachings and does not act upon them shall be likened to
a fool who built his house upon sand. The rain fell, the 27
swollen torrents came, and the winds blew and beat against
the house, and it fell; and disastrous was the fall."

When Jesus had concluded this discourse, the crowds 28
were filled with amazement at His teaching, for He had been 29
teaching them as one who had authority, and not as their
scribes taught.

8 Upon descending from the hill country He was followed 1
by immense crowds. And a leper came to Him, and 2
throwing himself at His feet, said,

"Master, if only you are willing, you are able to cleanse me."

So Jesus put out His hand and touched him, and said, 3

"I am willing: be cleansed."

Instantly he was cleansed from his leprosy; and Jesus said 4
to him,

"Be careful to tell no one, but go and show yourself to the
priest, and offer the gift which Moses appointed as evidence
for them" (Leviticus 14:4).

After His entry into Capernaum a captain came to Him, 5
and entreated Him.

"Sir," he said, "my servant at home is lying ill with paraly- 6
sis, and is suffering great pain."

"I will come and cure him," said Jesus. 7

"Sir," replied the captain, "I am not a fit person to receive 8
you under my roof: merely say the word, and my servant

will be cured. For I myself am also under authority, and 9
have soldiers under me. To one I say 'Go,' and he goes, to
another, 'Come,' and he comes, and to my slave 'Do this or
that,' and he does it."

Jesus listened to this reply, and was astonished, and said to 10
the people following Him,

"I solemnly tell you that in no Israelite have I found faith
as great as this. And I tell you that many will come from the 11
east and from the west and will take their seats with
Abraham, Isaac, and Jacob in the Kingdom of heaven, while 12
the natural heirs of the Kingdom will be driven out into the
darkness outside: there will be the weeping and the gnashing
of teeth."

And Jesus said to the captain, 13

"Go, and just as you have believed, so be it for you."

And the servant recovered precisely at that time.

After this Jesus went to the house of Peter, whose mother-in- 14
law He found ill in bed with fever. He touched her hand and 15
the fever left her: and then she rose and waited upon Him.

In the evening many demoniacs were brought to Him, and 16
with a word He expelled the demons: and He cured all persons who were ill, that this prediction of the prophet Isaiah 17
might be fulfilled,

"HE TOOK ON HIM OUR WEAKNESSES, AND BORE THE
BURDEN OF OUR DISEASES" (Isaiah 53:4).

Seeing great crowds about Him, Jesus had given directions 18
to cross to the other side of the lake, when a scribe came and 19
said to Him,

"Teacher, I will follow you wherever you go."

"Foxes have holes," replied Jesus, "and birds have nests; 20
but the Son of Man has nowhere to lay His head."

Another of the disciples said to Him, 21

"Master, allow me first to go and bury my father."

"Follow me," said Jesus, "and leave the dead to bury their 22 own dead."

Then He went on board a boat, and His disciples followed 23 Him. And suddenly there arose a great storm on the lake, so 24 that the waves threatened to engulf the boat; but He was asleep. So they came and woke Him, crying, 25

"Master, save us; we are drowning!"

He replied, "Why are you so easily frightened, you men of 26 little faith?"

Then He rose and reproved the winds and the waves, and there was a perfect calm; and the men, filled with amaze- 27 ment, exclaimed,

"What kind of man is this? Why, the very winds and waves obey Him!"

On His arrival at the other side, the country of the 28 Gadarenes, there met Him two men possessed by demons, coming from among the tombs: they were so dangerously fierce that no one was able to pass that way. They cried aloud, 29

"What hast Thou to do with us, Thou Son of God? Hast Thou come here to torment us before the time?"

Now at some distance from them a vast herd of swine was 30 feeding. So the demons entreated Him. 31

"If Thou drivest us out," they said, "send us into the herd of swine."

"Go," He replied. 32

Then they came out from the men and went into the swine, whereupon the entire herd instantly rushed down the steep into the lake and perished in the water. The swine- 33 herds fled, and went and told the whole story in the town, including what had happened to the demoniacs. So at once 34 the whole population came out to meet Jesus; and when they saw Him, they besought Him to leave their district.

9 Accordingly He went on board, and crossing over came 1
to His own town.

Here they brought to Him a paralyzed man, lying on a bed. 2
Seeing their faith, Jesus said to the paralytic,

"Take courage, my child; your sins are pardoned."

"Such language is impious," said some of the scribes 3
to themselves.

Knowing their thoughts, Jesus said, 4

"Why are you cherishing evil thoughts in your hearts?
Why, which is easier?—to say 'Your sins are pardoned,' or to 5
say 'Rise up and walk'? But, to prove to you that the Son of 6
Man has authority on earth to pardon sins"—

He then says to the paralytic,

"Rise, and take up your bed and go home."

And he got up, and went home. And the crowd were 7
awestruck when they saw it, and ascribed the glory to God 8
for entrusting such power to men.

Passing on thence, Jesus saw a man called Matthew sitting 9
at the Toll Office, and said to him,

"Follow me."

And he arose and followed Him.

When Jesus was reclining at table, a large number of 10
tax-gatherers and sinners were of the party with Him and
His disciples. The Pharisees noticed this, and they inquired 11
of His disciples,

"Why does your Teacher eat with the tax-gatherers
and sinners?"

He heard the question and replied, 12

"It is not men in good health who require a doctor, but
those who are ill. But go and learn what this means, 'IT IS 13
MERCY THAT I DESIRE, NOT SACRIFICE' (Hosea 6:6); for I
did not come to call the righteous, but sinners."

At that time John's disciples came and asked Jesus, 14

"Why do we and the Pharisees fast, but your disciples do not?"

"Can the bridegroom's party mourn," He replied, "as long 15 as the bridegroom is with them? Other days will come when the bridegroom has been taken from them, and then they will fast. No one ever mends an old cloak with a patch of 16 unshrunk cloth. Otherwise, the added patch tears away some of the garment, and a worse hole is made. Nor do peo- 17 ple pour new wine into old wineskins. Otherwise, the skins split, the wine escapes, and the skins perish. But they put new wine into fresh skins, and both are saved."

While He was thus speaking, a ruler came up and bowing 18 profoundly said,

"My daughter is just dead; but come and put your hand upon her and she will return to life."

And Jesus rose and followed him, as did also His disciples. 19

Now a woman who for twelve years had been afflicted 20 with hemorrhage came behind Him and touched the tassel of His cloak; for she said to herself, 21

"If I but touch His cloak, I shall be cured."

And Jesus turned and saw her, and said, 22

"Take courage, daughter; your faith has cured you."

And the woman was restored to health from that moment.

Entering the ruler's house, Jesus saw the flute-players and 23 the crowd loudly wailing, and He said, 24

"Go out of the room; the little girl is not dead, but asleep."

And they laughed at Him. When, however, the place was 25 cleared of the crowd, Jesus went in, and on His taking the little girl by the hand, she rose up. And the report of this 26 spread throughout all that district.

As Jesus passed on, two blind men followed Him, shouting 27 and saying,

"Pity us, Son of David."

And when He had gone indoors, they came to Him. 28

"Do you believe that I can do this?" He asked them.

"Yes, Master," they replied.

So He touched their eyes and said, 29

"According to your faith let it be to you."

Then their eyes were opened. And assuming a stern tone 30
Jesus said to them,

"Be careful to let no one know."

But they went out and spread His fame in all that district. 31

And as they were leaving His presence a dumb demoniac 32
was brought to Him. When the demon was expelled, the dumb 33
man could speak. And the crowds exclaimed in astonishment,

"Never was such a thing seen in Israel." But the Pharisees 34
maintained,

"It is by the power of the Prince of the demons that he
drives out the demons."

And Jesus went round all the towns and villages, teaching 35
in their synagogues and proclaiming the gospel of the Kingdom, and curing every kind of disease and infirmity. And 36
when He saw the crowds, He was touched with pity for them,
because they were distracted and dejected, like sheep without a shepherd.

Then He said to His disciples, 37

"The harvest is abundant, but the reapers are few; there- 38
fore entreat the owner of the harvest to send out reapers into
His fields."

10 Then He called to Him His twelve disciples and gave 1
them authority to drive out foul spirits, and to cure
every kind of disease and infirmity.

Now the names of the twelve apostles were these: first, 2
Simon called Peter, and his brother Andrew; James the son of

Zebedee, and his brother John; Philip and Bartholomew, 3
Thomas and Matthew the tax-gatherer, James the son of
Alphaeus, and Thaddaeus, Simon the Cananaean, and Judas 4
Iscariot, who also betrayed Him.

These twelve Jesus sent on a mission, after giving them 5
their instructions:

"Go not," He said, "among the Gentiles, and enter no
Samaritan town; but, instead of that, go to the lost sheep of 6
Israel's race. And as you go, preach and say, 'The Kingdom of 7
heaven is close at hand.' Cure the sick, raise the dead to life, 8
cleanse lepers, drive out demons: you have received without
payment, give without payment.

"Provide no gold, nor silver nor copper to carry in your 9
girdles; no bag for your journey, nor extra inner garment, nor 10
shoes, nor stick; for the laborer deserves his food.

"Whatever town or village you enter, inquire who is a 11
deserving man; and make his house your home till you leave
the place. When you enter the house, salute it; and if the 12
house deserves it, let your peace come upon it; if not, let 13
your peace return to you. And whoever refuses to receive you 14
or even to listen to your message, as you leave that house or
town, shake off the very dust that is on your feet. I solemnly 15
tell you that it will be more endurable for the land of Sodom
and Gomorrah on the day of judgment than for that town.

"Remember it is I who am sending you out, as sheep into 16
the midst of wolves; prove yourselves therefore as sagacious
[wise] as serpents, and as innocent as doves. But beware 17
of men; for they will deliver you up to appear before
Sanhedrins, and will flog you in their synagogues; and you 18
will even be put on trial before governors and kings for my
sake, to bear witness to them and to the Gentiles. But when 19
they have delivered you up, have no anxiety as to how you
shall speak or what you shall say; for at that very time it shall

be given you what to say; for it is not you who will speak: it 20
will be the Spirit of your Father speaking through you.
Brother will betray brother to death, and father betray child; 21
and children will rise against their own parents and will put
them to death. And you will be objects of universal hatred 22
because you are called by my name; but he who stands firm
to the end shall be saved. Whenever they persecute you in 23
one town, escape to the next; for I tell you in truth that you
will not have gone the round of all the towns of Israel before
the Son of Man comes.

"The learner is not superior to his teacher, nor the servant 24
to his master. Enough for the learner to be on a level with his 25
teacher, and for the servant to be on a level with his master. If
they have called the master of the house Beelzebul, how
much more will they slander his servants. Fear them not, 26
however; there is nothing veiled which will not be uncovered, nor secret which will not become known. What I tell 27
you in the dark, speak in daylight; and what is whispered
into your ear, proclaim upon the roofs of the houses.

"And do not fear those who kill the body, but cannot kill 28
the soul; rather fear Him who is able to destroy both soul and
body in Gehenna. Do not two sparrows sell for a half penny? 29
Yet not one of them falls to the ground without your Father's
leave. But as for you, the very hairs on your heads are all 30
numbered. Away then with fear; you are more precious than 31
a multitude of sparrows.

"Every man who acknowledges me before men I also will 32
acknowledge before my Father who is in heaven. But who- 33
ever disowns me before men I also will disown before my
Father who is in heaven.

"Do not suppose that I came to bring peace to the earth: 34
I did not come to bring peace, but a sword. For I came to set 35
a man against his father, A DAUGHTER AGAINST HER

MOTHER, AND A DAUGHTER-IN-LAW AGAINST HER
MOTHER-IN-LAW; AND A MAN'S OWN FAMILY WILL BE 36
HIS FOES (Micah 7:6). Any one who loves father or mother 37
more than me is not worthy of me, and any one who loves
son or daughter more than me is not worthy of me; and any 38
one who does not take up his cross and follow where I lead is
not worthy of me. He who finds his life shall lose it, and he 39
who loses his life for my sake shall find it.

"Whoever receives you receives me, and whoever receives 40
me receives Him who sent me. Every one who receives a 41
prophet because he is a prophet will receive a prophet's
reward, and every one who receives a righteous man
because he is a righteous man will receive a righteous man's
reward. And whoever gives one of these little ones even a cup 42
of cold water to drink because he is a disciple, I solemnly tell
you that he will not lose his reward."

11 When Jesus had concluded His instructions to His 1
twelve disciples, He left in order to teach and to proclaim His message in the neighboring towns.

Now John had heard in prison about the Christ's deeds, 2
and he sent a message by his disciples and inquired of Him: 3

"Are you the Coming One, or is it some one else that we are
to expect?"

"Go and report to John what you see and hear," replied 4
Jesus; "blind men receive sight, and cripples walk; lepers are 5
cleansed, and the deaf hear; the dead are raised to life, and
the poor have the gospel proclaimed to them. Blessed is 6
every one who does not take offense at my claims."

When the messengers had taken their leave, Jesus proceeded 7
to say to the multitude concerning John,

"What did you go out to the desert to gaze at? A reed

23

waving in the wind? But what did you go out to see? A man 8
finely dressed? Those who wear fine clothes are to be found
in kings' palaces. But why did you go? To see a prophet? Yes, 9
I tell you, and far more than a prophet. This is he of whom it 10
is written,

"'SEE, I AM SENDING MY MESSENGER BEFORE THY FACE,
AND HE SHALL MAKE THY ROAD READY BEFORE
THEE' (Malachi 3:1).

"I solemnly tell you that among all of woman born no 11
greater has ever been raised up than John the Baptist; yet the
least in the Kingdom of heaven is greater than he. But from 12
the time of John the Baptist till now, the Kingdom of heaven
has been enduring violent assault, and the violent have been
seizing it by force. For all the prophets and the Law taught 13
until John. And (if you are willing to receive it) he is the Elijah 14
who was to come. Listen, every one who has ears! 15

"To what shall I compare the present generation? It is like 16
children sitting in the open places, who call to their playmates.

"'We have played the flute to you,' they say, 'and you have 17
not danced: we have sung dirges, and you have not beaten
your breasts.'

"For John came neither eating nor drinking, and they say, 18
'He has a demon.' The Son of Man came eating and drinking, 19
and they exclaim, 'See this man!—given to gluttony and
tippling [drinking alcohol habitually], a friend of tax-gatherers
and sinners!' And yet Wisdom is vindicated by her actions."

Then began He to upbraid the towns where His many 20
mighty works had been done—because they had not repented.

"Woe to thee, Chorazin!" He cried. "Woe to thee, Bethsaida! 21
For had the mighty works been done in Tyre and Sidon which
have been done in both of you, they would long ere [before]
now have repented in sackcloth and ashes. Only I tell you 22
that it will be more endurable for Tyre and Sidon on the day

of judgment than for you. And thou, Capernaum, shalt thou 23
be exalted even to heaven? Even to Hades shalt thou descend.
For had the mighty works been done in Sodom which have
been done in thee, that city would have survived until now. I 24
tell you all, that it will be more endurable for the land of
Sodom on the day of judgment than for thee."

About that time Jesus exclaimed, 25

"I praise Thee, Father, Lord of heaven and of earth, that
Thou hast hidden these things from sages and men of discernment, and hast unveiled them to babes. Yes, Father, for 26
such has been Thy gracious will.

"All things have been handed over to me by my Father, and 27
no one fully knows the Son except the Father, nor does any
one fully know the Father except the Son and all to whom the
Son chooses to reveal Him.

"Come to me, all you toiling and burdened ones, and I will 28
give you rest. Take my yoke upon you and learn from me; for 29
I am gentle and lowly in heart, and you shall find rest for
your souls. For my yoke is easy, and my burden is light." 30

12 About that time Jesus passed on the sabbath through 1
the wheat fields; and His disciples became hungry,
and began to gather ears of wheat and eat them. But the 2
Pharisees saw it and said to Him,

"Look! your disciples are doing what the Law forbids them
to do on the sabbath."

"Have you never read," He replied, "what David did when 3
he and his men were hungry? how he entered the house of 4
God and ate the Showbread, which it was not lawful for him
or his men but only for the priests to eat (1 Samuel 21:1-6)?
And have you not read in the Law how on the sabbath the 5
priests in the Temple break the sabbath without incurring

guilt? But I tell you that there is here One who is greater than 6
the Temple. And if you knew what this means, 'IT IS MERCY 7
I DESIRE, NOT SACRIFICE' (Hosea 6:6), you would not have
condemned those who are without guilt. For the Son of Man 8
is the Lord of the sabbath."

Departing thence, He went to their synagogue, where there 9
was a man with a shriveled hand. And they questioned Him, 10

"Is it right to cure people on the sabbath?"

Their intention was to bring a charge against Him.

"Which of you is there," He replied, "who, if he has but a 11
single sheep and it falls into a hole on the sabbath, will not
lay hold of it and lift it out? Is not a man, however, worth 12
far more than a sheep? Therefore it is right to do good on
the sabbath."

Then He said to the man, 13

"Stretch out your hand."

And he stretched it out, and it was restored quite sound
like the other.

Then the Pharisees after leaving the synagogue consulted 14
together against Him, how they might destroy Him. Aware of 15
this, Jesus departed elsewhere; and a great number of people
followed Him, all of whom He cured. But He gave them strict 16
injunctions not to blaze abroad His doings: that those words 17
of the prophet Isaiah might be fulfilled,

"THIS IS MY SERVANT WHOM I HAVE CHOSEN, 18
MY BELOVED ONE IN WHOM MY SOUL TAKES PLEASURE.
I WILL PUT MY SPIRIT UPON HIM,
AND HE WILL ANNOUNCE JUSTICE TO THE NATIONS.
HE WILL NOT WRANGLE OR CRY ALOUD, 19
NOR WILL HIS VOICE BE HEARD IN THE BROADWAYS.
A CRUSHED REED HE WILL NOT BREAK, 20
NOR WILL HE QUENCH THE SMOLDERING WICK,
UNTIL HE HAS LED ON JUSTICE TO VICTORY.

AND ON HIS NAME SHALL THE NATIONS REST THEIR 21
HOPES" (Isaiah 42:1-4).

At that time a demoniac was brought to Him, blind and 22
dumb; and He cured him, so that the dumb man could speak
and see. And the crowds of people were all filled with amaze- 23
ment and said,

"Can this be the Son of David?"

The Pharisees heard it and said, 24

"This man only expels demons by the power of Beelzebul,
the prince of demons."

Knowing their thoughts, He said to them, 25

"Every kingdom in which civil war rages suffers desolation; and every city or house in which there is internal strife
will be brought low. And if Satan expels Satan, he has begun 26
to make war on himself: how therefore shall his kingdom
last? And if it is by Beelzebul's power that I expel the demons, 27
by whose power do your disciples expel them? They therefore shall be your judges. But if it is by the power of the Spirit 28
of God that I expel the demons, it is evident that the
Kingdom of God has come upon you. Again, how can any 29
one enter the house of a strong man and carry off his goods,
unless first of all he masters and secures the strong man:
then will he ransack his house.

"The man who is not with me is against me, and he who is 30
not gathering with me is scattering. This is why I tell you that 31
men will find forgiveness for every other sin and impious
word, but that for impious speaking against the Holy Spirit
they shall find no forgiveness. And whoever shall speak 32
against the Son of Man may obtain forgiveness; but whoever
speaks against the Holy Spirit shall obtain forgiveness
neither in this nor in the coming age.

"Either grant the tree to be a good one and its fruits good, 33
or the tree worthless and its fruit worthless; for the tree is

known by its fruit. O brood of vipers, how can you speak 34
what is good when you are bad men? It is from the fullness of
the heart that the mouth speaks. A good man from his good 35
store produces good things, and a bad man from his bad
store produces bad things. I tell you that for every careless 36
word that men shall speak they will be held accountable on
the day of judgment. For each of you by his words shall be 37
justified, or by his words shall be condemned."

Then He was questioned by certain of the scribes and of 38
the Pharisees who said,

"Teacher, we wish to see a sign given by you."

"Wicked and apostate generation!" He replied, "they 39
clamor for a sign, but none shall be given to them except the
sign of the prophet Jonah. For just as JONAH WAS THREE 40
DAYS AND THREE NIGHTS IN THE SEA-MONSTER'S BELLY
(Jonah 1:17), so will the Son of Man be three days and three
nights in the heart of the earth. There will stand up men of 41
Nineveh at the judgment together with the present generation, and will condemn it; because they repented at the
preaching of Jonah; and mark! [look/take note] there is One
greater than Jonah here. The queen of the south will awake 42
at the judgment together with the present generation, and
will condemn it; because she came from the ends of the
earth to hear the wisdom of Solomon; and mark! [look/take
note] there is One greater than Solomon here.

"When the foul spirit has gone out of a man, it roams 43
about in the desert, seeking rest but finding none. Then it 44
says, 'I will return to my house that I left'; and it comes and
finds it unoccupied, swept clean, and in good order. Then it 45
goes and brings back with it seven other spirits more wicked
than itself, and they come in and dwell there; and in the end
that man's condition becomes worse than it was at first. So
will it be also with the present wicked generation."

While He was addressing the people, His mother and His 46
brothers were standing on the edge of the crowd desiring to
speak to Him. So some one told Him, 47

"Your mother and your brothers are standing outside, and
desire to speak to you."

"Who is my mother?" He said to the man; "and who are 48
my brothers?"

And pointing to His disciples He added, 49

"See here are my mother and my brothers. To obey my 50
Father who is in heaven—that is to be my brother and my
sister and my mother."

13 That same day Jesus had left the house and was sit- 1
ting on the shore of the lake, when a vast multitude of 2
people crowded round Him. He therefore went on board a
boat and sat there, while all the people stood on the shore.
He then spoke many things to them in parables. 3

"A sower went out," He said, "to sow. As he sowed, some of 4
the seed fell by the way-side, and the birds came and pecked
it up. Some fell on rocky ground, where it had but scanty soil. 5
It quickly showed itself above ground, because it had no
depth of earth; but when the sun was risen, it was scorched 6
by the heat, and through having no root it withered up. Some 7
fell among the thorns; but the thorns sprang up and stifled it.
But a portion fell upon good ground and gave a return, some 8
a hundred for one, some sixty, some thirty. Listen, every one 9
who has ears!"

And His disciples came and asked Him, 10

"Why do you speak to them in parables?"

"Because," He replied, "while to you it is granted to know 11
the secrets of the Kingdom of heaven, to them it is not. For 12
whoever has, to him more shall be given, and he shall have

abundance; but whoever has not, from him even what he has shall be taken away. I speak to them in parables for this 13 reason, that while looking they do not see, and while hearing they neither hear nor understand. And in regard to them the 14 prophecy of Isaiah is being fulfilled:

"'YOU WILL HEAR AND HEAR AND BY NO MEANS UNDERSTAND,

AND YOU WILL LOOK AND LOOK AND BY NO MEANS SEE.

FOR THIS PEOPLE'S MIND IS STUPEFIED, 15

THEIR HEARING HAS BECOME DULL,

AND THEIR EYES HAVE CLOSED;

LEST THEY SHOULD EVER SEE WITH THEIR EYES,

AND HEAR WITH THEIR EARS,

AND UNDERSTAND WITH THEIR MINDS,

AND TURN BACK,

SO THAT I MIGHT HEAL THEM' (Isaiah 6:9-10).

"But as for you, blessed are your eyes, for they see, and 16 your ears, for they hear. For I tell you in truth that many 17 prophets and holy men have longed to see the sights you see, and have not seen them, and to hear the words you hear, and have not heard them.

"To you, then, I will explain the parable of the sower. When 18 a man hears the word concerning the Kingdom and does not 19 understand it, the Evil One comes and catches away what has been sown in his heart. This is he who received the seed by the road-side. He who received the seed on rocky ground 20 is the man who hears the word and immediately receives it with joy. It has struck no root, however, within him. He con- 21 tinues for a time, but when suffering comes or persecution because of the word, he at once turns against it. He who 22 received the seed among the thorns is the man who hears the word, but the cares of the present age and the delusion of riches quite stifle the word, and it becomes unfruitful. But 23 he who received the seed on good ground is he who hears and understands. Such hearers give a return, and yield one a hundred, another sixty, another thirty fold."

Another parable He put before them. 24

"The Kingdom of heaven," He said, "may be compared to a man who has sown good seed in his field; but during the 25 night his enemy comes, and over the first seed he sows dar- nel among the wheat, and goes away. When the blade shoots 26 up and the grain is formed, then appears the darnel also.

"So the farmer's men come and ask him, 27

"'Master, was it not good seed that you sowed on your land? Where, then, does the darnel come from?'

"'Some enemy has done this,' he said. 28

"'Shall we go and collect it?' the men inquire.

"'No,' he replied, 'for fear that while collecting the darnel 29 you should at the same time root up the wheat with it. Leave 30 both to grow together until the harvest, and at harvest-time I will direct the reapers to collect the darnel first and make it up into bundles to burn, but to bring all the wheat into my barn.'"

Another parable He put before them. 31

"The Kingdom of heaven," He said, "is like a mustard- seed, which a man takes and sows in his ground. It is the 32 smallest of all seeds, and yet when full-grown it is larger than any herb and forms a tree, so that the birds come and roost in its branches."

Another parable He spoke to them. 33

"The Kingdom of heaven," He said, "is like yeast which a woman takes and buries in three measures of flour, for it to work there till the whole is leavened."

All this Jesus spoke to the people in parables, and except 34 in parables He spoke nothing to them, in fulfillment of the 35 saying of the prophet,

"I WILL OPEN MY MOUTH IN PARABLES:
I WILL UTTER THINGS KEPT HIDDEN SINCE THE
CREATION OF ALL THINGS" (Psalm 78:2).

When He had dismissed the people and had returned to 36
the house, His disciples came to Him with the request,

"Explain to us the parable of the darnel sown in the field."

"The sower of the good seed," He replied, "is the Son of 37
Man; the field is the world; the good seed—these are the sons 38
of the Kingdom; the darnel, the sons of the Evil One. The 39
enemy who sowed the darnel is the devil; the harvest is the
close of the age; the reapers are the angels. As then the darnel 40
is collected together and burned up with fire, so will it be at
the close of the age. The Son of Man will commission His 41
angels, and they will gather out of His Kingdom all causes of
sin and all who violate His laws; and these they will throw into 42
the fiery furnace. There will be the weeping and the gnashing
of teeth. Then will the righteous shine out like the sun in their 43
Father's Kingdom. Listen, every one who has ears!

"The Kingdom of heaven is like treasure buried in the field, 44
which a man finds, but buries again, and, in his joy about
it, goes and sells all he has and buys that piece of ground.

"Again, the Kingdom of heaven is like a jewel merchant 45
who is in quest of choice pearls. He finds one most costly 46
pearl; he goes away, and though it costs all he has, he buys it.

"Again, the Kingdom of heaven is like a draw-net let down 47
into the sea, which encloses fish of all sorts. When it is full, 48
they haul it up on the beach, and sit down and collect the
good fish in baskets, while the worthless they throw away. So 49
will it be at the close of the age. The angels will go forth and
separate the wicked from among the righteous, and will 50
throw them into the fiery furnace. There will be the weeping
and the gnashing of teeth.

"Have you understood all this?" He asked. 51

"Yes," they said.

"Then remember," He said, "that every scribe well trained 52
for the Kingdom of heaven is like a householder who brings
out of his storehouse new things and old."

Jesus concluded this series of parables and then departed. 53
And He came into His own country and proceeded to teach 54
in their synagogue, so that they were filled with astonishment and exclaimed,

"Where did he obtain such wisdom, and these wondrous
powers? Is not this the carpenter's son? Is not his mother 55
called Mary? And are not his brothers, James, Joseph, Simon
and Judah? And his sisters—are they not all living here 56
among us? Where, then, did he get all this?"

So they turned against Him. 57

But Jesus said to them,

"There is no prophet left without honor except in his own
country and among his own family."

And He performed but few mighty deeds there because of 58
their want of faith.

14 About that time Herod the Tetrarch heard of the fame 1
of Jesus, and he said to his courtiers, 2

"This is John the Baptist: he has come back to life; and that
is why these miraculous powers are working in him."

For Herod had arrested John, and had put him in chains 3
and imprisoned him, for the sake of Herodias (his brother
Philip's wife), because John would say to him, 4

"It is not lawful for you to have her."

And he would have liked to put him to death, but was 5
afraid of the people, because they regarded John as a
prophet. But when Herod's birthday came, the daughter of 6
Herodias danced before all the company, and so pleased

Herod that with an oath he promised to give her whatever 7
she asked. So she, instructed by her mother, said, 8

"Give me here on a dish the head of John the Baptist."

The king was deeply vexed, yet because of his repeated oath 9
and of the guests at his table he ordered it to be given her, and 10
he sent and beheaded John in the prison. The head was 11
brought on a dish and given to the young girl, and she took it
to her mother. Then John's disciples went and removed the 12
body and buried it, and came and informed Jesus.

Upon receiving these tidings, Jesus went away by boat to 13
an uninhabited and secluded district; but the people heard
of it and followed Him in crowds from the towns by land. So 14
Jesus left the boat and saw an immense multitude, and felt
compassion for them, and cured those of them who were out
of health. But when evening was come, the disciples came to 15
Him, and said,

"This is an uninhabited place, and the best of the day is
now gone; send the people away to go into the villages and
buy something to eat."

"They need not go away," replied Jesus; "you yourselves 16
must give them something to eat."

"We have nothing here," they said, "but five loaves and a 17
couple of fish."

"Bring them here to me," He said, and He told all the peo- 18
ple to sit down on the grass. 19

Then He took the five loaves and the two fish, and after
looking up to heaven and blessing them, He broke up the
loaves and gave them to the disciples, and the disciples
distributed them to the people. So all ate, and were fully 20
satisfied. The broken portions that remained over they
gathered up, filling twelve baskets. Those who had eaten 21
were about five thousand adult men, without reckoning
women and children.

Immediately afterwards He made the disciples go on 22
board the boat and cross to the opposite shore, leaving Him
to dismiss the people. When He had done this, He climbed 23
the hill to pray in solitude. Night came on, and He was there
alone. Meanwhile the boat was far out on the lake, buffeted 24
and tossed by the waves, the wind being adverse.

But towards daybreak He went to them, walking over the 25
waves. When the disciples saw Him walking on the waves, 26
they were greatly alarmed.

"It is a ghost," they exclaimed, and they cried out with terror.

But instantly Jesus spoke to them, and said, 27

"There is no danger; it is I; do not be afraid."

"Master," answered Peter, "if it is you, bid me come to you 28
upon the water."

"Come," said Jesus. 29

Then Peter climbed down from the boat and walked upon
the water to go to Him. But when he felt the wind he grew 30
frightened, and beginning to sink he cried out,

"Master, save me."

Instantly Jesus stretched out His hand and caught hold of 31
him, saying to him,

"Man of little faith, why did you doubt?"

So they climbed into the boat, and the wind lulled; and the 32
men on board fell down before Him and said, 33

"You are indeed God's Son."

When they had crossed over, they put ashore at Gennesaret; 34
and the men of the place, recognizing Him, sent word to all 35
the country round. So they brought to Him all who were ill,
and entreated Him that they might but touch the tassel of 36
His outer garment; and all who did so were restored to
perfect health.

15 Then there came to Jesus some Pharisees and scribes 1 from Jerusalem, who inquired,

"Why do your disciples transgress the tradition of the 2 elders by not washing their hands before meals?"

"Why do you, too," He retorted, "transgress God's com- 3 mands for the sake of your tradition? God said, 'HONOR THY 4 FATHER AND THY MOTHER' (Exodus 20:12); and 'LET HIM WHO REVILES FATHER OR MOTHER BE PUT TO DEATH' (Exodus 21:17); but you say: 'If a man says to his father or 5 mother, "This thing is consecrated, otherwise you should have received it from me," he shall be absolved from honoring his 6 father'; and so you have rendered futile God's word for the sake of your tradition. Hypocrites! Well did Isaiah prophesy 7 of you,

"'THIS PEOPLE HONORS ME WITH THEIR LIPS, 8
WHILE THEIR HEART IS FAR FROM ME;
IN VAIN DO THEY WORSHIP ME, 9
WHILE GIVING AS DOCTRINES THE MERE PRECEPTS OF MEN'" (Isaiah 29:13).

Then, when He had called the people to Him, Jesus said, 10

"Hear and understand. It is not what goes into a man's 11 mouth that makes him unclean, but it is what comes out of his mouth that makes him unclean."

Then His disciples came and said to Him, 12

"Do you know that the Pharisees turned against you when they heard those words?"

"Every plant," He replied, "which my Heavenly Father has 13 not planted will be rooted up. Leave them alone. They are 14 blind guides of the blind; and if a blind man leads a blind man, both will fall into some pit."

"Explain to us this parable," said Peter. 15

"Are you," He answered, "still without intelligence? Do 16 you not understand that whatever enters the mouth passes 17 into the stomach and is afterwards ejected from the body? But the things that come out of the mouth proceed from the 18 heart, and it is these that defile the man. For out of the heart 19 proceed wicked scheming, murder, adultery, fornication, theft, perjury, slander. These are the things which make a 20 man unclean; but eating with unwashed hands does not make unclean."

Leaving that place, Jesus withdrew into the neighborhood 21 of Tyre and Sidon. Here a Canaanitish woman of the district 22 came out and kept crying—

"Master, Son of David, pity me; my daughter is cruelly harassed by a demon."

But He answered her not a word. Then the disciples came 23 up, and begged Him, saying,

"Send her away, because she keeps crying behind us."

"I have been sent only to the lost sheep of the house of 24 Israel," He replied.

Then she came and threw herself at His feet and en- 25 treated Him.

"Master, help me," she said.

"It is not right," He said, "to take the children's bread and 26 throw it to the dogs."

"Be it so, Master," she said, "for even the dogs eat the 27 scraps which fall from their masters' tables."

"O woman," replied Jesus, "great is your faith: be it done to 28 you as you desire."

And from that moment her daughter was restored to health.

Moving from that district, Jesus went along by the lake of 29 Galilee; and ascending the hill, He sat there. And great 30 crowds came to Him, bringing with them those who were crippled, blind, dumb, or maimed, and many besides, and they hastened to lay them at His feet. And He cured them, so 31 that the people were amazed to see the dumb speaking, the maimed with their hands perfect, the lame walking, and the blind seeing; and they gave the glory to the God of Israel.

Then Jesus called His disciples to Him and said, 32

"My heart yearns over this mass of people, for it is now the third day that they have been with me and they have nothing to eat. I am unwilling to send them away hungry, lest they should faint on the road."

"Where can we," asked the disciples, "get bread enough in 33 this remote place to satisfy so vast a multitude?"

"How many loaves have you?" Jesus asked. 34

"Seven," they said, "and a few small fish."

So He bade all the people sit down on the ground, and He 35 took the seven loaves and the fish, and after giving thanks He 36 broke them and then distributed them to the disciples, and they to the people. And they all ate and were satisfied. The 37 broken portions that remained over they took up—seven full baskets. Those who ate were four thousand men, without 38 reckoning women and children.

He then dismissed the people, went on board the boat, 39 and came into the district of Magadan.

16 Now the Pharisees and Sadducees came to Him; and, 1 to make trial of Him, they asked Him to show them a sign from heaven. He replied, 2

{"In the evening you say, 'It will be fine weather, for the sky is red'; and in the morning, 'It will be rough weather to-day, 3 for the sky is red and murky.' You learn how to distinguish the aspect of the sky, but the signs of the times you cannot.} A 4 wicked and apostate generation are eager for a sign; but none shall be given to them except the sign of Jonah."

And He left them and went away.

When the disciples arrived at the other side of the lake, 5

they found that they had forgotten to bring any bread; and 6
when Jesus said to them, "See to it and beware of the leaven
of the Pharisees and Sadducees," they reasoned with one 7
another and remarked,

"We have not brought any bread."

Jesus perceived this and said, 8

"What is this discussion among you, you men of little
faith, about having no bread? Do you not yet understand? 9
nor even remember the five thousand men and the five
loaves, and how many basketfuls you carried away, nor the 10
four thousand and the seven loaves, and how many hampers
you carried away? How is it you do not understand that it 11
was not about bread that I spoke to you? But beware of the
leaven of the Pharisees and Sadducees."

Then they perceived that He had not warned them 12
against leaven, but against the teaching of the Pharisees
and Sadducees.

When He arrived in the neighborhood of Caesarea 13
Philippi, Jesus questioned His disciples.

"Who do people say that the Son of Man is?" He asked.

"Some say John the Baptist," they replied; "others Elijah; 14
others Jeremiah or one of the prophets."

"But you, who do you say that I am?" He asked again. 15

"You," replied Simon Peter, "are the Christ, the Son of the 16
living God."

"Blessed are you, Simon Bar-Jonah," said Jesus; "for mere 17
human nature has not revealed this to you, but my Father in
heaven. And I tell you that you are Peter, and that upon this 18
rock I will build my church, and the might of Hades shall not
triumph over it. I will give you the keys of the Kingdom of 19
heaven; and whatever you bind on earth shall remain bound
in heaven, and whatever you loose on earth shall remain
loosed in heaven."

Then He instructed His disciples to tell no one that He was 20 the Christ.

From this time Jesus began to explain to His disciples that 21 He must go to Jerusalem, and suffer much cruelty from the elders and the high priests and the scribes, and be put to death, and on the third day be raised to life again. Then Peter 22 took Him aside and began to remonstrate [plead in protest] with Him.

"Master," he said, "God forbid; this shall not be your lot."

But He turned and said to Peter, 23

"Get behind me, Satan; you are a hindrance to me, because your thoughts are not God's thoughts, but men's."

Then Jesus said to His disciples, 24

"If any one wishes to follow me, let him renounce self and take up his cross, and so be my follower. For whoever desires 25 to save his life shall lose it, and whoever loses his life for my sake shall find it. Why, what benefit will it be to a man if he 26 gains the whole world but forfeits his life? Or what shall a man give to buy back his life? For the Son of Man is to come 27 in the glory of His Father with His angels, and then will He requite every man according to his actions. I tell you in truth 28 that some of those who are standing here will not taste death till they have seen the Son of Man coming in His Kingdom."

17 Six days later, Jesus took with Him Peter and the 1 brothers James and John, and brought them up a high mountain to a solitary place. There in their presence 2 His form underwent a change; His face shone like the sun, and His raiment became as white as the light. And suddenly 3 Moses and Elijah appeared to them conversing with Him.

Then Peter said to Jesus, 4

"Master, it is well for us to be here. If you approve, I will put up three tents here, one for you, one for Moses, and one for Elijah."

He was still speaking when a luminous cloud spread over them; and a voice was heard from within the cloud, which said, 5

"This is My Son the Beloved, in whom is My delight. Listen to Him."

On hearing this voice, the disciples fell on their faces and were filled with terror. But Jesus came and touched them, and said, 6, 7

"Rise, and have no fear."

So they looked up, and saw no one but Jesus. 8

As they were descending the mountain, Jesus laid a command upon them. 9

"Tell no one," He said, "of the sight you have seen till the Son of Man has risen from the dead."

"Why, then," asked the disciples, "do the scribes say that Elijah must first come?" 10

"Elijah was indeed to come," He replied, "and would reform everything. But I tell you that he has already come, and they did not recognize him, but dealt with him as they chose. And the Son of Man is about to be treated by them in the same way." 11, 12

Then it dawned upon the disciples that it was John the Baptist about whom He had spoken to them. 13

When they returned to the people, there came to Him a man who fell on his knees before Him and besought Him. 14

"Master," he said, "have pity on my son, for he is an epileptic and suffers badly. Often he falls into the fire and often into the water. I brought him to your disciples, and they were not able to cure him." 15, 16

"O unbelieving and perverse generation!" replied Jesus; "how long shall I be with you? how long must I bear with you? Bring him to me." 17

Then Jesus rebuked the demon, and it came out and left 18
him; and the boy was cured from that moment.

Then the disciples came to Jesus privately and asked Him, 19
"Why could not we expel the demon?"

"Because your faith is so small," He replied; "for I declare 20
to you in truth that if you have faith like a mustard-seed, you
shall say to this mountain, 'Remove from this place to that,'
and it will remove; and nothing shall be impossible to you."
{But an evil spirit of this kind is driven out only by prayer 21
and fasting.}

As they were traveling about in Galilee, Jesus said to them, 22

"The Son of Man is about to be betrayed into the hands of
men; they will put Him to death, but on the third day He will 23
be raised to life again."

And they were exceedingly distressed.

After their arrival at Capernaum the collectors of the half- 24
shekel came and asked Peter,

"Does not your teacher pay the half-shekel?"

"Yes," he replied, and then went into the house. 25

But before he spoke a word Jesus said,

"What think you, Simon? From whom do this world's kings
receive customs or capitation tax [poll tax]? from their own
children, or from others?"

"From others," he replied. 26

"Then the children go free," said Jesus. "However, lest we 27
offend them, go and throw a hook into the lake, and take the
first fish that comes up. When you open its mouth, you will
find a shekel in it: bring that coin and give it to them for
yourself and me."

18 Just then the disciples came to Jesus and asked, "Who 1
ranks higher than others in the Kingdom of heaven?"

So He called a young child to Him, and placing him in the 2
midst of them, said, 3

"In truth I tell you that unless you turn and become like
little children, you will in no case be admitted into the Kingdom of heaven. Whoever therefore shall humble himself as 4
this young child, is the one who is greatest in the Kingdom of
heaven. And whoever for my sake receives one young child 5
such as this, receives me. But whoever shall occasion the fall 6
of one of these little ones who believe in me, it would be better for him to have a millstone hung round his neck and to
be drowned in the depths of the sea.

"Woe to the world because of causes of stumbling! They 7
cannot but occur, but woe to the man through whom such
cause does occur! If your hand or your foot is to cause your 8
fall, cut it off and away with it. It is better for you to enter
crippled in hand or foot into Life than possessing two
sound hands or feet to be thrown into the fire eternal. And 9
if your eye is to cause your fall, tear it out and away with
it; it is better for you to enter with only one eye into Life
than possessing two eyes to be thrown into the Gehenna
of fire.

"Beware of despising one of these little ones, for I tell you 10
that in heaven their angels continually behold the face of my
Father who is in heaven. What do you yourselves think? 12
Suppose a man has a hundred sheep and one of them strays
away, will he not leave the ninety-nine on the hills and go
and look for the stray one? And if he succeeds in finding it, in 13
truth I tell you that he rejoices over it more than he does over
the ninety-nine that have not gone astray. Just so it is the will 14
of your Father in heaven that not one of these little ones
should be lost.

"If your brother acts wrongly towards you, go and point 15
out his fault to him when only you and he are there. If he

listens to you, you have gained your brother. But if he will 16
not listen to you, go again, and ask one or two to come with
you, that every word may be confirmed by two or three
witnesses. If he refuses to hear them, appeal to the church; 17
and if he refuses to hear even the church, regard him just as
you regard a heathen or a tax-gatherer. I in truth tell you all 18
that whatever you bind on earth will in heaven remain
bound, and whatever you loose on earth will in heaven remain loosed. I also in truth tell you that if two of you here on 19
earth agree together concerning anything that they shall ask,
the prayer shall be granted by my Father who is in heaven.
For where there are two or three assembled in my name, 20
there am I in the midst of them."

At this point Peter came to Him with the question, 21

"Master, how often shall my brother act wrongly towards
me and I forgive him? seven times?"

"I do not say seven times," answered Jesus, "but seventy 22
times seven.

"For this reason the Kingdom of heaven may be compared 23
to a king who determined to have a settlement of accounts
with his servants. But as soon as he began the settlement, 24
one was brought before him who owed ten thousand talents,
and was unable to pay. So his master ordered that he and his 25
wife and children and everything that he had should be sold,
and payment be made. The servant therefore falling down, 26
prostrated himself at his feet and entreated him.

"'Only give me time,' he said, 'and I will pay you the whole.'

"Whereupon his master, touched with compassion, set 27
him free and forgave him the debt. But no sooner had the 28
servant gone out, than he met with one of his fellow servants
who owed him one hundred shillings; and seizing him by the
throat and nearly strangling him he exclaimed,

"'Pay me all you owe.'

"His fellow servant therefore fell at his feet and entreated him: 29
"'Only give me time,' he said, 'and I will pay you.'"

"He would not, however, but went and threw him into 30
prison until he should pay what was due. His fellow servants, 31
therefore, seeing what had happened, were exceedingly angry;
and they came and told their master all that had occurred. At 32
once his master called him and said,

"'Wicked servant, I forgave you all that debt, because you
entreated me: ought not you also to have had pity on your 33
fellow servant, just as I had pity on you?'

"So his master, greatly incensed, handed him over to the 34
torturers until he should pay all he owed him.

"In the same way my heavenly Father will deal with you all, 35
if you do not from the heart each one forgive his brother."

19 When Jesus had finished these sayings, He removed 1
from Galilee and came into that part of Judaea which
lay beyond the Jordan. And a vast multitude followed Him, 2
and He cured them there.

Then came some of the Pharisees to Him to put Him to the 3
proof by the question,

"Has a man a right to divorce his wife for any sort of reason?"

"Have you not read," He replied, "that He who made them 4
'MADE THEM' from the beginning 'MALE AND FEMALE'
(Genesis 1:27), and said, 'FOR THIS REASON A MAN SHALL 5
LEAVE HIS FATHER AND MOTHER AND CLING TO HIS
WIFE, AND THE TWO SHALL BE ONE'? (Genesis 2:24). Thus 6
they are no longer two, but one. What therefore God has
joined together, let not man separate."

"Why then," said they, "did Moses command the husband 7
to give her a written notice of divorce, and send her away?"
(Deuteronomy 24:1).

"Moses," He replied, "in consideration of your stubborn 8 hearts permitted you to put away your wives, but it was not so from the beginning. I tell you that whoever divorces his 9 wife for any reason except her unchastity, and marries another woman, commits adultery."

"If this is a man's position in regard to his wife," said the 10 disciples to Him, "it is better not to marry."

"It is not every man," He replied, "who can receive this teach- 11 ing, but only those on whom the grace has been bestowed. There are men who from their birth have been disabled from 12 marriage, others who have been so disabled by men, and others who have disabled themselves for the sake of the Kingdom of heaven. He who is able to receive this, let him receive it."

Then young children were brought to Him that He should 13 put His hands on them and pray; but the disciples interfered. Jesus, however, said, 14

"Let the little children come to me, and do not hinder them; for it is to those who are childlike that the Kingdom of heaven belongs."

So He laid His hands upon them and went away. 15

"Teacher," said one man, coming up to Him, "what good 16 thing shall I do in order to win the life eternal?"

"Why do you ask me," He replied, "about the thing that is 17 good? There is One who is truly good. But if you desire to enter into Life, keep the commandments."

"Which commandments?" he asked. 18

Jesus answered,

"'THOU SHALT NOT KILL'; 'THOU SHALT NOT COMMIT ADULTERY'; 'THOU SHALT NOT STEAL'; 'THOU SHALT NOT LIE IN GIVING EVIDENCE'; 'HONOR THY FATHER 19 AND THY MOTHER' (Exodus 20:12-16; Deuteronomy 5:16-20); and 'THOU SHALT LOVE THY NEIGHBOR AS MUCH AS THYSELF'" (Leviticus 19:18).

"All of these," said the young man, "I have carefully 20
obeyed. What do I still lack?"

"If you wish and intend to be perfect," replied Jesus, "go 21
and sell all that you have, and give to the poor, and you shall
have wealth in heaven; and come and follow me."

On hearing these words the young man went away sad; for 22
he had much property.

So Jesus said to His disciples, 23

"I tell you in truth that it will be hard for a rich man to
enter the Kingdom of heaven. Yes, I tell you, it is easier for a 24
camel to go through the eye of a needle than for a rich man
to enter the Kingdom of God."

These words utterly amazed the disciples, and they asked, 25
"Who then can be saved?"

Jesus looked at them and said, 26

"With men this is impossible, but with God everything
is possible."

Then Peter said to Jesus, 27

"See, we have given up everything and followed you; what
then shall be our reward?"

"I tell you in truth," replied Jesus, "that in the new creation, 28
when the Son of Man has taken His seat on His glorious
throne, all of you who have followed me shall also sit on
twelve thrones and judge the twelve tribes of Israel. And 29
whoever has forsaken houses, or brothers or sisters, or father
or mother, or children or lands, for my sake, shall receive
many times as much and shall have as his inheritance
eternal life.

"But many who are now first shall be last, and many who 30
are now last shall be first.

20 "For the Kingdom of heaven is like the owner of an 1
estate who went out early in the morning to hire
men to work in his vineyard, and having made an agreement 2
with them for a shilling a day, sent them into his vineyard.
Going out about nine o'clock he saw others loitering in the 3
market-place. To these also he said, 4

"'You also, go into the vineyard, and whatever is right I will
give you.'

"So they went. Again about twelve, and about three 5
o'clock, he went out and did the same. And going out about 6
five o'clock he found others loitering, and he asked them,

'Why have you been standing here all day long, doing nothing?'

"'Because no one has hired us,' they replied. 7

"'You also, go into the vineyard,' he said.

"When evening came, the owner of the vineyard said to 8
his steward,

"'Call the men and pay them their wages. Begin with the
last set and finish with the first.'

"When those came who had begun at five o'clock, they 9
received a shilling apiece; and when the first came, they 10
expected to get more, but they also each got the shilling. So 11
when they had received it, they grumbled against the
employer, saying, 12

"'These who came last have done only one hour's work,
and you have put them on a level with us who have worked
the whole day and have borne the scorching heat.'

"'My friend,' he answered to one of them, 'I am doing you 13
no injustice. Did you not agree with me for a shilling? Take 14
your money and go. I choose to give this last comer just as
much as I give you. Have I not a right to do what I choose 15
with my own property? Or are you envious because I
am generous?'

"So the last shall be first, and the first last." 16

Jesus was now going up to Jerusalem, and He took the 17 twelve disciples aside by themselves, and on the way He said to them,

"We are going up to Jerusalem, and there the Son of Man 18 shall be betrayed to the high priests and scribes. They shall condemn Him to death, and hand Him over to the Gentiles 19 to be mocked and scourged and crucified; and on the third day He shall be raised to life."

Then the mother of the sons of Zebedee came to Him with 20 her sons, and knelt before Him to make a request of Him.

"What is it you wish for?" He asked. 21

"Command," she replied, "that these my two sons may sit one at your right hand and one at your left in your Kingdom."

"You know not what you are asking," said Jesus; "can you 22 drink out of the cup from which I am about to drink?"

"We can," they replied.

"You shall drink out of my cup," He said, "but a seat at my 23 right hand or at my left it is not mine to give, but it belongs to those for whom it has been reserved by my Father."

The other ten heard of this, and their indignation was 24 aroused against the two brothers. But Jesus called them to 25 Him, and said,

"You know that the rulers of the Gentiles lord it over them, and their great men exercise authority over them. Not so 26 shall it be among you; but whoever would be great among you must be your servant, and whoever would be first 27 among you must be your bondservant; just as the Son of 28 Man came not to be served but to serve, and to give His life as the redemption-price for many."

As they were leaving Jericho, with an immense crowd 29 following Him, two blind men sitting by the roadside heard 30 that it was Jesus who was passing by, and cried aloud,

"Master, Son of David, pity us."

The people angrily tried to silence them, but they cried all 31
the louder.

"Master, Son of David, pity us," they said.

So Jesus stood still and summoned them. 32

"What shall I do for you?" He asked.

"Master, let our eyes be opened," they replied. 33

Moved with compassion, Jesus touched their eyes, and 34
immediately they regained their sight and followed Him.

21 When they were come near Jerusalem and had 1
arrived at Bethphagé and the Mount of Olives, Jesus
sent two of the disciples in front, saying to them, 2

"Go to the village you see facing you, and at once you will
find a she-ass tied up and a colt with it. Untie it and bring
them to me. And if any one says anything to you, say, 'The 3
Master needs them,' and he will at once send them."

This took place in order that the prophet's prediction 4
might be fulfilled:

"TELL THE DAUGHTER OF ZION, 5

'SEE, THY KING IS COMING TO THEE,

GENTLE, AND MOUNTED ON AN ASS,

ON A COLT THE FOAL OF A BEAST OF BURDEN'" (Isaiah
62:11; Zechariah 9:9).

So the disciples went and did as Jesus had instructed 6
them: they brought the she-ass and the foal, and threw their 7
outer garments on them. So He sat thereon; and most of the 8
crowd kept spreading their garments along the road, while
others cut branches from the trees and carpeted the road
with them, and the multitudes—some of the people preced- 9
ing Him, and some following—sang aloud,

"HOSANNA TO THE SON OF DAVID!

BLESSED BE HE WHO COMES IN THE LORD'S NAME! HOSANNA IN THE HIGHEST!" (Psalm 118:26).

When He entered Jerusalem, the whole city was thrown 10 into commotion, every one inquiring,

"Who is this?"

"This is Jesus, the prophet, from Nazareth in Galilee," re- 11 plied the crowds.

Entering the Temple, Jesus drove out all who were buying 12 and selling there, and overturned the money-changers' tables and the seats of the dove-dealers.

"It is written," He said, "'MY HOUSE SHALL BE CALLED 13 THE HOUSE OF PRAYER' (Isaiah 56:7), but you are making it A ROBBERS' CAVE" (Jeremiah 7:11).

And the blind and the lame came to Him in the Temple, 14 and He cured them.

But when the high priests and the scribes saw the won- 15 derful things that He had done and the children who were crying aloud in the Temple, "HOSANNA TO THE SON OF DAVID," they were filled with indignation.

"Do you hear," they asked Him, "what these children 16 are saying?"

"Yes," He replied; "have you never read, 'OUT OF THE MOUTHS OF INFANTS AND OF BABES AT THE BREAST THOU HAST PERFECTED PRAISE'?" (Psalm 8:2).

So He left them and went out of the city to Bethany and 17 passed the night there.

Early in the morning as He was on His way to return to the 18 city He was hungry, and seeing a fig-tree on the road-side He 19 went up to it, but found nothing on it but leaves.

"On you," He said, "no fruit shall ever grow again."

And immediately the fig-tree withered away.

When the disciples saw it they exclaimed in astonishment, 20 "How in a moment the fig-tree has withered away!"

"I tell you in truth," said Jesus, "that if you have faith and 21
waver not, you shall not only perform such a miracle as
this of the fig-tree, but even if you say to this mountain,
'Arise, and hurl yourself into the sea,' it shall be done: and 22
everything, whatever it be, that you ask for in your prayers, if
you have faith, you shall obtain."

He entered the Temple; and while He was teaching, the 23
high priests and the elders of the people came to Him and
asked Him,

"By what authority are you doing these things? and who
gave you this authority?"

"I also will put a question to you," replied Jesus, "and if you 24
answer me, I in turn will tell you by what authority I do these
things. John's baptism, whence was it?—was it from heaven 25
or from men?"

So they debated the matter among themselves.

"If we say 'from heaven,'" they argued, "he will say, 'Why
then did you not believe him?' and if we say 'from men' we 26
have the people to fear, for they all hold John to have been
a prophet."

So they answered Jesus, 27

"We do not know."

"Nor do I tell you," He replied, "by what authority I do
these things.

"But give me your judgment. There was a man who had 28
two sons. He came to the first of them, and said,

"'My son, go and work in the vineyard to-day.'

"'I will not,' he replied. 29

"But afterwards he was sorry, and went. He came to the 30
second and spoke in the same manner. His answer was,

"'I will go, Sir.'

"But he did not go. Which of the two did as his father 31
desired?"

"The first," they said.

"I tell you," replied Jesus, "that the tax-gatherers and the harlots are entering the Kingdom of God in front of you. For 32 John came to you and kept to the path of righteousness, and you did not believe him: the tax-gatherers and the harlots did believe him, and you, though you saw this, did not even repent afterwards and believe him.

"Listen to another parable. There was a householder who 33 planted a vineyard, made a fence round it, dug a wine-tank in it, and built a watchtower; then let the place to vine-dressers, and went abroad. When vintage-time approached, 34 he sent his servants to the vine-dressers to receive his share of the grapes; but the vine-dressers seized the servants, and 35 one they cruelly beat, one they killed, one they pelted with stones. Again he sent another party of servants more numer- 36 ous than the first; and these they treated in the same manner. Later still he sent to them his son, saying, 37

"'They will respect my son.'

"But the vine-dressers, when they saw the son, said to 38 one another,

"'Here is the heir: come, let us kill him and get his inheritance.'

"So they seized him, flung him out of the vineyard, and 39 killed him. When, then, the owner of the vineyard comes, 40 what will he do to those vine-dressers?"

"He will put the wretches to a wretched death," was the 41 reply, "and will let out the vineyard to other vine-dressers, who will render the produce to him at the vintage season."

"Have you never read in the scriptures," said Jesus, 42

"'THE STONE WHICH THE BUILDERS REJECTED
HAS BECOME THE CORNERSTONE:
THIS CAME FROM THE LORD,
AND IT IS WONDERFUL IN OUR EYES'? (Psalm 118:22-23).

"That, I tell you, is the reason why the Kingdom of God will 43
be taken away from you, and given to a nation producing the
fruits of it. He who falls on this stone will be severely hurt; 44
but he on whom it falls will be utterly crushed."

After listening to His parables the high priests and the 45
Pharisees perceived that He was speaking about them;
but though they were eager to lay hands upon Him, they 46
were afraid of the people, for by them He was regarded as
a prophet.

22 Again Jesus spoke to them in parables. 1
"The Kingdom of heaven," He said, "may be com- 2
pared to a king who celebrated the marriage of his son, and 3
sent his servants to call the invited guests to the wedding
feast, but they were unwilling to come.

"Again he sent other servants with a message to those who 4
were invited.

"'My banquet is now ready,' he said, 'my bullocks and
fat cattle are killed, and every preparation is made: come to
the wedding.'

"They, however, gave no heed, but went, one to his home 5
in the country, another to his business; and the rest seized 6
the king's servants, maltreated them, and murdered them.
So the king's anger was stirred, and he sent his troops and 7
destroyed those murderers and burned their city. Then he 8
said to his servants,

"'The wedding banquet is ready, but those who were invited were unworthy of it. Go out therefore to the byways, 9
and invite everybody you meet to the wedding.'

"So they went out into the roads and gathered together all 10
they could find, both bad and good, and the banqueting-hall
was filled with guests.

"Now the king came in to see the guests; and among them 11 he noticed one who was not wearing a wedding robe.

"'My friend,' he said, 'how is it that you came in here 12 without a wedding robe?'

"The man was speechless. Then the king said to the servants, 13

"'Bind him hand and foot and fling him into the darkness outside: there will be the weeping and the gnashing of teeth.'

"For there are many called, but few chosen." 14

Then the Pharisees went and consulted together how 15 they might entrap Him in His talk. So they sent to Him their 16 disciples together with the Herodians; who said,

"Rabbi, we know that you are truthful and that you truly teach God's Way; and you pay no special regard to any one, since you do not consider men's outward appearance. Give 17 us your judgment therefore: is it allowable for us to pay a poll-tax to Caesar, or not?"

Perceiving their wickedness, Jesus replied, 18

"Why are you hypocrites trying to ensnare me? Show me 19 the tribute coin."

So they brought Him a shilling.

"Whose likeness and inscription," He asked, "is this?" 20

"Caesar's," they replied. 21

"Pay therefore," He rejoined, "what is Caesar's to Caesar; and what is God's to God."

They heard this, and were astonished; then left Him, and 22 went their way.

On the same day a party of Sadducees came to Him, con- 23 tending that there is no resurrection. And they put this case to Him.

"Rabbi," they said, "Moses enjoined, 'IF A MAN DIE CHILD- 24 LESS, HIS BROTHER SHALL MARRY HIS WIDOW, AND RAISE UP A FAMILY FOR HIM' (Deuteronomy 25:5). Now we had 25 among us seven brothers. The eldest of them married, but

died childless, leaving his wife to his brother. So also did the 26
second and the third, down to the seventh. The woman also 27
died, after surviving them all. At the resurrection, therefore, 28
whose wife of the seven will she be? for they all married her."

The reply of Jesus was, 29

"You are in error through ignorance of the scriptures and
of the power of God. In the resurrection, neither do men 30
marry nor are women given in marriage, but they are like
angels in heaven. But as to the resurrection of the dead, have 31
you never read what was spoken to you by God, 'I AM THE 32
GOD OF ABRAHAM, AND THE GOD OF ISAAC, AND THE
GOD OF JACOB'? (Exodus 3:6). He is not the God of the dead,
but of the living."

All the crowd heard this, and were filled with amazement 33
at His teaching.

Now the Pharisees came up when they heard that He had 34
silenced the Sadducees, and one of them, an expounder of 35
the Law, asked Him as a test question,

"Rabbi, which is the greatest commandment in the Law?" 36

He answered, "'THOU SHALT LOVE THE LORD THY GOD 37
WITH THY WHOLE HEART, THY WHOLE SOUL, AND THY
WHOLE MIND' (Deuteronomy 6:5). This is the greatest and 38
foremost commandment. And the second is similar to 39
it: 'THOU SHALT LOVE THY NEIGHBOR AS MUCH AS
THYSELF' (Leviticus 19:18). The whole of the Law and the 40
prophets is summed up in these two commandments."

While the Pharisees were still assembled there, Jesus put a 41
question to them.

"What think you about the Christ," He said, "whose son is He?" 42

"David's," they replied.

"How then," He asked, "does David, in the Spirit, call Him 43
Lord, when he says,

"'THE LORD SAID TO MY LORD, 44

SIT AT MY RIGHT HAND
UNTIL I HAVE PUT THY FOES BENEATH THY FEET'?
(Psalm 110:1).

"If therefore David calls Him 'Lord,' how can He be his 45
son?" No one could say a word in reply; nor from that day did 46
any one venture to put a question to Him.

23 Then Jesus addressed the crowds and His disciples. 1
"The scribes," He said, "and the Pharisees sit in the 2
chair of Moses. Therefore do and observe everything that 3
they command you; but do not imitate their actions, for they
talk but do nothing. Heavy and cumbrous burdens they 4
bind together and load men's shoulders with, while as for
themselves, not with one finger do they choose to shift them.
Everything they do is with a view to being observed by men; 5
for they widen their phylacteries [small leather cases
containing scripture passages], and make their tassels large,
and love the best places at dinner-parties, and the best seats 6
in the synagogues, and like to be bowed to in places of public 7
resort, and to be addressed by men as 'Rabbi.'

"As for you, do not accept the title of 'Rabbi,' for One alone 8
is your teacher, and you are all brothers. And call no one on 9
earth 'father,' for One alone is your Father—the heavenly
Father. And do not accept the name of 'leaders,' for your 10
leader is One alone—the Christ. He who is the greatest 11
among you shall be your servant; and one who uplifts him- 12
self shall be humbled, while one who humbles himself shall
be uplifted.

"But woe to you, scribes and Pharisees, hypocrites, for you 13
lock the door of the Kingdom of heaven against men; you
yourselves do not enter, nor do you allow those to enter who
are seeking to do so.

"Woe to you, scribes and Pharisees, hypocrites, for you 15
scour sea and land in order to make one proselyte; and when
he is gained, you make him twice as much a son of Gehenna
as yourselves.

"Woe to you, you blind guides, who say, 16

"'Whoever swears by the sanctuary, it is nothing; but
whoever swears by the gold of the sanctuary, is bound by
the oath.'

"Blind fools! Why, which is greater—the gold, or the sanc- 17
tuary which has made the gold holy? And you say, 18

"'Whoever swears by the altar, it is nothing; but whoever
swears by the offering lying on it, is bound by the oath.'

"You are blind! Why, which is greater—the offering, or the 19
altar which makes the offering holy? He who swears by 20
the altar swears both by it and by everything on it; he who 21
swears by the sanctuary swears both by it and by Him who
dwells in it; and he who swears by heaven swears both by the 22
throne of God and by Him who sits upon it.

"Woe to you, scribes and Pharisees, hypocrites, for you pay 23
the tithe on mint, dill, and cumin, while you have neglected
the weightier requirements of the Law—justice, mercy, and
faithful dealing. These things you ought to have done, yet
without leaving the others undone. You blind guides, strain- 24
ing out the gnat while you gulp down the camel!

"Woe to you, scribes and Pharisees, hypocrites, for you 25
wash clean the outside of the cup and dish, while within they
are full of greed and self-indulgence. Blind Pharisee, first 26
wash clean the inside of the cup and dish, that the outside
may be clean also.

"Woe to you, scribes and Pharisees, hypocrites, for you are 27
just like whitewashed sepulchers, the outside of which
pleases the eye, though inside they are full of dead men's
bones and of all that is unclean. The same is true of you: 28

outwardly you seem to the human eye to be good and honest men, but, within, you are full of insincerity and lawlessness.

"Woe to you, scribes and Pharisees, hypocrites, for you build the sepulchers of the prophets and keep in order the tombs of the righteous; and your boast is, 29 30

"'If we had lived in the time of our forefathers, we should not have shared with them in the murder of the prophets.'

"So you bear witness against yourselves that you are descendants of those who murdered the prophets. Fill up the measure of your forefathers. O serpents, O brood of vipers, how are you to escape condemnation to Gehenna? 31 32 33

"For this reason I am sending to you prophets and wise men and scribes. Some of them you will put to death—nay, crucify; some of them you will flog in your synagogues and chase from town to town; that all the innocent blood shed upon earth may come on you, from the blood of righteous Abel to the blood of Zechariah the son of Barachiah whom you murdered between the sanctuary and the altar. I tell you in solemn truth that all these things will come upon the present generation. 34 35 36

"O Jerusalem! Jerusalem! You that murder the prophets and stone those who have been sent to you! How often have I desired to gather your children to me, as a hen gathers her chickens under her wings, and you would not come! See, your house will now be left to you desolate! For I tell you that you will never see me again until you say, 'BLESSED BE HE WHO COMES IN THE NAME OF THE LORD'" (Psalm 118:26). 37 38 39

24 Jesus had left the Temple and was going on His way, when His disciples came and called His attention to the Temple buildings. 1

"You see all these?" He replied; "in solemn truth I tell you 2 that there will not be left here one stone upon another that shall not be pulled down."

Now when He was seated on the Mount of Olives, away 3 from the crowd, the disciples came to Him, and said,

"Tell us when this will be; and what will be the sign of your coming and of the close of the age?"

"Take care that no one misleads you," answered Jesus; "for 4 many will come assuming my name and saying, 'I am the 5 Christ'; and they will mislead many. And you are to hear of 6 wars and rumors of wars. See that you be not alarmed, for such things must be; but the end is not yet. FOR NATION 7 WILL RISE IN ARMS AGAINST NATION, KINGDOM AGAINST KINGDOM (Isaiah 19:2), and there will be famines and earthquakes in various places; but all these are but like 8 the earliest pains of childbirth.

"At that time they will deliver you up to punishment and 9 will put you to death; and you will be objects of hatred to all the nations on account of my name. Then will many turn 10 against me, and they will betray one another and hate one another. Many false prophets will rise up and mislead many; 11 and because of the spread of lawlessness the love of the great 12 majority will grow cold; but he who stands firm to the end 13 shall be saved. And this gospel of the Kingdom shall be pro- 14 claimed throughout the whole world to set the evidence before all the Gentiles; and then the end will come.

"When, then, you see (to use the language of the prophet 15 Daniel) the 'ABOMINATION OF DESOLATION' (Daniel 9:27) standing in the holy place"—let the reader observe those words—"then let those who are in Judaea escape to the hills; 16 any one on the roof should not go down to fetch his things 17 from the house; nor any one in the fields go home to fetch 18 his cloak. Alas for the women who at that time are with child 19 or have infants at the breast!

"But pray that your flight may not be in winter, nor on the 20
Sabbath; for it WILL BE A TIME OF GREAT SUFFERING, 21
SUCH AS NEVER HAS BEEN FROM THE BEGINNING OF
THE WORLD TILL NOW (Daniel 12:1), and assuredly never
will be again. And if those days had not been cut short, no 22
one would escape; but for the sake of the elect those days
will be cut short.

"If at that time any one should say to you, 'See, here is the 23
Christ!' or 'Here!' give no credence to it. For there will rise up 24
false Christs and false prophets, displaying wonderful signs
and prodigies, so as to deceive, if possible, even the elect.
Remember, I have forewarned you. If therefore they should 25
say to you, 'See, He is in the desert!' do not go out there: or 26
'See, He is in the inner-room!' do not believe it. For just as 27
the lightning flashes in the east and shoots to the west, so
will be the coming of the Son of Man. Wherever the dead 28
body is, there will the vultures flock together.

"But immediately after those times of distress THE SUN 29
WILL BE DARKENED, THE MOON WILL NOT SHED HER
LIGHT, THE STARS WILL FALL FROM HEAVEN, AND THE
FORCES WHICH CONTROL THE HEAVENS WILL BE
DISORDERED (Isaiah 13:10, 34:4). Then shall appear the 30
Sign of the Son of Man in the sky; and THEN SHALL ALL THE
NATIONS OF THE EARTH LAMENT (Zechariah 12:12), when
they see the SON OF MAN COMING ON THE CLOUDS OF
HEAVEN (Daniel 7:13) with great power and glory. And He 31
will send out His angels with A LOUD TRUMPET-BLAST
(Isaiah 27:13), and THEY WILL BRING together the elect to
Him FROM NORTH, SOUTH, EAST AND WEST—FROM
ONE EXTREMITY OF THE WORLD TO THE OTHER
(Deuteronomy 28:64, 30:4).

"Now learn from the fig-tree the lesson it teaches. As soon 32
as its branches have become soft and it is bursting into leaf,

you all know that summer is near. So also, when you see all 33
these signs, you may be sure that it is near, at your very door.
I tell you in solemn truth that the present generation will cer- 34
tainly not pass away until all this has taken place. Sky and 35
earth will pass away, but my words shall not pass away.

"But as to that day and hour no one knows—not even the 36
angels of heaven, nor the Son, but the Father alone. For as it 37
was in the time of Noah (Genesis 7), so it will be at the coming of the Son of Man. At that time, before the deluge, men 38
were busy eating and drinking, taking wives or giving them,
up to the very day when Noah entered the ark, nor did they 39
realize any danger till the deluge came and swept them all
away; so will it be at the coming of the Son of Man. Then will 40
two men be in the field: one will be taken away, and one left
behind. Two women will be grinding at the millstone: one 41
will be taken away, and one left behind. Keep watch there- 42
fore, for you do not know the day on which your Lord is coming. But of this be assured, that if the master of the house had 43
known the hour at which the robber was coming, he would
have kept awake, and not have allowed his house to be broken into. Therefore you also must be ready; for it is at a time 44
when you do not expect Him that the Son of Man will come.

"Who therefore is the faithful and prudent servant whom 45
his master has put in charge of his household to give them
their rations at the appointed time? Blessed is that servant 46
whom his master when he comes shall find so doing! In 47
solemn truth I tell you that he will give him the management
of all his property. But if the man, being a bad servant, 48
should say in his heart, 'My master is a long time in coming,'
and should begin to beat his fellow servants, while he eats 49
and drinks with drunkards; the master of that servant will 50
arrive on a day when he is not expecting him and at an hour
of which he is unaware. He will cut him asunder, and will 51

assign him a place among the hypocrites: there will be the weeping and the gnashing of teeth.

25

"Then will the Kingdom of heaven be found to be like 1 ten bridesmaids who took their torches and went out to meet the bridegroom. Five of them were foolish and five 2 were wise. For the foolish, when they took their torches, did 3 not provide themselves with oil; but the wise, besides their 4 torches, took oil in their flasks. The bridegroom was a long 5 time in coming, so that meanwhile they all became drowsy and fell asleep. But at midnight there was a loud cry, 6

"'The bridegroom! Go out and meet him!'

"Then all those bridesmaids roused themselves and 7 trimmed their torches.

"'Give us some of your oil,' said the foolish ones to the 8 wise, 'for our torches are going out.'

"'But perhaps,' replied the wise, 'there will not be enough for 9 all of us. Go to the dealers rather, and buy some for yourselves.'

"So they went to buy. But meanwhile the bridegroom 10 came; those bridesmaids who were ready went in with him to the wedding banquet; and the door was shut.

"Afterwards the other bridesmaids came and cried, 11

"'Sir, Sir, open the door to us.'

"'In truth I tell you,' he replied, 'I do not know you.' 12

"Keep watch therefore; for you know neither the day nor 13 the hour.

"Why, it is like a man who, when going on his travels, 14 called his servants and entrusted his property to their care. To one he gave five talents, to another two, to another one— 15 to each according to his capacity; and then started from home. Without delay the one who had received the five 16 talents went and employed them in business, and gained

five more. In the same way he who had the two gained two 17
more. But the man who had received the one went and dug 18
a hole and buried his master's money.

"After a long lapse of time the master of those servants 19
returned, and had a reckoning with them. The one who had 20
received the five talents came and brought five more, and said,

"'Sir, it was five talents that you entrusted to me: see, I
have gained five more.'

"'You have done well, good and trustworthy servant,' 21
replied his master; 'you have been trustworthy in the
management of a little, I will put you in charge of much.
Come and share the joy of your master.'

"The second, who had received the two talents, came and said, 22

"'Sir, it was two talents you entrusted to me: see, I have
gained two more.'

"'Good and trustworthy servant, you have done well,' his 23
master replied; 'you have been trustworthy in the management of a little, I will put you in charge of much. Come and
share the joy of your master.'

"Next, the man who had the one talent in his keeping 24
came and said,

"'Sir, I knew you to be a severe man, reaping where you
had not sown and garnering [gathering up and storing] what
you had not winnowed [blowing the chaff from grain]. So 25
being afraid I went and buried your talent in the ground:
here you have what belongs to you.'

"'You bad and slothful servant,' replied his master, 'did you 26
know that I reap where I have not sown, and garner what I
have not winnowed? Your duty, then, was to deposit my 27
money in some bank, and so when I came I should have
got back my money with interest. So take away the talent 28
from him, and give it to the man who has the ten.' (For to 29
every one who has, more shall be given, and he shall have

abundance; but from him who has nothing, even what he has shall be taken away.) 'But as for this worthless servant, put him out into the darkness outside: there will be the weeping and the gnashing of teeth.' 30

"When the Son of Man comes in His glory, and all the angels with Him, then will He sit upon His glorious throne, and all the nations will be gathered into His presence. And He will separate them from one another, just as a shepherd separates the sheep from the goats; and will make the sheep stand at His right hand, and the goats at His left. 31 32 33

"Then the King will say to those at His right, 34

"'Come, my Father's blessed ones, inherit the kingdom prepared for you ever since the creation of the world. For I was hungry, and you gave me food; I was thirsty, and you gave me drink; I was a stranger, and you gave me a welcome; I was ill-clad, and you clothed me; I was ill, and you visited me; I was in prison, and you came to see me.' 35 36

"'When, Lord,' the righteous will reply, 'did we see Thee hungry, and feed Thee; or thirsty, and give Thee drink? When did we see Thee a stranger, and give Thee a welcome? or ill-clad, and clothe Thee? When did we see Thee ill or in prison, and come to see Thee?' 37 38 39

"And the King will answer them, 40

"'In truth I tell you that in so far as you rendered such services to one of the humblest of these my brethren, you rendered them to myself.'

"Then will He say to those at His left, 41

"'Be gone from me, with the curse resting upon you, into the eternal fire, which has been prepared for the devil and his angels. For I was hungry, and you gave me nothing to eat; thirsty, and you gave me nothing to drink; a stranger, and you gave me no welcome; ill-clad, and you clothed me not; ill or in prison, and you visited me not.' 42 43

"Then will they also answer, 44

"'Lord, when did we see Thee hungry or thirsty or a stranger or ill-clad or ill or in prison, and not come to serve Thee?'

"Then He will reply, 45

"'In truth I tell you that in so far as you withheld such services from one of the humblest of these, you withheld them from me.'

"And these shall go away into eternal punishment, but the 46 righteous into eternal life."

26 When Jesus had ended all these sayings, He said 1 to His disciples:

"You know that in two days' time the Passover comes. And 2 the Son of Man will be delivered up to be crucified."

Then the high priests and elders of the people assembled 3 in the court of the palace of the high priest Caiaphas, and 4 consulted how to get Jesus into their power by stratagem and to put Him to death. But they said, 5

"Not during the festival, lest there be a riot among the people."

Now when Jesus was come to Bethany and was at the 6 house of Simon the Leper, a woman came to Him with an 7 alabaster jar of very costly perfume, which she poured over His head as He reclined at table.

"Why such waste?" indignantly exclaimed the disciples on 8 seeing it; "this might have been sold for a considerable sum, 9 and the money given to the poor."

Jesus heard it, and said to them, 10

"Why are you vexing her? It is a gracious thing that she has done to me. The poor you always have with you, but me you 11 have not always. In pouring this ointment over me, her object 12 was to prepare me for burial. In solemn truth I tell you that 13 wherever in the whole world this gospel shall be proclaimed, this deed of hers shall be spoken of in memory of her."

At that time one of the Twelve, called Judas Iscariot, went 14 to the high priests and said, "What are you willing to give me 15 if I betray him to you?"

So they weighed out to him thirty shekels (Zechariah 11:12), and from that moment he was on the watch for an 16 opportunity to betray Him.

On the first day of the Unleavened Bread the disciples 17 came to Jesus with the question,

"Where shall we make preparations for you to eat the Passover?"

"Go into the city," He replied, "to a certain man, and tell 18 him, 'The Teacher says, My time is close at hand. It is at your house that I shall keep the Passover with my disciples.'"

The disciples did as Jesus directed them, and got the 19 Passover ready.

When evening came, He was at table with the twelve 20 disciples, and the meal was proceeding, when Jesus said, 21

"In solemn truth I tell you that one of you will betray me."

Intensely grieved they began one after another to ask Him, 22 "Can it be I, Master?"

"One who has dipped his fingers in the bowl with me," He 23 answered, "is the man who will betray me. The Son of Man 24 goes His way as is written concerning Him; but alas for that man by whom the Son of Man is betrayed! It were better for that man if he had never been born."

Then Judas, the disciple who was betraying Him, asked, 25 "Can it be I, Rabbi?"

"It is you," He replied.

During the meal Jesus took a Passover loaf, blessed it and 26 broke it. He then gave it to the disciples, saying,

"Take this and eat it: it is my body."

And He took a cup, and after a thanksgiving gave it to 27
them, saying,

"Drink from it, all of you; for this is my blood, poured out 28
for many for the forgiveness of sins—the blood of the
covenant. I tell you that I will never again drink the juice of 29
the vine till the day when I drink the new wine with you in
my Father's Kingdom."

So they sang a hymn and went out to the Mount of Olives. 30

Then said Jesus, 31

"This night all of you will turn against me; for it is written,
'I WILL STRIKE THE SHEPHERD, AND THE SHEEP OF
THE FLOCK WILL BE SCATTERED IN ALL DIRECTIONS'
(Zechariah 13:7). But after I have risen to life again I will go 32
before you into Galilee."

"All may turn against you," said Peter, "but I will never do so." 33

"In truth I tell you," replied Jesus, "that this very night, 34
before the cock crows, you will three times disown me."

"Even if I must die with you," declared Peter, "I will never 35
disown you."

In like manner protested all the disciples.

Then Jesus came with them to a place called Gethsemane. 36
And He said to the disciples,

"Sit down here, whilst [while] I go yonder and there pray."

And He took with Him Peter and the two sons of Zebedee. 37
Then He began to be full of anguish and distress, and He said 38
to them,

"My soul is crushed with anguish to the point of death;
wait here, and watch with me."

Going forward a short distance He fell on His face and 39
prayed. "My Father," He said, "if it is possible, let this cup pass
away from me; nevertheless, not as I will, but as Thou willest."

Then He came to the disciples and found them asleep, and 40
He said to Peter,

"So none of you could keep awake with me for a single hour! Keep awake, and pray that you may not enter into 41 temptation: the spirit is right willing, but the body is frail."

Again a second time He went away and prayed, 42

"My Father, if it is impossible for this cup to pass without my drinking it, Thy will be done."

He came and again found them asleep, for they were very 43 weary. So He left them, and went away once more and 44 prayed a third time, again using the same words. Then He 45 came to the disciples and said,

"Sleep on and rest.—See, the moment is close at hand when the Son of Man is to be betrayed into the hands of sinful men. Rouse yourselves. Let us be going. My betrayer is 46 close at hand."

While He was still speaking, Judas, one of the Twelve, 47 came up, accompanied by a great crowd of men armed with swords and bludgeons, sent by the high priests and elders of the people. Now the betrayer had agreed upon a signal with 48 them, saying,

"The one whom I kiss is the man: lay hold of him."

So he went straight to Jesus and said, 49

"Peace to you, Rabbi!"

And he kissed Him affectionately.

"Friend," said Jesus, "carry out your intention." 50

Then they came and laid their hands on Jesus and seized Him. But one of those with Jesus drew his sword and struck 51 the high priest's servant, cutting off his ear.

"Put back your sword again," said Jesus, "for all who draw 52 the sword shall perish by the sword. Or do you suppose I 53 cannot entreat my Father and He would instantly send to my help more than twelve legions of angels? In that case how 54 are the scriptures to be fulfilled which declare that thus it must be?"

Then said Jesus to the crowds, 55

"Have you come out as if to fight with a robber, with swords and bludgeons to take me? Day after day I have been sitting teaching in the Temple, and you did not arrest me. But 56 all this has taken place in order that the writings of the prophets may be fulfilled."

Then the disciples all left Him and fled.

But the officers who had laid hold of Jesus led Him away to 57 Caiaphas the high priest, at whose house the scribes and the elders had assembled. And Peter kept following Him at a 58 distance, till he came to the court of the high priest's palace, where he entered and sat down among the police officers to see the issue.

Meanwhile the high priests and the whole Sanhedrin were 59 seeking false testimony against Jesus in order to put Him to death; but they could find none, although many false wit- 60 nesses came forward. At length there came two who testified, 61

"This man said, 'I am able to pull down the sanctuary of God and three days afterwards to build a new one.'"

Then the high priest stood up and asked Him, 62

"Have you no answer to make? What is this evidence they are bringing against you?"

Jesus, however, remained silent. Again the high priest 63 addressed Him.

"In the name of the living God," he said, "I now put you on your oath: tell us whether you are the Christ, the Son of God."

"I am He," replied Jesus. "And I tell you all that, hereafter, 64 you will see THE SON OF MAN SITTING AT THE RIGHT HAND of the Divine Power, AND COMING ON THE CLOUDS OF HEAVEN" (Psalm 110:1; Daniel 7:13).

Then the high priest tore his clothes and exclaimed, 65

"Impious words! What further need have we of witnesses! See, you have now heard His impiety. What is your verdict?" 66

"He deserves to die," they replied.

Then they spat in His face, and struck Him—some with 67
the fist, some with the open hand—saying, 68

"Christ, prove yourself a prophet by telling us who it was
that struck you."

Peter meanwhile was sitting outside in the court of the palace, 69
when one of the maidservants came over to him and said,

"You too were with Jesus the Galilaean."

He denied it before them all, saying, 70

"I do not know what you mean."

Soon afterwards he went out and stood in the gateway, when 71
another girl saw him, and said, addressing the people there,

"This man was with Jesus the Nazarene."

Again he denied it with an oath. 72

"I do not know the man," he said.

A short time afterwards the people standing there came 73
and said to Peter,

"Certainly you too are one of them, for your accent shows it."

Then he began with curses and oaths to declare, 74

"I do not know the man."

Immediately a cock crowed, and Peter recollected the 75
words of Jesus, how He had said,

"Before the cock crows you will three times disown me."

And he went out and wept aloud, bitterly.

27 When morning came all the high priests and the 1
elders of the people consulted together against Jesus
to put Him to death; and binding Him they led Him away 2
and handed Him over to Pilate the governor.

Then when Judas, who had betrayed Him, saw that He was 3
condemned, smitten with remorse he brought back the
thirty shekels to the high priests and elders and said, 4

"I have sinned in betraying to death one who is innocent."

"What does that matter to us?" they replied; "it is your business."

Flinging the shekels into the sanctuary, he left the place, 5 and went and hanged himself. When the high priests had 6 gathered up the money, they said,

"It is illegal to put it into the treasury, because it is the price of blood."

So after consulting together they spent the money in the pur- 7 chase of the Potter's Field as a burial place for people not belonging to the city; for which reason that piece of ground 8 received the name, which it still bears, of "the Field of Blood."

Then were fulfilled the words spoken by the prophet 9 Jeremiah, "AND I TOOK THE THIRTY SHEKELS, THE PRICE OF THE ONE WHO WAS PRICED—ON WHOM SOME OF THE ISRAELITES HAD SET A PRICE, AND GAVE THEM FOR 10 THE POTTER'S FIELD, AS THE LORD DIRECTED ME" (Zechariah 11:13).

Meanwhile Jesus was brought before the governor, and the 11 latter put the question, "Are you the King of the Jews?"

"I am," He answered.

When, however, the high priests and the elders brought 12 their charges against Him, He said not a word in reply.

"Do you not hear," asked Pilate, "what a mass of evidence 13 they are bringing against you?"

But He made no reply to a single accusation, so that the 14 governor was greatly astonished.

Now it was the governor's custom at the festival to release 15 some one prisoner, whomsoever the populace desired; and 16 at this time they had a notorious prisoner called Barabbas. So when they were now assembled Pilate appealed to them. 17

"Whom shall I release to you," he said, "Barabbas, or Jesus the so-called Christ?"

For he knew that it was from envious hatred that Jesus had 18 been brought before him.

While he was sitting on the tribunal a message came to 19 him from his wife.

"Have nothing to do with that innocent man," she said, "for during the night I have suffered terribly in a dream through him."

The high priests, however, and the elders persuaded the 20 crowd to ask for Barabbas and to demand the death of Jesus. So when the governor in reply asked them, "Which of the 21 two shall I release to you?"—they cried,

"Barabbas!"

"What then," said Pilate, "shall I do with Jesus, the so- 22 called Christ?"

With one voice they shouted,

"Let him be crucified!"

"But what crime has he committed?" asked Pilate. 23

They, however, kept on furiously shouting,

"Let him be crucified!"

So when he saw that he could gain nothing, but that on the 24 contrary there was a riot threatening, he took some water and washed his hands in sight of them all, saying,

"I am not responsible for this bloodshed: you must answer for it."

"His blood," replied all the people, "be on us and on 25 our children!"

Then he released Barabbas to them; but he had Jesus 26 scourged, and gave Him up to be crucified.

Then the governor's soldiers took Jesus into the 27 Praetorium, and called together the whole battalion to make sport of Him. Stripping off His garments, they put on Him a 28 scarlet cloak. They twisted a wreath of thorny twigs and put 29 it on His head, and as a scepter they put a cane in His right hand, and kneeling to Him they shouted in mockery,

"Hail, King of the Jews!"

Then they spat upon Him, and taking the cane they re- 30
peatedly struck Him on the head with it. At last, having fin- 31
ished their sport, they took off the cloak, clothed Him again
in His own garments, and led Him away for crucifixion.

Going out they met a Cyrenean named Simon, whom they 32
compelled to carry the cross of Jesus; and so they came to a 33
place called Golgotha, which means "skull-ground." Here 34
they gave Jesus a mixture of wine and gall to drink, but
having tasted it He refused to drink it. After crucifying Him, 35
they divided His garments among them by lot, and sat down 36
there on guard. Over His head they placed a written state- 37
ment of the charge against Him:

THIS IS JESUS THE KING OF THE JEWS

At the same time two robbers were crucified with Him, 38
one at His right hand and the other at His left.

And the passers-by reviled Him. They shook their heads at 39
Him and said, 40

"You who would pull down the sanctuary and build a new
one within three days, save yourself. If you are God's Son,
come down from the cross."

In like manner the high priests also, together with the 41
scribes and the elders, taunted Him.

"He saved others," they said, "himself he cannot save! He 42
is the King of Israel! Let him now come down from the
cross, and we will believe in him. His trust is in God: let 43
God deliver him now, if He will have him; for he said, 'I am
God's Son.'"

Insults of the same kind were heaped on Him even by the 44
robbers who were crucified with Him.

Now from noon until three o'clock in the afternoon there 45 was darkness over the whole land; and about three o'clock 46 Jesus cried out in a loud voice,

"ELI, ELI, LEMA SABACHTHANI?" that is to say, "MY GOD, MY GOD, WHY HAST THOU FORSAKEN ME?" (Psalm 22:1).

"The man is calling for Elijah," said some of the bystanders. 47

One of them ran forthwith [immediately/at once], and fill- 48 ing a sponge with sour wine put it on the end of a cane and offered it Him to drink; while the rest said, 49

"Stay! Let us see whether Elijah is coming to deliver him."

Then Jesus uttered another loud cry, and yielded up 50 His spirit.

Immediately the curtain of the sanctuary was torn in two 51 from top to bottom: the earth quaked; the rocks split; the 52 tombs opened; and many of the saints who were asleep in death awoke. And coming out of their tombs after Christ's 53 resurrection, they entered the holy city and showed them-selves to many.

As for the captain and his soldiers who were with him 54 keeping guard over Jesus, when they witnessed the earth-quake and the other occurrences, they were filled with terror, and exclaimed,

"Assuredly he was God's Son."

And there were there, looking on from a distance, a 55 number of women who had followed Jesus from Galilee in attendance upon Him; among them being Mary of Magdala, 56 Mary the mother of James and Joses, and the mother of the sons of Zebedee.

Towards sunset there came a wealthy man from 57 Arimathaea, named Joseph, who had himself become a disciple of Jesus. He went to Pilate and begged to have the 58 body of Jesus, and Pilate ordered it to be given to him. So 59 Joseph took the body and wrapped it in clean linen. He then 60 laid it in his own new tomb which he had hewn in the solid rock, and after rolling a great stone against the door of the tomb he went home. Mary of Magdala and the other Mary 61 were both present there, sitting opposite to the sepulcher.

On the next day, the day after the Preparation, the high 62 priests and the Pharisees came in a body to Pilate.

"Sir," they said, "we recollect that while still alive that 63 impostor said: 'After three days I shall rise to life again.' So 64 give orders for the sepulcher to be securely guarded till the third day, for fear his disciples should go and steal the body and then tell the people that he has come back to life; and so the last imposture will be more serious than the first."

"You can have a guard," said Pilate: "go and make all safe, 65 as best you can."

So they went there and made the sepulcher secure, sealing 66 the stone, besides setting the guard.

28 After the sabbath, in the early dawn of the first day of 1 the week, Mary of Magdala and the other Mary came to see the sepulcher. But to their surprise there had been a great 2 earthquake; for an angel of the Lord had descended from heaven, and had come and rolled back the stone, and was sitting upon it. His appearance was like lightning, and his raiment 3 white as snow. For fear of him the guards trembled violently, 4 and became like dead men. But the angel said to the women, 5

"Dismiss your fears. I know that it is Jesus that you are looking for—the crucified One. He is not here: He has come 6 back to life, as He foretold. Come and see the place where He lay. And go quickly and tell His disciples that He has risen 7 from the dead and is going before you into Galilee: there you shall see Him. Remember, I have told you."

They quickly left the tomb and ran, still terrified but full 8

of great joy, to carry the news to His disciples. And then 9
suddenly they saw Jesus coming to meet them.

"Peace be to you," He said.

And they came and clasped His feet, bowing to the ground
before Him. Then He said, 10

"Dismiss all fear! Go and take word to my brethren to go
into Galilee; there they shall see me."

While they went on this errand, some of the guards came 11
into the city and reported to the high priests all that had
happened. So the latter held a conference with the elders, 12
and after consultation with them they heavily bribed the
soldiers, telling them to say, 13

"His disciples came during the night and stole his body
while we were asleep."

"And if this," they added, "is reported to the governor, we 14
will satisfy him and screen you from punishment."

So they took the money and did as they were instructed; 15
and this story was spread about among the Jews, and is
current to this day.

As for the eleven disciples, they departed for Galilee, 16
to the hill where Jesus had arranged to meet them. There 17
they saw Him and prostrated themselves before Him. Yet
some doubted.

Jesus, however, came near and said to them, 18

"All authority in heaven and on earth has been given to
me. Go therefore and make disciples of all the nations; bap- 19
tize them into the name of the Father, and of the Son, and of
the Holy Spirit; and teach them to observe every command 20
which I have given you. And remember, I am with you
always, day by day, until the close of the age."

THE GOSPEL ACCORDING TO ST. MARK

1 The beginning of the gospel of Jesus Christ the Son of God. 1
As it is written in Isaiah the prophet, 2
"SEE, I AM SENDING MY MESSENGER BEFORE THY FACE,
WHO WILL PREPARE THY WAY" (Malachi 3:1);
"THE VOICE OF ONE CRYING ALOUD: 3
'IN THE DESERT PREPARE A ROAD FOR THE LORD:
MAKE HIS HIGHWAYS STRAIGHT'" (Isaiah 40:3).

So John the Baptizer came, and was in the desert, pro- 4
claiming a baptism of the penitent for forgiveness of sins.
There went out to him people of all classes from Judaea, and 5
from the inhabitants of Jerusalem, and were baptized by him
in the river Jordan, making open confession of their sins.

John's clothing was of camel's hair, and he wore a leather girdle; 6
and his food was locusts and wild honey. His proclamation was, 7

"There is One coming after me mightier than I—One
whose sandal-strap I am unworthy to stoop down and unfasten. I have baptized you with water, but He will baptize 8
you with the Holy Spirit."

At that time Jesus came from Nazareth in Galilee and was 9
baptized by John in the Jordan; and immediately on His 10
coming up out of the water He saw the sky parting asunder,
and the Spirit like a dove coming down upon Him; and a 11
voice came from the sky, saying,

"Thou art My Son, the Beloved: in Thee is My delight"
(Psalm 2:7; Isaiah 42:1).

At once the Spirit impelled Him to go out into the desert, 12
where He remained for forty days, tempted by Satan; and He 13
was among the wild beasts, but the angels waited upon Him.

Then, after John had been thrown into prison, Jesus came 14
into Galilee proclaiming the gospel of God.

"The time has fully come," He said, "and the Kingdom of 15
God is close at hand: repent, and believe this good news."

One day, passing along the shore of the Lake of Galilee, He 16
saw Simon and Andrew, Simon's brother, throwing their nets
in the lake; for they were fishermen.

"Come and follow me," said Jesus, "and I will make you 17
fishers for men."

At once they left their nets and followed Him. Going on a 18
little farther He saw James the son of Zebedee and his brother 19
John: they also were in their boat mending their nets, and He 20
immediately called them. They therefore left their father
Zebedee in the boat with the hired men, and followed Him.

So they came to Capernaum. And on the next sabbath He 21
went to the synagogue and began to teach. The people listened 22
with amazement to His teaching; for there was authority about
it: it was very different from that of the scribes. All at once, a 23
man with a foul spirit in their synagogue screamed out:

"What have you to do with us, Jesus the Nazarene? Have you 24
come to destroy us? I know who you are—God's Holy One."

But Jesus rebuked the spirit, saying, 25

"Silence! come out of him."

So the foul spirit, after throwing the man into convulsions, 26
came out of him with a loud cry. And all were awe-struck, so 27
that they began to ask one another,

"What does this mean? Here is a new sort of teaching—
and a tone of authority! Even to foul spirits he issues orders and they obey him!"

And His fame spread at once everywhere through all the 28
surrounding country of Galilee.

Then on leaving the synagogue they came at once, with 29
James and John, to the house of Simon and Andrew. Now 30

Simon's mother-in-law was ill in bed with a fever, and without delay they told Him about her. So He went to her, and 31 taking her hand He raised her to her feet: the fever left her, and she began to wait upon them.

When it was evening, after sunset people came bringing 32 Him all who were ill and the demoniacs; and the whole town 33 was assembled at the door. And He cured numbers of people 34 who were ill with various diseases, and He drove out many demons; not allowing the demons to speak, because they knew Him.

In the morning He rose early, while it was still quite dark, 35 and leaving the house He went away to a solitary place and there prayed. And Simon and the others searched every- 36 where for Him. When they found Him they said, 37

"Every one is looking for you."

He replied, "Let us go elsewhere, to the neighboring coun- 38 try towns, in order that I may preach there also; because for that purpose I came forth."

And He went through all Galilee, preaching in the 39 synagogues and expelling the demons.

One day there came a leper to Jesus entreating Him, and 40 pleading on his knees.

"If you are willing," he said, "you are able to cleanse me."

Moved with pity Jesus reached out His hand and touched him. 41

"I am willing," He said, "be cleansed."

The leprosy at once left him, and he was cleansed. Jesus at 42 once sent him away, sternly charging him, and saying, 43

"Be careful not to tell any one, but go and show yourself to 44 the Priest, and for your purification present the offerings that Moses appointed as evidence to them."

But the man went out, and began to tell every one and to 45 spread the news in all directions, so that it was no longer possible for Jesus to go openly into any town. He had to remain outside in unfrequented places, and people came to Him from all parts.

2 After some days He entered Capernaum again, and it soon became known that He was at home; and such numbers of people came together that there was no longer room for them even round the door. He was speaking the word to them, when there came a party of people bringing a paralyzed man— four men carrying him. Finding themselves unable, however, to bring him to Jesus because of the crowd, they untiled the roof just over His head, and after clearing an opening they lowered the mat on which the paralytic was lying.

Seeing their faith, Jesus said to the paralytic,

"My son, your sins are pardoned."

Now there were some of the scribes sitting there, who reasoned in their hearts,

"Why does this man use such words? he is blaspheming. Who can pardon sins but One—that is, God?"

At once becoming aware that they were thus reasoning in their minds, Jesus asked them,

"Why do you thus argue in your minds? Which is easier?— to say to this paralytic, 'Your sins are pardoned,' or to say, 'Rise, take up your mat, and walk'? But that you may know that the Son of Man has authority on earth to pardon sins"—

He turned to the paralytic, and said,

"To you I say, 'Rise, take up your mat and go home.'"

The man rose, and immediately under the eyes of all took up his mat and went out, so that they were all filled with astonishment, gave the glory to God, and said,

"We never saw anything like this."

Again He went out to the shore of the lake, and the whole multitude kept coming to Him, and He taught them. And as

He passed by, He saw Levi the son of Alphaeus sitting at the toll office, and said to him,

"Follow me."

So he rose and followed Him.

When He was at table in Levi's house, a large number of 15
tax-gatherers and sinners were at table with Jesus and His
disciples; for there were many such who followed Him. But 16
when the scribes of the Pharisee sect saw Him eating with
the sinners and the tax-gatherers, they said to His disciples,

"He is eating and drinking with the tax-gatherers and sinners!"

Jesus heard the words, and He said, 17

"It is not the healthy who require a doctor, but the sick: I
did not come to call the righteous, but sinners."

Now John's disciples and those of the Pharisees were keep- 18
ing a fast. And they came and asked Him,

"How is it that John's disciples and those of the Pharisees
are fasting, and yours are not?"

"Can the bridegroom's party fast while the bridegroom is 19
among them?" replied Jesus. "As long as they have the bridegroom with them, fasting is impossible. But a time will come 20
when the bridegroom will be taken away from them; then
they will fast. No one mends an old garment with a patch of 21
unshrunk cloth. Otherwise, the added patch tears away from
it—the new from the old—and a worse hole is made. And no 22
one pours new wine into old wineskins. Otherwise the wine
will burst the skins, and both wine and skins are lost. New
wine needs fresh skins!"

One sabbath He was walking through the wheat fields, 23
when His disciples began to pluck the ears of wheat as they
went. So the Pharisees said to Him, 24

"Look! why are they doing what on the sabbath is unlawful?"

"Have you never read," Jesus replied, "what David did 25
when he had need and he and his men were hungry: how 26

he entered the house of God in the high-priesthood of Abiathar, and ate the Presented Loaves—which none but the priests are allowed to eat—and gave some to his men also?" (1 Samuel 21:6).

And Jesus said to them: 27

"The sabbath was made for man, not man for the sabbath; so that the Son of Man is Lord even of the sabbath."   28

3 At another time when He went to the synagogue, there   1
was a man there with one hand shriveled up. They closely   2
watched Him to see whether He would cure him on the sabbath, so as to have a charge to bring against Him.

"Come forward," said He to the man with the shriveled hand.   3

Then he asked them,   4

"Are we allowed to do good on the sabbath, or to do evil? to save a life, or to destroy one?"

They remained silent. Grieved and indignant at the hardening of their hearts, He looked round on them with anger,   5
and said to the man,

"Stretch out your hand."

He stretched it out, and the hand was completely restored. But the Pharisees left the synagogue and at once held a consultation with the Herodians against Jesus, to devise some   6
means of destroying Him.

So Jesus withdrew with His disciples to the lake, and a vast   7
crowd of people from Galilee followed Him. And from Judaea and Jerusalem and Idumaea and from beyond the   8
Jordan and from the district of Tyre and Sidon there came to Him a vast crowd, hearing of all that He was doing. Therefore   9
He gave directions to His disciples to keep a small boat always ready because of the throng, to prevent their crushing Him. For He had cured many of the people, so that all   10

who had any ailments pressed upon Him, to touch Him. And 11
the foul spirits, whenever they saw Him, threw themselves
down at His feet, screaming out:

"You are the Son of God."

But He absolutely forbade them to say who He was. 12

Then He went up the hill, and called those whom He 13
Himself chose, and they came to Him. And He appointed 14
twelve of them, that they might be with Him, and that He
might send them forth to preach, with authority to expel the 15
demons. These twelve were Simon (to whom He gave the sur- 16
name of Peter), James the son of Zebedee and John the 17
brother of James (these two He surnamed Boanerges, that is
"Sons of Thunder"), Andrew, Philip, Bartholomew, Matthew, 18
Thomas, James the son of Alphaeus, Thaddaeus, Simon the
Cananaean, and Judas Iscariot, the man who betrayed Him. 19

And He went into a house. But again the crowd assembled, 20
so that there was no opportunity for them even to snatch a
meal. Hearing of this, His relatives set out to seize Him by 21
force, for they said,

"He is out of his mind."

The scribes, too, who had come down from Jerusalem, said, 22
"He has Beelzebul in him; and it is by the power of the
prince of the demons that he expels the demons."

So He called them to Him, and with a parable He appealed 23
to them, saying,

"How is it possible for Satan to expel Satan? For if civil war 24
breaks out in a kingdom, nothing can make that kingdom
last; and if a family splits into parties, that family cannot 25
continue. So if Satan has risen in arms and has made war 26
upon himself, stand he cannot, but meets his end. Indeed, 27
no one can go into a strong man's house and carry off his
property, unless he first binds the strong man, and then he
will plunder his house. In truth I tell you that all their sins 28

may be pardoned to the sons of men, and all their blasphemies, however they may have blasphemed; but whoever 29 blasphemes against the Holy Spirit remains for ever unpardoned: he is guilty of an eternal sin."

This was because they said, 30

"He is possessed by a foul spirit."

By this time His mother and His brothers arrive, and standing outside they send a message to Him to call Him. Now a 32 crowd was sitting round Him; so they tell Him, 31

"Your mother and your brothers and sisters are outside, inquiring for you."

"Who are my mother and my brothers?" He replied. 33

And, fixing His eyes on the people who were sitting round 34 Him in a circle, He said,

"Here are my mother and my brothers. For wherever there 35 is one who has been obedient to God, there is my brother, my sister, and my mother."

4 Once more He began to teach by the side of the lake, 1 and a vast multitude of people came together to listen to Him. He therefore went on board the boat and sat there, a little way from the land; and all the people were on the shore close to the water. Then He taught them much by means of 2 parables; and in His teaching He said,

"Listen! A sower went out to sow. As he sowed, some of the 3 seed fell by the way-side, and the birds came and pecked it 4 up. Some fell on the rocky ground where it found but little 5 earth, and it shot up quickly because it had no depth of soil; but when the sun was risen, it was scorched, and through 6 having no root it withered away. Some, again, fell among the 7 thorns; and the thorns sprang up and stifled it, so that it yielded no crop. But some of the seed fell into good ground, 8 and gave a return: it came up and increased, and yielded thirty, sixty, or a hundred fold."

"Listen," He added, "every one who has ears to hear!" 9

When He was alone, the Twelve and the others who were 10
about Him asked Him to explain His parables.

"To you," He replied, "has been entrusted the secret truth 11
concerning the Kingdom of God; but to those others outside
your number all this is spoken in parables, that

"'THEY MAY LOOK AND LOOK, BUT NOT SEE, 12
AND LISTEN AND LISTEN BUT NOT UNDERSTAND,
LEST PERCHANCE THEY SHOULD TURN AND BE PAR-
DONED' (Isaiah 6:10).

"Do you all miss the meaning of this parable?" He added; 13
"how then will you understand the rest of my parables?

"What the sower sows is the word. Those who receive the 14
seed by the way-side are those in whom the word is sown, 15
but, when they have heard it, Satan comes at once and carries away the word sown in them. In the same way those who 16
receive the seed on the rocky places are those who, when
they have heard the word, at once accept it joyfully, but they 17
have no root within them. They last for a time; then, when
suffering or persecution comes because of the word, they
stumble and fall. Others there are who receive the seed 18
among the thorns: these are they who have heard the word,
but worldly cares and the deceitfulness of wealth and 19
absorption in other attractions come in and stifle the word,
and it becomes unfruitful. Those, on the other hand, who 20
have received the seed on the good ground, are all who hear
the word and welcome it, and yield a return of thirty, sixty, or
a hundred fold."

He went on to say, 21

"Is the lamp brought in to be put under the bushel-
measure, or under the bed? Is it not that it may be placed on

the lampstand? Why, there is nothing hidden except to be 22
disclosed, nor has anything been made a secret but that it
may come to light. Listen, every one who has ears to hear!" 23

He also said to them, 24

"Take care what you hear. With what measure you measure, it will be measured to you, and that with interest. For he 25
who has will have more given him; and from him who has
not, even what he has will be taken away."

Another saying of His was this: 26

"The Kingdom of God is as if a man scattered seed over the
ground: he spends days and nights, now awake, now asleep, 27
while the seed sprouts and grows tall, he knows not how. Of 28
itself the land produces the crop—first the blade, then the
ear; afterwards the perfect grain in the ear. But no sooner is 29
the crop ripe, than he sends the reapers, because the time of
harvest has come."

Another saying of His was this: 30

"How are we to picture the Kingdom of God? or by what
parable shall we represent it? It is like a mustard-seed, 31
which, when sown in the earth, is the smallest of all the seeds
in the world; yet when sown it springs up and becomes 32
larger than all the herbs, and throws out great branches, so
that the birds roost under its shadow."

With many such parables He would speak the word to 33
them according to their capacity for receiving it. But except 34
in parables He spoke nothing to them; while to His own disciples He explained everything, in private.

The same day, in the evening, He said to them, 35

"Let us cross to the other side."

So they got away from the crowd, and took Him, as He was, 36
in the boat; and other boats accompanied Him. But a heavy 37
squall came on, and the waves were now dashing into the
boat, so that it was fast filling. But He Himself was in the stern 38

asleep, with His head on the cushion: so they woke Him.

"Rabbi," they cried, "is it nothing to you that we are drowning?"

So He roused Himself and rebuked the wind, and said to 39
the waves,

"Silence! Be still!"

The wind sank, and there was perfect calm.

"Why are you so timid?" He asked; "have you still no faith?" 40

Then they were filled with terror, and began to say to 41
one another,

"Who then is this? For even wind and sea obey Him."

5 So they arrived at the opposite shore of the lake, in the 1
country of the Gerasenes. At once, on His landing, there 2
came from the tombs to meet Him a man possessed by a foul
spirit. This man lived among the tombs, nor could any one 3
now secure him even with a chain; for many a time he had 4
been left securely bound in fetters and chains, but afterwards the chains lay torn link from link, and the fetters in
fragments, and there was no one strong enough to master
him. And constantly, day and night, he remained among the 5
tombs or on the hills, shrieking, and mangling himself with
sharp stones. When he saw Jesus in the distance, he ran and 6
threw himself at His feet, crying out in a loud voice, 7

"What hast Thou to do with me, Jesus, Son of God Most
High? In God's name I implore Thee not to torment me."

For He had said to him, 8

"Foul spirit, come out of the man."

Jesus also questioned him. 9

"What is your name?" He said.

"Legion," he replied, "for there are a host of us."

And he earnestly entreated Him not to send them away 10
out of the country.

Feeding there, on the mountain slope, was a great herd of swine. So they besought Jesus.

"Send us to the swine," they said, "that we may enter them."

He gave them leave; and the foul spirits came out and entered the swine; and the herd—about two thousand in number—rushed headlong down the steep into the lake and were drowned in the lake. The swineherds fled, and spread the news in town and country. So the people went to see what had happened. And when they came to Jesus, they beheld the demoniac quietly seated, clothed and of sane mind—the man who had had the legion: and they were awe-struck. And those who had seen it told them what had happened to the demoniac, and all about the swine. Then they began to entreat Him to depart from their district.

As He was embarking, the man who had been possessed asked permission to accompany Him. But He would not allow it.

"Go home to your family," He said, "and report to them all that the Lord has done for you, and the mercy He has shown you."

The man departed, and proclaimed everywhere in Decapolis all that Jesus had done for him; and all were astonished.

When Jesus had re-crossed in the boat to the other side, a vast multitude collected round Him; and He was on the shore of the lake, when there came one of the rulers of the synagogue (he was called Jairus) who, on beholding Him, threw himself at His feet, and besought Him with many entreaties.

"My little daughter," he said, "is at the point of death: I pray you come and lay your hands upon her, that she may recover and live."

And Jesus went with him. And a dense crowd followed Him, and thronged Him on all sides.

Now a woman who for twelve years had been troubled with hemorrhage, and had suffered much from a number of

doctors and had spent all she had without receiving benefit
but rather growing worse, heard of Jesus. And she came in 27
the crowd behind Him and touched His cloak; for she said, 28

"If I but touch His clothes, I shall be cured."

In a moment the flow of her blood ceased, and she felt in 29
herself that her complaint was cured. Immediately Jesus, 30
well knowing that healing power had gone from Him, turned
round in the crowd and asked,

"Who touched my clothes?"

"You see the multitude pressing you on all sides," His dis- 31
ciples exclaimed, "and yet you ask, 'Who touched me?'"

But He continued looking about to see the person who 32
had done this, until the woman, frightened and trembling, 33
knowing what had happened to her, came and threw herself
at His feet, and told Him all the truth.

"Daughter," He said, "your faith has cured you: go in 34
peace, and be free from your complaint."

While He is yet speaking, men come from the house to the 35
ruler, and say,

"Your daughter is dead: why trouble the Rabbi further?"

But Jesus, disregarding their words, said to the ruler, 36

"Do not be afraid: only have faith."

And He allowed no one to accompany Him except Peter 37
and the brothers James and John. So they come to the ruler's 38
house. Here He gazes on a scene of uproar, with people
weeping aloud and wailing. He goes in. 39

"Why all this outcry and loud weeping?" He asks; "the
child is asleep, not dead."

And they jeered at Him. But He puts them all out, takes the 40
child's father and mother and those He has brought with
Him, and enters the room where the child lies. Then, taking 41
her by the hand, He says to her,

"Talithà, koum"; that is to say, "Little girl, I bid you to wake!"

Instantly the little girl rises to her feet and begins to walk 42
(for she was twelve years old). They were at once beside
themselves with utter astonishment; but He gave strict 43
injunctions that the matter should not be made known, and
directed them to give her something to eat.

6 Leaving that place He came into His own country, 1
accompanied by His disciples. On the sabbath He be- 2
gan to teach in the synagogue; and many, as they heard Him,
were astonished.

"Where did he acquire all this?" they asked. "What is this
wisdom that has been given to him? And what are these miracles which his hands perform? Is not this the carpenter, 3
Mary's son, the brother of James and Joses, Jude and Simon?
And do not his sisters live here among us?"

So they took offense at Him. But Jesus said to them, 4

"There is no prophet without honor except in his own
country, and among his own relatives, and in his own home."

And He could not do any miracle there, except that He laid 5
His hands on a few sick folk and cured them; and He won- 6
dered at their unbelief. So He went round the adjacent
villages, teaching.

Then summoning the Twelve to Him, He proceeded to 7
send them out by twos, and gave them authority over the
foul spirits. He charged them to take nothing for the journey 8
except a stick; no bread, no bag, and not a penny in their
pockets, but to go wearing sandals. 9

"And do not," He said, "put on an extra inner garment.
Wherever you enter a house, make it your home till you leave 10
that place. But wherever they will not receive you or listen to 11
you, when you leave shake off the very dust from under your
feet as a protest against them."

So they set out, and preached, in order that men might 12 repent. Many demons they expelled, and many invalids they 13 anointed with oil and cured.

King Herod heard of all this (for the name of Jesus had 14 become widely known), and he said,

"John the Baptizer has come back to life, and that is why these miraculous powers are working in him."

Others asserted that He was Elijah. 15

Others again said,

"He is a prophet, like one of the great prophets."

But when Herod heard of Him, he said, 16

"That John, whom I beheaded, has come back to life."

For Herod himself had sent and arrested John, and had 17 kept him in prison in chains, for the sake of Herodias, his brother Philip's wife; because he had married her. For John 18 told Herod,

"You have no right to be living with your brother's wife."

Therefore Herodias bore a grudge against him and wished 19 to take his life, but could not; for Herod stood in awe of John, 20 knowing him to be an upright and holy man, and he protected him. After listening to him he was in great perplexity, and yet he found a pleasure in listening. At length 21 Herodias found her opportunity. Herod on his birthday gave a banquet to the nobles of his court and to the tribunes [magistrates] and the principal people in Galilee, at which 22 Herodias's own daughter came in and danced, and so charmed Herod and his guests that he said to her,

"Ask me for anything you please, and I will give it to you."

He even swore to her, 23

"Whatever you ask me for I will give you, up to half my kingdom."

She at once went out and said to her mother: 24

"What shall I ask for?"

"The head of John the Baptizer," she replied.

The girl immediately came in, in haste, to the King and made her request. 25

"My desire is," she said, "that you will give me, here and now, on a dish, the head of John the Baptist."

Then the King, though intensely sorry, yet for the sake of his oaths, and of his guests, would not break faith with her. 26 He at once sent a soldier of his guard with orders to bring 27 John's head. So he went and beheaded him in the prison, and 28 brought his head on a dish and gave it to the young girl, who gave it to her mother. When John's disciples heard of it, they 29 came and took away his body and laid it in a tomb.

When the apostles reassembled round Jesus, they reported 30 to Him all they had done and all they had taught. Then He 31 said to them,

"Come away, all of you, to a quiet place, and rest awhile."

For there were many coming and going, so that they had no time even for meals. Accordingly they went away in the boat 32 to a solitary place. But the people saw them going, and many 33 recognized them; so they hastened there on foot from all the neighboring towns, and arrived before them. So when Jesus 34 landed, He saw a vast multitude; and His heart was moved with pity for them, because they were like sheep without a shepherd, and He proceeded to teach them many things.

By this time it was late: so His disciples came to Him, and said, 35

"This is a lonely place, and the hour is now late: send them 36 away that they may go to the farms and villages near and buy themselves something to eat."

"Give them food yourselves," He replied. 37

"Are we," they asked, "to go and buy two hundred shillings' worth of bread and give them food?"

"How many loaves have you?" He inquired; "go and see." 38 So they found out, and said,

"Five; and a couple of fish."

So He directed them to make all recline in companies 39
on the green grass. And they settled down in groups of 40
hundreds and of fifties. Then He took the five loaves and the 41
two fish, and lifting His eyes to heaven He blessed the food.
Then He broke the loaves into portions, which He handed to
the disciples to distribute; giving pieces also of the two fish
to them all. All ate and were fully satisfied. And they took up 42
broken portions enough to fill twelve baskets, besides pieces 43
of the fish. Those who ate the bread were five thousand men. 44

Immediately afterwards He made His disciples go on 45
board the boat and cross over to Bethsaida, leaving Him
behind to dismiss the crowd. He then bade the people 46
farewell, and went away up the hill to pray.

When evening was come, the boat was half way across the 47
lake, while He Himself was on shore alone. But seeing them 48
distressed with rowing (for the wind was against them), about
the fourth watch of the night He came towards them walking
on the lake, as if intending to pass them. They saw Him walk- 49
ing on the water, and thinking that it was a ghost they cried
out; for they all saw Him and were terrified. He, however, 50
immediately spoke to them.

"There is no danger," He said; "it is I; do not be alarmed."

Then He went up to them and entered the boat, and the 51
wind lulled; and they were beside themselves with amazement; for they had not learned the lesson taught by the 52
loaves, but their minds were dull.

Having crossed over they drew to land at Gennesaret and 53
made fast to the shore. But no sooner had they left the boat 54
than the people immediately recognized Him. And they 55
scoured the whole district, and began to bring to Him on their
mats those who were ill wherever they heard He was. And 56
enter wherever He might—village or town or hamlet—they

laid their sick in the open places, and entreated Him to let them touch were it but the tassel of His robe; and all, whoever touched Him, were restored to health.

7 Then the Pharisees, with certain scribes who had come 1 from Jerusalem, came to Him in a body. They had 2 noticed that some of His disciples were eating their food with "unclean" (that is to say, unwashed) hands. (For the Pharisees 3 and all the Jews—being, as they are, zealous for the traditions of the elders—never eat without first carefully washing their hands, and when they come from market they will not eat 4 without bathing first; and they have a good many other customs which they have received traditionally and cling to, such as the washing of cups and pots and of bronze vessels, and of beds.) So the Pharisees and scribes put the question to Him: 5

"Why do your disciples transgress the traditions of the elders, and eat their food with unclean hands?"

"Rightly did Isaiah prophesy of you hypocrites," He 6 replied; "as it is written,

"'THIS PEOPLE HONOR ME WITH THEIR LIPS,
WHILE THEIR HEART IS FAR FROM ME:
IN VAIN DO THEY WORSHIP ME 7
WHILE THEY LAY DOWN PRECEPTS WHICH ARE MERE
HUMAN RULES' (Isaiah 29:13).

"You neglect God's commandment: you hold fast to 8 men's traditions."

"Praiseworthy indeed!" He added, "to set at naught God's 9 commandment in order to observe your own traditions! For 10 Moses said, 'HONOR THY FATHER AND THY MOTHER' (Exodus 20:12), and again, 'HE WHO REVILES FATHER OR MOTHER, LET HIM BE PUT TO DEATH' (Exodus 21:17). But 11 you say, 'If a man says to his father or mother, This thing is

Korban (that is consecrated to God); otherwise you should have received it from me—' you no longer allow him to do 12 anything for his father or mother, thus nullifying God's pre- 13 cept by your tradition which you have handed down. And many things of that kind you do."

Then Jesus called the people to Him again. 14

"Listen to me, all of you," He said, "and understand. There 15 is nothing outside a man which entering into him can make him unclean; but it is the things which come out of a man that make him unclean."

After He had left the crowd and gone indoors, His disciples 17 began to ask Him about this parable.

"Is it so that you also are without understanding?" He re- 18 plied; "do you not see that anything whatever that enters a man from outside cannot make him unclean, because it does 19 not go into his heart, but into his stomach, and passes away?"

By these words Jesus pronounced all kinds of food clean.

"It is what comes out of a man," He added, "that makes 20 him unclean. For from within, out of men's hearts, their evil 21 purposes proceed—fornication, theft, murder, adultery, cov- 22 etousness, wickedness, deceit, licentiousness, envy, slander, pride, reckless folly: all these wicked things come out from 23 within and make a man unclean."

Then He rose and left that place and went into the neigh- 24 borhood of Tyre and Sidon.

Here He entered a house and wished no one to know it, but He could not escape observation. Forthwith [immediately/at 25 once] a woman whose little daughter was possessed by a foul spirit heard of Him, and came and flung herself at His feet. She was a Gentile woman, a Syro-phoenician by nation, 26 and she begged Him to expel the demon from her daughter.

"Let the children first eat all they want," He said; "it is not 27 right to take the children's bread and throw it to the dogs."

"True, sir," she replied, "but even the dogs under the table 28
eat the children's scraps."

"For those words of yours, go home," He replied; "the 29
demon has gone out of your daughter."

So she went home, and found the child laid on the bed, 30
and the demon gone.

Returning from the neighborhood of Tyre, He came by way 31
of Sidon to the Lake of Galilee, passing through the district of
Decapolis. Here they brought to Him a deaf man who stam- 32
mered, on whom they begged Him to lay His hands. So Jesus 33
taking him aside, apart from the crowd, put His fingers into
his ears, and spat, and moistened his tongue; and looking up 34
to heaven He sighed, and said to him,

"Ephphatha" (that is, "Open!").

And the man's ears were opened, and his tongue became 35
untied, and he began to speak perfectly. Then Jesus charged 36
them to tell no one; but the more He charged them, all the
more did they spread the news far and wide. The amazement 37
was extreme.

"How well he has done everything," they exclaimed; "he
even makes deaf men hear and dumb men speak!"

8 About that time there was again an immense crowd, 1
and they found themselves with nothing to eat. So He
called His disciples to Him. "My heart aches for the people," 2
He said; "for this is now the third day they have remained
with me, and they have nothing to eat. If I were to send them 3
home hungry, they would faint on the way, some of them
having come a great distance."

"Where can we possibly get bread here in this remote 4
place to satisfy such a crowd?" answered His disciples.

"How many loaves have you?" He asked. 5

"Seven," they said.

So He passed the word to the people to sit down on the ground. Then taking the seven loaves He blessed them, and broke them into portions and proceeded to give them to His disciples for them to distribute, and they distributed them to the people. They had also a few small fish. He blessed them, and He told His disciples to distribute these also. So the people ate an abundant meal; and what remained over they took up—seven large baskets of broken pieces. The number fed were about four thousand. Then He sent them away, and at once going on board with His disciples He came into the district of Dalmanutha.

The Pharisees followed Him and began to dispute with Him, asking Him for a sign from heaven, to make trial of Him. But with a deep and troubled sigh, He said,

"Why do the men of to-day ask for a sign? In truth I tell you that no sign shall be given to the men of to-day."

So He left them, went on board again, and crossed to the other side of the lake.

Now they had forgotten to take bread, nor had they more than a single loaf with them in the boat; and when He admonished them "See that you are on your guard against the leaven of the Pharisees and the leaven of Herod," they reasoned with one another and remarked,

"We have no bread!"

He perceived what they were saying, and He said to them,

"What is this discussion about having no bread? Do you not yet see and understand? Are you so dull of mind? YOU HAVE EYES! CAN YOU NOT SEE? YOU HAVE EARS! CAN YOU NOT HEAR? (Jeremiah 5:21) and have you no memory? When I broke up the five loaves for the five thousand men, how many baskets did you take up full of broken portions?"

"Twelve," they said.

"And when the seven for the four thousand, how many 20
hampers full of portions did you take away?"

"Seven," they answered.

"Do you not yet understand?" He said. 21

And they came to Bethsaida. And a blind man was brought 22
to Jesus and they entreated Him to touch him. So He took the 23
blind man by the arm and brought him out of the village,
and spitting into his eyes He put His hands on him and
asked him,

"Can you see anything?"

He looked up and said, 24

"I can see people: I see them like trees—only walking."

Then for the second time He put His hands on the man's 25
eyes, and the man, looking steadily, recovered his sight and
saw everything distinctly. So He sent him home, and added, 26

"Do not even go into the village."

From that place Jesus and His disciples went to the villages 27
belonging to Caesarea Philippi. On the way He began to ask
His disciples,

"Who do people say that I am?"

"John the Baptist," they replied, "but others say Elijah, and 28
others, that you are one of the prophets."

Then He asked them, 29

"But you yourselves, who do you say that I am?"

"You are the Christ," answered Peter.

And He strictly forbade them to tell this about Him to any one. 30

And now for the first time He told them, 31

"The Son of Man must suffer much cruelty, and be rejected by the elders and the high priests and the scribes, and
be put to death, and on the third day rise to life."

This He told them plainly; whereupon Peter took Him 32
aside, and began to remonstrate [plead in protest] with Him.
But turning round and seeing His disciples, He rebuked Peter. 33

"Get behind me, Satan," He said, "for your thoughts are not God's thoughts, but men's."

Then calling to Him the crowd and also His disciples, He 34 said to them,

"If any one wishes to follow me, let him renounce self and take up his cross, and so be my follower. For whoever desires 35 to save his life shall lose it, but he who loses his life for my sake, and for the sake of the gospel, shall save it. Why, what does it 36 benefit a man to gain the whole world and forfeit his life? For 37 what could a man give to buy back his life? Every one who has 38 been ashamed of me and my teachings in this apostate and sinful age, of him the Son of Man also will be ashamed when He comes in His Father's glory with the holy angels."

9 He went on to say, 1
"I tell you in truth that some of those who are standing here will not taste death till they have seen the Kingdom of God already come in power."

Six days later, Jesus took with Him Peter, James, and John, 2 and brought them alone, apart from the rest, up a high mountain; and in their presence His appearance underwent a change. His garments also became dazzling with brilliant 3 whiteness—such whiteness as no bleaching on earth could give. Moreover there appeared to them Elijah accompanied 4 by Moses; and the two were conversing with Jesus, when 5 Peter said to Jesus,

"Rabbi, it is well that we are here. Let us put up three tents—one for you, one for Moses, and one for Elijah."

For he knew not what to say: they were filled with such 6 awe. Then there came a cloud spreading over them, and a 7 voice issued from the cloud,

"This is my Son, the Beloved: listen to Him."

Instantly they looked round, and now they could no longer 8
see any one, but only Jesus with them.

As they were coming down from the mountain, He very 9
strictly forbade them to tell any one what they had seen
"until after the Son of Man has risen from among the dead."
So they kept the matter to themselves, although discussing 10
one with another what was meant by this rising from the
dead. They also asked Him, 11

"How is it that the scribes say that Elijah must first come?"

"Elijah," He replied, "does indeed come first and reforms 12
everything; but how is it that it is written of the Son of Man
that He will endure much suffering and be held in contempt?
Yet I tell you that not only has Elijah come, but they have 13
also done to him whatever they chose, as the scriptures say
about him."

As they came to rejoin the disciples, they saw an immense 14
crowd surrounding them and a party of scribes disputing
with them. Immediately the whole multitude on behold- 15
ing Him where awe-struck, and they ran forward and
greeted Him.

"What are you discussing?" He asked them. 16

"Rabbi," answered one of the crowd, "I have brought you 17
my son. He has a dumb spirit in him; and wherever it comes 18
upon him, it dashes him to the ground, and he foams at the
mouth and grinds his teeth, and he is pining away. I begged
your disciples to expel it, but they were unable."

"O unbelieving generation!" replied Jesus; "how long must I 19
be with you? how long must I bear with you? Bring him to me."

So they brought him to Jesus. And the spirit, when he saw 20
Jesus, immediately threw the youth into convulsions, so that
he fell on the ground and rolled about, foaming at the
mouth. Then Jesus asked the father, 21

"How long has he been like this?"

"From early childhood," he said; "and often it has thrown 22 him into the fire or into pools of water to destroy him. But, if you can, have pity on us and help us."

"'If I can!'" replied Jesus; "Why, everything is possible to 23 him who believes."

Immediately the father cried out, 24

"I do believe: aid my weak faith."

Then Jesus, seeing that a crowd was rapidly gathering, 25 rebuked the foul spirit, and said to it,

"Dumb and deaf spirit, I command you, come out of him and never enter into him again."

So with a loud cry it threw the boy into fit after fit, and 26 came out. The boy looked as if he were dead, so that most of them said he was dead; but Jesus took his hand and raised 27 him up, and he stood on his feet.

After the return of Jesus to the house His disciples asked 28 Him privately,

"How is it that we could not expel the spirit?"

"An evil spirit of this kind," He answered, "can be driven 29 out only by prayer."

Departing thence they passed through Galilee, and He was 30 unwilling that any one should know it; for He was teaching 31 His disciples, and telling them,

"The Son of Man is to be betrayed into the hands of men, and they will put Him to death; and after being put to death, in three days He will rise to life again."

They, however, did not understand what He meant, and 32 were afraid to question Him.

So they came to Capernaum; and when in the house He 33 asked them,

"What were you arguing about on the way?"

They remained silent; for on the way they had debated 34 with one another who was the chief of them. Then sitting 35 down He called the Twelve, and said to them,

"If any one wishes to be first, he must be last of all and servant of all."

And taking a young child He set him in their midst, then 36 threw His arms round him and said,

"Whoever for my sake receives one such young child as 37 this, receives me; and whoever receives me, receives not so much me as Him who sent me."

"Rabbi," said John to Him, "we saw a man making use of 38 your name to expel demons, and we tried to hinder him, because he did not follow us."

"Hinder him not," replied Jesus, "for there is no one who will 39 perform a miracle in my name and be able the next minute to speak evil of me. He who is not against us is for us; and who- 40 ever gives you a cup of water to drink because you belong to 41 Christ, I tell you that he will certainly not lose his reward.

"Whoever shall occasion the fall of one of these little ones 42 who believe, it would be better for him if with a millstone hanging round his neck he had been thrown into the sea. If 43 your hand should cause you to fall, cut it off; it would be better for you to enter into Life maimed, than possessing both your hands to go into Gehenna, into the fire which can- not be put out. Or if your foot should cause you to fall, cut it 45 off: it would be better for you to enter into Life crippled, than possessing both your feet to be thrown into Gehenna. Or if 47 your eye should cause you to fall, tear it out. It would be better for you to enter into the Kingdom of God with one eye than possessing two eyes to be thrown into Gehenna, where 48 THEIR WORM DOES NOT DIE AND THE FIRE IS NOT PUT OUT (Isaiah 66:24). Every one shall be salted with fire. Salt is 49 a good thing, but if the salt should become tasteless, with 50 what will you restore the saltness? Have salt within you and live at peace with one another."

10 Setting out from that place, He enters the district of 1 Judaea and crosses the Jordan: again the people flock to Him, and again, as usual, He taught them. Presently a 2 party of Pharisees come to Him with the question—seeking to entrap Him,

"May a man divorce his wife?"

"What rule did Moses lay down for you?" He answered. 3

"Moses," they said, "permitted a man to draw up a written no- 4 tice of divorce, and to send his wife away" (Deuteronomy 24:1).

"It was in consideration of your stubborn hearts," said 5 Jesus, "that Moses made this law for you; but at the creation 6 'MALE AND FEMALE DID GOD MAKE THEM (Genesis 1:27) FOR THIS REASON A MAN SHALL LEAVE HIS FATHER AND 7 HIS MOTHER, AND SHALL CLING TO HIS WIFE, AND THE 8 TWO SHALL BE ONE' (Genesis 2:24); so that they are two no longer, but 'ONE.' What, therefore, God has joined together 9 let no man separate."

Indoors the disciples began questioning Jesus again on the 10 same subject. He replied, 11

"Whoever divorces his wife and marries another woman, commits adultery against his first wife; and if a woman 12 divorces her husband and marries another man, she commits adultery."

One day people were bringing young children to Jesus 13 for Him to touch them, but the disciples interfered. Jesus, 14 however, on seeing this, was moved to indignation, and said to them,

"Let the little children come to me: do not hinder them; for to those who are childlike the Kingdom of God belongs. In 15 truth I tell you that whoever does not receive the Kingdom of God like a little child will certainly not enter it."

Then He took them in His arms and blessed them lovingly, 16 laying His hands upon them.

As He went out on the road, there came a man running up 17
to Him, who knelt at His feet and asked,

"Good Rabbi, what am I to do in order to inherit eternal life?"

"Why do you call me good?" asked Jesus in reply; "there is 18
no one good except One—that is, God. You know the com- 19
mandments—'DO NOT MURDER'; 'DO NOT COMMIT
ADULTERY'; 'DO NOT STEAL'; 'DO NOT LIE IN GIVING EVI-
DENCE'; 'DO NOT DEFRAUD'; 'HONOR THY FATHER AND
THY MOTHER'" (Deuteronomy 5:16-20).

"Rabbi," he replied, "all these commandments I have care- 20
fully obeyed from my youth."

Then Jesus looked at him and loved him, and said, 21

"One thing is lacking in you: go, sell all you possess and
give the proceeds to the poor, and you shall have riches in
heaven; and come and follow me."

At these words his brow darkened, and he went away sad; 22
for he possessed great wealth.

Then looking round on His disciples Jesus said, 23

"How hard will it be for the possessors of riches to enter
the Kingdom of God!"

The disciples were amazed at His words. Jesus, however, 24
said again,

"Children, how hard it is to enter the Kingdom of God! It is 25
easier for a camel to go through the eye of a needle than for
a rich man to enter the Kingdom of God."

They were astonished beyond measure, and said to 26
one another,

"Who, then, can be saved?"

Jesus looking on them said, 27

"With men it is impossible, but not with God; for everything is possible with God."

Peter said to Him, "See, we gave up everything and have 28
followed you."

"In truth I tell you," replied Jesus, "that there is no one who 29 has forsaken house or brothers or sisters, or mother or father, or children or lands, for my sake and for the sake of the gospel, but will receive a hundred times as much now in 30 this present life—houses, brothers, sisters, mothers, children, lands—and persecution with them—and in the coming age eternal life. But many who are now first will be last, and the 31 last, first."

They were on the road going up to Jerusalem, and Jesus 32 was walking ahead of them; they were awe-struck, and those who followed did so in fear. Then, once more calling to Him the Twelve, He began to tell them what was about to happen to Him.

"See," He said, "we are going up to Jerusalem, where the Son 33 of Man will be betrayed to the high priests and the scribes. They will condemn Him to death, and will hand Him over to the Gentiles; they will mock Him, spit on Him, scourge Him, and 34 put Him to death; but on the third day He will rise to life again."

Then James and John, the sons of Zebedee, came up to 35 Him and said,

"Rabbi, we wish you would grant us what we may ask of you."

"What would you have me do for you?" He asked. 36

"Allow us," they replied, "to sit one at your right hand and 37 the other at your left hand, in your glory."

"You know not," said He, "what you are asking. Are you able 38 to drink out of the cup from which I am to drink, or to be baptized with the baptism with which I am to be baptized?"

"We are able," they replied. 39

"Out of the cup," said Jesus, "from which I am to drink you shall drink, and with the baptism with which I am to be baptized you shall be baptized; but as to sitting at my right hand 40 or at my left, that is not mine to give: it will be for those for whom it has been reserved."

The other ten, hearing of it, were at first highly indignant 41
with James and John. Jesus, however, called them to Him 42
and said to them,

"You are aware how those who are deemed rulers among
the Gentiles lord it over them, and their great men make
them feel their authority; but it is not so among you. No, 43
whoever would be great among you must be your servant;
and whoever would be first among you must be the bond- 44
servant of all. For indeed the Son of Man did not come to be 45
served, but to serve others, and to give His life as the
redemption-price for many."

They came to Jericho; and as He was leaving that town— 46
Himself and His disciples and a great crowd—Bartimaeus (the
son of Timaeus), a blind beggar, was sitting by the way-side.
Hearing that it was Jesus the Nazarene, he began to cry out, 47

"Son of David, Jesus, have pity on me."

Many angrily told him to leave off shouting; but he only 48
cried out all the louder,

"Son of David, have pity on me."

Then Jesus stood still. 49

"Call him," He said.

So they called the blind man.

"Cheer up," they said; "rise, he is calling you."

The man flung away his cloak, sprang to his feet, and came 50
to Jesus.

"What shall I do for you?" said Jesus. 51

"Rabboni," replied the blind man, "let me recover my sight."

"Go," said Jesus, "your faith has cured you." 52

Instantly he regained his sight, and followed Him along
the road.

11 When they were getting near Jerusalem and had 1 arrived at Bethphagé and Bethany, at the Mount of Olives, Jesus sent two of His disciples on in front, with 2 these instructions:

"Go to the village facing you, and immediately on entering it you will find an ass's colt tied up which no one has ever yet ridden: untie it and bring it here. And if any one asks you, 3 'Why are you doing that?' say, 'The Lord needs it, and will send it back here without delay.'"

So they went and found a young ass tied up at the front 4 door of a house. They were untying it, when some of the 5 bystanders called out,

"What are you doing, untying the colt?"

And they told them what Jesus had said, and they let them 6 take it.

So they brought the colt to Jesus, and threw their garments 7 over it; and He mounted. Then many spread their garments 8 to carpet the road, and others leafy branches which they had cut down in the fields; while those who led the way and 9 those who followed kept shouting

"HOSANNA!

BLESSED BE HE WHO COMES IN THE LORD'S NAME (Psalm 118:26).

Blessings on the coming Kingdom of our forefather David! 10 HOSANNA IN THE HIGHEST!" (Psalm 148:1).

So He came into Jerusalem and entered the Temple; and 11 after looking round upon everything there, the hour being now late He went out to Bethany with the Twelve.

The next day, after they had left Bethany, He was hungry. 12 In the distance He saw a fig-tree in full leaf, and went to see 13 whether perhaps He could find some figs on it. When, however, He came to it, He found nothing but leaves (for it was not fig time); and He said to the tree, 14

"Let no one ever again eat fruit from thee!"

And His disciples heard this.

They came to Jerusalem, and entering the Temple He be- 15
gan to drive out the buyers and sellers, and upset the money-
changers' tables and the stools of the dealers in doves, and 16
would not allow any one to carry any vessel through the
Temple. And He remonstrated [pleaded in protest] with them. 17

"Is it not written," He said,

"'MY HOUSE SHALL BE CALLED A HOUSE OF PRAYER
FOR ALL THE NATIONS'? (Isaiah 56:7). But you have made it
what it now is—A ROBBERS' CAVE" (Jeremiah 7:11).

This the high priests and scribes heard, and they sought 18
means to destroy Him. For they were afraid of Him, because
all the people were amazed at His teaching. When evening 19
came on, Jesus and His disciples used to leave the city.

In the early morning, as they passed by, they saw the fig-tree 20
withered to the roots; and Peter, recollecting, said to Him, 21

"Look, Rabbi, the fig-tree which you cursed is withered up."

Jesus said to them, 22

"Have faith in God. I tell you in truth that if any one shall 23
say to this mountain, 'Arise, and hurl yourself into the sea,'
and has no doubt about it in his heart, but steadfastly
believes that what he says will happen, it shall be granted
him. That is why I tell you, whatever you pray and ask for, if 24
you believe that you have received it, it shall be yours.
Whenever you stand praying, if you have a grievance against 25
any one, forgive it, so that your Father in heaven may also
forgive you your offenses."

They came again to Jerusalem; and as He was walking in 27
the Temple, the high priests and the scribes and elders came 28
and asked Him,

"By what authority are you doing these things? Who gave
you authority to do them?"

"And I will put a question to you," replied Jesus; "answer 29
me, and then I will tell you by what authority I do these
things. John's Baptism—was it from heaven or from men? 30
Answer me."

So they debated the matter with one another. 31

"Suppose we say, 'from heaven,'" they argued, "he will
ask, 'Why, then, did you not believe him?' Or should we say, 32
'from men'?"—

They were afraid of the people; for all agreed in holding
John to have been really a prophet. So they answered Jesus, 33

"We do not know."

"Nor do I tell you," said Jesus, "by what authority I do
these things."

12 Then He began to speak to them in parables. 1
"There was once a man," He said, "who planted a
vineyard, fenced it round, dug a pit for the wine-vat, and
built a watchtower. Then he let the place to vine-dressers
and went abroad. At vintage-time he sent one of his servants 2
to receive from the vine-dressers a share of the vintage. But 3
they seized him, beat him cruelly and sent him away empty-
handed. Again he sent to them another servant; and him 4
they wounded in the head and treated shamefully. Yet a third 5
he sent, and him they killed. And he sent many besides, and
them also they ill-treated, beating some and killing others.
He had still one left whom he could send, a dearly-loved son: 6
he sent him last of all, saying,

"'They will treat my son with respect.'

"But those men—the vine-dressers—said to one another, 7

"'Here is the heir: come, let us kill him, and then the inheritance shall be ours.'

"So they seized him and killed him, and flung his body 8

outside the vineyard. What, therefore, will the owner of the 9
vineyard do?"

"He will come and put the vine-dressers to death, and will
give the vineyard to others."

"Have you not read even this passage," He added, 10
"'THE STONE WHICH THE BUILDERS REJECTED
HAS BECOME THE CORNERSTONE:
THIS CAME FROM THE LORD, 11
AND IT IS WONDERFUL IN OUR EYES'?" (Psalm 118:22-23).

Now they were looking out for an opportunity to seize 12
Him, but were afraid of the people; for they saw that in this
parable He had referred to themselves. So they left Him and
went away.

Their next step was to send to Him some of the Pharisees 13
and of Herod's partisans to entrap Him in conversation. So 14
they came to Him.

"Rabbi," they said, "we know that you are a truthful man
and you pay no special regard to any one, since you do not
consider men's outward appearance, but teach God's way
truly. Is it allowable to pay poll-tax to Caesar, or not? Shall we 15
pay, or shall we refuse to pay?"

But He, knowing their hypocrisy, replied,

"Why try to ensnare me? Bring me a shilling for me to look at."
They brought one; and He asked them, 16

"Whose is this likeness and this inscription?"

"Caesar's," they replied.

"What is Caesar's," replied Jesus, "pay to Caesar—and 17
what is God's, pay to God."

And they wondered exceedingly at Him.

Then came to Him a party of Sadducees, a sect which 18
denies that there is any resurrection, and they proceeded to
question Him.

"Rabbi," they said, "Moses made it a law for us: 'IF A 19

MAN'S BROTHER SHOULD DIE AND LEAVE A WIFE, BUT NO CHILD, THE MAN SHALL MARRY THE WIDOW AND RAISE UP A FAMILY FOR HIS BROTHER' (Deuteronomy 25:5-6). There were once seven brothers, the eldest of whom 20 took a wife, but at his death left no family. The second mar- 21 ried the widow, and died, leaving no family; and the third did the same. And so did the rest of the seven, all dying childless. 22 Finally the woman also died. At the resurrection whose wife 23 will she be? For they all seven married her."

"Is not this the cause of your error," replied Jesus—"your 24 ignorance alike of the scriptures and of the power of God? For when they have risen from the dead, men do not marry 25 and women are not given in marriage, but they are as angels are in heaven. But as to the dead rising to life, have you never 26 read in the Book of Moses, in the passage about the bush, how God said to him, 'I AM THE GOD OF ABRAHAM, AND THE GOD OF ISAAC, AND THE GOD OF JACOB'? (Exodus 3:2-6). He is not the God of dead, but of living men. You are 27 in grave error."

Then one of the scribes, who had heard them disputing 28 and well knew that Jesus had given them an answer to the point, came forward and asked Him,

"Which is the chief of all the commandments?"

"The chief commandment," replied Jesus, "is this: 'HEAR, 29 O ISRAEL! THE LORD OUR GOD IS ONE LORD; AND THOU 30 SHALT LOVE THE LORD THY GOD WITH THY WHOLE HEART, THY WHOLE SOUL, THY WHOLE MIND, AND THY WHOLE STRENGTH' (Deuteronomy 6:4-5).

"The second is this: 'THOU SHALT LOVE THY NEIGHBOR 31 AS THYSELF' (Leviticus 19:18).

"There is no other commandment greater than these."

And the scribe said to Him, 32

"Rightly, in very truth, Rabbi, have you said that HE

STANDS ALONE, AND THERE IS NO OTHER THAN HE; and 33
TO LOVE HIM WITH ALL ONE'S HEART, WITH ALL ONE'S
UNDERSTANDING, AND WITH ALL ONE'S STRENGTH,
AND TO LOVE ONE'S NEIGHBOR NO LESS THAN ONESELF,
is far better than all our WHOLE BURNT-OFFERINGS AND
SACRIFICES" (1 Samuel 15:22).

Perceiving that the scribe had answered wisely, Jesus said 34
to him,

"You are not far from the Kingdom of God."

No one from that time forward ventured to put any question to Him.

Now, while teaching in the Temple, Jesus asked, 35

"How is it the scribes say that the Christ is a son of David?
David himself, taught by the Holy Spirit, said, 36

"'THE LORD SAID TO MY LORD,
SIT AT MY RIGHT HAND,
UNTIL I HAVE MADE THY FOES A FOOTSTOOL UNDER
THY FEET' (Psalm 110:1).

"David himself calls Him 'Lord': how then can He be his son?" 37
And the mass of the people heard Jesus gladly.

And in the course of His teaching He said, 38

"Be on your guard against the scribes who like to walk
about in long robes and to be bowed to in places of public
resort, and to occupy the best places in the synagogues and at 39
dinner-parties, and who swallow up the property of widows 40
and then mask their wickedness by making long prayers: the
heavier the punishment these men shall receive."

Having taken a seat opposite the treasury, He observed 41
how the people were dropping money into the treasury, and
that many of the wealthy threw in large sums. But there 42
came one poor widow and dropped in two small coins,
together equal in value to a mite. So He called His disciples 43
to Him, and said,

"I tell you in truth that this widow, poor as she is, has thrown in more than all the other contributors to the treasury; for they have all contributed what they could well spare, 44 but she out of her need has thrown in all she possessed—all she had to live on."

13

As He was leaving the Temple, one of His disciples 1 exclaimed,

"Look, Rabbi, what wonderful stones! what wonderful buildings!"

"You see all these great buildings?" Jesus replied; "not 2 one stone will be left here resting upon another, and not thrown down."

He was sitting on the Mount of Olives opposite to the 3 Temple, when Peter, James, John, and Andrew, apart from the others asked Him,

"Tell us, when will these things be? and what will be the 4 sign when all these predictions are about to be fulfilled?"

So Jesus began to tell them: 5

"Take care that no one misleads you. Many will come in 6 my name and say, 'I am he'; and they will mislead many. But when you hear of wars and rumors of wars, do not be 7 alarmed: come they must, but the end is not yet. For 8 NATION WILL RISE IN ARMS AGAINST NATION, AND KINGDOM AGAINST KINGDOM (Isaiah 19:2). There will be earthquakes in various places; there will be famines. These miseries are but like the early pains of childbirth.

"You yourselves must be on your guard. They will deliver 9 you up to Sanhedrins; you will be brought into synagogues and cruelly beaten; and you will stand before governors and kings for my sake, to be witnesses to them for me. But the 10 gospel must be preached to all nations first. When, however, 11 they are marching you along under arrest, do not be anxious beforehand about what you are to say, but speak whatever shall be given you when the time comes: for it will not be you who speak, but the Holy Spirit.

"Brother will betray brother to death, and fathers will 12 betray children; and CHILDREN WILL RISE AGAINST THEIR PARENTS (Micah 7:6) and have them put to death. You will 13 be objects of universal hatred because you are called by my name, but those who stand firm to the end shall be saved.

"But when you see the ABOMINATION OF DESOLATION 14 (Daniel 9:27) standing where he ought not"—let the reader observe these words—"then let those in Judaea escape to the hills; let him who is on the roof not come down and 15 enter the house to fetch anything out of it; and let not him 16 who is in the field turn back to pick up his outer garment. And alas for the women who at that time are with child or 17 have infants at the breast!

"But pray that it may not come in the winter. For those will 18 be times of SUFFERING THE LIKE OF WHICH HAS NEVER 19 BEEN FROM THE FIRST CREATION OF GOD'S WORLD UNTIL NOW (Daniel 12:1), and assuredly never will be again; and but for the fact that the Lord has cut short those 20 days, no one would escape; but for the sake of His elect whom He has chosen for Himself He has cut short the days.

"At that time if any one says to you, 'See, here is the Christ!' 21 or 'See, He is there!' do not believe it. For there will rise 22 up false Christs and false prophets, displaying signs and prodigies with a view to lead astray, if possible, even the elect. Do you, however, be on your guard: I have forewarned 23 you of everything.

"But at that time, after that distress, THE SUN WILL 24 BE DARKENED AND THE MOON WILL NOT SHED HER LIGHT; THE STARS WILL BE SEEN FALLING FROM HEAVEN 25

(Isaiah 13:10), AND THE FORCES WHICH ARE IN THE HEAVENS WILL BE DISORDERED (Isaiah 34:4). And then will 26 they see THE SON OF MAN COMING IN CLOUDS (Daniel 7:13) with great power and glory. Then He will send forth the 27 angels and gather together His elect from north, south, east and west—from the farthest bounds of earth and heaven.

"Learn from the fig-tree the lesson it teaches. As soon as its 28 branch has become soft and it is bursting into leaf, you know that summer is near. So also do you, when you see these 29 things happening, be sure that He is near, at your very door. I tell you in truth that the present generation will not pass 30 away until all these things have happened. Sky and earth will 31 pass away, but my words shall not pass away.

"But as to that day or the hour no one knows—not even 32 the angels in heaven, not even the Son, but the Father alone. Take care, be on the alert, and pray; for you do not know 33 when it will happen. It is like a man gone abroad, who has 34 left his house, and given the management to his servants— to each one his special duty—and has ordered the porter to keep awake. Keep watch therefore, for you know not when 35 the master of the house is coming—in the evening, at mid-night, at cock-crow, or at dawn. Beware lest He should arrive 36 unexpectedly and find you asleep. And what I say to you I say 37 to all—'Keep watch!'"

14 It was now two days before the Passover and the feast 1 of Unleavened Bread, and the high priests and scribes were bent on finding how to seize Him by craft and put Him to death. But they said, 2

"Not during the festival, for fear there should be a riot among the people."

Now when He was at Bethany, in the house of Simon the 3

leper, while He was at table, there came a woman with an alabaster jar of pure spikenard, very costly: she broke the jar and poured the perfume over his head. But there were some 4 who said to one another with indignation,

"Why has the perfume been thus wasted? For it might 5 have been sold for fifteen pounds or more, and the money given to the poor."

And they were very angry with her. But Jesus said, 6

"Leave her alone: Why are you troubling her? She has done me a most gracious service. You always have the poor among 7 you, and whenever you choose you can do acts of kindness to them; but me you have not always. What she could she 8 did: she has perfumed by body in preparation for my burial. And I solemnly tell you that wherever in the whole world the 9 gospel shall be proclaimed, this which she has done shall also be told in remembrance of her."

But Judas Iscariot, one of the Twelve, went to the high 10 priests to betray Jesus to them. They gladly listened to his 11 proposal, and promised to give him a sum of money. So he looked out for an opportunity to betray Him.

On the first day of the feast of Unleavened Bread—the day 12 for killing the Passover lamb—His disciples asked Him,

"Where shall we go and prepare for you to eat the Passover?"

So He sent two of His disciples with instructions, saying, 13

"Go into the city, and you will meet a man carrying a pitcher of water: follow him, and whatever house he enters, 14 tell the master of the house, 'The Rabbi asks, Where is my room where I can eat the Passover with my disciples?' Then 15 he will himself show you a large room upstairs, ready furnished: there make preparation for us."

So the disciples went out and came to the city, and found 16 everything just as He had told them; and they got the Passover ready.

When it was evening, He came with the Twelve. And while 17
they were at table Jesus said, 18

"I tell you in truth that one of you will betray me—one who
is eating with me."

They were filled with sorrow, and began asking Him, one 19
by one,

"Not I, is it?"

"It is one of the Twelve," He replied; "he who is dipping his 20
fingers in the dish with me. For the Son of Man is going His 21
way as it is written about Him; but woe to the man by whom
the Son of Man is betrayed! It were a happy thing for that
man, had he never been born."

Also during the meal He took a loaf, blessed it, and broke 22
it. He then gave it to them, saying,

"Take this, it is my body."

Then He took a cup, gave thanks, and handed it to them, 23
and they all of them drank from it.

"This is my blood," He said, "which is to be poured out on 24
behalf of many—the blood that ratifies the covenant. I tell 25
you that never again shall I drink the produce of the vine till
I drink the new wine in the Kingdom of God."

After singing the hymn, they went out to the Mount 26
of Olives.

Then said Jesus to them, 27

"All of you are about to turn against me, for it is written, 'I
WILL STRIKE DOWN THE SHEPHERD, AND THE SHEEP
WILL BE SCATTERED IN ALL DIRECTIONS' (Zechariah
13:7). But after I have risen to life again I will go before you 28
into Galilee."

"All may turn against you," said Peter, "yet I will never do so." 29

"I tell you in truth," replied Jesus, "that to-day—this 30
night—before the cock crows twice, you yourself will three
times disown me."

"Even if I must die with you," declared Peter again and 31
again, "I will never disown you."

In like manner protested also all the disciples.

So they came to a place called Gethsemane. There He said 32
to His disciples,

"Sit down here till I have prayed."

Then He took with Him Peter and James and John, and 33
began to be full of terror and distress, and He said to them, 34

"My heart is crushed with anguish to the point of death:
wait here and keep awake."

Going forward a short distance He threw Himself upon His 35
face, and prayed that, if it were possible, He might be spared
that time of agony; and He said, 36

"Abba! Father! all things are possible for Thee: take this
cup away from me: and yet not what I will, but what
Thou willest."

Then He came and found them asleep, and He said to Peter, 37

"Simon, are you asleep? Were you not able to keep awake a
single hour? Keep awake, all of you, and pray, that you may 38
not come into temptation: the spirit is right willing, but the
flesh is frail."

He again went away and prayed, using the very same 39
words. When He returned He again found them asleep, for 40
they were very weary; and they knew not how to answer
Him. A third time He came, and then He said, 41

"Sleep on and rest.—Enough! the hour has come. Even
now they are betraying the Son of Man into the hands of sinful men. Rouse yourselves, let us be going: my betrayer is 42
close at hand."

Immediately, while He was still speaking, Judas, one of the 43
Twelve, came and with him a crowd of men armed with swords
and cudgels [clubs], sent by the high priests and scribes and
elders. Now the betrayer had arranged a signal with them. 44

"The one I kiss," he said, "is the man: lay hold of him, and take him safely away."

So he came, and going straight to Jesus he said, "Rabbi!" 45
and kissed Him affectionately; whereupon they laid hands 46
on Him and held him firmly. But one of those who stood by 47
drew his sword and struck a blow at the high priest's servant,
cutting off his ear.

"Have you come out," said Jesus, "with swords and cudgels 48
[clubs] to arrest me, as if you had to fight with a robber? Day 49
after day I used to be among you in the Temple teaching, and
you never seized me. But this is happening in order that the
scriptures may be fulfilled."

Then His friends all forsook Him and fled. One youth 50
indeed did follow Him, wearing only a linen cloth round his 51
bare body. Of him they laid hold, but he left the linen cloth in 52
their hands and ran away naked.

So they led Jesus away to the high priest, and with him 53
there assembled all the high priests, elders, and scribes.
Peter followed Jesus at a distance, as far as the court of the 54
high priest's palace, where he remained, sitting among the
officers, and warming himself by the fire.

Meanwhile the high priests and the entire Sanhedrin were 55
endeavoring to get evidence against Jesus in order to put
Him to death, but could find none; for though many gave 56
false testimony against Him, their statements did not tally.
Then some came forward as witnesses and falsely declared, 57

"We have heard him say, 'I will pull down this sanctuary 58
built by human hands, and three days afterwards I will erect
another built without hands.'"

But not even in this form was their testimony consistent. 59

At last the high priest stood up, and advancing into the 60
midst of them all, asked Jesus,

"Have you no answer to make? What is this that these

witnesses allege against you?"

But He remained silent, and gave no reply. A second time 61
the high priest questioned Him.

"Are you the Christ, the Son of the Blessed One?" he said.

"I am," replied Jesus, "and you all shall see THE SON OF 62
MAN SITTING AT THE RIGHT HAND of the Divine Power,
AND COMING AMID THE CLOUDS OF HEAVEN" (Psalm
110:1; Daniel 7:13).

Rending his clothing the high priest exclaimed, 63

"What need have we of witnesses after that? You all heard 64
his impious words. What is your judgment?"

Then with one voice they condemned Him as deserving of
death. Thereupon some began to spit on Him, and to blind- 65
fold Him, while striking Him with their fists and crying,

"Prove that you are a prophet."

The officers too struck Him with open hands.

Now while Peter was below in the court, one of the high 66
priest's maidservants came, and seeing Peter warming him- 67
self she looked at him and said,

"You also were with Jesus, the Nazarene."

But he denied it, and said, 68

"I don't know, I don't understand—What do you mean?"

And then he went out into the forecourt. Just then a cock
crowed. Again the maidservant saw him, and again began to 69
say to the people standing by,

"He is one of them."

A second time he repeatedly denied it. Soon afterwards 70
the bystanders again accused Peter, saying,

"You are surely one of them, for indeed you are a Galilaean."

But he broke out into curses and oaths, declaring, "I know 71
nothing of the man you are talking about."

No sooner had he spoken than a cock crowed for the 72
second time, and Peter recollected the words of Jesus,

"Before the cock crows twice, you will three times disown me."

And as he thought of it, he wept aloud.

15 At earliest dawn, after the high priests had held a 1 consultation with the elders and scribes, they and the entire Sanhedrin bound Jesus and took Him away and handed Him over to Pilate. So Pilate questioned Him. 2

"Are you the King of the Jews?" he asked.

"I am," replied Jesus.

Then, as the high priests went on heaping accusations on 3 Him, Pilate again asked Him, 4

"Do you make no reply? Listen to the many charges they are bringing against you,"

But Jesus made no further answer: so that Pilate wondered. 5

Now at the festival it was customary for Pilate to release to 6 the Jews any one prisoner whom they might beg for; and at 7 this time a man named Barabbas was in prison among the insurgents—persons who in the insurrection had committed murder. So the people came crowding up, asking Pilate 8 to grant them the usual favor.

"Shall I release for you the King of the Jews?" answered Pilate. 9

For he could see that it was out of sheer spite that the high 10 priests had handed Him over. But the high priests urged on 11 the crowd to get him to release Barabbas instead. And Pilate 12 again asked them, "What, then, shall I do to the man you call the King of the Jews?" They once more shouted out, 13

"Crucify him!"

"But what crime has he committed?" asked Pilate. 14

But all the more they shouted,

"Crucify him!"

So Pilate, wishing to satisfy the mob, released Barabbas 15 to them, and then scourged Jesus and handed Him over for crucifixion.

Then the soldiers led Him away into the court of the 16 palace (the Praetorium), and calling together the whole battalion they arrayed Him in purple, placed on His head a 17 wreath of thorny twigs which they had twisted, and went on 18 to salute Him with shouts of "Hail, King of the Jews." Then 19 they began to beat Him on the head with a cane, to spit on Him, and to do Him homage on bended knees. At last, hav- 20 ing finished their sport, they took the robe off Him, put His own clothes on Him, and led Him out to crucify Him.

One Simon, a Cyrenean, the father of Alexander and 21 Rufus, was passing along, coming from the country: him they compelled to carry His cross. So they brought Him to 22 the place called Golgotha, which, being translated, means "Skull-ground." Here they offered Him wine mixed with 23 myrrh; but He refused it. Then they crucified Him, and they 24 divided His garments among them, drawing lots to decide what each should take. It was nine o'clock in the morning 25 when they crucified Him. And the written inscription of the 26 charge against Him was:

THE KING OF THE JEWS.

And together with Jesus they crucified two robbers, one at 27 His right hand and one at His left. And all the passers-by 29 reviled Him. They shook their heads at Him and said,

"Ah! you who were for destroying the sanctuary and building a new one in three days, come down from the cross and 30 save yourself."

In the same way the high priests also, as well as the scribes, 31 kept on scoffing at Him, saying to one another,

"He has saved others: himself he cannot save! This Christ, 32
the King of Israel, let him come down now from the cross,
that we may see and believe."

Even the men crucified with Him heaped insults on Him.

At noon there came a darkness over the whole land, last- 33
ing till three o'clock in the afternoon. And at three o'clock 34
Jesus cried out with a loud voice,

"ELÔI, ELÔI, LAMA SABACHTHANI?" which means,
"MY GOD, MY GOD, WHY HAST THOU FORSAKEN ME?"
(Psalm 22:1).

Some of the bystanders, hearing Him, said, 35
"Listen, he is calling for Elijah!"

Then a man ran to fill a sponge with sour wine, and he put 36
it on the end of a cane and placed it to the lips of Jesus, saying at the same time,

"Wait! let us see whether Elijah will come and take
him down."

But Jesus uttered a loud cry and yielded up His spirit. 37

And the curtain of the sanctuary was torn in two, from top 38
to bottom.

When the centurion who stood in front of the cross saw 39
that He was dead, he exclaimed,

"This man was indeed Son of God."

There were also women looking on from a distance; 40
among them being both Mary of Magdala and Mary the
mother of James the little and of Joses, and Salome—all of 41
whom in the Galilaean days had habitually been with Him
and attended upon Him, as well as many other women who
had come up to Jerusalem with Him.

Towards sunset, as it was the Preparation—that is, the day 42
preceding the sabbath—Joseph of Arimathaea came, a 43
highly respected member of the council, who himself was
living in expectation of the Kingdom of God. He summoned

up courage to go in to see Pilate and beg for the body of Jesus. But Pilate could hardly believe that He was already 44 dead. And he called for the centurion and inquired whether He had been long dead; having ascertained the fact from 45 the centurion he granted the body to Joseph. Then Joseph 46 bought a sheet of linen, took Him down, wrapped Him in the sheet and laid Him in a tomb hewn in the rock; after which he rolled a stone against the entrance to the tomb. Mary of 47 Magdala and Mary the mother of Joses were looking on to see where He was put.

16 When the sabbath was over, Mary of Magdala, Mary 1 the mother of James, and Salome, bought spices, in order to come and anoint His body. So, very soon after sun- 2 rise on the first day of the week, they came to the tomb; and 3 they said to one another,

"Who will roll away the stone for us from the entrance to the tomb?"

But then, looking up, they saw that the stone was 4 already rolled back: it was of immense size. Upon entering 5 the tomb, they saw a young man sitting at their right hand, clothed in a long white robe. They were terrified. But he said 6 to them,

"Do not be terrified. It is Jesus you are looking for—the Nazarene, the crucified one. He has come back to life: He is not here: this is the place where they laid Him. But go and tell 7 His disciples and Peter that He is going before you into Galilee: and that there you will see Him, as He told you."

So they came out, and fled from the tomb, for they were 8 trembling and amazed; and they said not a word to any one, for they were afraid.

{Now when He rose to life early on the first day of the week, 9
He appeared first to Mary of Magdala, from whom He had
expelled seven demons. She brought the tidings to those 10
who had been with Him, who were now mourning and
weeping. But they, when they were told that He was alive and 11
that He had been seen by her, could not believe it.

Afterwards He showed Himself in another form to two of 12
them as they were walking, on their way into the country.
These, again, went and told the news to the rest; but they did 13
not believe them either.

Later still He showed Himself to the eleven themselves 14
whilst [while] they were at table, and He upbraided them
with their unbelief and obstinacy in not believing those who
had seen Him alive. Then He said to them, 15

"Go the whole world over, and proclaim the gospel to all
mankind. He who believes and is baptized shall be saved, 16
but he who disbelieves will be condemned. And signs shall 17
attend those who believe, even such as these: by my name
they shall expel demons; they shall speak new languages;
they shall take up venomous snakes; and even if they drink 18
any deadly poison, it shall do them no harm whatever; they
shall lay their hands on the sick, and these shall recover."

So the Lord Jesus after having thus spoken to them was 19
taken up into heaven, and He sat down at the right hand of
God. And they went out and preached everywhere, the Lord 20
working with them and confirming their message by the
signs which accompanied it.}

THE GOSPEL ACCORDING TO
ST. LUKE

1 Seeing that many have attempted to draw up a narrative 1
of the events that have been accomplished among us on 2
the authority of those who were from the beginning eye-
witnesses and became devoted to the service of the divine
message, it has seemed right to me also, after careful investi- 3
gation of the facts from their beginning, to write for you,
most noble Theophilus, a connected account, that you may 4
fully know the truth of what you have been taught by word
of mouth.

There was in the time of Herod, king of Judaea, a priest of 5
the name of Zechariah, belonging to the order of Abijah. He
had a wife who was a descendant of Aaron, and her name
was Elizabeth. They were both of them upright before God, 6
blamelessly obeying all the Lord's precepts and ordinances.
But they had no child, because Elizabeth was barren; and 7
both of them were far advanced in life.

Now while he was doing priestly duty before God in the 8
prescribed course of his order, it fell to his lot—according to 9
the custom of the priesthood—to go into the sanctuary of the
Lord and burn the incense; and the whole multitude of the 10
people were outside praying at the hour of incense. Then 11
there appeared to him an angel of the Lord standing on the
right side of the altar of incense; and Zechariah on seeing 12
him was startled and terrified. But the angel said to him, 13

"Do not be frightened, Zechariah, for your petition has
been heard: your wife Elizabeth will bear you a son, and you
shall call his name John. You shall have gladness and intense 14
joy, and many will rejoice over his birth. For he will be great 15

in the sight of the Lord; no wine or fermented drink shall he ever drink; but he will be filled with the Holy Spirit from the very hour of his birth. Many of the sons of Israel will he turn 16 to the Lord their God; and he will go before Him in the spirit 17 and power of Elijah, to turn fathers' hearts to the children, and cause the rebellious to walk in the wisdom of the upright, to make a people perfectly ready for the Lord."

"How am I to know this?" asked Zechariah, "for I am an old 18 man, and my wife is far advanced in years."

"I am Gabriel, who stand in the presence of God," 19 answered the angel, "and I have been sent to speak with you and tell you this good news. And now you shall be dumb and 20 unable to speak until the day when this takes place; because you have not believed my words—words which will be fulfilled at their appointed time."

Meanwhile the people were waiting for Zechariah, and 21 were surprised that he stayed so long in the sanctuary. And 22 when he came out, he was unable to speak to them; and they knew that he must have seen a vision in the sanctuary; but he made signs to them and continued dumb.

When his days of service were at an end, he went to his 23 home; and in course of time his wife Elizabeth conceived, 24 and kept herself secluded five months.

"Thus has the Lord dealt with me at this time," she said; 25 "He has graciously taken away my reproach among men."

Now in the sixth month the angel Gabriel was sent from 26 God to a town in Galilee called Nazareth, to a maiden 27 betrothed to a man of the name of Joseph, a descendant of David. The maiden's name was Mary.

So Gabriel went in and said to her, 28

"Hail, favored one! the Lord be with you."

She was greatly startled at his words, and wondered what 29 such a greeting meant. But the angel said, 30

"Do not be frightened, Mary, for you have found favor with God. You will conceive in your womb and bear a son; and you 31 are to call His name JESUS. He will be great, and He will be 32 called 'Son of the Most High.' And the Lord God will give Him the throne of His forefather David; and He will be King over the 33 House of Jacob for ever, and of His reign there will be no end."

"How can this be," Mary replied, "seeing that I have 34 no husband?"

The angel answered, 35

"The Holy Spirit will come upon you, and the power of the Most High will overshadow you; and for this reason your off-spring will be called holy, 'the Son of God.' And see, your rel- 36 ative Elizabeth—she also has conceived a son in her old age; and this is the sixth month with her who was called barren. For no promise from God will be impossible of fulfillment." 37

"I am the Lord's maidservant," Mary replied; "may it be 38 with me in accordance with your words!"

And then the angel left her.

Not long after this, Mary made herself ready and went in 39 haste into the hill country to a town in Judah. Here she came 40 to the house of Zechariah and greeted Elizabeth; and as soon 41 as Elizabeth heard Mary's greeting, the babe leapt within her. And Elizabeth was filled with the Holy Spirit, and uttered a 42 loud cry of joy.

"Blest among women are you," she said, "and blest is the fruit of your womb! But why is this honor done me, that the 43 mother of my Lord should come to me? For, the moment 44 your greeting reached my ears, the babe within me leapt for joy. And blessed is she who believed, for the word spoken to 45 her from the Lord shall be fulfilled."

Then Mary said: 46

"My soul extols the Lord,
And my spirit triumphs in God my Savior; 47

Because He has looked on His maidservant in her 48
lowly position,
For from this time forward all generations will account
me happy,
Because the mighty One has done great things for me— 49
Holy is His name!—
And His compassion is, generation after generation, 50
Upon those who fear Him.
He has displayed His might with His arm. 51
He has scattered those who were haughty in the thoughts
of their hearts.
He has cast monarchs down from their thrones, 52
And exalted men of low estate.
The hungry He has satisfied with choice gifts, 53
But the rich He has sent empty-handed away.
His servant Israel He has helped, 54
Remembering His compassion—
As He promised our forefathers— 55
To Abraham and his posterity for ever."

So Mary stayed with Elizabeth about three months, and 56
then returned home.

Now when Elizabeth's full time was come, she gave birth to 57
a son; and her neighbors and relatives heard how the Lord 58
had shown great compassion to her; and they rejoiced with
her. And on the eighth day they came to circumcise the 59
child, and were going to call him Zechariah, after his father.

His mother, however, said, 60

"No, he is to be called John."

"There is not one of your family," they said, "who has 61
that name."

They asked his father by signs what he wished him to be 62
called. So he asked for a writing-tablet, and wrote, 63

"His name is John."

And they all wondered. Instantly his mouth and his 64
tongue were set free, and he began to speak and bless God.
And all who lived round about them were filled with awe, 65
and throughout the hill country of Judaea reports of all these
things were spread abroad. All who heard the story treasured 66
it in their memories.

"What, then, will this child be?" they said.

For the Lord's hand was indeed with him.

And Zechariah his father was filled with the Holy Spirit, 67
and he prophesied, saying,

"Blessed be the Lord, the God of Israel, 68
Because He has not forgotten His people but has effected
   redemption for them,
And has raised up a mighty Deliverer for us 69
In the house of David His servant—
As He has spoken from of old by the lips of His holy prophets— 70
To deliver us from our foes and from the power of all who 71
   hate us,
Dealing pitifully with our forefathers, 72
And to remember His holy covenant,
The oath which He swore to Abraham our forefather, 73
To grant us to be rescued from the power of our foes 74
And so render worship to Him free from fear,
In holiness and uprightness before Him all our days. 75
And you, O child, shall be called Prophet of the Most High; 76
For you shall go in front before the Lord to prepare the way
   for Him,
To give to His people a knowledge of salvation 77
In the forgiveness of their sins,
Through the tender compassion of our God, 78
Whereby a new day from on high will break on us,
Dawning on those who now dwell in the darkness and 79
   shadow of death—

To direct our feet into the path of peace."

And the child grew and became strong in character, and 80
lived in the desert till the time came for him to appear
publicly to Israel.

2 In those days an edict was issued by Caesar Augustus 1
for a census of the whole Empire. It was the first census 2
made during the governorship of Quirinius in Syria; and all 3
went to be registered—every one to the town to which he
belonged. So Joseph went up from Galilee, from the town of 4
Nazareth, to Judaea, to David's town of Bethlehem, because
he was of the house and lineage of David, to have himself 5
registered together with Mary, who was betrothed to him
and was with child. While they were there, her full time 6
came, and she gave birth to her first-born son, and wrapped 7
Him round, and laid Him in a manger, because there was no
room for them in the inn.

Now there were shepherds in the same part of the country 8
keeping watch over their sheep by night in the open fields,
when suddenly an angel of the Lord stood by them, and the 9
glory of the Lord shone round them; and they were filled
with terror. But the angel said to them, 10

"Put away all fear; for I am bringing you good news of great
joy—joy for all the people. For a Savior who is the Christ is 11
born to you to-day, in the town of David. And this is the 12
token for you: you will find a babe wrapped in swaddling
clothes and lying in a manger."

And immediately there was with the angel a multitude of 13
the host of heaven praising God and saying,

"Glory be to God in the highest heavens, 14
And on earth peace among men in whom He is well pleased!"

Then, as soon as the angels had left them and returned to 15
heaven, the shepherds said to one another,

"Let us now go as far as Bethlehem and see what this
occurrence is that the Lord has made known to us."

So they came in haste and found Mary and Joseph, with 16
the babe lying in the manger. And when they saw the child, 17
they told what had been said to them about Him; and all 18
who listened were astonished at what the shepherds told
them. But Mary treasured up all their story, often dwelling 19
on it in her mind. And the shepherds returned, glorifying 20
and praising God for all that they had heard and seen, agree-
ing as it did with what had been told to them.

When eight days had passed and the time for circumcising 21
Him had come, He was called JESUS, the name given Him by
the angel before His conception in the womb.

And when the days for their purification appointed by the 22
law of Moses had passed, they took Him up to Jerusalem to
present Him to the Lord, as it is written in the Law of the Lord: 23

"EVERY FIRST-BORN MALE SHALL BE CALLED HOLY TO
THE LORD" (Exodus 13:2);

And also to offer a sacrifice, as commanded in the Law of 24
the Lord,

"A PAIR OF TURTLE DOVES OR TWO YOUNG PIGEONS"
(Leviticus 12:8).

Now there was a man in Jerusalem of the name of Symeon, 25
an upright and God-fearing man, who was waiting for the
consolation of Israel; and the Holy Spirit was upon him. To 26
him it had been revealed by the Holy Spirit that he should
not see death until he had seen the Lord's Anointed One. Led 27
by the Spirit he came to the Temple; and when the parents
brought in the babe Jesus to carry out with regard to Him the
custom of the Law, he took Him up in his arms and blessed 28
God and said,

"Now, O Sovereign Lord, Thou dost release Thy servant in 29
    peace, in fulfillment of Thy word,
Because mine eyes have seen Thy salvation, 30
Which Thou hast made ready in the sight of all nations— 31
A light to shine upon the Gentiles, 32
And the glory of Thy people Israel."

And while the child's father and mother were wondering at 33
the words of Symeon concerning Him, Symeon blessed 34
them and said to Mary the mother,

"This child is appointed for the falling and for the uprising
of many in Israel and for a sign to be spoken against; and a 35
sword will pierce through your own soul also; that the reasonings in many hearts may be revealed."

There was also Anna, a prophetess, the daughter of 36
Phanuel, belonging to the tribe of Asher. She was of a very
great age, having had after her maidenhood seven years of
married life, and then being a widow of eighty-four years. She 37
was never absent from the Temple, but worshiped, by day and
by night, with fasting and prayer. And coming up just at that 38
moment, she gave thanks to God, and spoke about the child
to all who were expecting the redemption of Jerusalem.

Then, as soon as they had accomplished all that the 39
Law required, they returned to Galilee to their own town of
Nazareth. And the child grew and became strong and full of 40
wisdom, and the grace of God rested upon Him.

Now His parents used to go up year by year to Jerusalem at 41
the feast of the Passover. And when He was twelve years old 42
they went up as was customary at the time of the feast, and, 43
after staying the full number of days, they started back home;
but the boy Jesus remained behind in Jerusalem. His parents
did not discover this, but supposing Him to be in the caravan, 44
they proceeded a day's journey. Then they searched up and
down for Him among their relatives and acquaintances; but 45

being unable to find Him they returned to Jerusalem, making anxious inquiry for Him.

On the third day they found Him in the Temple sitting 46 among the rabbis, both listening to them and asking them questions, while all who heard Him were astonished at His 47 intelligence and at the answers He gave. When they saw 48 Him, they were amazed, and His mother said to Him,

"My child, why have you behaved thus to us? Your father and I have been searching for you in sore anxiety."

"Why is it that you have been searching for me?" He replied; 49 "did you not know that I must be in my Father's house?"

But they did not understand the meaning of these words. 50

Then He went down with them and came to Nazareth, 51 and was obedient to them; but His mother carefully treasured up all these incidents in her heart. And Jesus increased 52 both in wisdom and in stature, and in favor with God and man.

3 Now in the fifteenth year of the reign of Tiberius Caesar, 1 Pontius Pilate being Governor of Judaea, Herod Tetrarch of Galilee, his brother Philip Tetrarch of Ituraea and Trachonitis, and Lysanias Tetrarch of Abilene, during the 2 high-priesthood of Annas and Caiaphas, a message from God came to John, the son of Zechariah, in the desert. So 3 John went into all the district of the Jordan proclaiming a baptism of repentance for the forgiveness of sins; as it is 4 written in the book of the prophet Isaiah,

"THE VOICE OF ONE CRYING ALOUD:
'IN THE DESERT PREPARE A ROAD FOR THE LORD:
MAKE HIS HIGHWAYS STRAIGHT.
EVERY RAVINE SHALL BE FILLED UP, 5
AND EVERY MOUNTAIN AND HILL LEVELED DOWN,

THE CROOKED PLACES SHALL BE TURNED INTO
STRAIGHT ROADS,
AND THE RUGGED WAYS INTO SMOOTH;
AND THEN SHALL ALL MANKIND SEE GOD'S SALVATION'" 6
(Isaiah 40:3-5).

So John said to the crowds who came out to be baptized 7
by him,

"O brood of vipers, who has warned you to flee from the
coming wrath? Let your lives then prove your change of 8
heart; and do not begin to say to yourselves, 'We have
Abraham as our forefather,' for I tell you that God can raise
up children for Abraham from these stones. And even now 9
the ax is lying at the root of the trees, so that every tree which
does not produce good fruit will be hewn down and thrown
into the fire."

The crowds asked him, 10
"What, then, are we to do?"

"Let the man who has two tunics," he answered, "give one 11
to the man who has none; and let the man who has food
share it with others."

There came also a party of tax-gatherers to be baptized, 12
and they asked him,
"Rabbi, what are we to do?"

"Do not exact more than the legal amount," he replied. 13
Soldiers also inquired of him, 14
"And we, what are we to do?"
His answer was,
"Neither intimidate any one nor lay false charges; and be
content with your pay."

And while the people were in suspense, and all were 15
debating in their minds whether John might possibly be the
Christ, he answered by saying to them all, 16
"I am baptizing you with water, but One mightier than I is

coming, whose very sandal-strap I am not worthy to unfasten: He will baptize you in the Holy Spirit and in fire. His 17 winnowing shovel is in His hand to clear out His threshing-floor, and to gather the wheat into His storehouse; but the chaff He will burn up in fire unquenchable."

With many exhortations besides these he declared the 18 gospel to the people. (But Herod the Tetrarch, being rebuked 19 by him about Herodias, his brother's wife, and about all the wicked deeds that he had done, now added this to crown all, 20 that he threw John into prison.)

Now when all the people had been baptized, and Jesus 21 also had been baptized and was praying, the sky opened, 22 and the Holy Spirit came down in bodily shape, like a dove, upon Him, and a voice came from heaven,

"THOU ART MY SON, THE BELOVED: IN THEE IS MY DELIGHT."

And Jesus, when He began His ministry, was about thirty 23 years old. He was the son (it was supposed) of Joseph, son of Heli, son of Matthat, son of Levi, son of Melchi, son of Jannai, 24 son of Joseph, son of Mattathias, son of Amos, son of 25 Nahum, son of Esli, son of Naggai, son of Mahath, son 26 of Mattathias, son of Semien, son of Josech, son of Joda, son 27 of Johanan, son of Resa, son of Zerubbabel, son of Shealtiel, son of Neri, son of Melchi, son of Addi, son of Cosam, son of 28 Elmadam, son of Er, son of Jushua, son of Eliezar, son 29 of Jorim, son of Maththat, son of Levi, son of Symeon, son of Judah, son of Joseph, son of Jonam, son of Eliakim, son of 30 Melea, son of Menna, son of Mattatha, son of Nathan, son of 31 David, son of Jesse, son of Obed, son of Boaz, son of Salmon, 32 son of Nahshon, son of Amminadab, son of Admin, son of 33 Arni, son of Hezron, son of Perez, son of Judah, son of Jacob, 34 son of Isaac, son of Abraham, son of Terah, son of Nahor, son of Serug, son of Reu, son of Peleg, son of Eber, son of Shelah, 35

son of Cainan, son of Arpachshad, son of Shem, son of Noah, 36
son of Lamech, son of Methuselah, son of Enoch, son of 37
Jared, son of Mahalalel, son of Kenan, son of Enosh, son 38
of Seth, son of Adam, son of God.

4 Then Jesus, full of the Holy Spirit, returned from the 1
Jordan, and was led about by the Spirit in the desert for 2
forty days, tempted all the while by the devil. During those
days He ate nothing, and at the close of them He suffered
from hunger.

Then the devil said to Him, 3

"If you are God's Son, tell this stone to become bread."

"It is written," replied Jesus, "'IT IS NOT ON BREAD 4
ALONE THAT A MAN SHALL LIVE'" (Deuteronomy 8:3).

The devil next led Him up and caused Him to see at a glance 5
all the kingdoms of the world. And the devil said to Him, 6

"To you will I give all this power and this splendor; for it has
been handed over to me, and on whomsoever I will I bestow
it. If therefore you do homage to me, it shall all be yours." 7

Jesus answered him, 8

"It is written, 'TO THE LORD THY GOD THOU SHALT DO
HOMAGE, AND TO HIM ALONE SHALT THOU RENDER
WORSHIP'" (Deuteronomy 6:13).

Then he brought Him to Jerusalem and set Him on the 9
summit of the Temple, and said to Him,

"If you are God's Son, throw yourself down from here; for 10
it is written,

'HE WILL GIVE ORDERS TO HIS ANGELS CONCERNING
THEE, TO GUARD THEE';
and 11

'ON THEIR HANDS THEY SHALL BEAR THEE UP,
LEST EVER THOU SHOULDST STRIKE THY FOOT

AGAINST A STONE'" (Psalm 91:11-12).

The reply of Jesus was, 12

"It is said, 'THOU SHALT NOT PUT THE LORD THY GOD TO THE PROOF'" (Deuteronomy 6:16).

So the devil, having fully tried every kind of temptation on Him, left Him for a time. 13

Then Jesus returned in the Spirit's power to Galilee; and His 14 fame spread through all the adjacent districts. And He pro- 15 ceeded to teach in their synagogues, winning praise from all.

He came to Nazareth also, where He had been brought 16 up; and, as was His custom, He went to the synagogue on the sabbath, and stood up to read. And there was handed to 17 Him the book of the prophet Isaiah. Opening the book, He found the place where it was written,

"THE SPIRIT OF THE LORD IS UPON ME, 18

BECAUSE HE HAS ANOINTED ME TO PROCLAIM GOOD NEWS TO THE POOR;

HE HAS SENT ME TO ANNOUNCE RELEASE TO THE PRISONERS

AND RECOVERY OF SIGHT TO THE BLIND:

TO FREE THOSE WHOM TYRANNY HAS CRUSHED,

TO PROCLAIM THE YEAR OF ACCEPTANCE WITH THE 19 LORD" (Isaiah 61:1-2).

And rolling up the book, He returned it to the attendant, 20 and sat down. And the eyes of all in the synagogue were fixed on Him.

Then He proceeded to say to them, 21

"To-day is this scripture fulfilled in your hearing."

And they all spoke well of Him, wondering at the words of 22 grace which fell from His lips, while they asked one another,

"Is not this Joseph's son?"

"Doubtless," said He, "you will quote to me the proverb, 23

'Physician, cure yourself: all that we hear that you have done at Capernaum, do here also in your own country',

"I tell you in truth," He added, "that no prophet is welcomed among his own people. And I tell you that there was many a widow in Israel in the time of Elijah, when there was no rain for three years and six months and there came a severe famine over all the land; and yet to not one of them was Elijah sent, but only to a widow at Zarephath of Sidon (1 Kings 17). And there was also many a leper in Israel in the time of the prophet Elisha, and yet not one of them was cleansed, but only Naaman the Syrian" (2 Kings 5). 24 25 26 27

Then all in the synagogue, while listening to these words, were filled with fury. They rose, hurried Him outside the town, and brought Him to the brow of the hill on which their town was built, to hurl Him down; but He passed through the midst of them and went His way. 28 29 30

So He came down to Capernaum, a town in Galilee. There He taught the people on the sabbath; and they were exceedingly struck by His teaching, because He spoke with the language of authority. 31 32

In the synagogue there was a man possessed by the spirit of a foul demon. With a loud voice he cried out, 33

"Ha! Jesus the Nazarene, what have you to do with us? I know who you are—God's Holy One!" 34

But Jesus rebuked the demon. 35

"Silence!" He exclaimed; "come out of him."

Upon this, the demon hurled the man into the midst of them, and came out of him without doing him any harm. All were awestruck; and they asked one another, 36

"What sort of language is this? For with authority and power He gives orders to the foul spirits and they come out."

And the talk about Him spread into every part of the neighboring country. 37

Now when He rose and left the synagogue He went to 38
Simon's house. Simon's mother-in-law was suffering from an
acute attack of fever; and they consulted Him about her.
Then standing over her He rebuked the fever, and it left her; 39
and she at once rose and waited on them.

At sunset all who had persons suffering from any illness 40
brought them to Him, and He laid His hands on them all,
one by one, and cured them. Demons also came out of 41
many, loudly calling out,

"You are the Son of God."

But He rebuked them and forbade them to speak, because
they knew Him to be the Christ.

Next morning, at daybreak, He left the town and went away 42
to a solitary place; but the people flocked out to find Him,
and, coming to the place where He was, they tried to detain
Him that He might not leave them. But He said to them, 43

"I have to tell the gospel of the Kingdom of God to the
other towns also, because for this purpose I was sent."

So for some time He preached in the synagogues in Judaea. 44

5 On one occasion the crowd was pressing on Him and 1
listening to God's message, while He was standing by the
lake of Gennesaret. And He saw two fishing-boats drawn up on 2
the beach (for the men had gone out of them and were washing the nets), and going on board one of them, which was 3
Simon's, He asked him to push out a little from the land. Then
He sat down and taught the crowd of people from the boat.

When He had finished speaking, He said to Simon, 4

"Push out into deep water, and all of you let down your
nets for a haul."

"Rabbi," replied Peter, "all night long we have worked hard 5 and caught nothing; but at your command I will let down the nets."

This they did, and enclosed a vast number of fish; and 6
their nets began to break. So they signaled to their partners 7
in the other boat to come and help them; they came, and
they filled both the boats so that they almost sank.

When Simon Peter saw this, he fell down at the knees of 8
Jesus, and exclaimed,

"Master, leave me, for I am a sinful man."

For he was awe-struck—he and all his companions—at 9
the haul of fish which they had taken; and so were Simon's 10
partners James and John, the sons of Zebedee.

But Jesus replied to Simon,

"Fear not: from this time you shall be a catcher of men."

Then, after bringing their boats to land, they left every- 11
thing and followed Him.

On another occasion, when He was in one of the towns, 12
there was a man there covered with leprosy, who, seeing
Jesus, threw himself at His feet and implored Him, saying,

"Master, if only you are willing, you are able to make
me clean."

Reaching out His hand and touching him, Jesus said, 13
"I am willing; be cleansed!"

And instantly the leprosy left him. He ordered him to tell 14
no one.

"But go," He said, "show yourself to the priest, and make
the offering for your cleansing which Moses appointed, as
evidence to them."

All the more, however, the report about Him spread 15
abroad, and great multitudes crowded to hear Him and to be
cured of their diseases; but Jesus Himself constantly with- 16
drew into the desert and there prayed.

One day He was teaching, and there were Pharisees and 17

teachers of the Law sitting there who had come from every village in Galilee and Judaea and from Jerusalem. And the power of the Lord was present that He might heal. And 18 a party of men came carrying a paralyzed man on a bed, and they tried to bring him in and lay him before Jesus. But 19 when they could find no way of doing so because of the crowd, they went up on the roof and let him down through the tiling—bed and all—into the midst, in front of Jesus. He 20 saw their faith and said to him,

"Friend, your sins are pardoned."

Then the scribes and Pharisees began to cavil [quibble], 21 asking,

"Who is this—uttering blasphemies? Who but God can pardon sins?"

Well aware of their reasonings, Jesus answered their ques- 22 tions by asking,

"What is this that you are debating in your hearts? Which 23 is easier?—to say, 'Your sins are pardoned,' or to say, 'Rise and walk'? But to prove to you that the Son of Man has 24 authority on earth to pardon sins"—

Turning to the paralytic He said,

"I bid you, arise, take up your bed, and go home."

Instantly he stood up in their presence, took up the mat on 25 which he had been lying, and went home, giving glory to God. All were seized with amazement, and they began to glo- 26 rify God. Awe-struck, they said,

"We have seen strange things to-day."

After this He went out and noticed a tax-gatherer, Levi by 27 name, sitting at the toll office; and He said to him,

"Follow me."

So he rose, left everything, and followed Him. 28

Now Levi gave a great reception at his house in honor of 29 Jesus, and there was a large party of tax-gatherers and others

at a table with them. The Pharisees and scribes of their party 30
expostulated [reasoned earnestly] with His disciples:

"Why are you eating and drinking with these tax-gatherers
and sinners?"

Jesus replied to them, 31

"It is not men in good health who require a physician, but
those who are ill. I have not come to call the righteous to 32
repentance, but sinners."

Again they said to Him, 33

"John's disciples fast often and pray, as do also those of the
Pharisees; but yours eat and drink."

"Can you compel the bridal party to fast," replied Jesus, "so 34
long as they have the bridegroom among them? But a time 35
will come, when the bridegroom is taken from them: then at
that time they will fast."

He also spoke in a parable to them. 36

"No one," He said, "tears a piece from a new garment to
mend an old one. If he does, he will not only spoil the new,
but the patch from the new will not match the old. Nor does 37
any one pour new wine into old wine-skins. If he does, the
new wine will burst the skins, the wine itself will escape, and
the skins perish. But new wine must be put into fresh wine- 38
skins. Nor does any one after drinking old wine wish for new; 39
for he says, 'The old is good.'"

6 Now on the sabbath, while He was passing through the 1
wheat fields, His disciples plucked the ears and rubbed
them with their hands to eat the grain. And some of the 2
Pharisees asked,

"Why are you doing what is unlawful on the sabbath?"

Jesus answered, "Have you never even read what David 3
did when he and his followers were hungry; how he entered 4

the house of God and took and ate the showbread and gave some to his followers—loaves which none but the priests are allowed to eat?" (1 Samuel 21:1-6).

"The Son of Man," He added, "is Lord of the sabbath." 5

On another sabbath He had gone to the synagogue and 6 was teaching there; and in the congregation was a man whose right hand was withered. The scribes and the 7 Pharisees were on the watch to see whether He would cure him on the sabbath, that they might be able to bring an accusation against Him. He knew their thoughts, and said to 8 the man with the withered hand,

"Rise, and stand there in the midst."

And he rose and stood there. Then Jesus said to them, 9

"I put it to you all whether we are allowed to do good on the sabbath, or to do evil; to save a life, or to destroy it."

And looking round upon them all He said to the man, 10

"Stretch out your hand."

He did so, and the hand was restored. But they were filled 11 with madness, and began to discuss what they should do to Jesus.

It was at about that time that He went into the hill country 12 to pray; and He remained all night in prayer to God. When it 13 was day, He called His disciples; and He selected from among them twelve, whom He also named apostles. These 14 were Simon, to whom He also gave the name of Peter, Andrew his brother, James, John, Philip, Bartholomew, Matthew, Thomas, James the son of Alphaeus, Simon called 15 the Zealot, James's son Judas, and Judas Iscariot (who 16 became a traitor).

With these He came down and took His stand on a level 17 place, where there was a great crowd of His disciples, and a multitude of people from every part of Judaea, from Jerusalem, and from the sea-side district of Tyre and Sidon,

who came to hear Him and to be cured of their diseases; and 18
those who were tormented by foul spirits were cured. The 19
whole crowd were eager to touch Him, because power went
forth from Him and cured every one.

Then fixing His eyes upon His disciples, Jesus said to them, 20
"Blessed are you poor, because the Kingdom of God is yours.

"Blessed are you who hunger now, because your hunger 21
shall be satisfied.

"Blessed are you who now weep aloud, because you
shall laugh.

"Blessed are you when men shall hate you and exclude 22
you from their society and insult you, and spurn your very
name as an evil thing, for the Son of Man's sake.

"Be glad at such a time, and leap for joy; for your reward 23
is great in heaven; for just so their forefathers behaved to
the prophets!

"But woe to you rich men, because you already have 24
your consolation!

"Woe to you who now have plenty to eat, because you will 25
be hungry!

"Woe to you who laugh now, because you will mourn and
weep aloud!

"Woe to you when all men speak well of you; for just so 26
their forefathers behaved to the false prophets!

"But to you who are listening to me I say, love your ene- 27
mies; seek the welfare of those who hate you; bless those 28
who curse you; pray for those who revile you. To him who 29
gives you a blow on one side of the face offer the other side
also; and to him who is robbing you of your outer garment
refuse not the under one also. To every one who asks, give; 30
and from him who takes away your property, do not demand
it back. And act towards your fellow men just as you would 31
have them act towards you.

"If you love those who love you, what credit is it to you? 32
Why, even bad men love those who love them. And if you are 33
kind to those who are kind to you, what credit is it to you?
Even bad men act thus. And if you lend to those from whom 34
you hope to receive, what credit is it to you? Even bad men
lend to their fellows so as to receive back an equal amount.
But love your enemies, be good to them, and lend without 35
hoping for any repayment. Then your recompense shall be
great, and you will be sons of the Most High; for He is kind to
the ungrateful and wicked. Be compassionate, just as your 36
Father is compassionate.

"Judge not, and you shall not be judged; condemn not, 37
and you shall not be condemned; pardon, and you shall be
pardoned; give, and gifts shall be bestowed on you. Full 38
measure, pressed, shaken down, and running over, shall they
pour into your laps; for with the same measure that you use
they shall measure to you in return."

He also spoke to them in a parable. 39

"Can a blind man lead a blind man?" He asked; "would not
both fall into the ditch? There is no learner superior to his 40
teacher; but he whose instruction is complete will be like
his teacher.

"And why look at the splinter in your brother's eye and not 41
notice the beam of timber in your own? How say to your 42
brother, 'Brother, let me take that splinter out of your eye,'
when all the while you do not see the beam in your own
eye? Hypocrite! take the beam out of your own eye first, and
then you will see clearly to take the splinter out of your
brother's eye.

"There is no good tree that yields worthless fruit, nor again 43
any worthless tree that yields good fruit. Every tree is known 44
by its fruit. It is not from thorns that men gather figs, nor
from the bramble that they can get a bunch of grapes. A good 45

man from the good stored up in his heart brings out what is good; and an evil man from the evil stored up brings out what is evil; from the fullness of his heart his mouth speaks.

"And why call me 'Master, Master,' and yet not do what I 46 tell you? If any one who comes to me, listens to my words 47 and puts them in practice, I will show you whom he is like. He is like a man who built a house, dug deep and laid the 48 foundation on the rock; and when a flood came, the torrent burst upon that house, but was unable to shake it, because it was securely built. But he who has heard and not obeyed is 49 like a man who built a house upon soft soil without a foundation. Against it the torrent burst, and immediately it collapsed, and terrible was the wreck and ruin of that house."

7 After He had ended all these words in the hearing of the 1 people, He went to Capernaum. Here an army captain's 2 servant, highly valued by his master, was ill and at the point of death; and the captain, hearing about Jesus, sent to Him 3 some of the Jewish elders, begging Him to come and restore his servant to health. And they, when they came to Jesus, 4 earnestly entreated Him, pleading,

"He deserves to have this favor granted him, for he loves our 5 nation, and at his own expense he built our synagogue for us."

Then Jesus went with them. But when He was not far from 6 the house, the captain sent friends to Him with the message:

"Sir, do not trouble yourself. I am not a fit person to receive you under my roof; and therefore I did not deem 7 myself worthy to come to you. Only speak the word, and let my young man be cured. For I too am a man obedient to 8 authority, and have soldiers under me; and I say to one, 'Go,' and he goes; to another, 'Come,' and he comes; and to my slave, 'Do this or that,' and he does it."

Jesus listened to the captain's message and was aston- 9
ished at him, and He turned and said to the crowd that
followed Him,

"I tell you that not even in Israel have I found faith like this."

And the friends who had been sent, on returning to the 10
house, found the servant in perfect health.

Shortly afterwards He went to a town called Nain, 11
attended by His disciples and a great crowd of people. And 12
just as He reached the gate of the town, they happened to be
bringing out for burial a dead man who was his mother's
only son; and she was a widow; and a great number of the
townspeople were with her. The Lord saw her, was moved 13
with pity for her, and said to her,

"Do not weep."

Then He went close and touched the bier [a coffin and its 14
supporting platform], and the bearers halted.

"Young man," He said, "I command you, awake!"

The dead man sat up and began to speak; and Jesus re- 15
stored him to his mother. All were awe-struck, and they gave 16
glory to God, saying,

"A prophet, a great prophet, has risen up among us."

And again,

"God has not forgotten His people."

And the report of what Jesus had done spread through the 17
whole of Judaea and all the surrounding districts.

John's disciples brought to John an account of all these things; 18
so he called two of his disciples and sent them to the Lord. 19

"Are you the Coming One?" he asked, "or is there another
whom we are to expect?"

The men came to Jesus and said, 20

"John the Baptist has sent us to you with this question:
"Are you the Coming One, or is there another whom we are
to expect?"

So then and there He cured many of diseases, severe pain, 21
and evil spirits, and to many who were blind He gave sight.
Then He answered the messengers, 22

"Go and report to John what you have seen and heard.
Blind men receive sight, the lame walk, lepers are cleansed,
deaf persons hear, the dead are raised to life, the poor have
the gospel preached to them. Blessed is every one who does 23
not take offense at my claims."

When John's messengers were gone, He proceeded to say 24
to the multitude concerning John,

"What did you go out into the desert to gaze at? A reed
waving in the wind? But what did you go out to see? A man 25
wearing fine clothes? People who are gorgeously dressed and
live in luxury are found in palaces. But what did you go out 26
to see? A prophet? Aye, I tell you, and far more than a
prophet. John is the man about whom it is written, 27

"'SEE, I AM SENDING MY MESSENGER BEFORE THY
FACE, AND HE SHALL MAKE READY THY WAY BEFORE
THEE' (Malachi 3:1).

"I tell you that among all of women born there is not one 28
greater than John. Yet one who is of least rank in the
Kingdom of God is greater than he."

And all the people, including the tax-gatherers, when they 29
listened to Him acknowledged the righteousness of God by
being baptized with John's baptism. But the Pharisees and 30
expounders of the Law frustrated God's purpose for them, by
refusing to be baptized by him.

"To what, then," said Jesus, "shall I compare the men of 31
the present generation, and what are they like? They are 32
like children sitting in the public square and calling out to
one another, 'We have played the flute to you, and you have
not danced: we have sung dirges, and you have not shown
sorrow.' For John the Baptist has come eating no bread and 33

drinking no wine, and you say, 'He has a demon!' The Son 34
of Man has come eating and drinking, and you say, 'See this
man! given to gluttony and tippling [drinking alcohol
habitually], a friend of tax-gatherers and sinners!' But wis- 35
dom is justified by all her children."

Now one of the Pharisees invited Him to a meal at his 36
house; so He entered the house and reclined at the table.
And there was a woman in the town who was a sinner. 37
Having learned that Jesus was at table in the Pharisee's
house she brought an alabaster jar of perfume, and, stand- 38
ing behind close to His feet, weeping, began to wet His feet
with her tears; and with her hair she wiped the tears away
again, while she lovingly kissed His feet and poured the perfume over them. Noticing this, the Pharisee, His host, said 39
to himself,

"This man, if he were really a prophet, would know who
and what sort of person this woman is who is touching Him,
that she is an immoral woman."

In answer to his thoughts Jesus said to him, 40

"Simon, I have a word to say to you."

"Rabbi, say on," he replied.

"There were once two men in debt to one money-lender," 41
said Jesus; "one owed him five hundred shillings and the
other fifty. But neither of them could pay anything; so he 42
freely forgave them both. Tell me, then, which of them will
love him most?"

"I suppose," replied Simon, "the one to whom he for- 43
gave most."

And Jesus said, "You have judged rightly."

Then turning towards the woman He said to Simon, 44

"Do you see this woman? I came into your house: you gave
me no water for my feet; but she has made my feet wet with
her tears, and then wiped the tears away with her hair. No 45

kiss did you give me; but she from the moment I came in has not left off tenderly kissing my feet. No oil did you pour even 46 on my head; but she has poured perfume upon my feet. This 47 is the reason why I tell you that her sins, her many sins, are forgiven—because she has loved much; but he who is forgiven little, loves little."

And He said to her, 48

"Your sins are forgiven."

Then the other guests began to say to themselves, 49

"Who can this man be who even forgives sins?"

But He said to the woman, 50

"Your faith has saved you: go, and be at peace."

8 Shortly after this He visited town after town, and village 1 after village, proclaiming His message and telling the good news of the Kingdom of God. The Twelve were with Him, and certain women whom He had delivered from evil 2 spirits and various diseases—Mary of Magdala, out of whom seven demons had gone, and Joanna the wife of Chuza, 3 Herod's steward, and Susanna, and many other women, who ministered to Jesus and His apostles.

Now when a great crowd was assembling, and was re- 4 ceiving additions from one town after another, He spoke a parable to them.

"A sower," He said, "went out to sow his seed; and as he 5 sowed, some of the seed fell by the way-side, and was trodden upon, or the birds pecked it up. Another part dropped 6 upon the rock, and after growing up it withered away for want of moisture. Another part fell among thorns, and the 7 thorns grew up with it and stifled it. But some of the seed fell 8 into good ground, and grew up and yielded a return of a hundred for one."

While thus speaking, He cried aloud and said,

"Listen, every one who has ears to hear!"

The disciples asked Him what this parable meant. 9

"To you," He replied, "it is granted to know the secrets of 10 the Kingdom of God; but all others are taught by parables, in order that they may see and yet not see, and may hear and yet not understand. The meaning of the parable is this. The 11 seed is the word. Those by the way-side are those who have 12 heard, and then the devil comes and carries away the word from their hearts, lest they should believe and be saved. Those on the rock are the people who on hearing the word 13 receive it joyfully; but they have no root: for a time they believe, but when trial comes they fall away. That which fell 14 among the thorns means those who have heard, but, as they go on their way, the word is stifled by the anxieties, the wealth and the pleasures of life, and they bring nothing to perfection. But that in the good ground means those who, 15 having listened to the word with open minds and in a right spirit, hold it fast, and endure, and yield a return.

"When any one lights a lamp, he does not cover it with a 16 vessel or hide it under a couch; he puts it on a lamp stand, that people who enter the room may see the light. There 17 is nothing hidden, which shall not be openly seen; nor anything secret, which shall not be known and come to light. Be careful, therefore, how you hear; for whoever has 18 anything, to him more shall be given, and whoever has nothing, even what he thinks he has shall be taken away from him."

Then came to Him His mother and His brothers, but could 19 not get near Him for the crowd. He was told, 20

"Your mother and brothers are standing on the edge of the crowd, and want to see you."

"My mother and my brothers," He replied, "are these, who 21
hear God's word and obey it."

One day He went on board a boat—both He and His disci- 22
ples; and He said to them,

"Let us cross over to the other side of the lake."

So they set sail. During the passage He fell asleep, and 23
there came down a squall of wind on the lake, so that the
boat began to fill and they were in deadly peril. So they came 24
and woke Him, crying,

"Rabbi, Rabbi, we are drowning."

Then He roused Himself and rebuked the wind and the
surging of the water, and they ceased and there was a calm.

"Where is your faith?" He asked them. 25

They were filled with terror and amazement, and said to
one another,

"Who, then, is this? for he gives orders both to wind and
waves, and they obey him."

Then they put in to shore in the country of the Gerasenes, 26
which lies opposite to Galilee. Here, on landing, He was met 27
by one of the townsmen who was possessed by demons: for
a long time he had not put on any garment, nor did he live in
a house, but among the tombs. When he saw Jesus, he called 28
out and fell down before Him, and cried aloud,

"What hast Thou to do with me, Jesus, Son of God Most
High? Do not torture me, I beseech Thee."

For already He had commanded the foul spirit to come 29
out of the man. Many a time it had seized and held the man;
and they had repeatedly put him in chains and fetters and
kept guard over him, but he would break the chains to
pieces, and, impelled by the demon, escape into the desert.

"What is your name?" Jesus asked him. 30

"Legion," he replied—because a great number of demons

had entered into him; and they besought Him not to com- 31
mand them to be gone to the abyss.

Now there was a great herd of swine there feeding on the 32
hillside; and the demons begged Him to give them leave to
go into them; and He gave them leave. The demons came 33
out of the man and left him, and entered into the swine; and
the herd rushed violently down the steep into the lake and
were drowned.

The swineherds, seeing what had happened, fled and 34
reported it both in town and country; whereupon the 35
people came out to see what had happened. They came to
Jesus, and they found the man from whom the demons had
gone out sitting at the feet of Jesus, clothed and in his right
mind; and they were awe-struck. Those who had seen it 36
told them how the demoniac had been cured. Then the 37
whole population of the Gerasenes and of the adjacent
districts begged Him to depart from them; for their terror
was extreme. So He went on board and returned.

The man from whom the demons had gone out had 38
begged to go with Him; but He sent him away.

"Return home," He said, "and tell there all that God has 39
done for you."

So he went away and published through the whole town
all that Jesus had done for him.

Now when Jesus returned, the people gave Him a warm 40
welcome; for they had all been looking out for Him. Just then 41
there came a man named Jairus, a ruler of the synagogue,
who threw himself at the feet of Jesus, and entreated Him to
come to his house; for he had an only daughter, about twelve 42
years old, and she was dying. So He went, and the dense
throng crowded on Him.

Now a woman, who for twelve years had been afflicted 43
with hemorrhage, and had spent on doctors all she had, but

none of them being able to cure her, came close behind Him 44
and touched the tassel of His robe; and instantly her flow of
blood stopped.

"Who is it that touched me?" Jesus asked. 45

And when all denied having done so, Peter and the rest said,

"Rabbi, the crowds are hemming you in and pressing on you."

"Some one has touched me," Jesus replied, "for I feel that 46
power has gone out from me."

Then the woman, perceiving that she had not escaped 47
notice, came trembling, and throwing herself down at His
feet she stated before all the people the reason why she had
touched Him, and how she was instantly cured.

"Daughter," said He, "your faith has cured you; go, and be 48
at peace."

While He was still speaking, some one came from the ruler 49
of the synagogue's house and said to him,

"Your daughter is dead; trouble the Rabbi no further."

Jesus heard the words and said to him, 50

"Have no fear. Only believe, and she shall recover."

So He came to the house, but allowed no one to go in with 51
Him but Peter and John and James and the girl's father and
mother. The people were all weeping aloud and beating their 52
breasts for her; but He said,

"Leave off wailing; for she is not dead, but asleep."

And they jeered at Him, knowing that she was dead. He, 53
however, took her by the hand and called aloud, 54

"Child, awake!"

And her spirit returned, and instantly she stood up; 55
and He directed them to give her some food. Her parents 56
were astounded; but He forbade them to mention the matter
to any one.

9 Then calling the Twelve together He conferred on them 1 power and authority over all the demons and to cure diseases; and sent them out to proclaim the Kingdom of God 2 and to cure the sick. And He commanded them, 3

"Take nothing for your journey—neither stick nor bag nor bread nor money; and do not have an extra under-garment. Whatever house you enter, make that your home, and from 4 it start afresh. Wherever they refuse to receive you, as you 5 leave that town shake off the very dust from your feet as a protest against them."

So they departed and visited village after village, spreading 6 the gospel and performing cures everywhere.

Now Herod the Tetrarch heard of all that was going on; and 7 he was bewildered, because it was said by some that John had come back to life, by others that Elijah had appeared, 8 and by others that one of the ancient Prophets had risen again. And Herod said, 9

"John I beheaded; but who is this, of whom I hear such reports?" And he sought to see Him.

The apostles, on their return, related to Jesus all they had 10 done. Then He took them and withdrew to a quiet retreat, to a town called Bethsaida. But the immense crowd, aware of 11 this, followed Him; and receiving them kindly He talked to them about the Kingdom of God, and those who needed healing He cured.

Now when the day began to decline, the Twelve came to 12 Him and said,

"Send the people away, that they may go to the villages and farms round about and find lodging and a supply of food; because here we are in an uninhabited district."

"You yourselves," He said, "must give them food." 13

"We have nothing," they replied, "but five loaves and a

couple of fish, unless indeed we were to go and buy provisions for all this host of people."

(For there were about five thousand men.) But He said to 14
His disciples,

"Make them sit down in parties of about fifty each."

They did so, making them all sit down. Then He took the 15
five loaves and the two fish, and looking up to heaven He 16
blessed them and broke them into portions, which He gave
to the disciples to distribute to the people. So they ate and 17
were fully satisfied, all of them; and what they had remaining
over was gathered up, twelve baskets of fragments.

One day when He was praying in retirement, the disciples 18
were with Him; and He asked them,

"Who do the people say that I am?"

"John the Baptist," they replied; "but others say Elijah; and 19
others that some one of the ancient prophets has come back
to life."

"But you," He asked, "who do you say that I am?" 20

"The Christ of God," replied Peter.

And Jesus strictly forbade them to tell this to any one; and 21
He said, 22

"The Son of Man must suffer much cruelty, be rejected by
the elders and high priests and scribes, and be put to death,
and on the third day be raised to life."

And He said to all, 23

"If any one wishes to follow me, let him renounce self and
take up his cross day by day, and so be my follower. For who- 24
ever desires to save his life shall lose it, and whoever loses his
life for my sake shall save it. Why, what benefit is it to a man 25
to have gained the whole world, but to have lost or forfeited
his own self? For whoever is ashamed of me and my teach- 26
ings, of him the Son of Man will be ashamed when He comes
in His own glory and in that of the Father and of the holy

angels. I tell you truly that there are some of those who stand 27
here who will certainly not taste death till they have seen the
Kingdom of God."

It was about eight days after saying this that Jesus, taking 28
with Him Peter, John, and James, went up the mountain to
pray. And while He was praying the appearance of His face 29
underwent a change, and His clothing became white and
radiant. And suddenly there were two men conversing with 30
Him, who were Moses and Elijah. They appeared in glory, 31
and were speaking about His departure, which He was to
effect in Jerusalem. Now Peter and the others were weighed 32
down with sleep; but, when they were fully awake, they
saw His glory, and the two men standing beside Him. And 33
when these were preparing to depart from Jesus, Peter said
to Him,

"Rabbi, we are thankful to you that we are here. Let us
put up three tents—one for you, one for Moses, and one
for Elijah."

He did not know what he was saying. But while he was 34
thus speaking, there came a cloud which spread over them;
and they were awe-struck as they entered the cloud. Then 35
there came a voice from within the cloud:

"This is My Son, My chosen One: listen to Him."

After this voice was heard, Jesus was found alone. 36

They kept it to themselves, and said not a word to any one
at that time about what they had seen.

On the following day, when they came down from the 37
mountain, a great crowd came to meet Him; and a man in 38
the crowd called out,

"Rabbi, I beg you to look on my son, for he is my only
child. At times a spirit seizes him and he suddenly cries out. 39
It convulses him, and makes him foam at the mouth, and
does not leave him till it has well-nigh covered him with

bruises. I entreated your disciples to drive out the spirit, but 40 they could not."

"O unbelieving and perverse generation!" replied Jesus; 41 "how long shall I be with you and bear with you? Bring your son here to me."

Now while the youth was coming, the spirit dashed him to 42 the ground and cruelly convulsed him. But Jesus rebuked the demon, cured the youth, and gave him back to his father. And all were awe-struck at the mighty power of God. 43

And while every one was expressing wonder at all that Jesus was doing, He said to His disciples,

"Store these my words in your memories, for the Son of 44 Man is about to be betrayed into the hands of men."

But they did not grasp His meaning: it was veiled from 45 them, so that they might not perceive it, and they were afraid to ask Him about it.

Now there arose a dispute among them, as to which of 46 them was the greatest. And Jesus, knowing the reasoning in 47 their hearts, took a young child and made him stand by His side and He said to them, 48

"Whoever for my sake receives this little child, receives me; and whoever receives me, receives Him who sent me. For the lowliest among you all—he is great."

"Rabbi," replied John, "we saw a man making use of your 49 name to expel demons; and we forbade him, because he does not follow with us."

"Do not forbid him," said Jesus, "for he who is not against 50 you is on your side."

Now when the time drew near for Him to be taken up into 51 heaven, He proceeded with fixed purpose towards Jerusalem. And He sent messengers in advance, who entered a village 52 of the Samaritans to make ready for Him. But the people 53 there would not receive Him, because He was evidently going

to Jerusalem. When the disciples James and John saw this, 54
they said,

"Master, do you wish us to order fire to come down from heaven and consume them?" (2 Kings 1:10).

But He turned and rebuked them. And they went to 55
another village. 56

As they proceeded on their way, a man came to Him 57
and said,

"I will follow you wherever you go."

"Foxes have holes," said Jesus, "and birds have nests; but 58
the Son of Man has nowhere to lay His head."

"Follow me," He said to another. 59

"Master," the man replied, "allow me first to go and bury my father."

"Leave the dead," said Jesus, "to bury their own dead; but 60
do you go and announce far and wide the Kingdom of God."

"Master," said yet another, "I will follow you; but allow me 61
first to go and say good-bye to my friends at home."

Jesus answered him, 62

"No one who has put his hand to the plow, and then looks behind him, is of use for the Kingdom of God."

10 After this the Lord appointed seventy others, and 1
sent them before Him, by twos, to go to every town or place which He Himself intended to visit. And He addressed 2
them thus:

"The harvest is abundant, but the reapers are few: therefore entreat the Owner of the harvest to send out more reapers into His fields. And now go. Remember that I am sending 3
you out as lambs into the midst of wolves. Carry no purse, 4
bag, nor change of shoes; and salute no one on your way.

"Whatever house you enter, first say, 'Peace be to this 5

house!' And if there is a lover of peace there, your peace shall 6
rest upon it; otherwise it shall come back upon you. And in 7
that same house stay, eating and drinking at their table; for
the laborer deserves his wages. Do not move from one house
to another.

"And whatever town you come to and they receive you, eat 8
what they put before you. Cure those who are ill in that town, 9
and tell them,

"'The Kingdom of God is at your door.'

"But whenever you come to a town and they will not 10
receive you, go out into the streets and say,

"'The very dust of your town that clings to our feet we wipe 11
off as a protest. Only be sure of this—the Kingdom of God is
close at hand.'

"I tell you that it will be more endurable for Sodom on the 12
great Day than for that town.

"Woe to thee, Chorazin! Woe to thee, Bethsaida! For 13
had the miracles been performed in Tyre and Sidon which
have been performed in you, long ere [before] now they
would have repented, sitting in sackcloth and ashes.
However, for Tyre and Sidon it will be more endurable at 14
the judgment than for you. And thou, Capernaum, shalt 15
thou be lifted as high as heaven? Thou shalt be brought
down as low as Hades.

"He who listens to you listens to me; and he who dis- 16
regards you disregards me, and he who disregards me disregards Him who sent me."

When the seventy returned, they exclaimed joyfully, 17

"Master, even the demons submit to us when we utter
your name."

And He said to them, "I saw Satan fall like a lightning-flash 18
out of heaven. I have given you power to tread serpents and 19
scorpions under foot, and to trample on all the power of the

enemy; and in no case shall anything do you harm. Nevertheless rejoice not at this, that the spirits submit to you; but rejoice that your names are enrolled in heaven." 20

At that hour Jesus was filled by the Holy Spirit with rapturous joy. 21

"I praise Thee," He exclaimed, "O Father, Lord of heaven and earth, that Thou hast hidden these things from sages and men of understanding, and hast revealed them to babes. Yes, Father, for such has been Thy gracious will. All things are delivered to me by my Father; and no one knows who the Son is but the Father, nor who the Father is but the Son and he to whom the Son may choose to reveal Him." 22

And He turned towards His disciples and said to them apart, 23

"Blessed are the eyes which see what you see! For I tell you that many prophets and kings have desired to see the things you see, and have not seen them, and to hear the things you hear, and have not heard them." 24

Then an expounder of the Law stood up to test Him with a question. 25

"Rabbi," he asked, "what shall I do to inherit eternal life?"

"What is written in the Law?" said Jesus; "how does it read?" 26

"'THOU SHALT LOVE THE LORD THY GOD,'" he replied, "'WITH THY WHOLE HEART, THY WHOLE SOUL, THY WHOLE STRENGTH, AND THY WHOLE MIND; AND THY NEIGHBOR AS MUCH AS THYSELF'" (Deuteronomy 6:5; Leviticus 19:18). 27

"A right answer," said Jesus; "do that, and you shall live." 28

But he, desiring to justify himself, said to Jesus, 29

"But what is meant by my 'neighbor'?"

Jesus replied, 30

"A man was once on his way down from Jerusalem to Jericho when he fell among robbers, who after both stripping and beating him went away, leaving him half dead. Now a priest happened to be going along that road, 31 and on seeing him passed by on the other side. In like manner a Levite also came to the place, and seeing him passed 32 by on the other side. But a certain Samaritan, being on a 33 journey, came where he lay, and seeing him was moved with pity. He went to him, and dressed his wounds with oil and 34 wine and bound them up. Then placing him on his own mule he brought him to an inn, and took care of him. The next day he took out two shillings and gave them to 35 the innkeeper.

"'Take care of him,' he said, 'and whatever further expense you are put to, I will repay you at my next visit.'

"Which of those three seems to you to have acted like a 36 neighbor to him who fell among the robbers?"

"The one who showed him pity," he replied. 37

"Go," said Jesus, "and act in the same way."

As they pursued their journey He came to a certain village, 38 where a woman named Martha welcomed Him to her house. She had a sister called Mary, who also seated herself at the 39 Lord's feet and listened to His teaching. Martha meanwhile 40 was busy and distracted in attending to her guests, and she came up to Him and said,

"Master, do you not care that my sister is leaving me to do all the serving? Tell her to assist me."

"Martha, Martha," replied Jesus, "you are anxious and 41 worried about a multitude of things; and yet only one thing 42 is needful. Mary has chosen the good portion and shall not be deprived of it."

11 At one place He was praying, and when He ceased, 1 one of His disciples said to Him,

"Master, teach us to pray, just as John taught his disciples."

So He said to them, 2

"When you pray, say, 'Father, may Thy name be kept holy; let Thy Kingdom come; give us day after day our bread 3 for the day; and forgive us our sins, for we ourselves also 4 forgive everyone who is indebted to us; and bring us not into temptation.'"

And He said to them, 5

"Which of you shall have a friend and shall go to him in the middle of the night and say,

"'Friend, lend me three loaves of bread; for a friend of 6 mine has just come to my house from a distance, and I have nothing for him to eat'?

"And he from indoors shall answer, 7

"'Do not pester me. The door is now barred, and I am here in bed with my children. I cannot get up and give you bread.'

"I tell you that even if he will not rise and give him the 8 loaves because he is his friend, at any rate because of his persistency he will rouse himself and give him whatever he wants.

"So I say to you, 'Ask, and it shall be given to you; seek, and 9 you shall find; knock, and the door shall be opened to you.' For every one who asks, receives; and he who seeks, finds; 10 and he who knocks shall have the door opened to him. What 11 father is there among you, who, if his son shall ask for bread, will offer him a stone? or if he asks for a fish, will instead of a fish offer him a snake? or if he asks for an egg, will offer him 12 a scorpion? If you, then, imperfect as you are, know how to 13 give your children gifts that are good for them, how much more will your Father who is in heaven give the Holy Spirit to those who ask Him!"

On one occasion He was expelling a dumb demon; and 14 when the demon was gone out the dumb man could speak, and the people were astonished. But some among them said, 15

"It is by the power of Beelzebul, the prince of the demons, that he expels the demons."

Others, to put Him to the test, asked Him for a sign from heaven. And, knowing their thoughts, He said to them, 16 17

"Every kingdom in which civil war rages goes to ruin: family attacks family and is overthrown. And if Satan has 18 engaged in conflict with himself, how shall his kingdom stand?—because you say that I expel demons by the power of Beelzebul. And if it is by the power of Beelzebul that I 19 expel the demons, by whom do your disciples expel them? They therefore shall be your judges. But if it is by the power 20 of God that I drive out the demons, it is evident that the Kingdom of God has come upon you.

"Whenever a strong man, fully armed and equipped, is 21 guarding his own house, he enjoys peaceful possession of his property; but as soon as another stronger than he attacks 22 him and overcomes him, he takes away that armor of his in which he trusted, and distributes the plunder. Whoever is 23 not with me is against me, and whoever is not gathering with me is scattering abroad.

"When a foul spirit has left a man, it roams about in the 24 desert, seeking rest; but, unable to find any, it says, 'I will return to the house I have left'; and when it comes, it finds 25 the house swept clean and in good order. Then it goes and 26 fetches seven other spirits more malignant than itself, and they enter and dwell there; and in the end that man's condition becomes worse than at first."

As He thus spoke a woman in the crowd called out in a 27 loud voice,

"Blessed is the mother who carried you, and the breasts that you have sucked."

"Nay rather," He replied, "they are blessed who hear the 28
word of God and carefully keep it."

Now when the crowds came thronging upon Him, He pro- 29
ceeded to say,

"The present generation is a wicked one: it requires some
sign, but no sign shall be given to it except that of Jonah. For 30
just as Jonah became a sign to the men of Nineveh, so the Son
of Man will be a sign to the present generation. The queen of 31
the south will arise at the judgment together with the men of
the present generation, and will condemn them; because she
came from the ends of the earth to hear the wisdom of
Solomon; and mark! [look/take note] One greater than
Solomon is here. There will arise men of Nineveh at the judg- 32
ment together with the present generation, and will condemn it; because they repented at the preaching of Jonah;
and mark! [look/take note] One greater than Jonah is here.

"When any one lights a lamp, he never puts it in the cellar 33
or under the bushel measure, but on the lampstand, that
people who come in may see the light. The lamp of the body 34
is the eye. When your eye is sound, your whole body is
lighted up; but when it is diseased, your body is dark.
Consider therefore whether the light that is in you is any- 35
thing but mere darkness. If, however, your whole body is full 36
of light, and has no part dark, it will be lighted, all of it, as
when the lamp with its bright shining gives you light."

When He had thus spoken, a Pharisee invited Him to a 37
meal at his house; so He entered and took His place at table.
Now the Pharisee saw to his surprise that He did not wash 38
before eating. The Master, however, said to him, 39

"Here we see how you Pharisees clean the outside of the
cup and plate, while the inside, your heart, is full of greed
and wickedness. Foolish men! Did not He who made the 40

outside make the inside also? But what is within, give in 41
charity, and behold all is clean for you.

"But woe to you Pharisees! for you pay tithes on your mint 42
and rue and every kind of garden vegetable, and are indiffer-
ent to justice and the love of God. These things you ought to
have done, yet without neglecting the others. Alas for you 43
Pharisees! for you love the best seats in the synagogues, and
you like to be bowed to in places of public resort. Woe to you! 44
for you are like tombs which lie hidden, and the people who
walk over them are not aware of them."

Hereupon one of the expounders of the Law exclaimed, 45
"Rabbi, in saying such things you reproach us also."

"Woe also to you expounders of the Law!" replied Jesus, 46
"for you load men with cumbrous burdens which you yourselves will not touch with one of your fingers. Woe to you! for 47
you build the tombs of the prophets, whom your forefathers
killed. It follows that you are witnesses to and approve of 48
your fathers' actions. They slew, you build.

"For this reason also the Wisdom of God has said, 'I will 49
send prophets and apostles to them, of whom they will
kill some and persecute others'; so that the blood of all the 50
prophets that has been shed from the creation of the world
may be required from the present generation. Yes, I tell you 51
that, from the blood of Abel down to the blood of Zechariah
who perished between the altar and the sanctuary, it shall all
be required from the present generation.

"Woe to you expounders of the Law! for you have taken 52
away the key of knowledge: you yourselves have not entered
in, and those who wanted to enter in you have hindered."

After He had left the house, the scribes and Pharisees 53
began a vehement attempt to entangle Him and make Him
give offhand answers on numerous points, lying in wait to 54
catch some unguarded expression from His lips.

12 Meanwhile the people had come streaming towards 1 Him by thousands, so that they were trampling one another under foot. And now He proceeded to say to His disciples first,

"Beware of the leaven of the Pharisees, that is to say, beware of hypocrisy. There is nothing that is covered up 2 which will not be uncovered, nor hidden which will not become known. Whatever therefore you have said in the 3 dark will be heard in the light; and what you have whispered within closed doors will be proclaimed from the house-tops.

"But to you who are my friends I say, 4

"'Be not afraid of those who kill the body and after that can do nothing further. I will show you whom to fear: fear Him 5 who after killing has power to throw into Gehenna: yes, I say to you, fear Him. Are not five sparrows sold for a penny? and 6 yet not one of them is a thing forgotten in God's sight. But 7 the very hairs on your heads are all counted. Away with fear: you are more precious than many sparrows.'

"And I tell you that every man who acknowledges me 8 before men, the Son of Man will also acknowledge before the angels of God. But whoever disowns me before men will be 9 disowned before the angels of God.

"Moreover every one who shall speak against the Son of 10 Man may obtain forgiveness; but he who blasphemes the Holy Spirit will never obtain forgiveness. And when they are 11 bringing you before synagogues and magistrates and gover-nors, do not anxiously ponder the manner or matter of your defense, nor what you are to say; for the Holy Spirit shall 12 teach you at that very moment what you must say."

Just then a man in the crowd appealed to Him. "Rabbi," he 13 said, "tell my brother to give me a share of the inheritance."

"Man," He replied "who made me a judge or arbitrator 14 over you?"

And to the people He said, 15

"Take care, be on your guard against all covetousness, for no one's life consists in the superabundance of his possessions."

And He spoke a parable to them. 16

"A certain rich man's lands," He said, "yielded abundant crops, and he debated within himself, saying, 17

"'What am I to do? for I have no place in which to store my crops.'

"And he said to himself, 18

"'This is what I will do: I will pull down my barns and build larger ones, and in them I will store up all my harvest and my goods; and I will say to my soul, 19

"'Soul, you have ample possessions laid up for many years to come: take your ease, eat, drink, enjoy yourself.'

"But God said to him, 20

"'Foolish man, this night they are demanding your soul from you; and these preparations—for whom shall they be?'

"So is it with him who amasses treasure for himself, but 21 has no riches in God."

Then turning to His disciples He said, "For this reason I 22 say to you, 'Do not be anxious for your lives, what you are to eat, and for your persons, what you are to put on.' For a 23 man's life is more than his food, and his person than his clothing. Look at the ravens. They do not sow or reap, and 24 they have neither store-chamber nor barn. And yet God feeds them. How far more precious are you than the birds! And which of you is able by anxious thought to add a foot to 25 his height? If, then, you are unable to do even a very little 26 thing, why be anxious about other matters? Look at the 27 lilies, how they grow. They neither toil nor spin. And yet I tell you that not even Solomon in all his magnificence was arrayed like one of these. But if God so clothes the grass 28 of the fields, that blooms to-day and to-morrow is feeding the oven, how much more will He clothe you, you men of little faith!

"Therefore, do not be asking what you are to eat or what 29 you are to drink; and do not waver between hope and fear. For the nations of the world seek all these things; your Father 30 knows that you need them. But seek His Kingdom, and these 31 things shall be given you in addition.

"Dismiss your fears, little flock: your Father finds pleasure 32 in giving you the Kingdom. Sell your possessions and give 33 alms. Provide yourselves with purses that will never wear out, wealth inexhaustible in heaven, where no thief can come nor moth consume. For where your wealth is, there 34 also will your heart be.

"Have your girdles on, and let your lamps be alight; and be 35 like men waiting for their master—on the look-out till he 36 shall return from the wedding feast—that, when he comes and knocks, they may open the door instantly. Blessed are 37 those servants whom their Master when He comes shall find on the watch. I tell you, in solemn truth, that He will tie an apron round Him, and will bid them recline at table while He comes and waits on them. And whether it be in the second 38 watch or in the third that He comes and finds them so, blessed are they. Of this be sure, that if the master of the 39 house had known at what time the robber was coming, he would have kept awake and not have allowed his house to be broken into. Be you also ready, for at an hour when you are 40 not expecting Him the Son of Man will come."

"Master," said Peter, "are you addressing this parable to us, 41 or to all alike?"

"Who, then," replied the Lord, "is the faithful and prudent 42 steward whom his master will put in charge of his household to serve out their rations at the proper times? Blessed is that 43 servant whom his master when he comes shall find so doing.

I tell you truly that he will put him in authority over all his 44
possessions. But if that servant should say in his heart, 'My 45
master is a long time in coming,' and should begin to beat
the menservants and maidservants, and to eat and drink,
drinking even to excess; that servant's master will come on a 46
day when he is not expecting him and at an hour that he
knows not of, and cut him asunder, and make him share the
lot of the unfaithful. And that servant who has been told his 47
master's will and yet made no preparation and did not obey
his will, will receive many lashes. But he who had not been 48
told it and yet did what deserved the scourge, will receive but
few lashes. To whomsoever much has been given, from him
much will be required; and to whom much has been
entrusted, of him the more will be demanded.

"I came to throw fire upon the earth, and what is my 49
desire? Oh that it were even now kindled! But I have a bap- 50
tism to undergo; and how am I pent up till it is accomplished! Do you suppose that I came to bring peace to 51
the earth? No, I tell you that I came to bring dissension. For 52
from this time there will be in one house five persons split
into parties. Three will form a party against two and two
against three; father against son and son against father; 53
mother attacking daughter and daughter her mother,
mother-in-law her daughter-in-law, and daughter-in-law
her mother-in-law" (Micah 7:6).

Then He said to the people also, 54

"When you see a cloud rising in the west, you immediately
say, 'There is to be a shower'; and it comes to pass. And when 55
you see a south wind blowing, you say, 'It will be burning
hot'; and it comes to pass. Hypocrites! You know how to read 56
the aspect of earth and sky. How is it you cannot read this
present time?

"Why, too, do you not of yourselves judge what is right? 57

For when, with your opponent, you are going before the 58
magistrate, on the way take pains to be quit of him; for fear
that he should drag you before the judge, and the judge hand
you over to the officer of the court, and the officer lodge you
in prison. Never, I tell you, will you get free till you have paid 59
the last mite."

13 Just at that time people came to tell Him about the 1
Galilaeans whose blood Pilate had mingled with
their sacrifices.

"Do you suppose," He asked in reply, "that those 2
Galilaeans were worse sinners than the mass of the
Galilaeans, because this happened to them? I assure you it
was not so. Nay, if you are not penitent, you will all lose your 3
lives just as they lost theirs. Or those eighteen persons whom 4
the tower in Siloam fell on and killed, do you suppose they
were offenders more than any one else in Jerusalem? I assure 5
you it was not so. Nay, I tell you if you do not repent, you will
all lose your lives just as they lost theirs."

And He told them this parable. 6

"A man," He said, "who had a fig-tree growing in his garden came to look for fruit on it and could find none. So he 7
said to the gardener,

"'See, this is the third year I have come to look for fruit on
this fig-tree and cannot find any. Cut it down. Why should so
much ground be actually wasted?'

"But the gardener pleaded, 8

"'Leave it, Sir, this year also, till I have dug round it and
manured it. If next year it bears fruit, well and good; if not, 9
then you shall cut it down.'"

Once He was teaching on the sabbath in one of the syna- 10
gogues where a woman was present who for eighteen years 11

had had a spirit of weakness: she was bent double, and was quite unable to raise herself. But Jesus saw her, and calling to her, He said to her, 12

"Woman, you are free from your weakness."

And He put His hands on her, and she immediately stood upright and began to give glory to God. 13

Then the ruler of the synagogue, indignant that Jesus had cured her on a sabbath, said to the crowd, 14

"There are six days in the week on which people ought to work. On those days therefore come and get yourselves cured, and not on the sabbath day."

But the Lord's reply to him was, 15

"Hypocrites, does not each of you on the sabbath untie his bullock or his ass from the stall and lead him to water? And this woman, daughter of Abraham as she is, whom Satan had bound for no less than eighteen years, was she not to be loosed from this chain because it is the sabbath day?" 16

When He said this, all His opponents were ashamed, while the whole multitude was delighted at the many glorious things continually done by Him. 17

This prompted Him to say, 18

"What is the Kingdom of God like? and to what shall I compare it? It is like a mustard-seed which a man drops into the soil in his garden, and it grows and becomes a tree in whose branches the birds roost." 19

And again He said, 20

"To what shall I compare the Kingdom of God? It is like leaven which a woman takes and buries in three measures of flour, to work there till the whole is leavened." 21

He was passing through town after town and village after village, teaching and steadily proceeding towards Jerusalem, when, some one asked Him, 22

"Sir, are there but few who are to be saved?" 23

"Strive your hardest to enter by the narrow gate," He 24
answered; "for many, I tell you, will try to find a way in and
will not succeed. As soon as the Master of the house has 25
risen and shut the door, and you have begun to stand outside and knock at the door and say,

"'Sir, open the door for us,'

"He will answer, 'I do not know where you come from.'

"Then you will plead, 26

"'We have eaten and drunk in your company, and you
have taught in our streets.'

"But He will reply, 27

"'I tell you that I do not know where you come from. Be
gone from me, all of you, wrongdoers!'

"There will be the weeping and gnashing of teeth, when 28
you see Abraham and Isaac and Jacob and all the prophets
inside the Kingdom of God, and yourselves thrown out.
They will come from east and west, from north and south, 29
and will sit down at the banquet in the Kingdom of God.
And mark! [look/take note] some now last will be first, and 30
some now first will be last."

Just at that time there came some Pharisees, who warned 31
Him, saying,

"Leave this place and continue your journey; Herod
means to kill you."

"Go," He replied, "and take this message to that fox: 32

"'See, to-day and to-morrow I am driving out demons and
effecting cures, and on the third day I finish.'

"Yet I must continue my journey to-day and to-morrow 33
and the day following; for it is not conceivable that a prophet
should perish outside of Jerusalem.

"O Jerusalem! Jerusalem! You that murder the prophets 34
and stone those who have been sent to you! How often have
I desired to gather your children to me, as a hen gathers her

brood under her wings, and you would not come! See, your 35
house is abandoned to you. I tell you that you will never see
me again until you say, 'BLESSED IS HE WHO COMES IN
THE NAME OF THE LORD!'" (Psalm 118:26).

14 One day—it was a sabbath—He entered the house of 1
one of the rulers of the Pharisee party to take a meal,
while they were closely watching Him. In front of Him was a 2
man suffering from dropsy. This led Jesus to ask the lawyers 3
and Pharisees,

"Is it allowable to cure people on the sabbath?"

They gave Him no answer; so He took hold of the man, cured 4
him, and sent him away. Then He turned to them and said, 5

"Which of you shall have a child or an ox fall into a well on
the sabbath day, and will not immediately lift him out?"

To this they could make no reply. 6

Then, when He noticed how the invited guests chose the 7
best places, He spoke this parable, and said to them,

"When any one invites you to a wedding banquet, do not 8
take the best place, lest perhaps some more honored guest
than you may have been asked, and the man who invited 9
you both will come and say to you, 'Make room for him,' and
then you, ashamed, will move to the lowest place. But, when 10
invited, take the lowest place, that when your host comes he
may say to you, 'Friend, come up higher.' This will be doing
you honor in the presence of all the other guests. For who- 11
ever uplifts himself shall be humbled, and he who humbles
himself shall be uplifted."

Also to His host, who had invited Him, He said, 12

"When you give a breakfast or a dinner, do not invite
your friends or brothers or relatives or rich neighbors, lest
perhaps they should in turn invite you, and so repay your

hospitality. But when you entertain, invite the poor, the crip- 13
pled, the lame, and the blind; and you will be blessed, 14
because they have no means of repaying you, but you will be
repaid at the resurrection of the righteous."

On hearing this, one of His fellow guests said to Him, 15
"Blessed is he who shall feast in God's Kingdom."

"A man once gave a great feast," replied Jesus, "to which he 16
invited a large number of guests. At dinner-time he sent his 17
servant with a message to those invited,

"'Come, for things are now ready.'

"But they all without exception began to excuse them- 18
selves. The first told him,

"'I have just purchased a piece of land, and must of necessity go and look at it. Pray hold me excused.'

"A second pleaded, 19

"'I have just bought five yoke of oxen, and am on my way
to try them. Pray hold me excused.'

"Another said, 20

"'I am just married. It is impossible for me to come.'

"So the servant came and brought these answers to his 21
master; and it stirred his anger.

"'Go out quickly,' he said, 'into the streets of the city—
the wide ones and the narrow, and fetch in poor men, the
crippled, blind, and lame: fetch them all in here.'

"Soon the servant reported, 22

"'Sir, what you ordered is done, and there is room still.'

"'Go out,' replied the master, 'to the high roads and 23
hedgerows, and compel the people to come in, so that my
house may be filled. For I tell you that not one of those who 24
were invited shall taste my feast.'"

On His journey vast crowds attended Him, towards whom 25
He turned and said,

"If any one comes to me who does not hate his father and 26 mother, wife and children, brothers and sisters, yes and his own life also, he cannot be a disciple of mine. No one who 27 does not carry his own cross and come after me can be a disciple of mine.

"Which of you, desiring to build a tower, does not sit down 28 first and calculate the cost, asking if he has the means to finish it? lest perhaps, when he has laid the foundation and is unable 29 to finish, all who see it shall begin to jeer at him, saying, 'This 30 man began to build, but could not finish.' Or what king, march- 31 ing to encounter another king in war, does not first sit down and deliberate whether he is able with ten thousand men to meet the one who is advancing against him with twenty thou- sand? If not, while the other is still a long way off, he sends 32 envoys and sues for peace. Just so no one of you who does not 33 bid farewell to all that belongs to him can be a disciple of mine.

"Salt is good: but if even the salt has become tasteless, how 34 will you restore its flavor? Neither for land nor for dunghill is 35 it of any use; they throw it away. Listen, every one who has ears to hear!"

15 Now the tax-gatherers and the sinners were every- 1 where in the habit of coming close to Him to listen to Him; and this led the Pharisees and the scribes to complain, 2

"He gives a welcome to sinners, and joins them at their meals!"

So in a parable He asked them, 3

"Which of you men, if he has a hundred sheep and has lost 4 one of them, does not leave the ninety-nine in their desert pasture and go in search of the lost one till he finds it? And 5 when he has found it, he lifts it on his shoulders, glad at heart. Then coming home he calls his friends and neighbors 6 together, and says, 'Rejoice with me, for I have found my sheep—the one I had lost.' I tell you that in the same way there will be rejoicing in heaven over one repentant sinner—more rejoicing than over ninety-nine blameless persons who have no need of repentance. 7

"Or what woman who has ten silver coins, if she loses one of them, does not light a lamp and sweep the house and search carefully till she finds it? And when she has found it, she calls together her friends and neighbors, and says, 8 9

"'Congratulate me, for I have found the coin which I had lost.'

"I tell you that in the same way there is rejoicing in the presence of the angels of God over one repentant sinner." 10

He went on to say, 11

"There was a man who had two sons. The younger of them said to his father, 12

"'Father, give me the share of the property that comes to me.'

"So he divided his property between them. No long time afterwards the younger son got all together and traveled to a distant country, where he wasted his money in debauchery [extreme indulgence of sensual appetites] and excess. At last, when he had spent everything, there came a terrible famine throughout that country, and he began to feel the pinch of want. So he hired himself to one of the inhabitants of that country, who sent him on to his farm to tend swine; and he longed to make a meal of the pods the swine were eating, but no one gave him any. 13 14 15 16

"On coming to his senses he said, 17

"'How many of my father's hired men have more bread than they want, while I here am dying of hunger! I will rise and go to my father, and will say to him, Father, I have sinned against heaven, and before you: I no longer deserve to be called a son of yours: treat me as one of your hired men.' 18 19

"So he rose and came to his father. But while he was still a 20 long way off, his father saw him and pitied him, and ran and threw his arms round his neck and kissed him.

"'Father,' cried the son, 'I have sinned against heaven 21 and before you: no longer do I deserve to be called a son of yours.'

"But the father said to his servants, 22

"'Fetch the best coat quickly and put it on him; and bring a ring for his finger and shoes for his feet. Fetch the fat calf 23 and kill it, and let us feast and enjoy ourselves; for my son 24 here was dead and has come to life again: he was lost and has been found.'

"And they began to be merry.

"Now his elder son was out on the farm; and when he 25 came near the house, he heard music and dancing. Then he 26 called one of the lads to him and asked what all this meant.

"'Your brother has come,' he replied; 'and your father has 27 had the fat calf killed, because he has got him home safe and sound.'

"Then he was angry and would not go in. But his father 28 came out and entreated him.

"'All these years,' replied the son, 'I have served you, and I 29 have never at any time disobeyed any of your orders, and yet you have never given me so much as a kid, for me to enjoy myself with my friends; but now that this son of yours is 30 come who has squandered your property among harlots, you have killed the fat calf for him.'

"'You, my dear son,' said the father, 'are always with me, 31 and all that is mine is also yours. We were bound to make 32 merry and rejoice, for this brother of yours was dead and has come back to life, he was lost and has been found.'"

16 He said also to His disciples: 1
"There was a rich man who had a steward about whom an accusation was brought to him, that he was wasting his property. He called him and said, 2

"'What is this I hear about you? Render an account of your stewardship, for I cannot let you hold it any longer.'

"Then the steward said to himself, 3

"'What am I to do? My master is taking away the steward-ship from me. I am not strong enough for field labor: to beg, I should be ashamed. Ah! I see what to do, in order that when 4 I am discharged from the stewardship people may give me a home in their houses.'

"So he called all his master's debtors, one by one, and 5 asked the first, 'How much are you in debt to my master?'

"'A hundred measures of oil,' he replied. 6

"'Here is your account,' said the steward: 'sit down quickly and alter it to fifty measures.'

"To a second he said, 7

"'And how much do you owe?'

"'A hundred quarters of wheat,' was the answer.

"'Here is your account,' said he: 'alter it to eighty.'

"And the master praised the dishonest steward for his 8 shrewdness; for in dealing with their fellows, the men of this world are shrewder than the sons of Light.

"And I charge you, so to use wealth tainted with dishon- 9 esty as to win friends who, when it fails, shall welcome you to the tents that never perish. The man who is honest in a 10 very small matter is honest in a great one also; and he who is dishonest in a very small matter is dishonest in a great one also. If therefore you have not proved yourselves honest in 11 dealing with wealth tainted with dishonesty, who will entrust to you the true good? And if you have not been honest with 12 what belongs to another, who will give you what is your own?

"No servant can serve two masters. For either he will hate 13 one and love the other, or else he will attach himself to one and think lightly of the other. You cannot be servants both of God and of money."

To all this the Pharisees listened, bitterly jeering at Him; 14 for they were lovers of money.

"You are persons," He said to them, "who boast of their 15 own goodness before men, but God sees your hearts; for what is exalted by men may be an abomination in God's sight. The Law and the prophets continued until John came: 16 from that time the gospel of the Kingdom of God has been spreading, and every one presses into it. And it is easier for 17 sky and earth to pass away than for the smallest detail of the Law to lapse. Any man who divorces his wife and marries 18 another commits adultery; and he who marries a woman so divorced from her husband commits adultery.

"There was once a rich man who used to array himself in 19 purple and fine linen, and enjoyed a splendid banquet every day, while at his outer door there lay a beggar, Lazarus by 20 name, covered with sores and longing to make a meal off the 21 scraps falling on the floor from the rich man's table. Nay, the dogs, too, used to come and lick his sores.

"In course of time the beggar died; and he was carried by 22 the angels to Abraham's bosom. The rich man also died, and was buried. And in Hades, being in torment, he looked and 23 saw Abraham in the far distance, and Lazarus resting in his arms. So he cried aloud, and said, 24

"'Father Abraham, take pity on me and send Lazarus to dip the tip of his finger in water and cool my tongue, for I am in agony in this flame.'

"'Remember, my son,' said Abraham, 'that you had good 25 fortune during your life, and that Lazarus in like manner had bad fortune. But he is comforted here now, while you are

in agony. Besides all this there is set a vast chasm between us 26
and you, in order that those who desire to cross from this side
to you, or from your side to us, may not be able to do so.'

"'I entreat you then, father,' said he, 'to send him to my 27
father's house. For I have five brothers. Let him earnestly 28
warn them, lest they also come to this place of torment.'

"'They have Moses and the prophets,' replied Abraham; 29
'let them hear them.'

"'No, father Abraham,' he pleaded; 'but if some one goes to 30
them from the dead, they will repent.'

"'If they are deaf to Moses and the prophets,' replied 31
Abraham, 'they would not be led to believe even if some one
should rise from the dead.'"

17

Jesus said to His disciples, 1
"It is inevitable that causes of stumbling should occur;
but woe to him through whom they occur! Better for him if 2
with a millstone hanging round his neck he had been hurled
into the sea, rather than that he should cause a single one of
these little ones to fall. Be on your guard. 3

"If your brother acts wrongly, reprove him; and if he is
sorry, forgive him; and if seven times in a day he acts wrongly 4
towards you, and seven times turns again to you and says, 'I
am sorry,' you must forgive him."

And the apostles said to the Lord, 5
"Increase our faith."

"If your faith," replied the Lord, "were merely like a 6
mustard-seed, you might say to this black mulberry-tree,
'Tear up your roots and plant yourself in the sea,' and
instantly it would obey you.

"Which of you who has a servant plowing, or tending 7
sheep, will say to him when he comes in from the farm,

'Come at once and take your place at table,' and will not 8
rather say to him, 'Get my dinner ready, gird yourself, and
wait upon me till I have finished my dinner, and then you
shall have yours'? Does he thank the servant for obeying his 9
orders? So you also, when you have obeyed all the orders 10
given you, must say,

"'There is no merit in our service: we have merely done
our duty.'"

As they pursued their journey to Jerusalem, He passed 11
between Samaria and Galilee. And as He entered a certain 12
village, ten men met Him who were lepers and stood at a distance. In loud voices they cried out, 13

"Jesus, Rabbi, take pity on us."

Perceiving this, He said to them, 14

"Go and show yourselves to the priests."

And while on their way to do this they were made clean.

One of them, seeing that he was cured, came back, glorify- 15
ing God in a loud voice, and he threw himself at the feet of 16
Jesus, thanking Him. He was a Samaritan.

"Were not all ten made clean?" Jesus asked; "but where are 17
the nine? Have none been found to come back and give glory 18
to God except this foreigner?"

And He said to him, 19

"Rise and go: your faith has cured you."

Being asked by the Pharisees when the Kingdom of God 20
was coming, He answered,

"The Kingdom of God does not so come that you can
watch closely for it. Nor shall they say, 'See here!' or 'See 21
there!'—for the Kingdom of God is within you."

Then, turning to His disciples, He said, 22

"There will come a time when you will wish you could see
but a single one of the days of the Son of Man, but will not
see one. And they will say to you, 'See there!' 'See here!' Do 23

not go in pursuit. For just as the lightning, when it flashes, 24
shoots across the sky, so will the Son of Man be on His day.
But first He must endure much suffering, and be rejected by 25
the present generation.

"And as it was in the time of Noah, so will it also be in the 26
time of the Son of Man. Men were eating and drinking, tak- 27
ing wives and giving wives, up to the very day Noah entered
the ark, and the deluge came and destroyed them all. As it 28
was also in the time of Lot; they were eating and drinking,
buying and selling, planting and building; but on the day 29
that Lot left Sodom, it rained fire and brimstone from the sky
and destroyed them all. Exactly so will it be on the day that 30
the veil is lifted from the Son of Man.

"On that day, if a man is on the roof and his goods indoors, 31
let him not go down to fetch them; and, in the same way, he
who is in the field, let him not turn back. Remember Lot's 32
wife. Any man who seeks to save his life shall lose it; but 33
whoever loses his life shall retain it. On that night, I tell you, 34
there will be two lying on one bed: one will be taken away
and the other left. There will be two women turning the mill 35
together: one will be taken away and the other left."

"Where, Master?" they inquired. 37

"Where the dead body is," He replied, "there also will the
vultures flock together."

18 He also taught them by a parable that they must 1
always pray and never lose heart.

"In a certain town," He said, "there was a judge who had 2
no fear of God and no respect for man. And in the same town 3
was a widow who repeatedly came and entreated him, saying,

"'Give me justice and stop my adversary.'

"For a time he would not, but afterwards he said to himself, 4

"'Though I have neither fear of God nor respect for man, yet because she annoys me I will give her justice, to prevent 5 her from constantly coming to pester me.'"

And the Lord said, 6

"Hear those words of the unjust judge. And will not God 7 avenge the wrongs of His own people who cry aloud to Him day and night, although He delays vengeance on their behalf? Yes, He will soon avenge their wrongs. Yet, when the 8 Son of Man comes, will He find faith on earth?"

And to some who relied on themselves as being righteous 9 men, and looked down upon all others, He addressed this parable.

"Two men went up to the Temple to pray, one a Pharisee 10 and the other a tax-gatherer. The Pharisee, standing erect, 11 prayed as follows by himself:

"'O God, I thank Thee that I am not like other people— I am not a thief nor a cheat nor an adulterer, nor even like this tax-gatherer. I fast twice a week. I pay the tithe on all my gains.' 12

"But the tax-gatherer, standing far back, would not so 13 much as lift his eyes to heaven, but kept beating his breast and saying,

"'O God, have mercy on me, sinner that I am.'

"I tell you that this man went home accounted by God 14 freer from guilt than the other; for every one who uplifts himself shall be humbled, but he who humbles himself shall be uplifted."

On one occasion people brought with them their infants, 15 for Him to touch them; but the disciples, noticing this, found fault with them. Jesus, however, called for the infants. 16

"Let the little children come to me," He said; "do not hinder them; for it is to those who are childlike that the Kingdom of God belongs. I tell you in truth that whoever does not receive 17 the Kingdom of God like a little child will certainly not enter it."

The question was put to Him by a ruler: "Good Rabbi, what shall I do to inherit eternal life?" 18

"Why do you call me good?" replied Jesus; "there is no one good but One, namely God. You know the Commandments: 'DO NOT COMMIT ADULTERY'; 'DO NOT MURDER'; 'DO NOT STEAL'; 'DO NOT LIE IN GIVING EVIDENCE'; 'HONOR THY FATHER AND THY MOTHER.'" 19 20

"All these," he replied, "I have carefully obeyed from my youth." 21

On receiving this answer Jesus said to him, 22

"There is still one thing wanting in you. Sell everything you possess and give the money to the poor, and you shall have wealth in heaven; and come and follow me."

But on hearing these words he was very sorrowful, for he was exceedingly rich. 23

Jesus looked at him, and said, 24

"How hard it will be for the possessors of riches to enter the Kingdom of God! Why, it is easier for a camel to go through a needle's eye than for a rich man to enter the Kingdom of God." 25

"Who, then, can be saved?" exclaimed the hearers. 26

"Things impossible to man," He replied, "are possible to God." 27

Then Peter said, 28

"See, we have given up our homes and have followed you."

"I tell you in truth," replied Jesus, "that there is no one who has left house or wife, or brothers or parents or children, for the sake of God's Kingdom, who shall not receive many times as much in this life, and in the age that is coming eternal life." 29 30

Then He drew the Twelve to Him and said, 31

"See, we are going up to Jerusalem, and everything written in the prophets about the Son of Man will be fulfilled. For He 32 will be handed over to the Gentiles, and be mocked, outraged and spat upon. They will scourge Him and put Him to death, and on the third day He will rise to life again." 33

Nothing of this did they understand. The words were a 34 mystery to them, nor could they see what He meant.

As Jesus came near to Jericho, there was a blind man sit- 35 ting by the wayside begging. He heard a crowd of people 36 going past, and inquired what it all meant.

"Jesus the Nazarene is passing by," they told him. 37

Then, at the top of his voice, he cried out, 38

"Jesus, son of David, take pity on me."

Those in front reproved him and tried to silence him; but 39 he continued shouting, louder than ever,

"Son of David, take pity on me."

So Jesus stopped and bade them bring the man to Him; 40 and when he had come close to Him He asked him,

"What shall I do for you?" 41

"Sir," he replied, "let me recover my sight."

"Recover your sight," said Jesus: "your faith has cured you." 42

No sooner were the words spoken than the man regained 43 his sight and followed Jesus, giving glory to God; and all the people, seeing it, gave praise to God.

19 So He entered Jericho and proceeded through the 1 town. There was a man there called Zacchaeus, who 2 was the chief collector of taxes, and was wealthy. He was 3 anxious to see what sort of man Jesus was; but he could not because of the crowd, for he was short in stature. So he ran 4 on in front and climbed up a mulberry tree to see Him; for He was about to pass that way.

As soon as Jesus came to the place, He looked up and said 5 to him,

"Zacchaeus, come down quickly, for I must stay at your house to-day."

So he came down in haste, and welcomed Him joyfully. When they saw this, they all began muttering with indignation, 6 7

"He has gone in to be the guest of a sinner!"

Zacchaeus, however, stood up, and addressing the Lord said, 8

"Here and now, Master, I give half my property to the poor, and if I have unjustly exacted money from any man, I pledge myself to repay to him four times the amount."

Jesus said to him, 9

"To-day salvation has come to this house, seeing that he too is a son of Abraham. For the Son of Man has come to seek and to save what is lost." 10

As they were listening to His words, He went on to teach them by a parable, because He was near to Jerusalem and they supposed that the Kingdom of God was going to appear immediately. So He said to them, 11

12

"A man of noble family traveled to a distant country to obtain the rank of king, and to return. And he called ten of his servants and gave each of them a pound, instructing them to trade with the money during his absence. 13

"Now his countrymen hated him, and sent a deputation [representatives] after him to say, 'We are not willing that he should become our king.' And upon his return, after he had obtained the sovereignty, he ordered those servants to whom he had given the money to be summoned before him, that he might learn their success in trading. 14

15

"So the first came and said, 16

"'Sir, your pound has produced ten pounds more.'

"'Well done, good servant,' he replied; 'because you have been faithful in a very small matter, be in authority over ten towns.' 17

"The second came, and said, 18

"'Your pound, Sir, has produced five pounds.'

"So he said to this one also, 19

"'And you, be the governor of five towns,'

"The next came. 20

"'Sir,' he said, 'here is your pound, which I have kept wrapped up in a cloth. For I was afraid of you, because you 21 are a severe man: you take up what you did not lay down, and you reap what you did not sow.'

"'By your own words,' he replied, 'I will judge you, you 22 bad servant. You knew me to be a severe man, taking up what I did not lay down, and reaping what I did not sow! Why, then, did you not put my money into a bank, that 23 when I came I might have received it back with interest?'

"And he said to those who stood by, 24

"'Take the pound from him and give it to him who has the ten pounds.'

"They said to him, 25

"'Sir, he already has ten pounds.'

"'I tell you that to every one who has anything, more shall 26 be given; and from him who has not anything, even what he has shall be taken away. But as for those enemies of mine 27 who were unwilling that I should become their king, bring them here and slay them in my presence.'"

After thus speaking, He journeyed onward, proceeding to 28 Jerusalem. And when he was come near Bethphagé and 29 Bethany, at the mount called the Olive-grove, He dispatched two of the disciples, saying to them,

"Go into the village facing you. On entering it you will find 30 an ass's colt tied up which no one has ever yet ridden: untie it, and bring it here. And if any one asks you, 'Why are you 31 untying the colt?' simply say, 'The Master needs it.'"

So those who were sent went and found things as He had 32

told them. And while they were untying the colt the owners 33
called out, "Why are you untying the colt?" and they replied, 34
"The Master needs it."

Then they brought it to Jesus, and after throwing their 35
outer garments on the colt they placed Jesus on it. So He 36
rode on, while they carpeted the road with their garments.
And when He was now getting near Jerusalem, and descend- 37
ing the Mount of Olives, the whole multitude of the disciples
began in their joy to praise God in loud voices for all the
mighty deeds they had witnessed, saying,

"BLESSED IS THE KING WHO COMES IN THE NAME OF 38
THE LORD (Psalm 118:26): in heaven peace, and glory in the
highest realms."

Thereupon some of the Pharisees in the crowd appealed 39
to Him, saying,

"Rabbi, reprove your disciples."

"I tell you," He replied, "that if they became silent, the very 40
stones would cry out."

When He came into full view of the city, He wept aloud 41
over it, and exclaimed, 42

"O that at this time thou only knewest what makes for peace!
But now it is hid from thine eyes. For the time is coming upon 43
thee when thy foes will throw up around thee earthworks
[fortifications made of piled up earth] and a wall, investing
[surrounding] thee and hemming thee in on every side. And 44
they will dash thee to the ground and thy children within thee,
and will not leave one stone upon another within thee;
because thou didst not recognize the time of thy visitation."

Then Jesus entered the Temple and proceeded to drive out 45
the dealers.

"It is written," He said, "'AND MY HOUSE SHALL BE THE 46
HOUSE OF PRAYER' (Isaiah 56:7), but you have made it A
ROBBERS' CAVE" (Jeremiah 7:11).

And day after day He taught in the Temple, while the high 47
priests and the scribes were devising some means of
destroying Him, as were also the leading men of the people.
But they could not find any way of doing it, for the people all 48
hung upon His lips.

20 On one of those days while He was teaching the 1
people in the Temple and preaching the gospel, the
high priests came upon Him, and the scribes, together with
the elders, and they asked Him, 2

"Tell us, by what authority are you doing these things?
Who is it that gave you this authority?"

"I also will put a question to you," He said; "was John's 3
baptism from heaven or from men?" 4

So they debated the matter with one another. 5

"If we say 'from heaven,'" they argued, "he will say, 'Why did
you not believe him?' And if we say 'from men,' the people will 6
all stone us; for they are convinced that John was a prophet."

And they answered that they did not know the origin of it. 7

"Nor do I tell you," said Jesus, "by what authority I do 8
these things."

Then He proceeded to speak a parable to the people. 9

"There was a man," He said, "who planted a vineyard, let it
out to vine-dressers, and went abroad for a considerable
time. At vintage-time he sent a servant to the vine-dressers, 10
for them to give him a share of the crop; but the vine-
dressers beat him cruelly and sent him away empty-handed.
Then he sent a second servant; and him too they beat and 11
ill-treated and sent away empty-handed. Then again he sent 12
a third; and this one also they wounded and drove away.
Then the owner of the vineyard said, 13

"'What am I to do? I will send my son—my dearly-loved

son: they will probably respect him.'

"But when the vine-dressers saw him, they discussed the 14 matter with one another, and said,

"'This is the heir: let us kill him, that the inheritance may be ours.'

"So they flung him out of the vineyard and killed him. 15 What, then, will the owner of the vineyard do to them? He 16 will come and put these vine-dressers to death, and give the vineyard to others."

"God forbid!" exclaimed the hearers.

He looked at them and said, 17

"What, then, does that mean which is written,

"'THE STONE WHICH THE BUILDERS REJECTED HAS BECOME THE CORNERSTONE'? (Psalm 118:22). Every one who falls on that stone will be severely hurt, but he 18 on whom it falls will be utterly crushed."

At this the scribes and the high priests wanted to lay hands 19 on Him, then and there; only they were afraid of the people. For they saw that in this parable He had referred to them.

So, watching their opportunity, they sent spies who were 20 to act the part of honest men, that they might fasten on some expression of His, so as to hand Him over to the ruling power and the governor's authority. So they put a question 21 to Him.

"Rabbi," they said, "we know that you say and teach what is right and that you make no distinctions between one man and another, but teach God's way truly. May one pay a tax to 22 Caesar, or not?"

But He saw through their knavery [trickery] and replied, 23

"Show me a shilling. Whose likeness and inscription does 24 it bear?"

"Caesar's," they said. 25

"Pay therefore," He replied, "what is Caesar's to Caesar—and what is God's to God."

There was nothing here that they could lay hold of before 26 the people, and marveling at His answer they said no more.

Some of the Sadducces (who deny that there is a resurrec- 27 tion) next came forward and asked Him, 28

"Rabbi, Moses made this a law for us, 'IF A MAN'S BROTHER DIE, LEAVING A WIFE BUT NO CHILDREN, THE MAN SHALL MARRY THE WIDOW AND RAISE UP A FAMILY FOR HIS BROTHER' (Deuteronomy 25:5). Now there were 29 seven brothers. The first of them took a wife and died child-less. The second and the third also took her; and all seven, 30 having done the same, left no children when they died. 31 Finally the woman also died. Whose wife, then, at the resur- 32 rection shall the woman be? for they all seven married her." 33

"People in this world," replied Jesus, "marry, and are given 34 in marriage. But as for those who are deemed worthy to find 35 a place in that other age and in the resurrection from among the dead, the men do not marry, and the women are not given in marriage. For indeed they cannot die again; they are 36 like angels, and are sons of God as being sons of the resur-rection. But that the dead rise to life even Moses clearly 37 implies in the passage about the Bush, where he calls the Lord 'THE GOD OF ABRAHAM, AND THE GOD OF ISAAC, AND THE GOD OF JACOB' (Exodus 3:2-6). He is not a God of 38 the dead, but of the living, for to Him all are living."

Then some of the scribes replied, 39

"Rabbi, you have spoken well."

From that time no one ventured to put a single question 40 to Him.

But He asked them, 41

"How is it they say that the Christ is son of David? Why, 42 David himself says in the book of Psalms,

"'THE LORD SAID TO MY LORD,
SIT AT MY RIGHT HAND
UNTIL I HAVE MADE THY FOES A FOOTSTOOL UNDER 43
THY FEET' (Psalm 110:1).

"David himself therefore calls Him 'Lord,' and how can He 44
be his son?"

Then, in the hearing of all the people, He said to the disciples, 45
"Beware of the scribes, who like to walk about in long 46
robes, and love to be bowed to in places of public resort and
to occupy the best places in the synagogues or at dinner-
parties; who swallow up the property of widows and by way 47
of excuse make long prayers. The heavier the punishment
these men will receive."

21 Looking up He saw the people putting their gifts into 1
the treasury—the rich people. He also saw a poor 2
widow dropping in two mites, and He said, 3

"In truth I tell you that this widow, so poor, has thrown in
more than any of them. For from what they could well spare 4
they have all of them contributed to the offerings, but she in
her neediness has thrown in all she had to live on."

When some were remarking about the Temple, how it 5
was embellished with beautiful stones and dedicated gifts,
He said,

"As to these things which you now admire, the time is 6
coming when there will not be one stone left here upon
another which will not be pulled down."

"Rabbi, when will this be?" they asked Him, "and what will 7
be the sign when these things are about to take place?"

"See to it," He replied, "that you are not misled; for many will 8
come in my name professing, 'I am He,' or saying, 'The time is
close at hand.' Have nothing to do with them. But when 9

you hear of wars and turmoils, be not afraid; for these things must happen first, but the end does not come immediately."

Then He said to them,   10

"NATION WILL RISE IN ARMS AGAINST NATION, AND KINGDOM AGAINST KINGDOM (Isaiah 19:2). And there will   11 be great earthquakes, and in places famines and pestilence; and there will be terrors and wonderful signs from heaven.

"But before all these things happen they will lay hands on   12 you and persecute you. They will deliver you up to syna-gogues and to prison, and you will be brought before kings and governors for my sake. In the end all this will be evi-   13 dence of your fidelity.

"Make up your minds, however, not to prepare a defense   14 beforehand, for I will give you utterance and wisdom which   15 none of your opponents will be able to withstand or reply to. You will be betrayed even by parents, brothers, relatives, and   16 friends; and some of you they will put to death. You will be   17 hated by all men because you are called by my name; and yet   18 not a hair of your heads shall perish. By your endurance you   19 shall win your souls.

"But when you see Jerusalem with armies encamping   20 round her on every side, then be certain that her desolation is close at hand. Then let those in Judaea escape to the hills; let those who are in the city leave it, and those in the   21 country not enter therein. For those are THE DAYS OF   22 VENGEANCE (Hosea 9:7) in order to fulfill all that is written.

"Alas for women who at that time are with child or have   23 infants at breast; for there will be great distress in the land, and anger towards this people. They will fall by the edge of   24 the sword, or be carried off into captivity among all the Gentiles. And Jerusalem will be trampled under foot by the Gentiles, till the times of the Gentiles have expired.

"There will be signs in sun, moon, and stars; and on earth   25 anguish among the nations in their bewilderment at the roaring of the sea and its billows; men's hearts fainting for fear, and for apprehension of what is coming on the world. For THE FORCES WHICH CONTROL THE HEAVENS WILL BE DISORDERED (Isaiah 34:4). And then shall they see the SON OF MAN COMING IN A CLOUD (Daniel 7:13) with great power and glory. But when all this is beginning to take place, look up. Lift up your heads, because your deliverance is drawing near." 26 27 28

And He spoke a parable to them. 29

"See," He said, "the fig-tree and all the trees. As soon as they have shot out their leaves, you know at a glance that summer is now near. So also, when you see these things happening, you may be sure that the Kingdom of God is near. I tell you in truth that the present generation will not pass away without all these things first taking place. Heaven and earth will pass away, but my words will not pass away. 30 31 32 33

"But take heed to yourselves, lest your souls be weighed down with self-indulgence and drunkenness or the anxieties of this life, and that day come upon you, suddenly, like a falling trap; for it will come on all the dwellers on the face of the whole earth (Isaiah 24:17). Beware of slumbering; at all times pray that you may be fully strengthened to escape from all these coming evils, and to take your stand in the presence of the Son of Man." 34 35 36

At this time He would teach in the Temple by day, but go out and spend the night on the mount called the Olive-grove. And all the people came to Him in the Temple, early in the morning, to listen to Him. 37 38

22 Meanwhile the festival of the Unleavened Bread, called the Passover, was approaching, and the high 1 2 priests and the scribes were contriving how to destroy Him. For they feared the people. But Satan entered into Judas (the 3 one called Iscariot—one of the Twelve); who went away and 4 conferred with the high priests and commanders as to how he should deliver Him up to them. They were glad, and they 5 agreed to pay him. He accepted their offer, and then looked 6 out for an opportunity to betray Him when the people were not there.

When the day of the Unleavened Bread came—the day for 7 the Passover lamb to be sacrificed—Jesus sent Peter and 8 John with instructions.

"Go," He said, "and prepare the Passover for us, that we may eat it."

"Where shall we prepare it?" they asked. 9

"You will no sooner have entered the city," He replied, "than 10 you will meet a man carrying a pitcher of water. Follow him into the house to which he goes, and say to the master of the house, 11

"'The Rabbi asks you, Where is the room where I can eat the Passover with my disciples?'

"And he will show you a large furnished room upstairs. 12 There make your preparations."

So they went and found all as He had told them; and they 13 got the Passover ready.

When the time was come, and He had taken His place at 14 table, and the apostles with Him, He said to them, 15

"Earnestly have I longed to eat this Passover with you before I suffer; for I tell you that I certainly shall not eat one again till 16 its full meaning is brought out in the Kingdom of God."

Then, having received a cup and given thanks, He said, 17

"Take this and share it among you; for I tell you that from 18 this time I will never drink the produce of the vine till the Kingdom of God has come."

Then, taking a loaf, He gave thanks and broke it, and 19 handed it to them, saying,

"This is my body which is being given on your behalf: this do in remembrance of me."

He handed them the cup in like manner, when the meal 20 was over.

"This cup," He said, "is the new covenant ratified by my blood which is to be poured out on your behalf. Yet the hand 21 of my betrayer is at the table with me. For indeed the Son of 22 Man goes on His predestined way; but woe to the man who is betraying Him!"

Thereupon they began to discuss with one another which 23 of them it could possibly be who was about to do this.

There arose also a dispute among them as to which of 24 them should be regarded as greatest. But He said to them, 25

"The kings of the Gentiles are their masters, and those who exercise authority over them are called 'Benefactors.' With you it is not so; but let the greatest among you be as the 26 younger, and the leader be like him who serves. For which is 27 the greater—he who sits at table, or he who waits on him? Is it not he who sits at table? But I am among you as he who waits. You, however, have remained with me amid my trials; 28 and I assign to you, as my Father has assigned to me, a 29 Kingdom—so that you may eat and drink at my table in 30 my Kingdom, and sit on thrones as judges over the twelve tribes of Israel.

"Simon, Simon, I tell you that Satan has obtained permis- 31 sion to have all of you to sift as wheat is sifted. But I have 32 prayed for yourself that your faith may not fail, and you, as soon as you have repented, must strengthen your brethren."

"Master," replied Peter, "with you I am ready to go both to 33 prison and to death."

"I tell you, Peter," said Jesus, "that the cock will not crow 34
to-day till you have three times denied that you know me."

Then He asked them, 35

"When I sent you out without purse or bag or shoes, was
there anything you needed?"

"No, nothing," they replied.

"But now," said He, "let the one who has a purse take it, and 36
he who has a bag must do the same. And let any one who has
no sword sell his coat and buy one. For I tell you that those 37
words of scripture must find their fulfillment in me: 'AND HE
WAS RECKONED AMONG THE LAWLESS' (Isaiah 53:12); for
indeed that saying about me has now its accomplishment."

"Master, here are two swords," they exclaimed. 38

"Enough!" He replied.

On going out, He proceeded as usual to the Mount of 39
Olives, and His disciples followed Him. When He arrived at 40
the place, He said to them,

"Pray that you may not come into temptation."

He Himself withdrew from them about a stone's throw, 41
and knelt down and prayed, saying,

"Father, if it be Thy will, take this cup away from me; yet 42
not my will but Thine be done!"

And there appeared to Him an angel from heaven, strength- 43
ening Him; while He—an agony of distress having come upon 44
Him—prayed all the more with intense earnestness, and His
sweat became like clots of blood dropping on the ground.

When He rose from His prayer and came to His disciples, 45
He found them sleeping for sorrow.

"Why are you sleeping?" He said; "rise up; and pray that 46
you may not come into temptation."

While He was still speaking there came a crowd, with the 47
man called Judas, one of the Twelve, at their head. And he
went up to Jesus to kiss Him.

"Judas," said Jesus, "are you betraying the Son of Man with 48
a kiss?"

Those who were about Him, seeing what was likely to hap- 49
pen, asked Him,

"Master, shall we strike with the sword?"

And one of them struck a blow at the high priest's servant 50
and cut off his right ear.

"Permit me thus far," said Jesus. 51

And He touched the ear and healed it.

Then Jesus said to the high priests and commanders of the 52
Temple and elders, who had come to arrest Him,

"Have you come out as if to fight with a robber, with
swords and cudgels [clubs]? While day after day I was with 53
you in the Temple, you did not lay hands upon me, but to
you belongs this hour and the power of darkness."

And they arrested Him and led Him away, and brought 54
Him into the high priest's house, while Peter followed a good
way behind. And when they had lighted a fire in the middle 55
of the court and had seated themselves in a group round it,
Peter was sitting among them, when a maidservant saw him 56
sitting by the fire, and, looking fixedly at him, she said,

"This man also was with Him."

But he denied it, and declared, 57

"Woman, I do not know Him."

Shortly afterwards a man saw him and said, 58

"You, too, are one of them."

"No, man, I am not," said Peter.

After an interval of about an hour some one else stoutly 59
maintained:

"Certainly this man also was with Him, for he is a Galilaean."

"I don't know what you mean, man," replied Peter. 60

No sooner had he spoken than a cock crowed. The Master 61

turned and looked on Peter; and Peter recollected the Master's words, how He had said to him,

"This very day, before the cock crows, you will disown me three times."

And he went out and wept bitterly. 62

Meanwhile the men who held Jesus in custody beat Him 63
in cruel sport, blindfolded Him, and then challenged Him. 64

"Prove to us," they said, "that you are a prophet, by telling us who it was that struck you."

And they said many other insulting things to Him, 65

As soon as it was day, the whole body of the elders, as well 66
as the high priests and the scribes, assembled. Then He was brought into their Sanhedrin, and they asked Him,

"Are you the Christ? Tell us." 67

"If I tell you," He replied, "you will not believe; and if I ask 68
you questions, you will not answer. But from this time for- 69
ward THE SON OF MAN WILL BE SEATED AT THE RIGHT HAND of the Divine Power" (Daniel 7:13; Psalm 110:1).

Thereupon they cried out with one voice, 70

"You, then, are the Son of God?"

"It is as you say," He answered; "I am."

"What need have we of further evidence?" they said; "for 71
we ourselves have heard it from his own lips."

23 Then the whole assembly rose and brought Him to 1
Pilate, and began to accuse Him. 2

"We have found this man," they said, "perverting our nation, forbidding the payment of tribute to Caesar, and claiming to be himself King Messiah."

Then Pilate asked Him, 3

"You, then, are the King of the Jews?"

"It is as you say," He replied.

Pilate said to the high priests and to the crowd. 4

"I can find no crime in this man."

But they violently insisted. 5

"He stirs up the people," they said, "throughout all Judaea with His teaching—even from Galilee (where He first started) to this city."

On hearing this, Pilate inquired, 6

"Is the man a Galilean?"

And learning that He belonged to Herod's jurisdiction he 7 sent Him to Herod, for he too was in Jerusalem at that time.

To Herod the sight of Jesus was a great gratification, for, 8 for a long time, he had been wanting to see Him, because he had heard so much about Him. He hoped also to see some miracle performed by Him. So he put a number of questions 9 to Him, but Jesus gave him no reply. Meanwhile the high 10 priests and the scribes were standing there and vehemently accusing Him. Laughing to scorn the claims of Jesus, Herod 11 (and his soldiers with him) made sport of Him, dressed Him in a gorgeous costume, and sent Him back to Pilate. And on 12 that very day Herod and Pilate became friends again, for they had been for some time at enmity.

Then calling together the high priests and the rulers and 13 the people, Pilate said, 14

"You have brought this man to me on a charge of corrupt- ing the loyalty of the people. But, you see, I have examined him in your presence and have discovered in the man no ground for the accusations which you bring against him. No, 15 nor does Herod; for he has sent him back to us; and, you see, there is nothing he has done that deserves death. I will there- 16 fore chastise him and release him."

Then the whole multitude burst out into a shout. 18

"Away with this man," they said, "and release Barabbas to us"—Barabbas! who had been lodged in gaol [jail] for some 19 time in connection with a riot which had occurred in the city, and for murder.

But Pilate once more addressed them, wishing to set Jesus free. They, however, persistently shouted, 20 21

"Crucify, crucify him!"

A third time he appealed to them: 22

"But what crime has the man committed? I have discovered in him nothing that deserves death. I will therefore chastise him and release him."

But they urgently insisted, demanding with frantic outcries that He should be crucified; and their clamor prevailed. So Pilate gave judgment, yielding to their demand. The man who was lying in prison charged with riot and murder and for whom they asked he set free, but Jesus he gave up to be dealt with as they desired. 23 24 25

As soon as they led Him away, they laid hold on one Simon, a Cyrenean, who was coming in from the country, and on his shoulders they put the cross, for him to carry it behind Jesus. A vast crowd of the people also followed Him, and of women who were beating their breasts and wailing for Him. But Jesus turned towards them and said, 26 27 28

"Daughters of Jerusalem, weep not for me, but weep for yourselves and for your children. For a time is coming when they will say, 'Blessed are the women who never bore children, and the breasts which have never given milk.' Then will they begin to say to the mountains, 'FALL ON US'; and to the hills, 'COVER US' (Hosea 10:8). For if they are doing these things with the green wood, what will be done with the dry?" 29 30 31

They brought also two others, criminals, to put them to death with Him. 32

When they reached the place called "The Skull," there they nailed Him to the cross, and the criminals also, one at His right hand and one at His left. But Jesus was praying, 33 34

"Father, forgive them, for they know not what they are doing."

And they divided His garments among them, drawing lots for them (Psalm 22:18); and the people stood looking on.   35

The rulers, too, repeatedly uttered their bitter taunts.

"This fellow," they said, "saved others: let him save himself, if he is God's Anointed, the Chosen One."

And the soldiers also made sport of Him, coming and   36
offering Him sour wine and saying,   37

"You the King of the Jews! Save yourself, then!"

There was moreover a writing over His head: 38

THIS IS THE KING OF THE JEWS.

Now one of the criminals who had been crucified insulted   39
Him, saying,

"Are not you the Christ? Save yourself and us."

But the other replied, reproving him,   40

"Do you not even fear God when you are suffering the
same punishment? And we indeed are suffering justly, for we   41
are getting our deserts [deserved reward or punishment] for
what we have done. But this man has done nothing amiss."

And he said,   42

"Jesus, remember me when you come in your Kingdom."

"I tell you in truth," replied Jesus, "that this very day you   43
shall be with me in Paradise."

It was now about noon, and a darkness came over the   44
whole land till three o'clock in the afternoon. The sun was   45
darkened, and the curtain of the sanctuary was torn down
the middle. Then Jesus cried out in a loud voice, and said,   46

"Father, TO THY HANDS I ENTRUST MY SPIRIT"
(Psalm 31:5).

And after uttering these words He yielded up His spirit.

The captain, seeing what had happened, gave glory to 47
God, saying,

"Beyond question this man was innocent."

And all the crowds that had come together to this sight, 48
after seeing all that had occurred, returned to the city beating their breasts. But all His acquaintances, and the women 49
who had been His followers after leaving Galilee, continued
standing at a distance and looking on.

There was a member of the council of the name of Joseph, 50
a good and upright man, who came from the Jewish town of 51
Arimathaea and was awaiting the coming of the Kingdom of
God. He had not concurred in the design or action of the
council, and now he went to Pilate and asked for the body of 52
Jesus. Then, taking it down, he wrapped it in a linen sheet 53
and laid it in a tomb in the rock, where no one else had yet
been put. It was the Preparation day, and the sabbath was 54
near at hand. The women—those who had come with Jesus 55
from Galilee—followed close behind, and saw the tomb and
how His body was placed. Then they returned, and prepared 56
spices and perfumes.

On the sabbath they rested in obedience to the
commandment.

24 And, on the first day of the week, at early dawn, they 1
came to the tomb, bringing the spices they had
prepared. But they found the stone rolled back from the 2
tomb, and on entering they found that the body of the Lord 3
Jesus was not there.

At this they were in great perplexity, when suddenly there 4
stood by them two men whose raiment flashed like lightning. The women were terrified; but, as they stood with 5
their faces bowed to the ground, the men said to them,

"Why do you search among the dead for Him who is living? He is not here. He has come back to life. Remember how He 6 spoke to you while He was still in Galilee, when He told you that the Son of Man must be betrayed into the hands of sin- 7 ful men, and be crucified, and on the third day rise again."

Then they remembered His words, and returning from the 8 tomb they reported all this to the eleven and to all the rest. 9

The women were Mary of Magdala, Joanna, and Mary the 10 mother of James; and they and the rest of the women related all this to the apostles. But the whole story seemed to them 11 an idle tale; they could not believe the women. Peter, how- 12 ever, rose and ran to the tomb. Stooping and looking in, he saw nothing but the linen wrappings: so he went away home, wondering what had happened.

On that same day two of the disciples were walking to 13 Emmaus, a village seven or eight miles from Jerusalem, and 14 were conversing about all these events; and, in the midst of 15 their conversation and discussion, Jesus Himself came and joined them, though they were prevented from recognizing 16 Him, and He asked them, 17

"What is it you are talking so earnestly about, as you walk?"

And they stood still, looking sad. Then one of them, 18 named Cleopas, answered,

"Are you a stranger lodging alone in Jerusalem, that you have known nothing of what has lately happened in the city?"

"What may that be?" He asked. 19

"All about Jesus the Nazarene," they said, "who was a prophet powerful in work and word before God and all the people; and how our high priests and rulers delivered Him up 20 to be sentenced to death, and crucified Him. We were hoping 21 that it was He who was about to ransom Israel. Yes, it was but the day before yesterday that this happened. Besides, some 22 of the women of our company have amazed us. They went to

the tomb at daybreak, and, finding that His body was not 23
there, they came and declared to us that they had even seen
a vision of angels who asserted that He was alive. Thereupon 24
some of our party went to the tomb and found things just as
the women had said; but Jesus Himself they did not see."

"O dull-witted men," He replied, "with minds so slow to 25
believe all that the prophets have spoken! Was there not 26
a necessity for the Christ thus to suffer, and then enter into
His glory?"

And beginning with Moses and all the prophets, He 27
explained to them the passages in scripture which referred
to Himself.

When they had come near the village to which they were 28
going, He appeared to be going farther. But they pressed 29
Him to remain with them.

"Because," said they, "it is getting towards evening, and
the day is nearly over."

So He went in to stay with them. But as soon as He had 30
sat down with them, and had taken the bread and had
blessed and broken it, and was handing it to them, their eyes 31
were opened and they recognized Him. But He vanished
from them.

"Were not our hearts," they said one to the other, "burning 32
within us while He talked to us on the way and explained the
scriptures to us?"

So they rose and without an hour's delay returned to 33
Jerusalem, and found the eleven and the rest met together,
who said to them, 34

"Yes, it is true: the Master has come back to life. He has
been seen by Simon."

Then they related what had happened on the way, and how 35
He had been recognized by them in the breaking of the bread.

While they were thus talking, He Himself stood in their 36 midst and said,

"Peace be to you!"

Startled, and in the utmost alarm, they thought they were 37 looking at a ghost; but He said to them, 38

"Why such alarm? And why are there such questionings in your minds? See my hands and my feet—it is my very self. 39 Feel me and see, for a ghost has not flesh and bones as you see I have."

And then He showed them His hands and His feet. 40

But, while they still could not believe it for joy and were 41 full of astonishment, He asked them,

"Have you any food here?"

And they gave Him a piece of broiled fish, and He took 42 it and ate it in their presence. 43

And He said to them, 44

"This is what I told you while I was still with you—that everything must be fulfilled that is written in the Law of Moses and in the prophets and the psalms concerning me."

Then He opened their minds to understand the scriptures, 45 and He said, 46

"Thus it is written that the Christ would suffer and on the third day rise from the dead; and that proclamation would be made, in His name, of repentance and forgiveness of sins to 47 all nations, beginning from Jerusalem. You are witnesses as to 48 this. And remember that I am about to send out my Father's 49 promised gift to rest upon you. But do you wait patiently in the city until you are endued with power from on high."

And He brought them out as far as Bethany, and then lifted 50 up His hands and blessed them. And while He was blessing 51 them, He parted from them and was carried up into heaven. They worshiped Him, and returned to Jerusalem with great joy. 52 Afterwards they were continually in the Temple, blessing God. 53

THE GOSPEL ACCORDING TO ST. JOHN

1 In the beginning was the Word, and the Word was with 1
God, and the Word was God. He was in the beginning 2
with God. All things came into being through Him, and 3
apart from Him nothing that now exists came into being. In 4
Him was Life, and that Life was the Light of men. The Light 5
shines on in the darkness, and the darkness has never over-
powered it.

There was a man sent from God, whose name was John. 6
He came as a witness, in order that he might give testimony 7
concerning the Light, so that all might believe through him.
He was not the Light, but he came that he might give testi- 8
mony concerning the Light. There was the true Light, which 9
lightens every man, coming into the world. He was in the 10
world, and the world came into existence through Him, and
the world did not recognize Him. He came to His own home, 11
and His own people gave Him no welcome. But to all who 12
have received Him—that is, to those who trust in His
name—He has given the privilege of becoming children of
God; who were begotten not by human descent, nor through 13
an impulse of the flesh, nor through the will of a human
father, but from God.

And the Word became flesh, and lived awhile in our midst, 14
so that we saw His glory, glory such as a father bestows on his
only son, full of grace and truth.

John gave testimony concerning Him and cried aloud, saying, 15
"This is He of whom I said, 'He who is coming after me has
taken precedence of me,' for He existed before me."

For it is from His fullness we have all received, and grace 16
upon grace. The Law was given through Moses; grace and 17
truth came through Jesus Christ. No human eye has ever 18
seen God: the only Son, who is God, who is in the Father's
bosom—He has made Him known.

This also is John's testimony, when the Jews sent to him 19
a deputation [representatives] of priests and Levites from
Jerusalem to ask him who he was. He avowed—he did not 20
conceal the truth, but avowed,

"I am not the Christ."

"What then?" they inquired; "are you Elijah?" 21

"I am not," he said.

"Are you the Prophet?"

"No," he answered.

So they pressed the question. 22

"Who are you?" they said—"that we may take an answer to
those who sent us. What account do you give of yourself?"

"I am THE VOICE," he replied, "OF ONE CRYING ALOUD, 23
'MAKE STRAIGHT THE LORD'S WAY IN THE DESERT,'"
fulfilling the words of the prophet Isaiah (Isaiah 40:3).

Some of those who had been sent were Pharisees. And 24
they questioned him. 25

"Why, then, do you baptize," they said, "if you are neither
the Christ nor Elijah nor the Prophet?"

"I baptize in water only," John answered, "but in your midst 26
stands One whom you do not know—He who is to come after 27
me, and whose sandal-strap I am not worthy to unfasten."

This conversation took place at Bethany beyond the 28
Jordan, where John was baptizing.

The next day John saw Jesus coming towards him 29
and exclaimed,

"Look, there is the Lamb of God who is to take away the sin
of the world! This is He about whom I said, 'After me is to 30

come One who has taken precedence of me, because He was before me.' I did not know Him; but that He may be openly 31 shown to Israel is the reason why I have come baptizing in water."

John also gave testimony by stating: 32

"I have seen the Spirit coming down like a dove out of heaven; and it rested on Him. I did not know Him, but He 33 who sent me to baptize in water said to me,

"'He on whom you see the Spirit coming down and resting is the One who baptizes in the Holy Spirit.'

"This I have seen, and I am become a witness that He is 34 the Son of God."

Again the next day John was standing with two of his 35 disciples, when he saw Jesus passing by, and said, 36

"Look! that is the Lamb of God!"

The two disciples heard his exclamation, and they 37 followed Jesus. Then Jesus turned round, and seeing them 38 following He asked them,

"What is your wish?"

"Rabbi," they replied ("Rabbi" means "Teacher"), "where are you staying?"

"Come and you shall see," He said. 39

So they went and saw where He was staying, and they remained and spent that day with Him. It was then about four o'clock in the afternoon.

Andrew, Simon Peter's brother, was one of the two who 40 heard John's exclamation and followed Jesus. He first found 41 his own brother Simon, and said to him,

"We have found the Messiah!" (which means the Christ).

He brought him to Jesus. Jesus looked at him and said, 42

"You are Simon, son of John: you shall be called Cephas" (which means "Peter," that is, "Rock").

The next day, having decided to leave for Galilee, Jesus 43

found Philip, and said to him: "Follow me." (Now Philip 44
came from Bethsaida, the town of Andrew and Peter.) Then 45
Philip found Nathanael, and said to him,

"We have found Him about whom Moses in the Law
wrote, as well as the prophets—Jesus, the son of Joseph, a
man of Nazareth."

"Can anything good come out of Nazareth?" replied 46
Nathanael.

"Come and see," said Philip.

Jesus saw Nathanael approaching, and said of him, 47

"Look! here is a true Israelite, in whom there is no guile!"

"How do you know me?" Nathanael asked. 48

"Before Philip called you," said Jesus, "when you were
under the fig-tree I saw you."

"Rabbi," cried Nathanael, "you are the Son of God, you are 49
Israel's King!"

"Because I said to you, 'I saw you under the fig-tree,'" 50
replied Jesus, "do you believe? You shall see greater things
than that."

"I tell you all in very truth," He added, "that you shall see 51
heaven opened wide, and God's angels going up, and coming down upon the Son of Man."

2 Two days later there was a wedding at Cana in Galilee, 1
which the mother of Jesus attended, and to which Jesus 2
also was invited and His disciples. Now the wine ran short; 3
whereupon the mother of Jesus said to Him,

"They have no wine."

"Leave it to me," He replied; "my hour has not yet come." 4

His mother said to the attendants, 5

"Whatever He tells you to do, do it."

Now there were six stone jars standing there (in accordance 6 with the Jewish regulations for purification), each large enough to hold twenty gallons or more. Jesus said to the 7 attendants,

"Fill the jars with water."

And they filled them to the brim. Then He said, 8

"Now, take some out, and carry it to the president of the feast."

So they carried some to him. And no sooner had the presi- 9 dent tested the water now turned into wine, than—not knowing where it came from, though the attendants who had drawn the water knew—he called to the bridegroom and said to him, 10

"Every one puts on the good wine first, and when people have drunk freely, then that which is inferior. But you have kept the good wine till now."

This, the first of His signs, Jesus performed at Cana in 11 Galilee, and thus displayed His glory; and His disciples believed in Him.

Afterwards He went down to Capernaum—He, and His 12 mother, and His brothers, and His disciples; and they made a short stay there. But the Jewish Passover was approaching, and 13 for this Jesus went up to Jerusalem. Now He found in the 14 Temple dealers in cattle and sheep and doves, and money-changers sitting there. So He plaited a whip of rushes, and 15 drove them all, with the sheep and bullocks, out of the Temple. The small coin of the brokers He poured on the ground and overturned their tables. And to the dove-dealers He said, 16

"Take these things away. Do not turn my Father's house into a market."

This recalled to His disciples the words of scripture, 17

"MY ZEAL FOR THY HOUSE WILL CONSUME ME" (Psalm 69:9).

So the Jews asked Him, 18

"What authority can you show us for doing this?"

"Demolish this sanctuary," said Jesus, "and in three days I will rebuild it." 19

"It has taken forty-six years," replied the Jews, "to build this sanctuary, and will you rebuild it in three days?" 20

But He was speaking of the sanctuary of His body. When, however, He had risen from the dead, His disciples recollected that He had said this; and they believed the scripture and the words which Jesus had spoken to them. 21 22

Now when He was in Jerusalem, at the festival of the Passover, many became believers in His name, beholding the signs which He wrought. But for His part, Jesus did not trust Himself to them, because He knew them all, and did not need any one's evidence concerning a man, for He of Himself knew what was in the man. 23 24 25

3 Now there was one of the Pharisees whose name was Nicodemus, a ruler among the Jews. He came to Jesus by night and said, 1 2

"Rabbi, we know that you are a teacher come from God; for no one can do these miracles which you are doing, unless God is with him."

"In very truth I tell you," answered Jesus, "that unless a man is born anew he cannot see the Kingdom of God." 3

"How is it possible," Nicodemus asked, "for a man to be born when he is old? Can he a second time enter his mother's womb and be born?" 4

"In very truth I tell you," replied Jesus, "that unless a man is born of water and the Spirit, he cannot enter the Kingdom of God. Whatever is born of the flesh is flesh, and whatever is born of the Spirit is spirit. Do not be astonished at my telling you, 'You must all be born anew.' The wind blows where it chooses, and you hear its sound, but you do not know where 5 6 7 8 it comes from or where it is going. So is it with every one who is born of the Spirit."

"How is all this possible?" asked Nicodemus. 9

"Are you," replied Jesus, "'the teacher of Israel,' and yet do 10 you not understand these things? In very truth I tell you that 11 we speak what we know, and give evidence concerning what we have witnessed, and yet you all reject our evidence. If I 12 have told you of things on earth and none of you believes me, how will you believe me if I tell you of things in heaven? There is no one who has gone up to heaven, except One who 13 has come down from heaven, namely the Son of Man whose home is in heaven. And just as Moses lifted high the serpent 14 in the desert, so must the Son of Man be lifted up, in order 15 that every one who trusts in Him may have eternal life."

For so greatly did God love the world that He gave His only 16 Son, that every one who trusts in Him may not perish but may have eternal life. God did not send His Son into the 17 world to judge the world, but that the world might be saved through Him. He who trusts in Him does not come up for 18 judgment. He who does not trust has already received sentence, because he has not his trust resting on the name of God's only Son. And this is the test by which men are 19 judged—the Light has come into the world, and men have loved the darkness rather than the Light, because their deeds have been wicked. For every wrongdoer hates the light, and 20 does not come into it, for fear his actions should be exposed. But he whose actions are true comes into the light, that his 21 actions may be plainly shown to have been done in God.

After this Jesus and His disciples went to Judaea; and there 22 He stayed in company with them and baptized. And John 23 too was baptizing at Aenon, near Salim, because there were many pools and streams there; and people came and received baptism. (For John was not yet thrown into prison.) 24

So, a discussion having arisen on the part of John's disciples 25
with a Jew about purification, they came to John and re- 26
ported to him,

"Rabbi, He who was with you on the other side of the
Jordan and to whom you bore testimony is now baptizing,
and great numbers of people are resorting to Him."

"A man cannot obtain anything," replied John, "unless it 27
has been granted to him from heaven. You yourselves can 28
bear witness to my having said, 'I am not the Christ,' but 'I
am His appointed forerunner.' He who has the bride is the 29
bridegroom; and the bridegroom's friend who stands by his
side and listens to him rejoices heartily on account of the
bridegroom's voice. This is my joy now complete. He must 30
grow greater, but I must grow less.

"He who comes from above is above all. He who springs 31
from the earth not only springs from the earth, but speaks of
the earth. He who comes from heaven is above all. What He 32
has seen and heard, to that He bears witness; but His evidence no one accepts. Any man who has accepted His 33
evidence has solemnly declared that God is true. For He 34
whom God has sent speaks God's words; God does not give
the Spirit in sparing measure. The Father loves the Son and 35
has entrusted everything to His hands. He who believes in 36
the Son has eternal life; he who disobeys the Son will not see
life, but God's anger remains upon him."

4 Now as soon as the Lord was aware that the Pharisees 1
had heard it said, "Jesus is gaining and baptizing more
disciples than John"—though Jesus Himself did not baptize 2
them, but His disciples did—He left Judaea and returned to 3
Galilee. His road lay through Samaria, and so He came to 4
Sychar, a town in Samaria near the piece of land that Jacob 5

gave to his son Joseph. Jacob's Well was there: so Jesus, tired 6
out with His journey, sat down by the well to rest. It was
about noon.

Presently there came a woman of Samaria to draw water. 7
Jesus asked her to give Him some water; for His disciples 8
were gone to the town to buy provisions.

"How is it," replied the woman, "that a Jew like you asks 9
me, who am a Samaritan woman, for water?"

(For Jews have no dealings with Samaritans.)

"If you had known God's free gift," replied Jesus, "and who 10
it is that said to you, 'Give me some water,' you would have
asked Him, and He would have given you living water."

"Sir," she said, "you have nothing to draw with, and the well 11
is deep; so where can you get the living water from? Are you 12
greater than our forefather Jacob, who gave us the well, and
himself drank from it, as did also his sons and his cattle?"

"Every one," replied Jesus, "who drinks this water will be 13
thirsty again; but whoever drinks the water that I shall give 14
him will never, never thirst. The water that I shall give him
will become a fountain within him of water springing up for
eternal life."

"Sir," said the woman, "give me that water, that I may 15
never be thirsty, nor continually be coming all the way here
to draw water."

"Go and call your husband," said Jesus; "and come back." 16

"I have no husband," she replied. 17

"You rightly say that you have no husband," said Jesus; "for 18
you have had five husbands, and the man you have at
present is not your husband. You have spoken the truth in
saying that."

"Sir," replied the woman, "I see that you are a prophet. Our 19
forefathers worshiped on this mountain, but you Jews say 20
that the place where people must worship is in Jerusalem."

"Believe me," said Jesus, "the time is coming when you will 21
worship the Father neither on this mountain nor in
Jerusalem. You worship that of which you know nothing. We 22
worship that which we know; for salvation comes from the
Jews. But a time is coming—indeed, has already come—when 23
true worshipers will worship the Father in spirit and truth; for
indeed the Father desires such worshipers. God is Spirit; and 24
those who worship Him must worship in spirit and truth."

"I know," replied the woman, "that Messiah is coming— 25
'the Christ,' as He is called. When He has come, He will tell
us everything."

"I am He," said Jesus—"I who am now talking to you." 26

Just then His disciples came, and were surprised to find 27
Him talking with a woman. Yet not one of them asked Him,
"What are you seeking?" or "Why are you talking with her?"

So the woman, leaving her pitcher, went away to the town, 28
and called the people.

"Come," she said, "and see a man who has told me every- 29
thing I have ever done. Can this be the Christ, do you think?"

They left the town and made their way to see Him. 30

Meanwhile the disciples were urging Jesus, 31

"Rabbi," they said, "eat something."

"I have food to eat," He replied, "of which you do not know." 32

So the disciples began questioning one another. 33

"Can it be," they said, "that some one has brought Him
something to eat?"

"My food," said Jesus, "is to do the will of Him who sent me, 34
and to accomplish His work. Are you not saying, 'It wants 35
four months yet to the harvest?' But look round, I tell you,
and observe these plains, how they are ripe for the harvest.
Already the reaper is getting pay and gathering in a crop in 36
preparation for eternal life, so that sower and reaper may
rejoice together. In this you see the real meaning of the 37

saying, 'One sows, but another reaps.' I have sent you to reap 38
a harvest which is not the result of your own labors. Others
have labored, and you are getting the benefit of their labor."

Of the Samaritan population of that town a good many 39
believed in Him because of the woman's statement,

"He told me all that I have ever done."

When the Samaritans came to Him, they asked Him to 40
stay with them; and He stayed there two days. Then a far 41
larger number of people believed because of His own words,
and they said to the woman, 42

"We no longer believe in Him simply because of your talk;
we have now heard for ourselves, and we know that this
really is the Savior of the world."

After the two days He departed, and went into Galilee; for 43
Jesus Himself declared that a prophet has no honor in his 44
own country. So when He reached Galilee, the Galilaeans 45
welcomed Him eagerly, having been eye-witnesses of all that
He had done in Jerusalem at the festival; for they also had
been to the festival.

So He came once more to Cana in Galilee, where He had 46
made the water wine.

Now there was a certain official of the king's court whose
son was ill at Capernaum. Having heard that Jesus had come 47
from Judaea to Galilee, he came to Him and begged Him to
go down and cure his son; for he was at the point of death.

"Unless you and others see signs and marvels," said Jesus, 48
"nothing will induce you to believe."

"Sir," pleaded the official, "come down before my child dies." 49

"You may return," replied Jesus; "your son is alive." 50

He believed the words of Jesus, and started back home;
and he was already on his way down when his servants met 51
him and told him that his son was alive. So he inquired of 52
them at what hour he had shown improvement.

"Yesterday, about one o'clock," they replied, "the fever left him."

Then the father recollected that that was the time at which 53 Jesus had said to him, "Your son is alive," and he and his whole household became believers.

This is the second sign that Jesus wrought after coming 54 from Judaea into Galilee.

5 After this there was a festival of the Jews, and Jesus went 1 up to Jerusalem. Now there is in Jerusalem near the 2 Sheep Gate a pool, called in Hebrew "Bethesda." It has five alcoves. In these there used to lie a great number of invalids, 3 and of people who were blind or lame or with withered limbs. And there was one man there who had been an 5 invalid for thirty-eight years. Jesus saw him lying there, and 6 knowing that he had been a long time in that condition, He asked him,

"Do you wish to be made strong again?"

"Sir," replied the sufferer, "I have no one to put me into the 7 pool when the water is disturbed; but while I am coming some one else steps down before me."

"Rise," said Jesus, "take up your mat and walk." 8

Instantly the man was restored to perfect health, and he 9 took up his mat and began to walk.

That day was a sabbath. So the Jews said to the man who 10 had been cured,

"It is the sabbath: you must not carry your mat."

"He who cured me," he replied, "said to me, 'Take up your 11 mat and walk.'"

"Who is it," they asked, "that said to you, 'Take up your mat 12 and walk'?"

But the man who had been cured did not know who it was; 13

for Jesus had passed out unnoticed, there being a crowd in the place.

Afterwards Jesus found him in the Temple and said to him, 14 "You are now restored to health. Do not sin any more, or a worse thing may befall you."

The man went away and told the Jews that it was Jesus 15 who had restored him to health; and on this account the 16 Jews began to persecute Jesus—because He did these things on the sabbath.

His reply was, 17

"My Father works unceasingly, and so do I."

The Jews therefore were all the more eager to put Him to 18 death, because He not only broke the sabbath, but also spoke of God as being in a special sense His Father, thus putting Himself on a level with God.

"In very truth I tell you," replied Jesus, "the Son can do 19 nothing of Himself—He can do only what He sees the Father doing; for whatever He does, the Son does in like manner. The Father loves the Son and reveals to Him all that He 20 Himself is doing. And greater deeds than these will He reveal to Him, in order that you may wonder. For just as the Father 21 awakens the dead and gives them life, so the Son also gives life to whom He wills. The Father indeed does not judge any 22 one, but He has entrusted the passing of judgment wholly to the Son, that all may honor the Son even as they honor the 23 Father. The man who honors not the Son honors not the Father who sent Him.

"In very truth I tell you that he who listens to my teaching 24 and believes Him who sent me has eternal life, and does not come under judgment, but has passed over out of death into life.

"In very truth I tell you that a time is coming—indeed, has 25 already come—when the dead will hear the voice of the Son

of God, and those who hear it will live. For just as the Father 26
has life in Himself, so He has also given to the Son to have life
in Himself. And He has conferred on Him authority to act as 27
judge, because He is the Son of Man. Wonder not at this. For 28
a time is coming when all who are in the graves will hear His 29
voice and will come forth—those who have done right to the
resurrection to life, and those whose actions have been evil
to the resurrection to judgment.

"I can of my own self do nothing. As I hear, so I judge; and 30
mine is a just judgment, because my own will I seek not to
do, but the will of Him who sent me.

"If I give evidence concerning myself, my evidence cannot 31
be accepted. There is Another who gives evidence concern- 32
ing me, and I know that the evidence is true which He offers
concerning me.

"You sent to John, and he has been a witness to the truth. 33
But the evidence on my behalf which I accept is not from 34
man; though I say all this that you may be saved. He was the 35
lamp that burned and shone, and for a time you were willing
to be gladdened by his light.

"But the evidence which I have is weightier than that of 36
John; for the work the Father has appointed me to complete—
the very work which I am doing—affords evidence about me
that the Father has sent me. And the Father who sent me has 37
Himself supplied evidence about me. Never have any of you
either heard His voice or seen what He is like. Nor have you 38
His word abiding within you, for you refuse to believe Him
whom He has sent.

"You search the scriptures, because you suppose that in 39
them you will find eternal life; it is those scriptures that yield
evidence about me; yet you are unwilling to come to me that 40
you may have life.

"I do not accept honor from man, but I know that in your 41

hearts you do not really love God. I am come in my Father's 42
name, and you do not receive me. If some one else comes in 43
his own name, you will receive him. How is it possible for you 44
to believe, while you receive honor from one another and
have no desire for the honor that comes from the only God?

"Do not suppose that I will accuse you to the Father. There 45
is one who accuses you, namely Moses, on whom your hope
rests. For if you believed Moses, you would believe me; for he 46
wrote about me. But if you disbelieve his writings, how are 47
you to believe my words?"

6 After this Jesus went away across the sea of Galilee (that 1
is, the sea of Tiberias). A vast multitude followed Him, 2
because they witnessed the signs He performed on those
who were ill.

Then Jesus went up the hill, and sat there with His disci- 3
ples. The Jewish festival, the Passover, was at hand. And 4
when He looked round and saw an immense crowd coming 5
towards Him, He said to Philip,

"Where shall we buy bread for all these people to eat?"

He said this to put Philip to the test, for He Himself knew 6
what He was going to do.

"Seven pounds' worth of bread," replied Philip, "is not 7
enough for them all to get even a scanty meal."

One of His disciples, Andrew, Simon Peter's brother, said 8
to Him,

"There is a boy here with five barley loaves and a couple of 9
fish: but what is that among so many?"

"Make the people sit down," said Jesus. 10

The ground was covered with thick grass; so they sat
down, the men numbering about five thousand. Then Jesus 11
took the loaves, and after giving thanks He distributed them

to those who were resting on the ground; and also the fish in like manner—as much as they desired.

When all were fully satisfied, He said to His disciples, 12 "Gather up the broken portions that remain over, so that nothing be lost."

Accordingly they gathered them up; and with the frag- 13 ments of the five barley loaves—the broken portions that remained over after they had done eating—they filled twelve baskets. Thereupon the people, having seen the sign He had 14 performed, said,

"This is indeed the Prophet who was to come into the world."

But perceiving that they were about to come and carry Him off by force to make Him a king, Jesus withdrew again 15 up the hill alone by Himself. When evening came on, His disciples went down to the lake. There they got on board a 16 boat, and pushed off to cross the lake to Capernaum. By this 17 time it had become dark, and Jesus had not yet joined them. The lake also was getting rough, because a strong wind was blowing. When, however, they had rowed three or four miles, 18 they saw Jesus walking on the water and coming near the 19 boat. They were terrified; but He called to them.

"It is I," He said; "do not be afraid." 20

Then they were willing to take Him on board; and in a 21 moment the boat reached the shore at the point to which they were going.

Next morning the crowd who were still standing about on 22 the other side of the lake found that there had been but one small boat there, and they had seen that Jesus did not go on board with His disciples, but that they went away without Him. Yet a number of small boats came from Tiberias to the 23 neighborhood of the place where they had eaten the bread after the Lord had given thanks. So when the crowd saw that 24 neither Jesus was there nor His disciples, they themselves got into the boats and came to Capernaum to look for Him.

So when they had crossed the lake and found Him, they 25 asked Him,

"Rabbi, when did you come here?"

"In very truth I tell you," replied Jesus, "that you are 26 searching for me not because you have seen signs, but because you ate the loaves and were satisfied. Work not for 27 the food that perishes, but for the food that lasts to eternal life—that food which will be the Son of Man's gift to you; for on Him the Father, God, has set His seal."

"What are we to do," they asked, "to carry out what 28 God requires?"

"This," replied Jesus, "is above all what God requires—that 29 you should be believers in Him whom He has sent."

"What sign, then," they asked, "do you perform for us to 30 see and become believers in you? What can you do? Our 31 forefathers ate the manna in the desert, as it is written, 'HE GAVE THEM BREAD OUT OF HEAVEN TO EAT'" (Exodus 16:15; Psalm 78:24).

"In very truth I tell you," replied Jesus, "that Moses did 32 not give you the bread out of heaven, but my Father is giving you the bread—the true bread—out of heaven. For God's 33 bread is that which comes down from heaven and gives life to the world."

"Sir," they said, "give us that bread for ever." 34

"I am the bread of life," replied Jesus; "he who comes to me 35 shall never hunger, and he who believes in me shall never thirst. But it is as I have said to you: you have seen me and 36 yet you do not believe. Every one whom the Father gives me 37 will come to me, and him who comes to me I will never drive away. For I have left heaven and have come down to earth 38 not to seek my own pleasure, but to do the will of Him who

sent me. And this is the will of Him who sent me, that of all 39
that He has given me I should lose nothing, but should raise
it to life on the last day. This is my Father's will, that every one 40
who beholds the Son of God and believes in Him should
have eternal life, and I will raise him to life on the last day."

Now the Jews began to murmur about Him because He 41
said "I am the bread which came down from heaven." And 42
they said,

"Is not this man Joseph's son? Is he not Jesus, whose father
and mother we know? What does he mean by now saying, 'I
am come down from heaven'?"

"Do not murmur to one another," replied Jesus; "no one 43
can come to me unless the Father who sent me draws him; 44
then I will raise him to life on the last day. It stands written 45
in the prophets, 'AND THEY SHALL ALL OF THEM BE
TAUGHT BY GOD' (Isaiah 54:13). Every one who listens to
the Father and learns from Him comes to me. No one has 46
ever seen the Father—except that He alone who is from
God has seen the Father.

"In very truth I tell you that he who believes has eternal 47
life. I am the bread of life. Your forefathers ate the manna in 48–
the desert, and they died. Here is the bread that comes down 50
from heaven, that a man may eat it and not die. I am the 51
living bread come down from heaven. If a man eats this
bread, he shall live for ever. Moreover the bread which I will
give for the life of the world is my flesh."

This led to an angry debate among the Jews. 52

"How can this man," they argued, "give us his flesh to eat?"

"In very truth I tell you," said Jesus, "that unless you eat the 53
flesh of the Son of Man and drink His blood, you have no life
in you. He who eats my flesh and drinks my blood has eter- 54
nal life, and I will raise him up on the last day. For my flesh is 55
true food, and my blood is true drink. He who eats my flesh 56

and drinks my blood abides in me and I in him. As the living 57
Father has sent me, and I live because of the Father, so also
he who eats me will live because of me. This is the bread 58
which came down out of heaven; it is unlike that which your
forefathers ate—for they ate and yet died. He who eats this
bread shall live for ever."

Jesus said all this in the synagogue while teaching 59
at Capernaum.

Many therefore of His disciples, when they heard it, said, 60
"This is hard to accept. Who can listen to such teaching?"

But, knowing in His heart that his disciples were murmur- 61
ing about it, Jesus asked them,

"Is this a stumbling-block to you? What, then, if you were 62
to see the Son of Man ascending again where He was before?
It is the Spirit which gives life. The flesh confers no benefit 63
whatever. The words I have spoken to you are spirit and are
life. But there are some of you who do not believe." 64

For Jesus knew from the beginning who those were that did
not believe, and who it was that would betray Him. So He added, 65

"That is why I told you that no one can come to me unless
it be granted him by the Father."

Thereupon many of His disciples left Him, and no longer 66
associated with Him.

Jesus therefore appealed to the Twelve. 67

"Will you go also?" He asked.

"Master," replied Simon Peter, "to whom shall we go? Your 68
teachings tell us of eternal life. And we have come to believe 69
and know that you are indeed the Holy One of God."

"Did not I choose you—the Twelve?" said Jesus, "and even 70
of you one is a devil."

He meant Judas, the son of Simon Iscariot. For he it was 71
who, though one of the Twelve, was about to betray Him.

7 After this Jesus moved from place to place in Galilee. He 1
would not go about in Judaea, because the Jews were
seeking to kill Him. But the Jewish festival of Tabernacles was 2
approaching. So His brothers said to Him, 3

"Leave these parts and go to Judaea, that your disciples
also may witness the works you perform. For no one acts in 4
secret while desiring to be known publicly. Since you are
doing these deeds, show yourself openly to the world."

For even His brothers were not believers in Him. 5

"My time," replied Jesus, "has not yet come, but for you 6
any time is suitable. The world cannot hate you; but it does 7
hate me, because I give testimony that its works are evil. As 8
for you, go up to the festival. I am not going up to this festival, because my time is not yet come."

Such was His answer, and He remained in Galilee. When, 9
however, His brothers had gone up to the festival, then He 10
also went up, not openly, but as it were privately.

Meanwhile the Jews at the festival were looking for Him 11
and were inquiring,

"Where is he?"

Among the mass of the people there was much muttered 12
debate about Him.

Some said,

"He is a good man."

Others said,

"Not so: he is imposing on the people."

Yet for fear of the Jews no one spoke out boldly about Him. 13

But when the festival was already half over, Jesus went up 14
to the Temple and began to teach. The Jews were astonished. 15

"How does this man know anything of books," they said,
"although he has never been taught?"

Jesus answered their question by saying, 16

"My teaching is not mine, but comes from Him who sent

me. If any one is willing to do His will, he shall know about 17
the teaching, whether it is from God or originates with me.
The man whose teaching originates with himself aims at his 18
own glory. He who aims at the glory of Him who sent him
teaches the truth, and there is no deception in him. Did not 19
Moses give you the Law? And yet not a man of you obeys the
Law. Why do you want to kill me?"

"You are possessed by a demon," replied the crowd. "Who 20
wants to kill you?"

"One deed I have done," replied Jesus, "and you are all full 21
of wonder. Well, then, Moses gave you the rite of circumci- 22
sion (not that it began with Moses, but with your earlier forefathers), and even on a sabbath day you circumcise a child.
If to save the Law of Moses from being broken a child is 23
circumcised even on a sabbath day, are you bitter against me
because I have restored a whole man to health on a sabbath
day? Do not judge superficially, but form a just judgment." 24

Some, however, of the people of Jerusalem said, 25

"Is not this the man they are wanting to kill? But here he is, 26
speaking out boldly, and they say nothing to him! Can the
rulers really have discovered that this man is the Christ? And 27
yet we know this man, and where he comes from; but as for
the Christ, when He comes, no one will know where He
comes from."

Jesus therefore, while teaching in the Temple, cried aloud, 28
and said,

"Yes, you know me, and you know where I am from. And
yet I have not come of my own accord; but there is One who
has really sent me, of whom you have no knowledge. I know 29
Him, because I came from Him, and He sent me."

On hearing this they wanted to arrest Him; yet not a hand 30
was laid on Him, because His time had not yet come. But 31
among the crowd a large number believed in Him.

"When the Christ comes," they said, "will He perform more signs than this teacher has performed?"

The Pharisees heard the people thus expressing their various doubts about Him, and the high priests and the Pharisees sent some officers to apprehend Him. So Jesus said, 32 33

"Still for a short time I shall be with you, and then I go my way to Him who sent me. You will look for me and will not find me, and where I am you cannot come." 34

The Jews therefore said to one another, 35

"Where is he about to betake [to go] himself, so that we shall not find him? Will he betake himself to the Dispersion among the Greeks, and teach the Greeks? What do those words of his mean, 'You will look for me, but will not find me, and where I am you cannot come'?" 36

On the last day of the festival—the great day—Jesus stood up and cried aloud, 37

"Whoever is thirsty," He said, "let him come to me, and let him drink who believes in me. 'From within Him'—as the scripture has said—'rivers of living water shall flow.'" 38

He referred to the Spirit which those who believed in Him were to receive; for the Spirit was not yet, because Jesus had not yet been glorified. 39

After listening to His words, some of the crowd began to say, 40
"This is beyond doubt the Prophet."

Others said, 41
"He is the Christ."

But others again,

"Not so: is the Christ to come from Galilee? Has not the scripture declared that the Christ is to come of the family of David (Psalm 89:3-4) and from Bethlehem, David's village?" (Micah 5:2). 42

So there was a dissension among the people on His 43

account. Some of them wanted to arrest Him, but no one 44
laid hands upon Him.

Meanwhile the officers returned to the high priests and 45
Pharisees, who asked them,

"Why have you not brought him?"

"No mere man has ever spoken as this man speaks," said 46
the officers.

"Are you deluded too?" replied the Pharisees; "has any one 47–
of the rulers or of the Pharisees believed in him? As for 49
this rabble [disorderly crowd] who understand nothing about
the Law, they are accursed!"

Nicodemus interposed—he who had formerly gone to 50
Jesus, being himself one of them.

"Does our Law," he asked, "judge a man without first hear- 51
ing what he has to say and ascertaining what he is doing?"

"Do you also come from Galilee?" they asked in reply. "Search 52
and see for yourself that no prophet is of Galilaean origin."

{So they went away to their several homes; 53

8 But Jesus went to the Mount of Olives. At break of day, 1
however, He returned to the Temple, and there the 2
people came to Him in crowds. He seated Himself; and was
teaching them when the scribes and the Pharisees brought 3
to Him a woman who had been found committing adultery.
They made her stand in the center of the court, and they put
the case to Him.

"Rabbi," they said, "this woman has been found in the very 4
act of committing adultery. Now, in the Law, Moses has 5
ordered us to stone such women to death. But what do
you say?"

They asked this in order to put Him to the test, so that they 6
might have some charge to bring against Him. But Jesus

stooped down and began to write with His finger on the ground. When, however, they persisted with their question, He raised His head and said to them, 7

"Let the sinless man among you be the first to throw a stone at her."

Then He stooped down again, and again began to write on 8 the ground. They listened to Him, and then, beginning with 9 the eldest, took their departure, one by one, till all were gone. And Jesus was left behind alone—and the woman in the center of the court. Then, raising His head, Jesus said to her, 10

"Where are they? Has no one condemned you?"

"No one, Sir," she replied. 11

"And I do not condemn you either," said Jesus; "go, and from this time do not sin any more."}

Once more Jesus addressed them. 12

"I am the Light of the world," He said; "the man who follows me shall not walk in the dark, but shall have the light of Life."

"You are giving evidence about yourself," said the 13 Pharisees; "your evidence is not valid."

"Even if I am giving evidence about myself," replied Jesus, 14 "my evidence is true; for I know where I came from and where I am going, but you know neither the one nor the other. You 15 judge according to appearances: I am judging no one. And 16 even if I do judge, my judgment is just; for I am not alone, but the Father who sent me is with me. In your own Law, too, it is 17 written that THE TESTIMONY OF TWO MEN IS TRUE (Deuteronomy 19:15). I am one giving testimony about myself, 18 and the Father who sent me gives testimony about me."

"Where is your Father?" they asked. 19

"You know my Father as little as you know me," He replied; "if you knew me, you would know my Father also."

These sayings He uttered in the treasury, while teaching in 20 the Temple; yet no one arrested Him, because His time had not yet come.

Again He said to them, 21

"I am going away. Then you will try to find me, but you will die in your sins. Where I am going, it is impossible for you to come."

The Jews began to ask one another, 22

"Is he going to kill himself, since he says, 'Where I am going, it is impossible for you to come'?"

"You," He continued, "are from below, I am from above: 23 you are of this present world, I am not of this present world. That is why I told you that you will die in your sins; for, 24 unless you believe that I am He, you will die in your sins."

"You—who are you?" they asked. 25

"How is it that I even speak to you at all?" replied Jesus. "Many things I have to speak and to judge concerning you. 26 But He who sent me is true, and what I have heard from Him I tell forth to the world."

They did not perceive that He was speaking to them of the 27 Father. So Jesus added, 28

"When you have lifted up the Son of Man, then you will know that I am He. Of myself I do nothing; but as the Father has taught me, so I speak. And He who sent me is with me. 29 He has not left me alone: for I do always what is pleasing to Him."

As He thus spoke, many became believers in Him. 30

Jesus therefore said to those of the Jews who had now 31 believed in Him,

"As for you, if you hold fast to my teaching, then you are truly my disciples; and you shall know the truth, and the 32 truth will make you free."

"We are descendants of Abraham," they answered, "and 33 have never at any time been in slavery to any one. What do those words of yours mean, 'You shall become free'?"

"In very truth I tell you," replied Jesus, "that every one who commits sin is the slave of sin. Now a slave does not remain always in His master's house, but a son does. If, then, the Son shall make you free, you will be free indeed. You are descendants of Abraham, I know; but you want to kill me, because my teaching gains no ground within you. I speak of what I have seen with the Father. You, then, also are doing what you have heard from your father." 34 35 36 37 38

"Our father is Abraham," they said. 39

"If you were Abraham's children," replied Jesus, "it is Abraham's deeds that you would be doing. But, in fact, you are longing to kill me, a man who has spoken to you the truth which I have heard from God. Abraham did not do that. You are doing the deeds of your father." 40 41

"We," they replied, "are not illegitimate children. We have one Father, namely God."

"If God were your Father," said Jesus, "you would love me; for it is from God that I came and I am now here. I have not come of myself, but He sent me. How is it you do not understand me when I speak? It is because you are unable to listen to my words. The father whose sons you are is the devil; and you desire to do what gives him pleasure. He was a murderer from the beginning, and does not stand firm in the truth—for there is no truth in him. Whenever he utters his lie, he speaks what is his own; for he is a liar, and the father of lies. But because I speak the truth, you do not believe me. Which of you convicts me of sin? If I speak the truth, why do you not believe me? Only he who is a child of God listens to God's words. You do not listen to them: and why? It is because you are not God's children." 42 43 44 45 46 47

"Are we not right," answered the Jews, "in saying that you are a Samaritan and are possessed by a demon?" 48

"I am not possessed by a demon," replied Jesus. "But I 49
honor my Father, and you dishonor me. I, however, am not 50
aiming at glory for myself: there is One who aims at glory for
me—and who judges. In very truth I tell you that if any one 51
obeys my teaching he shall never see death."

"Now," exclaimed the Jews, "we know that you are pos- 52
sessed of a demon. Abraham died, and so did the prophets,
and yet you say, 'If any one obeys my teaching, he shall never
taste death.' Are you really greater than our forefather 53
Abraham? For he died. And the prophets died. Whom do you
make yourself out to be?"

"Were I to glorify myself," answered Jesus, "I should have 54
no real glory. There is One who glorifies me—namely my
Father, who you say is your God. You do not know Him, but I 55
know Him; and were I to deny my knowledge of Him, I
should be like you, a liar. But I do know Him, and I obey His
teaching. Abraham your forefather rejoiced in the hope of 56
seeing my day: and he saw it, and was glad."

"You are not yet fifty years old," cried the Jews, "and have 57
you seen Abraham?"

"In very truth," answered Jesus, "I tell you that before 58
Abraham came into existence, I am."

Thereupon they took up stones to throw at Him, but He 59
hid Himself and went away out of the Temple.

9 As He passed by, He saw a man who had been blind 1
from his birth. So His disciples asked Him, 2
"Rabbi, who sinned—this man or his parents—that he was
born blind?"

"Neither he nor his parents sinned," answered Jesus, "but 3
he was born blind in order that God's work might be openly
shown in him. We must do the works of Him who sent me 4

while there is daylight. Night is coming on, when no one can 5
work. When I am in the world, I am the light of the world."

After thus speaking, He spat on the ground, and then, 6
kneading the dust and spittle into clay, He smeared the clay
over the man's eyes and said to him, 7

"Go and wash in the pool of Siloam"—the name
means "Sent."

So he went and washed his eyes, and returned seeing.

His neighbors, therefore, and the other people to whom he 8
had been a familiar sight as a beggar, began asking,

"Is not this the man who used to sit and beg?"

"Yes, it is," replied some of them. 9

"No, it is not," said others, "but he is like him."

But he said,

"I am the man."

"How then were your eyes opened?" they asked. 10

"He whose name is Jesus," he answered, "made clay and 11
smeared my eyes with it, and then told me to go to Siloam
and wash. So I went and washed and obtained sight."

"Where is he?" they inquired. 12

"I do not know," he said.

They brought him to the Pharisees—this man who had 13
been blind. Now the day on which Jesus made the clay and 14
opened the man's eyes was the sabbath. So the Pharisees in 15
their turn asked him how he had obtained his sight.

"He put clay on my eyes," he replied, "and I washed, and
now I can see."

This led some of the Pharisees to say, 16

"That man has not come from God, for he does not keep
the sabbath."

"How is it possible for a bad man to do such signs?"
argued others.

And there was a division among them. So again they asked 17
the once blind man,

"What do you say about his opening your eyes?"

"He is a prophet," he replied.

The Jews, however, did not believe the statement concern- 18
ing him—that he had been blind and had obtained his
sight—until they called his parents and asked them, 19

"Is this your son, who you say was born blind? How is it,
then, that he can now see?"

"We know," replied the parents, "that this is our son and 20
that he was born blind; but how it is that he can now see or 21
who has opened his eyes we do not know. Ask him himself;
he is of full age; he himself will give his own account of it."

This was their answer, because they were afraid of the Jews; 22
for the Jews had already settled among themselves that if any
one should acknowledge Jesus as the Christ, he should be
excluded from the synagogue. That was why his parents said, 23

"He is of full age: ask him himself."

A second time therefore they called the man who had 24
been blind, and said,

"Give God the praise: we know that that man is a sinner."

"Whether he is a sinner or not, I do not know," he replied; 25
"one thing I know—that I was once blind and that now I
can see."

"What did he do to you?" they asked; "how did he open 26
your eyes?"

"I have told you already," he replied, "and you did not lis- 27
ten to me. Why do you want to hear it again? Do you also
mean to be disciples of his?"

Then they railed at him, and said, 28

"You are that man's disciple, but we are disciples of Moses.
We know that God spoke to Moses; but as for this fellow we 29
do not know where he comes from."

"Why, this is marvelous!" the man replied; "you do not 30
know where he comes from, and yet he has opened my eyes!
We know that God does not listen to bad people, but that if 31
any one is a God-fearing man and does His will He listens to
him. From the beginning of the world such a thing was never 32
heard of as that any one should open the eyes of a man blind
from his birth. Had that man not come from God, he could 33
have done nothing."

"You," they replied, "were wholly begotten and born in sin, 34
and do you teach us?"

And they put him out of the synagogue.

Jesus heard that they had done this. So having found him, 35
He asked him,

"Do you believe in the Son of God?"

"Who is He, Master?" replied the man. "Tell me, so that I 36
may believe in Him."

"You have seen Him," said Jesus; "and not only so: He is 37
now speaking to you."

"I believe, Master," he said. 38

And he threw himself at His feet.

"I came into this world," said Jesus, "for judgment, that 39
those who do not see may see, and that those who do see
may become blind."

These words were heard by those of the Pharisees who 40
were present, and they asked Him,

"Are we also blind?"

"If you were blind," answered Jesus, "you would have no 41
sin; but as a matter of fact you boast that you see. So your
sin remains!"

10 "In very truth I tell you that the man who does not 1
enter the sheepfold by the door, but climbs over

some other way, is a thief and a robber. He who enters by the 2
door is the shepherd of the sheep. To him the porter opens 3
the door, and the sheep hear his voice; and he calls his own
sheep by their names and leads them out. When he has 4
brought his own sheep all out, he walks at the head of them;
and the sheep follow him, because they know his voice. But
a stranger they will by no means follow, but will run away 5
from him, because they do not know the voice of strangers."

Jesus spoke to them in this allegorical language, but they 6
did not understand what He meant.

Again therefore Jesus said to them, 7

"In very truth I tell you that I am the door of the sheep. All 8
who have come before me are thieves and robbers; but the
sheep would not listen to them. I am the door. If any one 9
enters by me, he will find safety, and will go in and out and
find pasture. The thief comes only to steal and kill and 10
destroy: I have come that they may have life, and may have
it in abundance.

"I am the good shepherd. The good shepherd lays down 11
his very life for the sheep. The hired servant, who is not the 12
shepherd and does not own the sheep, no sooner sees the
wolf coming than he leaves the sheep and runs away; and
the wolf worries and scatters them. For he is only a hired 13
servant and cares nothing for the sheep.

"I am the good shepherd. And I know my sheep and my 14
sheep know me, just as the Father knows me and I know the 15
Father; and I lay down my life for the sheep. I have also other 16
sheep—which do not belong to this fold. Those also I must
bring, and they will listen to my voice; and they shall become
one flock under one shepherd. For this reason my Father 17
loves me, because I am laying down my life to receive it back
again. No one is taking it away from me, but I myself am 18
laying it down. I am authorized to lay it down, and I am

authorized to receive it back again. This is the command I received from my Father."

Again there arose a division among the Jews because of these words. Many of them said, 19 20

"He is possessed by a demon and is mad. Why do you listen to him?"

Others argued, 21

"That is not the language of a demoniac: can a demon open blind men's eyes?"

The Re-dedication festival came on in Jerusalem. It was 22 winter, and Jesus was walking in the Temple in Solomon's 23 portico, when the Jews gathered round Him and asked Him, 24

"How long do you mean to keep us in suspense? If you are the Christ, tell us so plainly."

"I have told you," answered Jesus, "and you do not believe. 25 The deeds that I do in my Father's name—they bear witness about me. But you do not believe, because you are not my 26 sheep. My sheep listen to my voice, and I know them, and they 27 follow me. I give them eternal life, and they shall never perish, 28 nor shall any one wrest them from my hand. What my Father 29 has given me is greater than all, and no one is able to wrest anything from my Father's hand. I and the Father are one." 30

Again the Jews brought stones to throw at Him. Jesus 31 remonstrated [pleaded in protest] with them. 32

"Many good deeds from the Father have I shown you; for which of them will you stone me?"

"For no good deed," the Jews replied, "are we going to 33 stone you, but for blasphemy, and because you, who are only a man, are making yourself out to be God."

"Does it not stand written in your Law," replied Jesus, "'I 34 SAID, YOU ARE GODS' (Psalm 82:6)? If those to whom God's 35 word was addressed are called gods (and the scripture cannot be annulled), how is it that you say to one whom the 36

Father consecrated and sent into the world, 'You are blaspheming,' because I said, 'I am God's Son'? If the deeds I do 37 are not my Father's deeds, do not believe me. But if they are, 38 then even if you do not believe me, at least believe the deeds, that you may recognize and see clearly that the Father is in me, and that I am in the Father."

This made them once more try to arrest Him, but He withdrew out of their power. 39

Then He went away again to the other side of the Jordan, 40 to the place where John had been baptizing at first; and there He stayed. And many people came to Him. Their report was, 41

"John did not work any sign, but all that John said about this man was true."

And many became believers in Him there. 42

11 Now a certain man was lying ill, named Lazarus, of 1 Bethany, the village of Mary and her sister Martha. (This Mary, whose brother Lazarus was ill, was the one who 2 poured the perfume over the Lord and wiped His feet with her hair.) So the sisters sent to Him to say, 3

"Master, he whom you hold dear is ill."

Jesus received the message and said, 4

"This illness is not to end in death, but is to promote the glory of God, in order that the Son of God may be glorified by it."

Now Jesus loved Martha, and her sister, and Lazarus. 5 When, however, He heard that Lazarus was ill, He still 6 remained two days in the same place. Then, after that, He 7 said to the disciples,

"Let us return to Judaea."

"Rabbi," exclaimed the disciples, "the Jews have just been trying to stone you, and do you think of going back there again?" 8

"Are there not twelve hours in the day?" replied Jesus. "If 9 any one walks in the daytime, he does not stumble— because he sees the light of this world. But if a man walks by 10 night, he does stumble, because he has no light in him."

He said this, and afterwards He added, 11

"Our beloved Lazarus is sleeping, but I will go and wake him."

"Master," said the disciples, "if he is asleep he will recover." 12

Now Jesus had spoken of his death, but they thought He re- 13 ferred to the rest of natural sleep. So then He told them plainly, 14

"Lazarus is dead; and for your sakes I am glad I was not 15 there in order that you may believe. But let us go to him."

"Let us go also," Thomas (called The Twin) said to his fel- 16 low disciples, "that we may die with him."

On His arrival Jesus found that Lazarus had already been 17 four days in the tomb. Bethany was near Jerusalem, the dis- 18 tance being a little less than two miles; and a considerable 19 number of the Jews were with Martha and Mary, having come to express sympathy with them on the death of their brother. Martha, then, as soon as she heard the tidings, 20 "Jesus is coming," went to meet Him; but Mary remained sit- ting in the house. So Martha said to Jesus, 21

"Master, if you had been here, my brother would not have died. And even now I know that whatever you ask from God, 22 He will give you."

"Your brother shall rise again," replied Jesus. 23

"I know," said Martha, "that he will rise again at the resur- 24 rection, on the last day."

"I am the resurrection and the life," said Jesus; "he who 25 believes in me, even if he has died, shall live; and every one 26 who is living and is a believer in me shall never die. Do you believe this?"

"Yes, Master," she replied; "I believe that you are the 27

Christ, the Son of God, who was to come into the world."

After saying this, she went and called her sister Mary 28
privately, telling her,

"The Rabbi is here and is asking for you."

So she, on hearing that, rose up quickly to go to Him. Now 29
Jesus was not yet come into the village, but was still at the 30
place where Martha had met Him. So the Jews who were 31
with Mary in the house sympathizing with her, when they
saw that she had risen hastily and had gone out, followed
her, supposing that she was going to the tomb to wail there.

Mary, then, when she came to Jesus and saw Him, fell at 32
His feet and exclaimed,

"Master, if you had been here, my brother would not
have died."

Seeing her wailing, and the Jews in like manner wailing 33
who had come with her, Jesus, with deep emotion and
greatly troubled, asked them, 34

"Where have you laid him?"

"Master, come and see," was their reply.

Jesus burst into tears. 35

"See how dear he held him," said the Jews. 36

But others asked, 37

"Was not he who opened the blind man's eyes also able to
prevent this man from dying?"

Jesus, however, again with deep emotion, came to the 38
tomb. It was a cave, and a stone had been laid against the
mouth of it.

"Take away the stone," said Jesus. 39

Martha, the sister of the dead man, exclaimed,

"Master, by this time there is a foul smell; for it is the
fourth day since he died."

"Did I not promise you," replied Jesus, "that if you believe, 40
you shall see the glory of God?"

So they removed the stone. Then Jesus lifted up His eyes 41
and said,

"Father, I thank Thee that Thou hast heard me. I know that 42
Thou always hearest me; but for the sake of the crowd standing round I have said this—that they may believe that Thou
didst send me."

After speaking thus, He cried out in a loud voice, 43
"Lazarus, come forth."

The dead man came out, his hands and feet swathed in 44
bandages, and his face wrapped round with a kerchief.

"Untie him," said Jesus, "and let him go."

Thereupon a number of the Jews who had come to Mary 45
and had witnessed His deeds became believers in Him;
though some of them went off to the Pharisees, and told 46
them what He had done.

The high priests and the Pharisees therefore held a meet- 47
ing of the Sanhedrin. "What steps are we taking?" they asked
one another: "for this man is performing a great number of 48
signs. If we leave him alone in this way, everybody will
believe in him, and the Romans will come and blot out both
our place and our nation."

But one of them, named Caiaphas, being high priest that 49
year, said,

"You know nothing about it. You do not reflect that it is to 50
your interest that one man should die for the people rather
than the whole nation perish."

It was not of his own impulse that he thus spoke. But being 51
high priest that year he was inspired to declare that Jesus was
to die for the nation, and not for the nation only, but in order 52
to unite into one body all the far-scattered children of God.
So from that day forward they schemed to put Jesus to death. 53

Therefore Jesus no longer went about openly among the 54
Jews, but He left that neighborhood and went into the district

near the desert, to a town called Ephraim, and remained there with the disciples. The Jewish Passover was coming near, and 55 many from the country went up to Jerusalem before the Passover, to purify themselves. They therefore looked out for 56 Jesus, and asked one another as they stood in the Temple,

"What do you think?—will he come to the festival at all?"

Now the high priests and the Pharisees had issued orders 57 that if any one knew where He was, he should give information, so that they might arrest Him.

12 Jesus, however, six days before the Passover, came to 1 Bethany, where Lazarus was whom He had raised from the dead. So they gave a dinner there in honor of Jesus, 2 at which Martha waited at table, but Lazarus was one of those who were at table with Him. Mary then took a pound 3 weight of pure spikenard, very costly, and poured it over His feet, and wiped His feet with her hair, so that the house was filled with the fragrance of the perfume. Then said Judas 4 Iscariot, one of the Twelve, the one who was to betray Jesus,

"Why was not that perfume sold for three hundred 5 shillings and the money given to the poor?"

The reason he said this was not that he cared for the 6 poor, but that he was a thief, and that, being in charge of the money-box, he used to steal what was put into it. But 7 Jesus interposed.

"Leave her alone," He said, "let her keep it for the time of my preparation for burial. For the poor you always have with 8 you, but you have not me always."

Now it became widely known among the Jews that Jesus 9 was there; and they came not only on His account, but also in order to see Lazarus whom He had brought back to life. The high priests, however, consulted together to put Lazarus 10

also to death, for because of him many of the Jews left them 11
and became believers in Jesus.

The next day a great crowd of those who had come to the 12
festival, hearing that Jesus was coming to Jerusalem, took 13
branches of palm trees and went out to meet Him, shouting
as they went,

"HOSANNA! BLESSINGS ON HIM WHO COMES IN THE
NAME OF THE LORD (Psalm 118:26), on the King of Israel!"

And Jesus, having procured a young ass, sat upon it, just as 14
the scripture says,

"FEAR NOT, DAUGHTER OF ZION! SEE, THY KING IS 15
COMING RIDING ON AN ASS'S COLT" (Zechariah 9:9).

The meaning of this His disciples did not understand at 16
the time; but after Jesus was glorified they recollected that
this was written about Him, and that they had done this to
Him. The crowd, therefore, that had been present when 17
He called Lazarus out of the tomb and brought him back to
life, related what they had witnessed. This was why the 18
crowd came to meet Him, because they had heard of His
having performed that sign. The Pharisees therefore said to 19
one another,

"See how futile your efforts are! The world is gone
after him!"

Now some of those who were coming up to worship at the 20
festival were Greeks. They came to Philip, of Bethsaida in 21
Galilee, with the request,

"Sir, we wish to see Jesus."

Philip came and told Andrew: Andrew and Philip told 22
Jesus. His answer was, 23

"The time has come for the Son of Man to be glorified. In
very truth I tell you that unless a grain of wheat falls into the 24
ground and dies, it remains what it was—a single grain; but
that if it dies, it makes a rich yield. He who holds his life dear, 25

destroys it; and he who makes his life of no account in this world shall keep it to eternal life. If a man serves me, let him follow me; and where I am, there too shall my servant be. If a man serves me, the Father will honor him. Now is my soul full of trouble; and what shall I say? Father, save me from this hour. Yet for this very purpose I have come to this hour. Father, glorify Thy name." 26 27 28

Then there came a voice from the sky,

"I have glorified it and will glorify it again."

The crowd that stood by and heard it, said it had thundered. Others said, 29

"An angel spoke to him."

"It is not for my sake," said Jesus, "that that voice came, but for your sakes. Now comes judgment upon this world: now will the Prince of this world be driven out. And I—if I am lifted up from the earth—will draw all men to me." 30 31 32

He said this to indicate the kind of death He would die. The crowd answered Him, 33 34

"We have heard out of the Law that the Christ remains for ever. Why do you say that the Son of Man must be lifted up? Who is that Son of Man?"

"A little while longer," He replied, "the light will be among you. Live and act according to the light that you have, for fear darkness overtake you; for a man who walks in the dark does not know where he is going. Inasmuch as you have the light, believe in the light, so that you may become sons of light." 35 36

Jesus said this, and went away and hid Himself from them. Though He had performed so many signs in their presence, they did not believe in Him—in order that the words of Isaiah the prophet might be fulfilled, 37 38

"LORD, WHO HAS BELIEVED OUR PREACHING?
AND THE ARM OF THE LORD—TO WHOM HAS IT BEEN REVEALED?" (Isaiah 53:1).

For this reason they were unable to believe—because 39
Isaiah said again,

"HE HAS BLINDED THEIR EYES AND MADE THEIR 40
MINDS CALLOUS,

LEST THEY SHOULD SEE WITH THEIR EYES AND
PERCEIVE WITH THEIR MINDS,

AND SHOULD TURN,

AND I SHOULD HEAL THEM" (Isaiah 6:9-10).

Isaiah uttered these words because he saw His glory; and 41
he spoke of Him.

Nevertheless even from among the rulers many believed 42
in Him. But because of the Pharisees they did not avow their
belief, for fear they should be excommunicated. They loved 43
honor from men rather than honor from God.

But Jesus cried aloud, 44

"He who believes in me, believes not in me but in Him
who sent me; and he who sees me sees Him who sent me. I 45
have come like light into the world, in order that no one who 46
believes in me may remain in the dark. If any one hears my 47
teachings and regards them not, I do not judge him; for I did
not come to judge the world, but to save the world. He who 48
sets me at naught and does not receive my teachings is not
left without a judge: the words I have spoken will judge him
on the last day; because I have not spoken on my own 49
authority; but the Father who sent me, Himself gave me a
command what to say and in what words to speak. And
I know that His command is eternal life. What therefore I 50
speak, I speak just as the Father has bidden me."

13 Now before the feast of the Passover, Jesus knew that 1
the time had come for Him to leave this world and go
to the Father. Having loved His own who were in the world,

He loved them to the end. While supper was proceeding, the 2
devil having already suggested to Judas Iscariot, the son of
Simon, the thought of betraying Him, Jesus, knowing that 3
the Father had put everything into His hands, and that He
had come forth from God and was now going to God, rose 4
from table, threw off His upper garments, and took a towel
and tied it round Him. Then He poured water into a basin, 5
and proceeded to wash the feet of the disciples and to wipe
them with the towel which He had put round Him. When He 6
came to Simon Peter, Peter objected.

"Master," he said, "are you going to wash my feet?"

"What I am doing," answered Jesus, "for the present you 7
do not know, but afterwards you shall know."

"Never, so long as I live," said Peter, "shall you wash my feet." 8

"If I do not wash you," replied Jesus, "you have no share
with me."

"Master," said Peter, "wash not only my feet, but also my 9
hands and my head."

"Any one who has lately bathed," said Jesus, "does not need 10
to wash more than his feet, but is clean all over. And you my
disciples are clean, and yet this is not true of all of you."

For He knew who was betraying Him, and that was why 11
He said,

"You are not all of you clean."

So after He had washed their feet, put on His garments 12
again, and returned to the table, He said to them,

"Do you understand what I have done to you? You call me 13
'The Rabbi' and 'The Master,' and rightly so, for such I am. If
I, then, your Master and Rabbi, have washed your feet, it is 14
also your duty to wash one another's feet. For I have set you 15
an example in order that you may do what I have done to
you. In very truth I tell you that a servant is not superior to 16
his master, nor is a messenger superior to him who sent him.

If you know all this, blessed are you if you act accordingly. I 17
am not speaking of all of you. I know whom I have chosen, 18
but it is that the scripture may be fulfilled, which says, 'HE
WHO EATS MY BREAD HAS LIFTED UP HIS HEEL AGAINST
ME' (Psalm 41:9). From this time forward I tell you things 19
before they happen, in order that when they do happen you
may believe that I am He. In very truth I tell you that he who 20
receives any one I send receives me, and that he who
receives me receives Him who sent me."

After speaking thus Jesus was troubled in spirit and said 21
with deep earnestness,

"In very truth I tell you that one of you will betray me."

The disciples began looking at one another, at a loss to 22
know to which of them He was referring. There was at table 23
one of His disciples—one whom Jesus loved—reclining with
his head on Jesus' bosom. Making a sign therefore to him, 24
Simon Peter said,

"Tell us whom He means."

So he, having his head on Jesus' bosom, leaned back 25
and asked,

"Master, who is it?"

"It is the one," answered Jesus, "to whom I shall give this 26
piece of bread when I have dipped it."

Accordingly He dipped the piece of bread, and took it and
gave it to Judas, the son of Simon Iscariot. Then, after Judas 27
had received the piece of bread, Satan entered into him.

"What you are doing, do quickly," said Jesus to him.

But why He said this to him no one at the table under- 28
stood. Some supposed that because Judas had the money- 29
box Jesus meant, "Buy what we require for the festival," or
that he should give something to the poor. So Judas took the 30
piece of bread and immediately went out. And it was night.

When he was gone out, Jesus said, 31

"Now is the Son of Man glorified, and God is glorified in Him. Moreover God will glorify Him in Himself, and will 32 glorify Him without delay. Dear children, I am still with you 33 a little longer. You will seek me, but, as I said to the Jews, 'Where I am going you cannot come,' so for the present I say to you. A new commandment I give you, to love one 34 another; that as I have loved you, you also may love one another. It is by this that every one will know that you are my 35 disciples—if you love one another."

"Master," inquired Simon Peter, "where are you going?" 36

"Where I am going," replied Jesus, "you cannot follow me now, but you shall follow later."

"Master," asked Peter again, "why cannot I follow you 37 now? I will lay down my life on your behalf."

"You say you will lay down your life on my behalf!" said 38 Jesus; "in very truth I tell you that the cock will not crow before you have three times disowned me."

14 "Let not your hearts be troubled. Trust in God: trust 1 in me also. In my Father's house there are many 2 resting-places. Were it otherwise, I would have told you; for I am going to make ready a place for you. And if I go and 3 make ready a place for you, I will return and take you to be with me, that where I am you also may be. And where I am 4 going, you all know the way."

"Master," said Thomas, "we do not know where you are 5 going. How should we know the way?"

"I am the way, the truth, and the life," replied Jesus. "No 6 one comes to the Father except through me. If you had 7 known me, you would have known my Father also. From this time forward you know Him and have seen Him."

"Master," said Philip, "show us the Father: that is all we need." 8

"Have I been so long among you," Jesus answered, "and 9
yet you, Philip, do not know me? He who has seen me has
seen the Father. How can you say to me, 'Show us the
Father'? Do you not believe that I am in the Father and that 10
the Father is in me? The things that I tell you all I do not
speak on my own authority: but the Father dwelling within
me carries on His own work. Believe me, all of you, that I am 11
in the Father and that the Father is in me; or at any rate,
believe me because of what I do. In very truth I tell you that 12
he who trusts in me shall do the deeds I do; and he shall do
greater deeds than these, because I am going to the Father.
And whatever any of you ask in my name, I will do, in order 13
that the Father may be glorified in the Son. If you make any 14
request of me in my name, I will grant it.

"If you love me, you will obey my commandments. And I 15
will ask the Father, and He will give you another Advocate to 16
be for ever with you—the Spirit of truth. That Spirit the world 17
cannot receive, because it does not see Him or know Him.
You know Him, because He remains by your side and is in
you. I will not leave you bereaved: I am coming to you. Yet a 18
little while and the world will see me no more, but you will 19
see me: because I live, you also shall live. At that time you will 20
know that I am in my Father, and that you are in me, and that
I am in you. He who has my commandments and obeys 21
them is the one who loves me. And he who loves me will be
loved by my Father, and I will love him and will reveal myself
to him."

Judas (not Judas Iscariot) asked, 22

"Master, how is it that you will reveal yourself to us and not
to the world?"

"If any one loves me," replied Jesus, "he will obey my 23
teaching; and my Father will love him, and we will come to
him and make our home with him. He who has no love for 24

me does not obey my teaching; and yet the teaching to which you are listening is not mine, but is that of the Father who sent me.

"All this I have spoken to you while still with you. But the Advocate, the Holy Spirit whom the Father will send in my name, will teach you everything, and will bring to your memories all that I have said to you. Peace I leave with you: my own peace I give to you. Not as the world gives do I give to you. Let not your hearts be troubled or dismayed. 25 26 27

"You heard me say to you, 'I am going away, and I am coming back to you.' If you loved me, you would have rejoiced because I am going to the Father; for the Father is greater than I am. I have now told you before it comes to pass, that when it has come to pass you may believe. In future I shall not talk much with you, for the Prince of this world is coming. And yet in me he has nothing; but in order that the world may know that I love the Father, I thus act in accordance with the command which the Father gave me. Rise, let us be going." 28 29 30 31

15 "I am the true Vine, and my Father is the vine-dresser. Every branch in me that bears no fruit He takes away; and every branch that bears fruit He cleans, that it may bear more fruit. Already you are clean—through the teaching which I have given you. Continue in me, and let me continue in you. As the branch cannot bear fruit of itself if it does not continue in the vine, so you cannot if you do not continue in me. I am the Vine, you are the branches. He who continues in me and I in him bears abundant fruit, for apart from me you can do nothing. If any one does not continue in me, he is thrown away like the unfruitful branch, and then withers up. Such branches they gather up and throw into the fire and they are burned. 1 2 3 4 5 6

"If you continue in me and my sayings continue in you, 7
ask what you will and it shall be done for you. By this is God 8
glorified—by your bearing abundant fruit and being my
disciples. As the Father has loved me, I have also loved you: 9
continue in my love. If you obey my commands, you will 10
continue in my love, as I have obeyed my Father's commands and continue in His love.

"These things I have spoken to you that I may have joy in 11
you, and that your joy may become perfect. This is my 12
commandment to you, to love one another as I have loved
you. No one has greater love than this—that a man lay down 13
his life for his friends. You are my friends, if you do what I 14
command you. No longer do I call you servants, because a 15
servant does not know what his master is doing; but I have
called you friends, because all that I have heard from the
Father I have made known to you. It is not you who chose 16
me, but it is I who chose you and appointed you that you
might go and be fruitful and that your fruit might be lasting;
so that whatever petition you present to the Father in my
name He may give you.

"This I command you, to love one another. If the world 17
hates you, you know that it has first hated me. If you 18
belonged to the world, the world would love its own. But 19
because you do not belong to the world, and I have chosen
you out of the world—for that reason the world hates you.
Bear in mind what I said to you, 'A servant is not superior to 20
his master.' If they have persecuted me, they will also persecute you; if they have given heed to my teaching, they will
give heed to yours also. But they will inflict all this suffering 21
upon you on account of your bearing my name—because
they do not know Him who sent me.

"If I had not come and spoken to them, they would have 22
had no sin; but as it is they are without excuse for their sin.

He who hates me hates my Father also. If I had not done 23
among them such deeds as no one else ever did, they would 24
have had no sin; but now they have seen and also hated both
me and my Father. But this has been so, that the words writ- 25
ten in their Law might be fulfilled, 'THEY HAVE HATED ME
WITHOUT REASON' (Psalms 35:19, 69:4).

"When the Advocate is come whom I will send to you from 26
the Father—the Spirit of truth who comes forth from the
Father—He will be a witness concerning me. And you also 27
are witnesses, because you have been with me from the first.

16 "These things I have spoken to you in order to clear 1
stumbling-blocks out of your path. You will be 2
excluded from the synagogues; nay more, the time is coming
when any one who has murdered you will suppose he is
offering service to God. And they will do these things 3
because they have not known the Father or myself. But I 4
have spoken this to you that when the time for their accomplishment comes you may recollect that I told you. I did not,
however, tell you all this at first, because I was still with you.
But now I am returning to Him who sent me; yet not one of 5
you asks me where I am going. But grief has filled your hearts 6
because I have said all this to you.

"Yet I am telling you the truth—it is to your advantage that 7
I go away. For unless I go away, the Advocate will not come
to you; but if I go, I will send Him to you. And He, when He 8
comes, will bring conviction to the world alike of sin, of
righteousness, and of judgment;—of sin, because they do 9
not believe in me; of righteousness, because I am going to 10
the Father, and you will no longer see me; of judgment, 11
because the Prince of this world is under sentence.

"I have much more to say to you, but you are unable just now to bear it. But when He has come—the Spirit of truth—He will guide you into all the truth. For He will not speak of His own accord, but all that He hears He will speak, and He will make known the future to you. He will glorify me, because He will take of what is mine and will make it known to you. Everything that the Father has is mine; that is why I said that the Spirit of truth takes of what is mine and will make it known to you. 12 13 14 15

"A little while and you see me no more, and again a little while and you shall see me." 16

Some of His disciples therefore said to one another, 17

"What does this mean which He is telling us, 'A little while and you do not see me, and again a little while and you shall see me,' and 'Because I am going to the Father'?"

So they asked one another, 18

"What can that 'little while' mean which He speaks of? We do not understand His words."

Jesus perceived that they wanted to ask Him, and He said, 19

"Is this what you are questioning one another about—my saying, 'A little while and you do not see me, and again a little while and you shall see me'? In very truth I tell you that you will weep aloud and lament, but the world will be glad. You will mourn, but your grief will be turned into gladness. A woman, when she is in labor, has sorrow, because her time has come. But when she has given birth to the babe, she no longer remembers the pain, because of her joy at a child being born into the world. So you also now have sorrow; but I shall see you again, and your hearts will be glad, and your gladness no one will take away from you. You will put no questions to me then. 20 21 22 23

"In very truth I tell you that whatever you ask the Father for in my name He will give you. As yet you have not asked 24 for anything in my name: ask, and you shall receive, that your hearts may be filled with gladness.

"All this I have spoken to you in veiled language. The time 25 is coming when I shall no longer speak to you in veiled language, but will tell you about the Father in plain words. At 26 that time you will make your requests in my name; and I do not promise to ask the Father on your behalf, for the Father 27 Himself holds you dear, because you have loved me and have believed that I came from the Father. I came out from 28 the Father and have come into the world. Again I am leaving the world and am going to the Father."

"Ah, now you are using plain language," said His disci- 29 ples, "and are uttering no figure of speech! Now we know 30 that you have all knowledge, and do not need to be pressed with questions. Through this we believe that you came from God."

"You believe now," replied Jesus, "but mark! [look/take 31 note] the time is coming—indeed, has already come—for 32 you all to be dispersed each to his own home and to leave me alone. And yet I am not alone, for the Father is with me.

"I have spoken all this to you in order that in me you may 33 have peace. In the world you have affliction. But keep up your courage: I have won the victory over the world."

17 When Jesus had thus spoken, He raised His eyes 1 towards heaven and said,

"Father, the hour has come. Glorify Thy Son that the Son may glorify Thee; even as Thou hast given Him authority 2 over all mankind, so that on all whom Thou hast given Him He may bestow eternal life. And this is eternal life, to know 3 Thee the only true God, and Jesus Christ whom Thou hast 4 sent. I have glorified Thee on earth, having done perfectly

the work which Thou hast given me to do. And now, Father, 5
do Thou glorify me in Thine own presence, with the glory
that I had in Thy presence before the world existed.

"I have revealed Thy name to the men whom Thou gavest 6
me out of the world. Thine they were, and Thou gavest them
to me, and they have obeyed Thy teaching. Now they know 7
that whatever Thou hast given me is from Thee. For the truths 8
which Thou didst teach me I have taught them. And they have
received them, and have known for certain that I came out
from Thee, and have believed that thou didst send me.

"I am making petition for them: for the world I do not 9
make any petition, but for those whom Thou hast given me;
because they are Thine, and everything that is mine is Thine, 10
and everything Thine is mine: and I am crowned with glory
in them. I am now no longer in the world, but they are in the 11
world and I am coming to Thee.

"Holy Father, keep them true to Thy name, which Thou hast
given me, that they may be one, even as we are. While I was 12
with them, I kept them true to Thy name—the name Thou
hast given me to bear—and I kept watch over them, and none
of them is lost but the one doomed to destruction—that the
scripture may be fulfilled.

"But now I am coming to Thee, and I speak these words 13
while I am in the world, in order that they may have my gladness within them filling their hearts. I have given them Thy 14
word, and the world has hated them, because they do not
belong to the world, just as I do not. I do not ask that Thou 15
wilt remove them out of the world, but that Thou wilt protect
them from the Evil One. They do not belong to the world, 16
just as I do not. Consecrate them by the truth: Thy word is 17
truth. As Thou didst send me into the world, I also have sent 18
them into the world; and on their behalf I consecrate myself, 19
that they also may be consecrated by truth.

"Nor is it for them alone that I make petition, but also for 20
those who trust in me through their teaching; that they may 21
all be one, even as Thou art in me, O Father, and I am in
Thee; that they also may be in us; that the world may believe
that Thou didst send me. And the glory which Thou hast 22
given me I have given them, that they may be one, just as we
are one: I in them and Thou in me; that they may stand per- 23
fected in union; that the world may come to understand that
Thou didst send me and hast loved them even as Thou hast
loved me.

"Father, I desire that those whom Thou hast given me may 24
be with me where I am, that they may see my glory—my gift
from Thee, which Thou hast given me because Thou didst
love me before the creation of the world. And, righteous 25
Father, though the world has failed to recognize Thee, I have
known Thee, and these have perceived that Thou didst send
me. And I have made known Thy name to them and will 26
make it known, that the love with which Thou hast loved me
may be in them, and I in them."

18 After offering this prayer Jesus went out with His dis- 1
ciples to a place on the farther side of the Ravine of
the Cedars, where there was a garden, which He entered—
Himself and His disciples. Now Judas also, who was betray- 2
ing Him, knew the place, for Jesus had often resorted there
with His disciples. So Judas, taking the battalion and a 3
detachment of the Temple police sent by the high priests and
Pharisees, came there with lanterns and torches and
weapons. Jesus therefore, knowing all that was about to 4
befall Him, went out to meet them.

"Whom are you looking for?" He asked them.

"For Jesus the Nazarene," was the answer. 5

"I am he," He replied.

(Now Judas who was betraying Him was also standing with them.) As soon then as He said to them, "I am he," they 6 went backwards and fell to the ground. Again therefore He 7 asked them,

"Whom are you looking for?"

"For Jesus the Nazarene," they said.

"I have told you," replied Jesus, "that I am he. If therefore 8 you are looking for me, let these my disciples go their way."

It was that the scripture might be fulfilled which said, 9

"Of those whom Thou hast given me, I have not lost one."

Now Simon Peter, having a sword, drew it, and, aiming at 10 the high priest's servant, cut off his right ear. The servant's name was Malchus. Jesus therefore said to Peter, 11

"Put back your sword. Shall I refuse to drink the cup of sorrow which the Father has given me to drink?"

So the battalion and their tribune [magistrate] and the 12 Jewish police arrested Jesus and bound Him. They then 13 brought Him to Annas first; for Annas was the father-in-law of Caiaphas who was high priest that year.

(This was Caiaphas who had given the Jews the advice, 14

"It is to your interest that one man should die for the people.")

Simon Peter was following Jesus, and so also was another dis- 15 ciple. The latter was known to the high priest, and went in with Jesus into the court of the high priest's palace. But Peter 16 remained standing without at the door, till the disciple who was acquainted with the high priest came out and induced the portress [a woman porter/doorkeeper] to let Peter in. This led 17 the girl, the portress, to ask Peter,

"Are you also one of this man's disciples?"

"No, I am not," he replied.

Now because it was cold the servants and the police had 18 lighted a charcoal fire, and were standing and warming themselves; and Peter too remained with them, standing and warming himself.

So the high priest questioned Jesus about His disciples 19 and His teaching.

"I," replied Jesus, "have spoken openly to the world. I have 20 continually taught in some synagogue or in the Temple where all the Jews are wont [accustomed] to assemble, and I have said nothing in secret. Why do you question me? 21 Question those who heard what it was I said to them: these witnesses here know what I said."

Upon His saying this, one of the officers standing by struck 22 Him a blow, asking Him as he did so,

"Is that the way you answer the high priest?"

"If I have spoken wrongly," replied Jesus, "bear witness to 23 the wrong; but if rightly, why that blow?"

So Annas sent Him bound to Caiaphas the high priest. 24

But Simon Peter remained standing and warming himself. 25 So they said to him,

"Are you also one of his disciples?"

He denied it, and said,

"No, I am not."

One of the high priest's servants, a relative of the man 26 whose ear Peter had cut off, said,

"Did I not see you in the garden with him?"

Once more Peter denied it, and immediately a cock crowed. 27

So they brought Jesus from Caiaphas's house to the 28 Praetorium. It was the early morning, and they would not enter the Praetorium themselves for fear of defilement, that they might be able to eat the Passover. Accordingly Pilate 29 came out to them and inquired,

"What accusation have you to bring against this man?"

"If the man were not a criminal," they replied, "we would 30 not have handed him over to you."

"Take him yourselves," said Pilate, "and judge him by 31 your Law."

"We have no power," replied the Jews, "to put any man to death."

They said this that the words might be fulfilled in which 32 Jesus predicted the kind of death He was to die.

Re-entering the Praetorium, therefore, Pilate called Jesus 33 and asked Him,

"Are you the King of the Jews?"

"Do you say this of yourself, or have others told it you 34 about me?" replied Jesus.

"Am I a Jew?" exclaimed Pilate; "it is your own nation and 35 the high priests who have handed you over to me. What have you done?"

"My kingdom," replied Jesus, "does not belong to this 36 world. If my kingdom did belong to this world, my subjects would have fought to save me from being delivered up to the Jews. But, in fact, my kingdom has not this origin."

"So, then, you are a king!" rejoined Pilate. 37

"Yes," said Jesus, "you say truly that I am a king. For this purpose I was born, and for this purpose I have come into the world—to give testimony to the truth. Every one who is a friend of the truth listens to my voice."

"What is truth?" said Pilate. 38

So saying, he went out again to the Jews and told them,

"I find no crime in him. But you have a custom that I 39 should release one prisoner to you at the Passover. So shall I release to you the King of the Jews?"

With a roar of voices they again cried out, saying, 40

"Not this man, but Barabbas!"

Now Barabbas was a robber.

19 Then Pilate had Jesus taken and scourged. And the 1 soldiers, twisting twigs of thorn into a wreath, put it 2 on His head, and threw round Him a purple cloak. Then they came up to Him and said, 3

"Hail, King of the Jews!"

And they struck Him with the palms of their hands.

Once more Pilate came out and said to the Jews, 4

"See, I am bringing him out to you to let you clearly understand that I find no crime in him."

So Jesus came out, wearing the wreath of thorns and the 5 purple cloak. And Pilate said to them,

"See, there is the man."

As soon, then, as the high priests and the officers saw Him, 6 they shouted,

"To the cross! To the cross!"

"Take him yourselves and crucify him," said Pilate; "for I, at any rate, find no crime in him."

"We," replied the Jews, "have a Law, and in accordance 7 with that Law he ought to die, for having claimed to be the Son of God."

More alarmed than ever, Pilate no sooner heard these 8 words than he re-entered the Praetorium and began to ques- 9 tion Jesus.

"What is your origin?" he asked.

But Jesus gave him no answer.

"Do you refuse to speak even to me?" asked Pilate; "do you 10 not know that I have it in my power either to release you or to crucify you?"

"You would have had no power whatever over me," replied 11 Jesus, "had it not been granted you from above. On that account he who has delivered me up to you is more guilty than you are."

Upon receiving this answer, Pilate was for releasing Him. 12
But the Jews kept shouting,

"If you release this man you are no friend of Caesar's. Every one who sets himself up as king declares himself a rebel against Caesar."

On hearing this, Pilate brought Jesus out, and sat down on 13
the judge's seat in a place called the Pavement—or, in Hebrew, Gabbatha. It was the day of Preparation for the 14
Passover, about mid-day. Then he said to the Jews,

"There is your king!"

This caused a storm of outcries, 15

"Away with him! Away with him! Crucify him!"

"Am I to crucify your king?" Pilate asked.

"We have no king, except Caesar," answered the high priests.

Then Pilate gave Him up to them to be crucified. 16

Accordingly they took Jesus; and He went out carrying His 17
own cross, to the place called Skull-place—or, in Hebrew, Golgotha—where they nailed Him to a cross, and two others 18
at the same time, one on each side and Jesus in the middle. And Pilate wrote a notice and had it fastened to the top of the 19
cross. It ran thus:

JESUS THE NAZARENE, THE KING OF THE JEWS.

Many of the Jews read this notice, for the place where Jesus 20
was crucified was near the city, and the notice was in three languages—Hebrew, Latin, and Greek. The Jewish high priests 21
therefore remonstrated [pleaded in protest] with Pilate.

"You should not write 'The King of the Jews,'" they said, "but that he claimed to be King of the Jews."

"What I have written I have written," was Pilate's answer. 22

So the soldiers, as soon as they had crucified Jesus, took 23
His garments, including His tunic, and divided them into

four parts—one part for each soldier. The tunic was without seam, woven from the top in one piece. So they said to one another, 24

"Do not let us tear it. Let us draw lots for it."

This happened that the scripture might be fulfilled which says,

"THEY SHARED MY GARMENTS AMONG THEM, AND DREW LOTS FOR MY CLOTHING" (Psalm 22:18).

That was what the soldiers did.

Now standing close to the cross of Jesus were His mother 25 and His mother's sister, Mary the wife of Clopas, and Mary of Magdala. So Jesus, seeing His mother, and seeing the disci- 26 ple whom He loved standing near, said to His mother,

"Look, your son!"

Then He said to the disciple, 27

"Look, your mother!"

And from that time the disciple received her into his own home.

After this, Jesus, knowing that everything was now 28 brought to an end, said—that the scripture might be fulfilled (Psalm 69:21),

"I am thirsty."

There was a jar of wine standing there. With this wine they 29 filled a sponge, put it on the end of a stalk of hyssop, and lifted it to His mouth. As soon as Jesus had taken the wine, He said, 30

"It is finished."

And then, bowing His head, He yielded up His spirit.

Meanwhile the Jews, because it was the day of Preparation 31 for the Passover, and in order that the bodies might not remain on the crosses during the sabbath (for that sabbath was one of special solemnity), requested Pilate to have the legs of the dying men broken, and the bodies removed. Accordingly the 32 soldiers came and broke the legs of the first man, and also of

the other who had been crucified with Jesus. Then they came 33
to Jesus: but when they saw that He was already dead, they
refrained from breaking His legs. One of the soldiers, however, 34
made a thrust at His side with a lance, and immediately blood
and water flowed out. This statement is the testimony of an 35
eye-witness, and it is true. He knows that he is telling the
truth—in order that you also may believe. For all this took 36
place that the scripture might be fulfilled which declares,

"NOT ONE OF HIS BONES SHALL BE BROKEN" (Exodus
12:46; Psalm 34:20).

And again another scripture says, 37

"THEY SHALL LOOK ON HIM WHOM THEY HAVE
PIERCED" (Zechariah 12:10).

After this, Joseph of Arimathaea, who was a disciple of 38
Jesus, but for fear of the Jews a secret disciple, asked Pilate's
permission to carry away the body of Jesus; and Pilate gave
him leave. So he came and removed the body. Nicodemus 39
too—he who at first had visited Jesus by night—came bringing a mixture of myrrh and aloes, in weight about seventy or
eighty pounds. Taking down the body they wrapped it in 40
linen cloths along with the spices, in accordance with the
Jewish mode of preparing for burial. There was a garden at 41
the place where Jesus had been crucified, and in the garden
a new tomb, in which no one had yet been buried. Therefore, 42
because it was the day of Preparation for the Jewish Passover,
and the tomb was close at hand, they put Jesus there.

20 On the first day of the week, very early, while it was 1
still dark, Mary of Magdala came to the tomb and
saw that the stone had been removed from it. So she ran off 2
and found Simon Peter and the other disciple—the one who
was dear to Jesus—and said to them,

"They have taken the Lord out of the tomb, and we do not know where they have put Him."

Peter and the other disciple started at once to go to the tomb, both of them running, but the other disciple ran faster than Peter and reached it before he did. Stooping and looking in, he saw the linen cloths lying there, but he did not go in. Simon Peter, however, also came, following him, and entered the tomb. There he saw the wrappings as they lay; and the towel which had been placed on the head of Jesus, not lying with the cloths, but rolled round and round separately. Then the other disciple, who had been the first to come to the tomb, also went in and saw and was convinced. For until now they had not understood the scripture, that He must rise again from the dead (Psalm 16:10). Then the disciples returned home.

But Mary remained standing near the tomb, weeping aloud. She did not enter the tomb, but as she wept she stooped and looked in, and saw two angels clothed in white raiment, sitting one at the head and one at the feet where the body of Jesus had been. They spoke to her.

"Why are you weeping?" they asked.

"Because," she replied, "they have taken away my Lord, and I do not know where they have put Him."

While she was speaking, she turned round and saw Jesus standing there, but did not recognize Him.

"Why are you weeping?" He asked; "whom are you looking for?"

She, supposing that He was the gardener, replied,

"Sir, if you have carried him away, tell me where you have put him and I will remove him."

"Mary!" said Jesus.

She turned to Him.

"Rabboni!" she cried in Hebrew: the word means "Teacher."

"Do not cling to me," said Jesus, "for I have not yet ascended to the Father. But take this message to my brethren: 'I am ascending to my Father and your Father, to my God and your God.'" 17

Mary of Magdala came and brought word to the disciples. "I have seen the Lord," she said. 18

And she told them that He had said these things to her.

On that same first day of the week, when it was evening and, for fear of the Jews, the doors of the house where the disciples were had been locked, Jesus came and stood in their midst, and said to them, 19

"Peace be to you!"

Having said this He showed them His hands and His side; and the disciples were filled with joy at seeing the Lord. A second time, therefore, He said to them, 20 21

"Peace be to you! As the Father sent me, I also now send you."

Having said this He breathed upon them and said, 22

"Receive the Holy Spirit. If you remit the sins of any persons, they remain remitted to them. If you bind fast the sins of any, they remain bound." 23

Thomas, one of the Twelve—called "the Twin"—was not among them when Jesus came. So the rest of the disciples told him, 24 25

"We have seen the Lord!"

His reply was,

"Unless I see in His hands the wound made by the nails and put my finger into the wound, and put my hand into His side, I will never believe it."

A week later the disciples were again in the house, and Thomas was with them, when Jesus came—though the doors were locked—and stood in their midst, and said, 26

"Peace be to you."

Then He said to Thomas, 27

"Bring your finger here and see my hands; bring your hand and put it into my side; and be not incredulous but believe."

"My Lord and my God!" replied Thomas. 28

"Because you have seen me," replied Jesus, "you have 29 believed? Blessed are those who have not seen and yet have believed."

There were also many other signs which Jesus performed 30 in the presence of the disciples, which are not recorded in this book. But these have been recorded in order that you 31 may believe that Jesus is the Christ, the Son of God, and that, believing, you may have life through His name.

21 After this, Jesus again showed Himself to the disci- 1 ples. It was at the Lake of Tiberias. The circumstances were as follows.

Simon Peter was with Thomas (called "the Twin"), 2 Nathanael from Cana in Galilee, the sons of Zebedee, and two others of His disciples. And Simon Peter said to them, 3

"I am going fishing."

"We will go too," said they.

So they went on board their boat; but they caught nothing that night. Now when day was dawning, Jesus stood on the 4 beach, though the disciples did not know that it was Jesus. He called to them. 5

"Boys," He said, "have you any food there?"

"No," they answered.

"Throw the net in on the right of the boat," He said, "and 6 you will find fish."

So they threw the net in, and now they could scarcely drag it along for the quantity of fish. This made the disciple whom 7 Jesus loved say to Peter,

"It is the Lord."

Simon Peter therefore, when he heard the words, "It is the Lord," drew on his fisherman's shirt—for he had not been wearing it—put on his girdle, and sprang into the water. But the rest of the disciples came in the small boat (for they were not far from land—only about a hundred yards), dragging the net full of fish. 8

As soon as they landed, they saw a charcoal fire burning there, with fish broiling on it, and bread close by. Jesus told them to fetch some of the fish which they had just caught. So Simon Peter went on board the boat and drew the net ashore full of large fish, one hundred and fifty-three in number; yet, although there were so many, the net had not broken. 9 10 11

"Come to breakfast," said Jesus. 12

Now not one of the disciples ventured to ask Him who He was, for they felt sure that it was the Lord. Then Jesus came and took the bread and gave them some, and the fish likewise. This was now the third occasion on which Jesus showed Himself to the disciples after He had risen from the dead. 13 14

When they had finished breakfast, Jesus asked Simon Peter, "Simon, son of John, do you love me more than these others do?" 15

"Yes, Lord," was his answer; "you know that I love you."

"Then feed my lambs," replied Jesus.

Again a second time He asked him, "Simon, son of John, do you love me?" 16

"Yes, Lord," he said, "you know that I love you."

"Then be a shepherd to my sheep," He said.

A third time Jesus put the question: "Simon, son of John, do you love me?" 17

It grieved Peter that Jesus asked him the third time, "Do you love me?"

"Lord," he replied, "you know everything, you can see that I love you."

"Then feed my sheep," said Jesus. "In very truth I tell you 18 that whereas, when you were young, you used to put on your girdle and walk wherever you chose, when you have grown old you will stretch out your arms and some one else will put a girdle round you and carry you where you have no wish to go."

This He said to indicate by what kind of death that disciple 19 would bring glory to God. After speaking thus, He said to him,

"Follow me."

Peter turned round and noticed the disciple whom Jesus 20 loved following—the one who at the supper had leaned back on His breast and had asked,

"Master, who is it that is betraying you?"

On seeing him, Peter asked Jesus, 21

"And, Master, what about him?"

"If it is my will that he should remain till I come," replied 22 Jesus, "what concern is that of yours? Follow me yourself."

Hence the report spread among the brethren that that dis- 23 ciple would never die. Yet Jesus did not say, "He is not to die," but, "If it is my will that he should remain till I come, what concern is that of yours?"

This is the disciple who gives his testimony as to these 24 facts, and has written this history; and we know that his testimony is true. But there are many other things that Jesus 25 did—so vast a number indeed that if they were all described in detail, I suppose the world itself could not contain the books that would be written.

THE ACTS OF THE APOSTLES

Introduction

1 My former narrative, Theophilus, dealt with all that Jesus did and taught as a beginning, down to the day when, after giving instructions through the Holy Spirit to the apostles whom He had chosen, He was taken up to heaven. He had also, after His passion, shown Himself alive to them with many sure proofs, appearing to them at intervals during forty days, and speaking of the Kingdom of God. And while in their company He charged them not to leave Jerusalem, but to wait for the Father's promised gift. 1 2 3 4

"This you have heard of," He said, "from me. For John indeed baptized with water, but before many days have passed you shall be baptized with the Holy Spirit." 5

Now when they were with Him, they asked Him, 6

"Lord, is it the time for you to restore the kingdom to Israel?"

"It is not for you," He replied, "to know times or occasions which the Father has reserved within His own authority; but you shall receive power when the Holy Spirit has come upon you, and you shall be my witnesses in Jerusalem and in all Judaea and Samaria and to the remotest parts of the earth." 7 8

When He had said this, and while they were looking at Him, He was carried up, and a cloud closing beneath Him hid Him from their sight. And while they stood intently gazing into the sky as He went, suddenly there were two men in white garments standing by them, who said, 9 10 11

"Galilaeans, why stand looking into the sky? This same Jesus who has been taken up from you into heaven will come in just the same way as you have seen Him departing into heaven."

The Church in Jerusalem

Then they returned to Jerusalem from the mountain called the Olive-grove, which is near Jerusalem, about a mile off. They entered the city, and then went to the upper room which was now their fixed place for meeting. Their names were Peter, John, James and Andrew, Philip and Thomas, Bartholomew and Matthew, James the son of Alphaeus, Simon the Zealot, and Judas the brother of James. All of these with one mind continued earnest in prayer, together with some women, and Mary the mother of Jesus, and His brothers.

It was on one of these days that Peter stood up in the midst of the brethren—the entire number of persons present being about one hundred and twenty—and said,

"Brethren, it was necessary that the scripture should be fulfilled—the prediction which the Holy Spirit uttered by the lips of David, about Judas, who acted as guide to those who arrested Jesus. For Judas was reckoned as one of our number, and a share in this ministry was allotted to him."

(Now Judas, having bought a piece of ground with the money paid him for his wickedness, fell there with his face downwards, and, his body bursting open, he became disemboweled. This fact became widely known to the people of Jerusalem, so that the place received the name, in their language, of Akel-damach, which means "The Field of Blood.")

"For it is written in the Book of Psalms,

"'LET HIS HABITATION BE DESOLATE:

LET THERE BE NO ONE TO DWELL THERE' (Psalm 69:25); and

"'HIS WORK LET ANOTHER TAKE UP' (Psalm 109:8).

"It is necessary, therefore, that of the men who have been 21 with us all the time that the Lord Jesus went in and out among us—beginning from His baptism by John down to the day on 22 which He was taken up from us into heaven—one should be appointed to become a witness with us of His resurrection."

So they proposed two names, Joseph called Bar-Sabbas— 23 and surnamed Justus—and Matthias. And the brethren 24 prayed, saying,

"Thou, Lord, who knowest the hearts of all, show clearly which of these two Thou hast chosen to occupy the place in 25 this ministry and apostleship, from which Judas through transgression fell, in order to go to his own place."

Then they drew lots between them. The lot fell on Matthias, 26 and a place with the eleven apostles was voted to him.

2 Now, in the course of the day of Pentecost, they had all 1 met in one place; when suddenly there came from the 2 sky a sound as of a strong rushing blast of wind filling the whole house where they were sitting. And there appeared to 3 them tongues of what looked like fire, distributing themselves over the assembly; and on the head of each person a tongue alighted. They were all filled with the Holy Spirit, and 4 began to speak in other tongues according as the Spirit gave them words to utter.

Now there were Jews residing in Jerusalem, devout men 5 from every part of the world. So when this noise was heard, 6 they came crowding together, and were amazed because every one heard his own language spoken. They were beside 7 themselves with wonder, and exclaimed,

"Are not all these speakers Galilaeans? How, then, does 8 each of us hear his own native language spoken by them?

Parthians, Medes, Elamites, inhabitants of Mesopotamia, 9
of Judaea and Cappadocia, of Pontus and the Asian
Province, of Phrygia and Pamphylia, of Egypt and of the 10
parts of Africa towards Cyrene, visitors from Rome, both
Jews and converts, Cretans and Arabians, we all alike hear 11
these Galilaeans speaking in our own language about the
majesty of God."

They were all astounded and bewildered, and asked 12
one another,

"What can this mean?"

But others, scornfully jeering, said, 13

"They are brimful [full to the brim] of sweet wine."

Peter, however, together with the eleven, stood up and 14
addressed them in a loud voice.

"Men of Judaea, and all you inhabitants of Jerusalem," he
said, "let this be known to you, and attend to what I say.
These men are not drunken, as you suppose, it being only 15
nine o'clock in the morning. But that which was predicted 16
through the prophet Joel has happened:

"'AND IT SHALL COME TO PASS IN THE LAST DAYS,' 17
says God,
'THAT I WILL POUR OUT MY SPIRIT UPON ALL
MANKIND;
AND YOUR SONS AND YOUR DAUGHTERS SHALL
PROPHESY,
AND YOUR YOUNG MEN SHALL SEE VISIONS,
AND YOUR OLD MEN SHALL DREAM DREAMS;
AND EVEN UPON MY SERVANTS, BOTH MEN AND 18
WOMEN,
AT THAT TIME I WILL POUR OUT MY SPIRIT, AND THEY
SHALL PROPHESY.
I WILL DISPLAY MARVELS IN THE SKY ABOVE, 19
AND SIGNS ON THE EARTH BELOW,

BLOOD AND FIRE, AND CLOUD OF SMOKE.
THE SUN SHALL BE TURNED INTO DARKNESS 20
AND THE MOON INTO BLOOD,
TO USHER IN THE DAY OF THE LORD—
THAT GREAT AND ILLUSTRIOUS DAY;
AND EVERY ONE WHO CALLS ON THE NAME OF THE 21
LORD SHALL BE SAVED' (Joel 2:28-32).

"Listen, Israelites, to what I say. Jesus, the Nazarene, a 22
man accredited to you from God by mighty works and
marvels and signs which God did among you through Him,
as you yourselves know, this man—delivered up through 23
God's settled purpose and foreknowledge—you by the
hands of wicked men have nailed to a cross and have put to
death. But God has raised Him to life, ending the pangs of 24
death. It was not possible for Him to be held fast by death;
for David says in reference to Him, 25

"'I HAVE EVER FIXED MY EYES UPON THE LORD,
BECAUSE HE IS AT MY RIGHT HAND THAT I MAY
ABIDE UNSHAKEN.
FOR THIS CAUSE MY HEART IS GLAD AND MY TONGUE 26
EXULTS.
MY BODY ALSO SHALL REST IN HOPE.
FOR THOU WILT NOT LEAVE ME IN THE GRAVE 27
FORSAKEN,
NOR GIVE UP THY HOLY ONE TO UNDERGO DECAY.
THOU HAST MADE KNOWN TO ME THE PATH TO LIFE: 28
THOU WILT FILL ME WITH GLADNESS IN THY PRES-
ENCE' (Psalm 16:8-11).

"As to the patriarch David, I need hardly remind you, 29
brethren, that he died and was buried, and that we still have
his tomb among us. Being a prophet, however, and knowing 30
that God had solemnly sworn to him to seat a descendant of
his upon his throne (Psalm 132:11), with prophetic foresight 31

he spoke of the resurrection of the Christ, to the effect that He was not left forsaken in the grave, nor did His body undergo decay (Psalm 16:10). This Jesus God has raised to 32 life—a fact to which all of us testify.

"Being therefore lifted high by the right hand of God, He 33 has received from the Father the promised Holy Spirit, and has poured forth what you see and hear. For it was not David 34 that ascended into heaven but he says himself,

"'THE LORD SAID TO MY LORD.

SIT AT MY RIGHT HAND

UNTIL I MAKE THY FOES A FOOTSTOOL UNDER THY 35 FEET' (Psalm 110:1).

"Therefore let the whole House of Israel know beyond all 36 doubt that God has made Him both LORD and CHRIST— this Jesus whom you crucified."

Struck to the heart by these words, they said to Peter and 37 the rest of the apostles,

"Brethren, what are we to do?"

"Repent," replied Peter, "and be baptized, every one of 38 you, in the name of Jesus Christ, for the remission of your sins, and you shall receive the gift of the Holy Spirit. For to 39 you belongs the promise, and to your children, and to all who are far off, as many as the Lord our God may call."

And with many more appeals he solemnly declared and 40 entreated them, saying,

"Escape from this perverse generation."

Those, therefore, who joyfully welcomed his word were 41 baptized; and on that one day about three thousand persons were added to them; and they were constant in attendance 42 on the teaching of the apostles, and in the fellowship, the breaking of the bread, and at the prayers.

Awe came upon every one, and many marvels and signs 43 were wrought by the apostles. And all the believers kept 44

together, and had everything in common. They sold their 45
lands and other property, and distributed the proceeds
among all, according to every one's necessities. And day by 46
day attending constantly in the Temple with one accord, and
breaking bread at home, they took their meals with great
happiness and single-heartedness, praising God and being 47
regarded with favor by all the people. Also day by day the
Lord added to their number those whom He was saving.

3 One day Peter and John were going up to the Temple for 1
the hour of prayer—three o'clock—and, just then, some 2
men were carrying there one who had been lame from his
birth, whom they were wont [accustomed] to place every
day close to the gate of the Temple, called the Beautiful Gate,
to beg from the people as they went in. Seeing Peter and 3
John about to go into the Temple, he asked them for alms.
Peter fixing his eyes on him, as John did also, said, 4
   "Look at us."
So he looked and waited, expecting to receive something 5
from them.
   "I have no silver or gold," Peter said, "but what I have, I 6
give you. In the name of Jesus Christ, the Nazarene—walk!"
   Then taking his hand Peter lifted him up, and immediately 7
his feet and ankles were strengthened. Leaping up, he stood 8
upright and began to walk, and went into the Temple with
them, walking, leaping, and praising God. All the people saw 9
him walking and praising God; and recognizing him as the 10
man who used to sit at the Beautiful Gate of the Temple
asking for alms, they were filled with awe and amazement at
what had happened to him.
   While he still clung to Peter and John, the people, awe- 11
struck, ran up and crowded round them in what was known

as Solomon's portico. Peter, seeing this, spoke to the people. 12

"Israelites," he said, "why do you wonder at this? Or why gaze at us, as though by any power or piety of our own we had enabled him to walk? The God of Abraham, Isaac, and 13 Jacob, the God of our forefathers, has glorified His servant Jesus, whom you delivered up and disowned in the presence of Pilate, when he had decided to let Him go. Yes, you dis- 14 owned the holy and righteous One, and asked as a favor the release of a murderer. The Guide of Life you put to death; but 15 God has raised Him from the dead, of which we are wit- nesses. In virtue of faith in His name, His name has strength- 16 ened this man whom you behold and know; and the faith which He has bestowed has entirely restored this man, as you can all see.

"And now, brethren, I know that it was in ignorance that 17 you did it, as was the case with your rulers also. But in this 18 way God has fulfilled the declarations He made through all the prophets, that His Christ would suffer. Repent, therefore, 19 and reform your lives, so that the record of your sins may be canceled, and that there may come seasons of refreshment from the Lord, and that He may send the Christ appointed 20 beforehand for you—even Jesus. Heaven must receive Him 21 until those times of which God has spoken from the earliest ages through the lips of His holy prophets—the times of the reconstitution of all things. Moses declared, 22

"'THE LORD YOUR GOD WILL RAISE UP A PROPHET FOR YOU FROM AMONG YOUR BRETHREN AS HE HAS RAISED ME. IN ALL THAT HE SAYS TO YOU, YOU MUST LISTEN TO HIM. AND EVERY ONE WHO REFUSES TO LISTEN TO 23 THAT PROPHET SHALL BE UTTERLY DESTROYED FROM AMONG THE PEOPLE' (Deuteronomy 18:15-19). Yes, and all 24 the prophets from Samuel onwards who have spoken have also predicted these days.

"You are the heirs of the prophets, and of the Covenant 25
which God made with your forefathers when He said to
Abraham, 'AND THROUGH YOUR POSTERITY ALL THE
FAMILIES OF THE WORLD SHALL BE BLESSED' (Genesis
12:3, 22:18). It is to you first that God, after raising His 26
Servant from the grave, has sent Him to bless you, by causing every one of you to turn from his wickedness."

4 While they were saying this to the people, the 1
priests, the commander of the Temple guard, and the
Sadducees came upon them, highly incensed at their teach- 2
ing the people and proclaiming in the case of Jesus the
resurrection from the dead. They arrested the two apostles 3
and lodged them in custody till the next day; for it was
already evening. But many of those who had listened to their 4
preaching believed; the number of the men now grew to
about five thousand.

The next day a meeting was held in Jerusalem of their 5
rulers, elders, and scribes, with Annas the high priest, 6
Caiaphas, John, Alexander, and the other members of the
high priest's family. So they made the apostles stand forward 7
and demanded of them,

"By what power or in what name have you done this?"

Then Peter, filled with the Holy Spirit, replied, 8

"Rulers and elders of the people, if we to-day are under 9
examination concerning the benefit conferred on a man
helplessly lame, as to how this man has been cured, be it 10
known to you all, and to all the people of Israel, that through
the name of Jesus Christ the Nazarene, whom you crucified,
but whom God has raised from the dead—through that name
this man stands here before you in perfect health. This Jesus 11
is THE STONE TREATED WITH CONTEMPT BY YOU THE

BUILDERS, BUT IT HAS BEEN MADE THE CORNERSTONE (Psalm 118:22). And in no other is salvation to be found; for, 12 indeed, there is no second name under heaven that has been given to men through which we are to be saved."

As they looked on Peter and John so fearlessly outspoken— 13 and also discovered that they were illiterate persons, untrained in the schools—they were surprised; and now they recognized them as having been with Jesus. But seeing the 14 man who had been cured standing with them, they had no reply to make. So they ordered them to withdraw from the 15 Sanhedrin while they conferred among themselves.

"What are we to do with these men?" they asked one 16 another; "for the fact that a notable miracle has been performed by them is well known to every one in Jerusalem, and we cannot deny it. But to prevent the matter spreading any 17 further among the people, let us stop them by threats from speaking in future in this name to any man."

So they recalled the apostles, and ordered them altogether 18 to give up speaking or teaching in the name of Jesus. But 19 Peter and John replied,

"Whether it is right in God's sight to listen to you instead of listening to God, do you judge. As for us, what we have 20 seen and heard we cannot help speaking about."

The Court added further threats and then let them go, 21 being quite unable on account of the people to find any way of punishing them, because all men gave God the glory for what had happened. For the man was over forty years of age 22 on whom this miracle of healing had been performed.

After their release the two apostles went to their friends, 23 and told them all that the high priests and elders had said. And they, upon hearing the story, one and all lifted up their 24 voices to God and said,

"O Sovereign Lord, Thou didst make heaven and earth and

sea, and all that is in them, and didst say through the Holy   25
Spirit by the lips of our forefather David, Thy servant,

"'WHY HAVE THE NATIONS RAGED,
AND THE PEOPLES IMAGINED VAIN THINGS?
THE KINGS OF THE EARTH STOOD BY,   26
AND THE RULERS ASSEMBLED TOGETHER
AGAINST THE LORD AND AGAINST HIS ANOINTED'
(Psalm 2:1-2).

"They did indeed assemble in this city in hostility to Thy holy   27
servant Jesus whom Thou hadst anointed—Herod and Pontius
Pilate with the Gentiles and also the tribes of Israel—to do all   28
that Thy power and Thy will had predetermined should be
done. And now, Lord, listen to their threats, and enable Thy   29
servants to proclaim Thy word with fearless courage, whilst   30
[while] Thou stretchest out Thy hand to cure men, and to give
signs and marvels through the name of Thy holy servant Jesus."

When they had prayed, the place in which they were   31
assembled shook, and they were, one and all, filled with the
Holy Spirit, and spoke God's word with boldness.

Among all those who had embraced the faith there was   32
but one heart and soul, so that none of them claimed any of
his possessions as his own, but everything they had was
common property; while the apostles with great effect deliv-   33
ered their testimony as to the resurrection of the Lord Jesus;
and great grace was upon them all. And, in fact, there was   34
not a needy man among them, for all who were possessors of
lands or houses sold them, and brought the money which
they realized, and gave it to the apostles, and distribution   35
was made to every one according to his wants. In this way   36
Joseph, to whom the apostles gave the name of Barnabas—
signifying "Son of Encouragement"—a Levite, a native of
Cyprus, sold a farm which he had, and brought the money   37
and gave it to the apostles.

5 There was, however, a man of the name of Ananias who, 1
with his wife Sapphira, sold some property, but, with 2
her full knowledge and consent, dishonestly kept back part
of the price received for it, though he brought the rest and
gave it to the apostles.

"Ananias," said Peter, "why has Satan taken possession of 3
your heart, that you should try to deceive the Holy Spirit and
dishonestly keep back part of the price paid you for this
land? While it remained unsold, was not the land your own? 4
And when sold, was it not at your own disposal? How is it
that you have cherished this design in your heart? It is not to
men you have told this lie, but to God."

Upon hearing these words Ananias fell down dead, and all 5
who heard the words were awe-struck. The younger men, 6
however, rose, and wrapping the body up, carried it out and
buried it.

About three hours had passed, when his wife came in, 7
knowing nothing of what had happened. Peter at once ques- 8
tioned her.

"Tell me," he said, "whether you sold the land for so much."

"Yes," she replied, "for so much."

"How was it," replied Peter, "that you two agreed to put the 9
Spirit of the Lord to the test? The men who have buried your
husband are already at the door, and they will carry you out."

Instantly she fell down dead at his feet, and the young men 10
came in and found her dead. So they carried her out and
buried her by her husband's side. The whole church was 11
awe-struck, and so were all who heard of this incident.

Many signs and marvels continued to be done among the 12
people by the apostles; and by common consent they all met
in Solomon's portico. But none of the others dared to attach 13
themselves to them. Yet the people held them in high
honor—and more and more believers in the Lord joined 14

them, including great numbers both of men and of women—so that they would even bring out their sick friends 15 into the streets and lay them on light couches or mats, in order that when Peter came by, at least his shadow might fall on one or other of them. The inhabitants, too, of the towns in 16 the neighborhood of Jerusalem came in crowds, bringing sick persons and some who were harassed by foul spirits, and they were cured, one and all.

This roused the high priest. He and all his party—the sect 17 of the Sadducees—were filled with angry jealousy, and they 18 laid hands upon the apostles, and put them into the public gaol [jail]. But during the night an angel of the Lord opened 19 the prison doors and brought them out, and said,

"Go and stand in the Temple, and continue proclaiming to 20 the people all this message of Life."

On hearing this, they went into the Temple just before 21 daybreak, and began to teach.

So when the high priest and his party came, and had called together the Sanhedrin as well as all the elders of the sons of Israel, they sent to the gaol [jail] to fetch the apostles. But the officers went and could not find them in the prison. 22 So they came back and brought word, saying, 23

"The gaol [jail] we found quite safely locked, and the warders [guards] were on guard at the doors, but upon going in we found no one there."

When the commander of the Temple guards and the high 24 priests heard this statement, they were utterly at a loss with regard to it, wondering what would happen next. And some 25 one came and brought them word, saying,

"The men you put in prison are standing in the Temple, and teaching the people."

Upon this the commander went with the officers, and 26 brought the apostles; but without using violence; for they

were afraid of being stoned by the people. So they brought 27
them and set them before the Sanhedrin. And the high priest
questioned them.

"We strictly forbade you to teach in that name—did we 28
not?" he said. "And see, you have filled Jerusalem with your
teaching, and are trying to make us responsible for that
man's death!"

Peter and the other apostles replied, 29

"We must obey God rather than man. The God of our fore- 30
fathers has raised Jesus to life, whom you crucified and put
to death. God has exalted Him to His right hand as Guide 31
and Savior, to give Israel repentance and forgiveness of sins.
And we—and the Holy Spirit whom God has given to those 32
who obey Him—are witnesses as to these things."

Infuriated at getting this answer, they were disposed to kill 33
the apostles. But a Pharisee of the name of Gamaliel, a 34
teacher of the Law, held in honor by all the people, rose and
demanded that the men should be sent out of court for
a while.

"Israelites," he said, "be careful what you are about to do 35
in dealing with these men. Years ago Theudas appeared, pro- 36
fessing to be a person of importance, and a body of men,
some four hundred in number, joined him. He was killed,
and all his followers were dispersed and annihilated. After 37
him, at the time of the census, came Judas, the Galilaean,
and was the leader in a revolt. He too perished, and all his
followers were scattered. And now I tell you to hold aloof 38
from these men and leave them alone—for if this scheme or
work be of human origin, it will come to nothing. But if it is 39
really from God, you will be powerless to put them down—
lest perhaps you find yourselves to be actually fighting
against God."

His advice carried conviction. So they called the apostles 40 in, and—after flogging them—ordered them not to speak in the name of Jesus, and then let them go. They, therefore, left 41 the Sanhedrin and went their way, rejoicing that they had been deemed worthy to suffer disgrace on behalf of the Name. But they did not desist from teaching every day, in 42 the Temple or at home, and telling the gospel about Jesus, the Christ.

6 About this time, as the number of the disciples was 1 increasing, complaints were made by the Greek-speaking Jews against the Hebrews because their widows were habitually overlooked in the daily ministration. So 2 the Twelve called together the general body of the disciples and said,

"It does not seem fitting that we apostles should neglect the word of God and attend to the tables. Therefore, 3 brethren, pick out from among yourselves seven men of good repute, full of the Spirit and of wisdom, and we will appoint them to undertake this duty. But, as for us, we will 4 devote ourselves to prayer and to the ministry of the word."

The suggestion met with general approval, and they 5 selected Stephen, a man full of faith and of the Holy Spirit, Philip, Prochorus, Nicanor, Timon, Parmenas, and Nicolas, a proselyte of Antioch. These men they brought to the apos- 6 tles, and, after prayer, they laid their hands upon them.

Meanwhile God's word continued to spread, and the num- 7 ber of the disciples in Jerusalem very greatly increased, and very many priests became obedient to the faith. And 8 Stephen, full of grace and power, performed great marvels and signs among the people.

But some members of the synagogue called that of the 9 Libertines, and some Cyreneans, Alexandrians, and men of

Cilicia and Asia, were roused to encounter Stephen in debate. They were quite unable, however, to resist the wisdom and the Spirit with which he spoke. Then they privately put forward men who declared, 10 11

"We have heard him speak blasphemous words against Moses and against God."

In this way they excited the people, the elders, and the scribes. At length they came upon him, seized him with violence, and took him before the Sanhedrin. Here they brought forward false witnesses who declared, 12 13

"This fellow is incessantly speaking against the Holy Place and the Law. For we have heard him say that Jesus, the Nazarene, will pull this place down to the ground and will change the customs which Moses handed down to us." 14

At once the eyes of all who were sitting in the Sanhedrin were fastened on him, and they saw his face like the face of an angel. 15

7 Then the High Priest asked him, 1
"Are these statements true?"

The reply of Stephen was, 2

"Sirs—brethren and fathers—listen to me. The God of Glory appeared to our forefather Abraham when he was living in Mesopotamia, before he settled in Haran, and said to him, 3

"'Leave your country and your kindred, and go into whatever land I point out to you' (Genesis 12:1).

"Thereupon he left Chaldaea and settled in Haran till after the death of his father, when God caused him to remove into this country where you now live. But he gave him no possession in it, no, not a single square yard of ground (Deuteronomy 2:5). And yet He promised to bestow the land as 4 5 a permanent possession on him and his posterity after him—and promised this at a time when Abraham was childless (Genesis 17:8). And God declared that Abraham's posterity 6 should for four hundred years make their home in a country not their own, and be reduced to slavery and be oppressed.

"'And the nation, whichever it is, that enslaves them, I will 7 judge,' said God; 'and afterwards they shall come out' (Genesis 15:13-14), 'and they shall worship Me in this place' (Exodus 3:12).

"Then He gave him the covenant of circumcision (Genesis 8 17:10), and under this covenant he became the father of Isaac—whom he circumcised on the eighth day (Genesis 21:4). Isaac became the father of Jacob, and Jacob became the father of the twelve patriarchs.

"The patriarchs were jealous of Joseph and sold him into 9 slavery in Egypt (Genesis 37:11-28). But God was with him (Genesis 39:2-21) and delivered him from all his afflictions, 10 and gave him favor and wisdom when he stood before Pharaoh, king of Egypt, who appointed him governor over Egypt and all the royal household (Genesis 41:37, 40, 43, 55; Psalm 105:21). But there came a famine throughout the 11 whole of Egypt and Canaan—and great distress—so that our forefathers could find no food (Genesis 41:54). When, how- 12 ever, Jacob heard that there was wheat to be had, he sent our forefathers into Egypt (Genesis 42:1-2); that was the first time. On their second visit Joseph made himself known to 13 his brothers (Genesis 45:4), and Pharaoh was informed of Joseph's parentage. Then Joseph sent and invited his father 14 Jacob and all his family, numbering seventy-five persons (Genesis 45:9, 46:27), to come to him, and Jacob went down 15 into Egypt (Genesis 46:5-6). There he died, and so did our forefathers (Genesis 49:33; Exodus 1:6), and they were taken 16 to Shechem and were laid in the tomb which Abraham had bought from the sons of Hamor at Shechem for a sum of money paid in silver (Genesis 50:13; Joshua 24:32).

"But as the time drew near for the fulfillment of the 17 promise which God had made to Abraham, the people became many times more numerous in Egypt, until there 18 arose a foreign king over Egypt who knew nothing of Joseph (Exodus 1:7-8). He adopted a crafty policy towards our race, 19 and oppressed our forefathers, making them cast out their infants so that they might not be permitted to live (Exodus 1:10-22). At this time Moses was born—a wonderfully beau- 20 tiful child (Exodus 2:2); and for three months he was cared for in his father's house. At length he was cast out, but 21 Pharaoh's daughter adopted him, and brought him up as her own son (Exodus 2:5-10). So Moses was educated in all the 22 learning of the Egyptians, and possessed great influence through his eloquence and his achievements.

"And when he was just forty years old, it occurred to him 23 to visit his brethren the descendants of Israel. Seeing one of 24 them wrongfully treated he took his part, and secured justice for the ill-treated man by striking down the Egyptian. He 25 supposed his brethren to be aware that by him God was sending them deliverance; this, however, they did not understand. The next day, also, he came and found two of them 26 fighting, and he endeavored to make peace between them.

"'Sirs,' he said, 'you are brothers. Why are you wronging one another?'

"But the man who was doing the wrong resented his inter- 27 ference, and asked,

"'Who appointed you ruler and judge over us? Do you 28 mean to kill me as you killed the Egyptian yesterday?'

"Alarmed at this question, Moses fled from the country 29 and went to live in the land of Midian (Exodus 2:11-15). There he became the father of two sons.

"But at the end of forty years there appeared to him in the desert of Mount Sinai an angel in a flame of fire in a bush. When Moses saw this he wondered at the sight; but on his going up to look further, the voice of the Lord was heard, saying, 30 31 32

"'I am the God of your forefathers, the God of Abraham, of Isaac, and of Jacob.'

"Quaking with fear Moses did not dare gaze.

"'Take off your shoes,' said the Lord, 'for the spot on which you are standing is holy ground. I have seen, yes, I have seen the oppression of My people who are in Egypt and have heard their groans, and I have come down to deliver them. And now come, I will send you to Egypt' (Exodus 3:10). 33 34

"The Moses whom they rejected, asking him, 'Who appointed you ruler and judge?'—that same Moses we find God sending as a ruler and a deliverer by the help of the angel who appeared to him in the bush. This was he who brought them out, after performing marvels and signs in Egypt and at the Red Sea, and in the desert for forty years. This is the Moses who said to the descendants of Israel, 35 36 37

"'GOD WILL RAISE UP A PROPHET FOR YOU FROM AMONG YOUR BRETHREN, JUST AS HE RAISED ME' (Deuteronomy 18:15, 18).

"This is he who was among the congregation in the desert, together with the angel who spoke to him on Mount Sinai and with our forefathers, who received ever-living utterances to hand on to us. 38

"Our forefathers, however, would not submit to him, but spurned his authority and in their hearts turned back to Egypt. They said to Aaron, 39 40

"'Make gods for us, to march in front of us; for as for this Moses who brought us out of the land of Egypt, we do not know what has become of him' (Exodus 32:1-8).

"Moreover they made a calf at that time, and offered a 41

sacrifice to the idol, and kept rejoicing in the gods which their own hands had made. So God turned from them and 42 gave them up to the worship of the Host of heaven, as it is written in the book of the prophets,

"'DID YOU OFFER ME VICTIMS AND SACRIFICES
FORTY YEARS IN THE DESERT, O HOUSE OF ISRAEL?
NAY, YOU LIFTED UP MOLOCH'S TENT 43
AND THE STAR OF THE GOD REPHAN—
THE IMAGES WHICH YOU MADE IN ORDER TO WOR-
SHIP THEM;
AND I WILL REMOVE YOU BEYOND BABYLON' (Amos 5:25-27).

"Our forefathers had the tent of witness in the desert, 44 built as He who spoke to Moses had instructed him to make it in imitation of the model which he had seen. That tent 45 was bequeathed to the next generation of our forefathers. Under Joshua they brought it with them when they were taking possession of the land of the Gentile nations, whom God drove out before them. So it continued till David's time. David obtained favor with God, and asked leave to 46 provide a dwelling-place for the God of Jacob. But it was 47 Solomon who built a house for Him. Yet the Most High does 48 not dwell in buildings erected by men's hands. But, as the prophet declares,

"'THE SKY IS MY THRONE, 49
AND EARTH IS THE FOOTSTOOL FOR MY FEET.
WHAT KIND OF HOUSE WILL YOU BUILD FOR ME, SAYS
THE LORD,
OR WHAT RESTING-PLACE SHALL I HAVE?
DID NOT MY HAND FORM THIS UNIVERSE?' (Isaiah 50 66:1-2).

"O stiff-necked men, uncircumcised in heart and ears, you 51 are continually at strife with the Holy Spirit—just as your

forefathers were. Which of the prophets did not your fore- 52
fathers persecute? Yes, they killed those who foretold the
advent of the righteous One, whose betrayers and murderers
you have now become—you who received the Law given 53
through angels, and yet have not obeyed it."

As they listened to these words, they became infuriated 54
and gnashed their teeth at him. But, full of the Holy Spirit 55
and looking up to heaven, Stephen saw the glory of God, and
Jesus standing at God's right hand.

"I can see heaven wide open," he said, "and the Son of 56
Man standing at God's right hand."

Upon this, with a loud outcry they stopped their ears, 57
rushed upon Stephen in a body, dragged him out of the city, 58
and stoned him, the witnesses throwing off their outer garments and giving them into the care of a young man called
Saul. So they stoned Stephen, while he prayed, 59

"Lord Jesus, receive my spirit."

Then, rising on his knees, he cried aloud, 60
"Lord, do not reckon this sin against them."
And with these words he fell asleep.

8 And Saul fully approved of his murder. 1
That day a great persecution broke out against the
church in Jerusalem, and all except the apostles were
scattered throughout Judaea and Samaria. A party of devout 2
men buried Stephen, and made loud lamentation over him.
But Saul cruelly harassed the church. He went into house 3
after house, and, dragging off both men and women, threw
them into prison.

The Church in Judaea and Samaria

So those who were scattered abroad went from place to 4
place spreading the gospel of God's word; while Philip went 5
down to the city of Samaria and proclaimed Christ there.
Crowds of people with one accord gave attention to what they 6
heard from him, listening and witnessing the signs which he
wrought. For with a loud cry foul spirits came out of many 7
possessed by them, and many paralytics and lame persons
were restored to health. And there was great joy in that city. 8

Now for some time past there had been a man named 9
Simon living there, who had been practicing magic and aston-
ishing the Samaritans, pretending that he was more than
human. To him people of all classes paid attention, declaring, 10
"This man is the Power of God, known as the Great Power."

His influence over them arose, because he had, for a long 11
time, bewildered them by his sorceries. But when Philip 12
began to tell the gospel about the Kingdom of God and the
Name of Jesus Christ, and they embraced the faith, they were
baptized, men and women alike. Simon himself also 13
believed, and after being baptized remained in close attendance on Philip, and was full of amazement at seeing such
signs and such great miracles performed.

When the apostles in Jerusalem heard that the Samaritans 14
had accepted God's word, they sent Peter and John to visit
them. They, when they came down, prayed for them that 15
they might receive the Holy Spirit. For He had not as yet 16
fallen upon any of them: they had only been baptized into
the name of the Lord Jesus. Then the apostles laid their 17
hands upon them, and they received the Holy Spirit.

When, however, Simon saw that it was through the laying 18
on of the apostles' hands that the Spirit was bestowed, he
offered them money.

"Give me too," he said, "that power, so that every one on 19
whom I place my hands will receive the Holy Spirit."

"Perish your money and yourself," replied Peter, "because 20
you have imagined that you can obtain God's free gift with
money! No part or lot have you in this matter, for your heart 21
is not right in God's sight. Repent, therefore, of this wicked- 22
ness of yours, and pray to the Lord, in the hope that the purpose which is in your heart may perhaps be forgiven you. For 23
I perceive that you have fallen into the gall of bitterness and
the bondage of iniquity."

"Pray, both of you, to the Lord for me," answered Simon, 24
"that nothing of what you have said may come upon me."

So the apostles, after giving a solemn charge and deliver- 25
ing the Lord's word, traveled back to Jerusalem, making
known the gospel also in many of the Samaritan villages.
And an angel of the Lord said to Philip, 26

"Rise and proceed south to the road that runs down from
Jerusalem to Gaza, crossing the desert."

Upon this he rose and went. Now, as it happened, an 27
Ethiopian eunuch who was in a position of high authority
with Candace, queen of the Ethiopians, as her treasurer, had
visited Jerusalem to worship there, and was now on his way 28
home; and as he sat in his chariot he was reading the
prophet Isaiah. Then the Spirit said to Philip, 29

"Go and join that chariot."

So Philip ran up, and heard the eunuch reading the 30
prophet Isaiah.

"Do you understand what you are reading?" he asked.

"Why, how can I," replied the eunuch, "unless some one 31
explains it to me?"

And he earnestly invited Philip to come up and sit
with him.

The passage of scripture which he was reading was this: 32

"LIKE A SHEEP HE WAS LED TO SLAUGHTER,
AND AS A LAMB BEFORE ITS SHEARER IS DUMB,
SO HE OPENED NOT HIS MOUTH.
IN HIS HUMILIATION JUSTICE WAS DENIED HIM.   33
WHO WILL MAKE KNOWN HIS POSTERITY?
FOR HE IS DESTROYED FROM AMONG MEN" (Isaiah 53:7-8).

"Pray, of whom is the prophet speaking?" inquired the 34 eunuch; "of himself or of some one else?"

Then Philip began to speak, and, starting from that same 35 portion of scripture, told him the gospel about Jesus.

So they proceeded on their way till they came to some 36 water; and the eunuch exclaimed,

"See, here is water; what is there to prevent my being baptized?"

So he stopped the chariot; and both of them—Philip and 38 the eunuch—went down into the water, and Philip baptized him. But no sooner had they come up out of the water than 39 the Spirit of the Lord caught Philip away, and the eunuch did not see him again. With a glad heart he resumed his journey; but Philip found himself at Azotus. Then visiting town after 40 town he everywhere made known the gospel until he reached Caesarea.

9 Now Saul, whose every breath was a threat of destruction 1 for the disciples of the Lord, went to the high priest and 2 begged from him letters addressed to the synagogues in Damascus, in order that if he found any who were of the Way there, either men or women, he might bring them in chains to Jerusalem. But on the journey, as he was getting near Damascus, 3 suddenly there flashed round him a light from heaven; and falling to the ground he heard a voice which said to him,   4

"Saul, Saul, why are you persecuting Me?"

"Who art thou, Lord?" he asked. 5

"I am Jesus, whom you are persecuting," was the reply. "But rise and go to the city, and you will be told what you are 6 to do."

Meanwhile the men who traveled with Saul were standing 7 dumb with amazement, hearing the voice, but seeing no one. Then he rose from the ground, but when he had opened 8 his eyes, he could see nothing, and they led him by the hand and brought him to Damascus. And till the third day he 9 remained without sight, and did not eat or drink anything.

Now in Damascus there was a disciple of the name of 10 Ananias. The Lord spoke to him in a vision, saying,

"Ananias!"

"I am here, Lord," he answered.

"Rise," said the Lord, "and go to Straight Street, and 11 inquire at the house of Judas for a man called Saul, from Tarsus, for see, he is praying. He has seen a man called 12 Ananias come and lay his hands upon him so that he may recover his sight."

"Lord," answered Ananias, "I have heard about that man 13 from many, and about the great mischief he has done to Thy saints in Jerusalem; and here he is authorized by the high 14 priests to arrest all who call upon Thy name."

"Go," replied the Lord; "he is a chosen instrument of Mine 15 to carry My name to the Gentiles and to kings and to the sons of Israel. For I will let him know the great sufferings which he 16 must pass through for My sake."

So Ananias went and entered the house; and, laying his 17 hands upon Saul, said,

"Saul, brother, the Lord—even Jesus who appeared to you on your journey—has sent me, that you may recover your sight and be filled with the Holy Spirit."

Instantly there dropped from his eyes what seemed to be 18
scales, and he could see once more. Upon this he rose and
received baptism; after which he took food and regained 19
his strength.

Then he remained some little time with the disciples in
Damascus. And in the synagogues he began at once to pro- 20
claim Jesus as the Son of God; and his hearers were all 21
amazed, and began to ask one another,

"Is not this the man who in Jerusalem made havoc of those
who called upon that Name, and came here on purpose to
carry them off in chains to the high priests?"

Saul, however, gained power more and more, and as for 22
the Jews living in Damascus, he confounded them with his
proofs that Jesus is the Christ.

At length the Jews plotted to kill Saul; but information of 23
their intention was given to him. They even watched the 24
gates, day and night, in order to murder him; but his disci- 25
ples took him by night and let him down through the wall,
lowering him in a basket.

So he came to Jerusalem and made several attempts to 26
associate with the disciples, but they were all afraid of him,
being in doubt as to whether he was a disciple. Barnabas, 27
however, came to his assistance. He brought Saul to the
apostles, and related to them how, on his journey, he had
seen the Lord, and that the Lord had spoken to him, and how
in Damascus he had fearlessly taught in the name of Jesus.
Henceforth Saul was one of them, going in and out of the 28
city, and speaking fearlessly in the name of the Lord. And he 29
often talked with the Hellenists and had discussions with
them. But they tried to take his life. On learning this, the 30
brethren brought him down to Caesarea, and then sent him
by sea to Tarsus.

The church, however, throughout the whole of Judaea, 31

Galilee, and Samaria, had peace and was built up; and grew in numbers, living in the fear of the Lord and in the encouragement of the Holy Spirit.

Now Peter, as he went to town after town, came down also 32 to the saints at Lydda. There he found a man of the name of 33 Aeneas, who for eight years had kept his bed, being paralyzed. Peter said to him, 34

"Aeneas, Jesus Christ cures you. Rise and make your own bed."

He at once rose to his feet. And all the people of Lydda and 35 Sharon saw him; and they turned to the Lord.

Among the disciples at Joppa was a woman called Tabitha, 36 or, as the name may be translated, "Dorcas." Her life was full of the good and charitable actions which she was constantly doing. But it happened, just at that time, that she was taken 37 ill and died. After washing her body they laid it out in a room upstairs. Lydda, however, being near Joppa, the disciples, 38 who had heard that Peter was at Lydda, sent two men to him with an urgent request that he would come over to them without delay. So Peter rose and went with them. On his 39 arrival they took him upstairs, and the widows all stood by his side, weeping and showing him all the clothing and cloaks that Dorcas used to make while she was still with them. Peter, 40 however, putting every one out of the room, knelt down and prayed, and then turning to the body, he said,

"Tabitha, rise."

Dorcas opened her eyes, and, seeing Peter, sat up. Then, 41 giving her his hand, he raised her to her feet, and calling to him the saints and the widows, he gave her back to them alive. This became known throughout Joppa, and many 42 believed in the Lord; and Peter remained for a considerable 43 time at Joppa, staying at the house of a man called Simon, a tanner.

10 Now a captain of the Italian regiment, named 1
Cornelius, was quartered at Caesarea. He was reli- 2
gious and God-fearing—and so was every member of his
household. He was also liberal in his charities to the people,
and continually offered prayer to God. About three o'clock 3
one afternoon he had a vision, and distinctly saw an angel of
God enter his house, who called him by name, saying,

"Cornelius!"

Looking steadily at him, and being much alarmed, he said, 4
"What is it, Lord?"

"Your prayers and charities," he replied, "have gone up as
a memorial before God. And now send to Joppa and fetch 5
Simon, surnamed Peter. He is lodging with one Simon, a 6
tanner, who has a house close to the sea."

So when the angel who had been speaking to him was 7
gone, Cornelius called two of his servants and a God-fearing
soldier who was in constant attendance on him, and, after 8
telling them everything, he sent them to Joppa.

The next day, while they were still on their journey and 9
were getting near the town, about noon Peter went up on the
house-top to pray. He had got very hungry and wished for 10
some food; but, while they were preparing it, he fell into a
trance. The sky had opened to his view, and what seemed to 11
be an enormous sheet was descending, being let down to the
earth by ropes at the four corners. In it were all kinds of 12
quadrupeds, reptiles, and birds, and a voice came to him 13
which said,

"Rise, Peter, kill and eat."

"On no account, Lord," he replied; "for I have never yet 14
eaten anything unhallowed and unclean."

Again a second time a voice was heard which said, 15

"What God has cleansed, you must not regard as
unhallowed."

This took place three times, and immediately the sheet 16
was drawn up out of sight.

Now just while Peter was wondering as to the meaning of 17
the vision he had seen, the men sent by Cornelius, having by
inquiry found out Simon's house, came to the door and 18
called the servant, and asked,

"Is Simon, surnamed Peter, staying here?"

Peter was still pondering over the vision, when the Spirit 19
said to him,

"Three men are now inquiring for you. Rise, go down, and 20
go with them without any misgivings; for it is I who have sent
them to you."

So Peter went down and said to the men, 21

"I am the man you are inquiring for. What is the reason of
your coming?"

They said, 22

"Cornelius, a captain, an upright and God-fearing man,
of whom the whole Jewish nation speaks well, has been
divinely instructed by a holy angel to send for you to his
house and listen to what you have to say."

Upon hearing this, Peter invited them in, and gave them 23
a lodging.

The next day he set out with them, some of the brethren
from Joppa going with him, and the day after that they 24
reached Caesarea. There Cornelius was awaiting their
arrival, and had invited all his kinsmen and intimate friends
to be present. When Peter entered the house, Cornelius met 25
him, and falling at his feet did him homage. But Peter lifted 26
him up.

"Stand up," he said; "I myself also am but a man."

So Peter went in and conversed with him, and found a 27
large company assembled. He said to them, 28

"You are aware that a Jew is strictly forbidden to associate with a Gentile or visit him; but God has taught me to call no one unhallowed or unclean. Hence, when sent for, I came without raising any objection. I therefore ask why you sent for me." 29

"Just at this hour, three days ago," replied Cornelius, "I was offering afternoon prayer in my house, when suddenly a man in shining raiment stood in front of me, who said, 30 31

"'Cornelius, your prayer has been heard, and your acts of charity have been remembered by God. Send therefore to Joppa, and invite Simon, surnamed Peter, to come here. He is staying in the house of Simon, a tanner, close to the sea.' 32

"Immediately, therefore, I sent for you, and I thank you heartily for having come. That is why all of us are now assembled here in God's presence, to listen to what the Lord has commanded you to say." 33

Then Peter began to speak. 34

"I clearly see," he said, "that God makes no distinctions between one man and another; but that in every nation those who fear Him and live good lives are acceptable to Him. The word which He sent to the sons of Israel, when He announced the gospel of peace through Jesus Christ—He is Lord of all—that word you cannot but know; the story, I mean, which has spread through the length and breadth of Judaea, beginning in Galilee after the baptism which John proclaimed. It tells how God anointed Jesus of Nazareth with the Holy Spirit and with power, so that He went about doing good, and curing all who were oppressed by the devil—for God was with Him. 35 36 37 38

"And we are witnesses to all that He did both in the country of the Jews and in Jerusalem. But they even put Him to death by crucifixion. That same Jesus God raised to life on the third day, and permitted Him to appear, not to all the people, but to witnesses—men previously chosen by God—namely, 39 40 41 to us, who ate and drank with Him after He rose from the dead. And He has commanded us to preach to the people 42 and solemnly declare that this is He who has been appointed by God to be the judge of the living and the dead. To Him all 43 the prophets bear witness that through His name all who believe in Him receive the forgiveness of their sins."

While Peter was speaking these words, the Holy Spirit fell 44 on all who were listening to the word. And all the Jewish 45 believers who had come with Peter were astonished that on the Gentiles also the gift of the Holy Spirit was poured out. For they heard them speaking in tongues and extolling the 46 majesty of God. Then Peter said,

"Can any one forbid the use of the water for the baptism of 47 these people—men who have received the Holy Spirit just as we did?"

And he directed that they should be baptized in the name 48 of Jesus Christ. Then they begged him to remain with them for a time.

11 Now the apostles, and the brethren in various parts of 1 Judaea, heard that the Gentiles also had received God's word; and, when Peter returned to Jerusalem, the 2 party of circumcision found fault with him.

"You went into the houses of men uncircumcised," they 3 said, "and you ate with them."

Peter, however, explained the whole matter to them from 4 the beginning.

"While I was in the town of Joppa, offering prayer," he said, 5 "in a trance I saw a vision. There descended what seemed to be an enormous sheet, being let down from the sky by ropes at the four corners, and it came close to me. Fixing my 6 eyes on it, I examined it closely, and saw various kinds of

quadrupeds, wild beasts, reptiles, and birds. I also heard a 7
voice saying to me,

"'Rise, Peter, kill and eat.'

"'On no account, Lord,' I replied, 'for nothing unhallowed 8
or unclean has ever gone into my mouth.'

"But a voice answered, speaking a second time from 9
the sky,

"'What God has cleansed, you must not regard as
unhallowed.'

"This took place three times, and then everything was 10
drawn up again out of sight.

"Now at that very moment three men came to the house 11
where we were, having been sent from Caesarea to find me.
And the Spirit told me to accompany them without any 12
misgivings. There also went with me these six brethren who
are now present, and we entered the centurion's house. Then 13
he described to us how he had seen the angel standing in his
house and saying,

"'Send to Joppa, and fetch Simon, surnamed Peter. He will 14
teach you truths by which you and all your household will
be saved.'

"And," said Peter, "no sooner had I begun to speak than the 15
Holy Spirit fell upon them, just as He fell upon us at the first.
Then I remembered the Lord's words, how He said, 16

"'John baptized with water, but you shall be baptized in
the Holy Spirit.'

"If therefore God gave them the same gift as He gave us 17
when we first believed on the Lord Jesus Christ, why, who
was I to be able to thwart God?"

On hearing this they were silenced, and they extolled the 18
goodness of God, and said,

"So then, to the Gentiles also God has given the repentance which leads to Life."

The Church in Antioch

Those, however, who had been driven in various directions by the persecution which broke out on account of Stephen made their way to Phoenicia, Cyprus, and Antioch, delivering the word to none but Jews. But some of them were Cyprians and Cyreneans, who, on coming to Antioch, spoke to the Greeks also and told them the gospel concerning the Lord Jesus. The power of the Lord was with them, and there were a vast number who believed and turned to the Lord. 19 20 21

When tidings of this reached the ears of the church in Jerusalem, they sent Barnabas as far as Antioch. On arriving he was delighted to see the grace of God; and he encouraged them all to remain, with fixed resolve, faithful to the Lord. For he was a good man, and was full of the Holy Spirit and of faith; and the number of believers in the Lord greatly increased. 22 23 24

Then Barnabas paid a visit to Tarsus to try to find Saul. He succeeded, and brought him to Antioch; and for a whole year they were the guests of the church, and taught a large number of people. And it was in Antioch that the disciples first received the name of "Christians." 25 26

At that time certain prophets came down from Jerusalem to Antioch, one of whom, named Agabus, publicly predicted by the Spirit the speedy coming of a great famine throughout the world. (It came in the reign of Claudius.) So the disciples put aside money, every one in proportion to his means, for the relief of the brethren living in Judaea. This they did, forwarding their contributions to the elders by Barnabas and Saul. 27 28 29 30

12 Now, about that time, King Herod laid hands on certain members of the church, to do them violence; and James, John's brother, he beheaded. Finding that this gratified the Jews, he proceeded to seize Peter also: these were the days of Unleavened Bread. He had him arrested and lodged in gaol [jail], handing him over to the care of sixteen soldiers; he intended after the Passover to bring him out again to the people. So Peter was kept in gaol [jail]; but long and fervent prayer was offered to God by the church on his behalf.

Now when Herod was on the point of taking him out of prison, that very night Peter was asleep between two soldiers, bound with two chains, and guards were on duty outside the door. Suddenly an angel of the Lord stood by him, and a light shone in the cell; and, striking Peter on the side, he woke him and said,

"Rise quickly."

And the chains dropped off his wrists.

"Fasten your girdle," said the angel, "and tie on your sandals."

He did so. Then the angel said,

"Throw your cloak round you, and follow me."

So Peter went out, following him, yet could not believe that what the angel was doing was real, but supposed that he saw a vision. And passing the first guard and the second, they came to the iron gate leading into the city. This opened to them of itself; and, going out, they passed on through one street, and then suddenly the angel left him. Peter coming to himself said,

"Now I know for certain that the Lord has sent His angel and has rescued me from the power of Herod and from all that the Jewish people were anticipating."

So, on reflection, he went to the house of Mary, the mother of John surnamed Mark, where a large number of people were assembled, praying. When he knocked at the door in the gate, a maidservant named Rhoda came to answer the knock; and recognizing Peter's voice, for very joy she did not 14 open the door, but ran in and told them that Peter was standing there.

"You are mad," they said. 15

But she stoutly maintained that it was true.

"It is his guardian angel," they said.

Meanwhile Peter went on knocking, until at last they 16 opened the door and saw that it was really he, and were filled with amazement. But he motioned with his hand for silence, 17 and then described to them how the Lord had brought him out of the prison.

"Tell all this to James and the brethren," he added.

Then he left them, and went to another place.

When morning came, there was no little commotion 18 among the soldiers as to what could possibly have become of Peter. And when Herod had had him searched for and 19 could not find him, after questioning the guards he ordered them away to execution. He then went down from Judaea to Caesarea and remained there.

Now the people of Tyre and Sidon had incurred 20 Herod's violent displeasure. So they sent a large deputation [representatives] to wait on him; and having secured the good will of Blastus, his treasurer, they begged the king to be friendly with them again, because their country was dependent on his for its food supply. So, on an appointed 21 day, Herod, having arrayed himself in royal robes, took his seat on the tribunal [court], and was haranguing [fervently accusing] them; and the assembled people raised a shout, 22

"It is the voice of a god, and not of a man!"

Instantly an angel of the Lord struck him, because he had 23 not given the glory to God; and being eaten up by worms, he died.

But God's word prospered and spread. And Barnabas and 24
Saul returned from Jerusalem, having discharged their mis- 25
sion, and they brought with them John, surnamed Mark.

13 Now there were in Antioch, in the church there—as 1
prophets and teachers—Barnabas, Symeon surnamed "Niger," Lucius the Cyrenean, Manaen (who was
Herod the Tetrarch's foster-brother), and Saul. While they 2
were worshiping the Lord and fasting, the Holy Spirit said,

"Set me apart Barnabas and Saul for the work to which I
have called them."

So, after fasting and prayer and the laying on of hands, 3
they let them go.

First Missionary Tour of Barnabas and Saul

They therefore, being thus sent out by the Holy Spirit, 4
went down to Seleuceia, and from there sailed to Cyprus.
Having reached Salamis, they began to announce the word 5
of God in the synagogues of the Jews. And they had John as
their assistant.

When they had gone through the whole length of the 6
island as far as Paphos, they there met with a Jewish magician and false prophet, Bar-Jesus by name, who was a friend 7
of the proconsul [Roman governing official or provincial
governor] Sergius Paulus. The proconsul was a man of keen
intelligence. He sent for Barnabas and Saul, and asked to be
told the word of God. But Elymas (or "the Magician," for such 8
is the meaning of the name) opposed them, and tried to prevent the proconsul from accepting the faith. Then Saul, who 9
is also called Paul, was filled with the Holy Spirit, and, fixing
his eyes on Elymas, said, 10

"You who are full of every kind of craftiness and unscrupulous cunning—you son of the devil and foe to all that is right—will you never cease to misrepresent the straight paths of the Lord? The Lord's hand is now upon you, and you 11 will be blind for a time and unable to see the light of day."

Instantly there fell upon him a mist and a darkness, and, as he walked about, he begged people to lead him by the hand. Then the proconsul, seeing what had happened, 12 believed, being struck with amazement at the teaching of the Lord.

From Paphos, Paul and his party put out to sea and sailed 13 to Perga in Pamphylia. John, however, left them and returned to Jerusalem. But they themselves, passing through 14 from Perga, came to Pisidian Antioch.

Here, on the sabbath day, they went into the synagogue and sat down. After the reading of the Law and the prophets, 15 the rulers of the synagogue sent word to them.

"Brethren," they said, "if you have anything encouraging to say to the people, speak."

So Paul rose, and motioning with his hand for silence, said, 16 "Israelites, and you others who fear God, pay attention to me. The God of this people of Israel chose our forefathers, 17 and made the people great during their stay in Egypt, until with wondrous power He brought them out from that land. For about forty years He fed them like a nurse in the desert. 18 Then, after overthrowing seven nations in the land of 19 Canaan, He divided that country among them as their inheritance for about four hundred and fifty years; and afterwards 20 He gave them judges down to the time of the prophet Samuel. Next they asked for a king, and God gave them Saul 21 the son of Kish, a Benjamite, who reigned forty years. After 22 removing him, He raised up David to be their king, to whom He also bore witness when He said,

"'I have found David the son of Jesse, a man I love, who will obey all My commands.'

"It is from among David's descendants that God, in fulfill- 23 ment of His promise, has brought a Savior to Israel, even Jesus. Before the coming of Jesus, John had proclaimed to all 24 the people of Israel a baptism of repentance. But John, when 25 he was fulfilling his career, used to speak thus,

"'What do you suppose me to be? I am not the Christ. But there is One coming after me whose sandal I am not worthy to unfasten.'

"Brethren, descendants of the family of Abraham, and all 26 among you who fear God, to us has the word of this salvation been sent. For the people of Jerusalem and their rulers, by 27 the judgment they pronounced on Jesus, have actually ful- filled the predictions of the prophets which are read sabbath after sabbath, through ignorance of those predictions and of Him. Without having found Him guilty of any capital offense 28 they urged Pilate to have Him put to death; and when they 29 had carried out everything which had been written about Him, they took Him down from the cross and laid Him in a tomb.

"But God raised Him from the dead. And for many days He 30 appeared to the people who had gone up with Him from 31 Galilee to Jerusalem and are now witnesses concerning Him to the Jews. And we bring you the good news about the 32 promise made to our forefathers, that God has amply fulfilled 33 it to our children in raising up Jesus; as it is also written in the second psalm, 'THOU ART MY SON: TO-DAY I HAVE BECOME THY FATHER' (Psalm 2:7). And as to His having 34 raised Him from among the dead, never again to be in the position of one soon to return to decay, He speaks thus: 'I WILL GIVE YOU THE HOLY AND TRUSTWORTHY PROMISES MADE TO DAVID' (Isaiah 55:3). Because in 35 another psalm also He says, 'THOU WILT NOT GIVE UP THY HOLY ONE TO UNDERGO DECAY' (Psalm 16:10). For David, 36 after having been useful to his own generation in accordance with God's purpose, did fall asleep, was gathered to his fore-fathers, and did undergo decay. But He whom God raised to 37 life underwent no decay.

"Understand therefore, brethren, that through this Jesus 38 forgiveness of sins is announced to you; and in Him every 39 believer is absolved from all offenses, from which you could not be absolved under the Law of Moses. Beware, then, lest 40 what is spoken in the prophets should come true of you: 'BEHOLD, YOU DESPISERS, BE ASTONISHED AND PERISH, 41 BECAUSE I AM CARRYING ON A WORK IN YOUR TIME—A WORK WHICH YOU WILL UTTERLY REFUSE TO BELIEVE, THOUGH IT BE FULLY DECLARED TO YOU'" (Habakkuk 1:5).

As Paul and Barnabas were leaving the synagogue, the 42 people earnestly begged to have all this repeated to them on the following sabbath. And, when the congregation had bro- 43 ken up, many of the Jews and of the devout converts from heathenism continued with Paul and Barnabas, who talked to them and urged them to hold fast to the grace of God.

On the next sabbath almost the whole population of the 44 city came together to hear the word of the Lord. Seeing the 45 crowds, the Jews, filled with angry jealousy, opposed Paul's statements and abused him. Then, throwing off all reserve, 46 Paul and Barnabas said,

"We were bound to proclaim the word of God to you first. But since you spurn it and judge yourselves to be unworthy of eternal life—well, we turn to the Gentiles. For such is the 47 Lord's command to us.

"'I HAVE PLACED THEE AS A LIGHT TO THE GENTILES, IN ORDER THAT THOU MAYEST BE A SAVIOR TO THE ENDS OF THE EARTH'" (Isaiah 49:6).

The Gentiles listened with delight and extolled the Lord's 48
word; and all who were predestined to eternal life believed.

So the word of the Lord spread through the whole district. 49
But the Jews influenced the gentlewomen of rank who wor- 50
shiped with them, and also the leading men in the city, and
stirred up persecution against Paul and Barnabas and drove
them out of the district. The apostles shook off the dust from 51
their feet as a protest against them and came to Iconium;
and as for the disciples, they were more and more filled with 52
joy and with the Holy Spirit.

14 At Iconium the apostles went together to the Jewish 1
synagogue and preached, with the result that a great
number both of Jews and of Greeks believed. But the Jews 2
who had refused obedience stirred up the Gentiles and
embittered their minds against the brethren. For a consider- 3
able time, however, Paul and Barnabas remained there,
speaking freely and relying on the Lord, while He bore
witness to the word of His grace by permitting signs and
marvels to be done by them. At length the people of the city 4
split into parties, some siding with the Jews and some with
the apostles. And when a hostile movement was made by 5
both Gentiles and Jews, with the sanction of their magistrates, to maltreat and stone them, the apostles, having 6
become aware of it, made their escape into the Lycaonian
towns of Lystra and Derbe, and the neighboring country.
And there they continued to preach the gospel. 7

Now a man who had no power in his feet used to sit in the 8
streets of Lystra. He had been lame from his birth and had
never walked. This man heard Paul speaking. And the apostle, 9
looking steadily at him and perceiving that he had faith to be
cured, said in a loud voice, 10

"Stand upright upon your feet!"

So he sprang up and began to walk about. Then the 11
crowds, seeing what Paul had done, rent the air with their
shouts in the Lycaonian language, saying,

"The gods have come down to us in the form of men."

They called Barnabas "Zeus," and Paul, as being the prin- 12
cipal speaker, "Hermes." And the priest of Zeus—the temple 13
of Zeus being just outside the city—brought bullocks and
garlands to the gates, and in company with the crowd was
intending to offer sacrifices to them. But the apostles, 14
Barnabas and Paul, heard of it; and tearing their clothes they
rushed out into the crowd, exclaiming, 15

"Sirs, why are you doing all this? We also are but human
beings with natures like yours; and we bring you the good
news that you are to turn from these unreal things, to worship the living God, the Creator of earth and sky and sea and
of everything that is in them. In times gone by He allowed all 16
the nations to go their own ways; and yet by His beneficence 17
[charity] He has not left His existence unattested, in that He
sends you rain from heaven and fruitful seasons, satisfying
your hearts with food and gladness."

Even with words like these they had difficulty in prevent- 18
ing the thronging crowd from offering sacrifices to them.

But now a party of Jews came from Antioch and Iconium, 19
and, having won over the crowd, they stoned Paul and
dragged him out of the town, believing him to be dead.
When, however, the disciples had collected round him, he 20
rose and went back into the town. The next day he went with
Barnabas to Derbe. After proclaiming the gospel to the 21
people there and gaining a large number of converts, they
retraced their steps to Lystra, Iconium, and Antioch.
Everywhere they strengthened the disciples by encouraging 22
them to hold fast to the faith, and warned them, saying,

"It is through many afflictions that we must make our way into the Kingdom of God."

And in every church, after prayer and fasting, they 23 appointed elders, and commended them to the Lord on whom their faith rested.

Then passing through Pisidia they came into Pamphylia; 24 and after telling the word at Perga they came down to Attaleia. 25 Thence they sailed to Antioch, where they had previously 26 been commended to the grace of God in connection with the work which they had now completed. Upon their arrival they 27 called the church together and proceeded to report in detail all that God, working with them, had done, and how He had opened for the Gentiles a door of faith. And they remained a 28 considerable time in Antioch with the disciples.

15 But certain persons who had come down from 1 Judaea tried to convince the brethren, saying,

"Unless you are circumcised in accordance with the Mosaic custom, you cannot be saved."

Between these new-comers and Paul and Barnabas there 2 was no little disagreement and controversy, until at last it was decided that Paul and Barnabas and some other brethren should go up to consult the apostles and elders in Jerusalem on this matter. So they set out, being accompanied for a short 3 distance by the church; and as they passed through Phoenicia and Samaria, they told the whole story of the conversion of the Gentiles and inspired all the brethren with great joy.

Upon their arrival in Jerusalem they were cordially 4 received by the church, the apostles, and the elders; and they reported all that God, working with them, had done. But 5 certain men who belonged to the sect of the Pharisees and were now believers stood up in the assembly and said,

"Gentile believers ought to be circumcised and be ordered to keep the Law of Moses."

Then the apostles and elders met to consider the matter; 6 and after there had been a long discussion Peter rose. 7

"It is within your own knowledge," he said, "that God originally made choice among you that from my lips the Gentiles were to hear the word of the gospel, and believe. And God, who knows all hearts, gave His testi- 8 mony in their favor by bestowing the Holy Spirit on them just as He did on us; and He made no difference between 9 us and them, in that He cleansed their hearts by their faith. Now, therefore, why provoke God, by laying on the necks of 10 these disciples a yoke which neither our fathers nor we have been able to bear? On the contrary, we believe that it 11 is by the grace of the Lord Jesus that we, as well as they, shall be saved."

Then the whole assembly remained silent while they 12 listened to the statement made by Paul and Barnabas as to all the signs and marvels that God had done among the Gentiles by means of them.

When they had finished speaking, James said, 13

"Brethren, listen to me. Symeon has related how God first 14 looked graciously on the nations to take from among them a people to be called by His name. And this is in harmony with 15 the language of the prophets, which says:

""AFTERWARDS I WILL RETURN, AND WILL REBUILD 16 DAVID'S FALLEN TENT.

ITS RUINS I WILL REBUILD, AND I WILL SET IT UP AGAIN;

THAT THE REST OF MANKIND MAY SEEK AFTER THE 17 LORD—

EVEN ALL THE NATIONS WHICH ARE CALLED BY MY NAME," SAYS THE LORD, WHO HAS BEEN MAKING THESE 18

THINGS KNOWN FROM AGES LONG PAST' (Amos 9:11-12).

"My judgment, therefore, is against inflicting unexpected 19
vexation on those of the Gentiles who are turning to God.
Yet let us send them written instructions to abstain from 20
things polluted by connection with idolatry, from fornication, from flesh of strangled animals, and from blood. For 21
Moses from the earliest times has had his preachers in every
town, being read, as he is, sabbath after sabbath, in the various synagogues."

Thereupon it was decided by the apostles and elders, with 22
the approval of the whole church, to choose persons from
among themselves and send them to Antioch, with Paul and
Barnabas. Judas, called Barsabbas, and Silas, leading men
among the brethren, were selected, and they took with them 23
the following letter:

"The apostles and the elders of the brotherhood send
greeting to the Gentile brethren throughout Antioch, Syria,
and Cilicia. As we have been informed that certain persons 24
who have gone from our midst have disturbed you by their
teaching and have unsettled your minds, without having
received any such instructions from us; we have unani- 25
mously decided to select certain men and send them to you
in company with our beloved friends Barnabas and Paul,
who have endangered their lives for the sake of our Lord 26
Jesus Christ. We have therefore sent Judas and Silas, who are 27
themselves bringing you the same message by word of
mouth. For it has seemed good to the Holy Spirit and to us to 28
lay upon you no burden heavier than these necessary
requirements: you must abstain from things sacrificed to 29
idols, from blood, from flesh of strangled animals, and from
fornication. Keep yourselves clear of these things, and it will
be well with you. Farewell."

They, therefore, having been formally sent, came down to 30

Antioch, where they called together the whole assembly and delivered the letter. The people read it, and were delighted with 31 the comfort it brought them. And Judas and Silas, being them- 32 selves also prophets, gave the brethren a long and encouraging talk, and strengthened them in the faith. After spending some 33 time there they received an affectionate farewell from the brethren to return to those who had sent them. But Paul and 35 Barnabas remained in Antioch, teaching and, in company with many others, telling the gospel of the word of the Lord.

St. Paul's Second Missionary Tour

After a while Paul said to Barnabas, 36

"Come, let us return and visit the brethren in the various towns in which we have made known the Lord's word—to see how they fare."

Now Barnabas was bent on taking with them John, whose 37 other name was Mark, while Paul deemed it undesirable to 38 have as their companion one who had deserted them in Pamphylia and had not gone on with them to the work. So 39 there arose a sharp altercation between them, which resulted in their parting from one another, Barnabas taking Mark and setting sail for Cyprus. But Paul chose Silas, and set 40 out, commended by the brethren to the grace of the Lord; and he passed through Syria and Cilicia, strengthening 41 the churches.

16 He also came to Derbe and to Lystra. At Lystra he 1 found a disciple, Timothy by name—the son of a Christian Jewess, but of a Greek father. Timothy was well 2 spoken of by the brethren at Lystra and Iconium, and Paul, 3 desiring that he should accompany him on his journey, had him circumcised on account of the Jews in those parts, for they all knew that his father was a Greek.

As they journeyed on from town to town, they handed to 4 the brethren for their observance the decisions which had been arrived at by the apostles and elders in Jerusalem. So 5 the churches were strengthened in faith, and grew in numbers from day to day.

Then Paul and his companions passed through Phrygia 6 and Galatia, having been forbidden by the Holy Spirit to tell the word in the province of Asia. When they reached the 7 frontier of Mysia, they were about to enter Bithynia, but the Spirit of Jesus would not permit this. So, passing along 8 Mysia, they came to Troas.

And here, one night, Paul saw a vision. There stood a 9 Macedonian entreating him and saying,

"Come over to Macedonia and help us."

So when he had seen the vision, we immediately sought to 10 pass to Macedonia, confidently inferring that God had called us to preach the gospel to the people there.

Accordingly we put out to sea from Troas, and ran a 11 straight course to Samothrace. The next day we came to 12 Neapolis, and thence to Philippi, which is a city in Macedonia, the first in its district, and a Roman colony. And there we stayed some little time.

On the sabbath we went beyond the city gate to the river-13 side, where we had reason to believe that there was a place for prayer; and sitting down we talked with the women who had come together. Among our hearers was one named 14 Lydia, a dealer in purple. She belonged to the city of Thyatira, and was a worshiper of God. The Lord opened her heart, so that she gave attention to what Paul was saying. When she 15 and her household had been baptized, she urged us, saying,

"If in your judgment I am a believer in the Lord, come and stay at my house."

And she made us go there.

One day, as we were on our way to the place of prayer, a 16 slave girl met us who had a spirit of divination and was accustomed to bring her owners large profits by telling fortunes. She kept following close behind Paul and the rest of 17 us, crying aloud,

"These men are the servants of the Most High God, and are proclaiming to you the way of salvation."

This she persisted in for a considerable time, until Paul in 18 vexation turned round and said to the spirit,

"I command you in the name of Jesus Christ to depart from her."

And it departed immediately.

But when her owners saw that their hope of gain had also 19 departed, they seized Paul and Silas and dragged them off to the magistrates in the forum. Bringing them before the 20 praetors [Roman magistrates], they said,

"These men are creating a great disturbance in our city. They are Jews, and are teaching customs which we, as 21 Romans, are not permitted to adopt or practice."

The crowd, too, joined in the outcry against them: and the 22 praetors [Roman magistrates] ordered them to be stripped and beaten with rods; and, after severely flogging them, they 23 threw them into gaol [jail] and bade the gaoler [jailer] keep them safely. Having received an order like that, he lodged 24 them in the inner prison, and secured their feet in the stocks.

About midnight Paul and Silas were praying and singing 25 hymns to God, and the prisoners were listening to them, when suddenly there was such a violent shock of earthquake 26 that the prison shook to its foundations. Instantly the doors all flew open, and the chains fell off from every prisoner.

Starting up from sleep and seeing the doors of the gaol [jail] 27
wide open, the gaoler [jailer] drew his sword and was on the
point of killing himself, supposing that the prisoners had
escaped. But Paul shouted loudly to him, saying, 28

"Do yourself no injury: we are all here."

Then, calling for lights, he sprang in and fell trembling at 29
the feet of Paul and Silas; and, bringing them out of the 30
prison, he exclaimed,

"O sirs, what must I do to be saved?"

"Believe on the Lord Jesus," they replied, "and both you 31
and your household will be saved."

And they told the Lord's word to him as well as to all who 32
were in his house. Then he took them, even at that time of 33
night, and washed their wounds, and he and all his household
were immediately baptized. Then bringing the apostles up 34
into his house, he spread a meal for them, and was filled with
gladness, with his whole household, his faith resting on God.

In the morning the praetors [Roman magistrates] sent 35
their lictors [Roman officials of lower rank than magistrates]
with the order,

"Release those men."

So the gaoler [jailer] brought Paul word, saying, 36

"The praetors [Roman magistrates] have sent orders for
you to be released. Now therefore you can go, and proceed
on your way in peace."

But Paul said to them, 37

"After cruelly beating us in public, without trial, Roman
citizens though we are, they have thrown us into prison, and
are they now going to send us away privately? No, indeed! Let
them come in person and fetch us out."

This answer the lictors [Roman officials of lower rank than 38
magistrates] took back to the praetors [Roman magistrates],
who were alarmed when they were told that Paul and Silas

were Roman citizens. Accordingly they came and apologized 39
to them; and, bringing them out, asked them to leave the
city. Then Paul and Silas, having come out of the prison, 40
went to Lydia's house; and, after seeing the brethren and
encouraging them, they left Philippi.

17 Then, passing through Amphipolis and Apollonia, 1
they went to Thessalonica. Here there was a synagogue of the Jews. Paul—following his usual custom—betook 2
[went] himself to it, and for three successive sabbaths reasoned with them from the scriptures, which he clearly
explained, pointing out that it had been necessary for the 3
Christ to suffer and rise again from the dead, and insisting,

"The Jesus whom I am proclaiming to you is the Christ."

Some of the people were won over, and attached them- 4
selves to Paul and Silas, including a great number of God-
fearing Greeks and not a few prominent gentlewomen.

But the jealousy of the Jews was aroused, and, calling to 5
their aid some ill-conditioned and idle fellows, they got
together a riotous mob and filled the city with uproar. They
then attacked the house of Jason and searched for Paul and
Silas, to bring them out before the assembly of the people.
But, failing to find them, they dragged Jason and some of the 6
other brethren before the magistrates of the city, loudly
accusing them.

"These men," they said, "who have raised a tumult
throughout the Empire, have come here also. Jason has 7
received them into his house; and they all set Caesar's
enactments at defiance, declaring that there is another
King—one called Jesus."

Great was the excitement among the crowd, and among 8
the magistrates of the city, when they heard these charges.

They required Jason and the rest to find substantial bail, and 9 after that they let them go.

The brethren at once sent Paul and Silas away by night 10 to Beroea, and they, on their arrival, went to the synagogue of the Jews. The Jews at Beroea were of a nobler disposi- 11 tion than those in Thessalonica, for they very readily received the word, and day after day searched the scriptures to see whether it was as Paul stated. Many of them therefore 12 became believers, and so did not a few of the Greeks— gentlewomen of good position, and men.

As soon, however, as the Jews of Thessalonica learned that 13 God's word had been proclaimed by Paul at Beroea, they came there also, and incited the mob to a riot. Then the brethren 14 promptly sent Paul down to the sea-coast, but Silas and Timothy remained behind. Those who were escorting Paul went with 15 him as far as Athens, and then left him, taking a message from him to Silas and Timothy to join him as speedily as possible.

While Paul was waiting for them in Athens, his spirit was 16 stirred within him when he noticed that the city was full of idols. So he had discussions in the synagogue with the Jews 17 and the other worshipers, and in the market-place, day after day, with those whom he happened to meet there. A few of 18 the Epicurean and Stoic philosophers also encountered him. Some of them asked,

"What has this beggarly babbler to say?"

"His business," said others, "seems to be to cry up some foreign gods."

This was because he had been telling the gospel of Jesus and the resurrection. Then they took him and brought him 19 up to the Areopagus, asking him,

"May we be told what this new teaching of yours is? For 20 the things you are saying sound strange to us. We should therefore like to be told exactly what they mean."

(For all the Athenians and their foreign visitors used to devote 21 their whole leisure to telling or listening to the latest new thing.)

So Paul, taking his stand in the middle of the Areopagus, 22 spoke as follows:

"Men of Athens, I perceive that you are in every respect remarkably religious. For as I passed along and observed 23 your objects of worship, I found also an altar bearing the inscription,

TO AN UNKNOWN GOD.

"What, therefore, you in your ignorance revere, I now proclaim to you. The God who made the universe and every- 24 thing in it—He, being Lord of heaven and earth, does not dwell in sanctuaries built by men. Nor is He ministered to by 25 human hands, as though He needed anything; but He Himself gives to all men life and breath and all things. He 26 caused to spring from one forefather people of every race, for them to live on the whole surface of the earth, and marked out for them their appointed periods and the limits of their settlements; that they might seek God, if perhaps 27 they could grope for Him and find Him. Yes, though He is not far from any one of us. For it is in Him we live and move and 28 have our being; as in fact some of your own poets have said, 'For we are also His offspring.' Since then we are God's off- 29 spring, we ought not to imagine that His nature resembles gold or silver or stone, sculptured by the art and inventive faculty of man. Those times of ignorance God viewed with 30 indulgence. But now He commands all men everywhere to repent, seeing that He has appointed a day on which He will 31 judge the world in righteousness, in the person of a man whom He has destined for this work, giving assurance of this to all mankind by raising Him from the dead."

When they heard Paul speak of a resurrection of dead 32
men, some began to scoff. But others said,

"We will hear you again on that subject."

So Paul went away from them. A few, however, attached 33
themselves to him and believed, among them being 34
Dionysius a member of the council, a woman named
Damaris, and some others.

18 After this he left Athens and came to Corinth. Here he 1
found a Jew, a native of Pontus, by name Aquila. He 2
and his wife Priscilla had recently come from Italy because of
Claudius's edict expelling all the Jews from Rome. So Paul
paid them a visit; and because he was of the same trade— 3
that of tent-maker—he lodged with them and worked with
them. Sabbath after sabbath he preached in the synagogue 4
and tried to win over both Jews and Greeks.

Now at the time when Silas and Timothy arrived from 5
Macedonia, Paul was preaching fervently, solemnly affirm-
ing to the Jews that the Christ was Jesus. But upon their
opposing him with abusive language, he shook his clothes 6
by way of protest, and said to them,

"Your blood be upon your own heads! I am not responsible: in future I will go among the Gentiles."

So he left the place and went to the house of a person 7
called Titus Justus, a worshiper of God, whose house was
next door to the synagogue. And Crispus, the ruler of the 8
synagogue, believed in the Lord, and so did all his household; and from time to time many of the Corinthians who
heard Paul believed and received baptism. And, in a vision 9
by night, the Lord said to Paul,

"Dismiss your fears: go on speaking, and do not be silent. 10

I am with you, and no one shall attack you to injure you; for I have very many people in this city."

So Paul remained in Corinth for a year and six months, 11 teaching among them the word of God.

But when Gallio became proconsul [Roman governing 12 official or provincial governor] of Greece, the Jews with one accord made a dead set [a resolute attack] at Paul, and brought him before the court.

"This man," they said, "is inducing people to offer worship 13 to God in an unlawful manner."

Now when Paul was about to begin his defense, Gallio said 14 to the Jews,

"If it had been some wrongful act or piece of cunning knavery [trickery] I might reasonably have listened to you Jews. But since these are questions about words and names 15 and your Law, you yourselves must see to them. I refuse to be a judge in such matters."

So he drove them out of court. Then the people all set 16 upon Sosthenes, the ruler of the synagogue, and beat him in 17 front of the tribunal [court]. Gallio did not concern himself in the least about this.

After remaining a considerable time longer in Corinth, 18 Paul took leave of the brethren and set sail for Syria; and Priscilla and Aquila were with him. He had cut off his hair at Cenchreae, because he was bound by a vow. They put in at 19 Ephesus, and there Paul left his companions behind. As for himself, he went to the synagogue and had a discussion with the Jews. When they asked him to remain longer he did not 20 consent, but took leave of them with the promise, 21

"I will return to you, God willing."

So he set sail from Ephesus.

Landing at Caesarea, he went up to Jerusalem and greeted 22 the church, and then went down to Antioch.

St. Paul's Third Missionary Tour

After spending some time in Antioch, Paul set out on a 23
tour, visiting the whole of Galatia and Phrygia in order, and
strengthening all the disciples.

Meanwhile a Jew named Apollus came to Ephesus. He was 24
a native of Alexandria, an eloquent man and well versed in
the scriptures. He had been instructed in the way of the 25
Lord, and, being full of burning zeal, he used to speak and
teach accurately the facts about Jesus, though he knew of no
baptism but John's. He began to speak boldly in the syna- 26
gogue, and Priscilla and Aquila, after hearing him, took him
home and explained God's Way to him more accurately.
Then, as he had made up his mind to cross over to Greece, 27
the brethren wrote to the disciples in Corinth, begging them
to give him a kindly welcome. Upon his arrival he rendered
valuable help to those who through grace had believed; for 28
he powerfully and in public overcame the Jews in argument,
proving from the scriptures that Jesus is the Christ.

19 During the stay of Apollos in Corinth, Paul, after 1
passing through the inland districts, came to
Ephesus, where he found a few disciples.

"Did you receive the Holy Spirit when you first believed?" 2
he asked them.

"No," they replied, "we have not even heard that there is a
Holy Spirit."

"Into what, then, were you baptized?" he asked. 3

"Into John's baptism," they replied.

"John," he said, "administered a baptism of repentance, 4
bidding the people believe on One who was to come after
him; namely, on Jesus."

On hearing this, they were baptized into the name of the Lord Jesus; and when Paul laid his hands upon them, the Holy Spirit came on them, and they began to speak in tongues and to prophesy. They numbered in all about twelve men.

Afterwards he went into the synagogue. There for three months he continued to preach fearlessly, reasoning persuasively concerning the Kingdom of God. But some grew obstinate in unbelief and spoke evil of the Way before all the congregation. So Paul left them, and, taking with him those who were disciples, held discussions daily in the lecture-hall of Tyrannus. This went on for two years, so that all the inhabitants of the province of Asia, Jews as well as Greeks, heard the Lord's message.

God also brought about extraordinary miracles through Paul. Towels or aprons, for instance, which Paul had handled, would be carried to the sick, and they would recover from their ailments, and the evil spirits would leave them.

But there were also some wandering Jewish exorcists who undertook to invoke the name of Jesus over those who had the evil spirits, saying,

"I command you by that Jesus whom Paul preaches."

There were seven sons of one Sceva, a Jew of high-priestly family, who were doing this.

"Jesus I acknowledge," the evil spirit answered, "and Paul I know, but who are you?"

And the man in whom the evil spirit was sprang on them, overmastered them, and treated them with such violence that they fled from the house stripped of their clothes and wounded. All the people of Ephesus, Jews as well as Greeks, came to know of this. There was widespread awe, and they began to hold the name of the Lord Jesus in high honor.

Many also of those who believed came confessing without reserve their practices, and not a few of those who had practiced magical arts brought their books together and burned them in the presence of all. The total value was reckoned and found to be fifty thousand silver pieces. Thus 20 mightily did the Lord's word spread and triumph!

When matters had reached this point, Paul, guided by the 21 Spirit, decided to travel through Macedonia and Greece and go to Jerusalem.

"After that," he said, "I must also see Rome."

But he sent two of his assistants, Timothy and Erastus, 22 to Macedonia, while he himself remained for a while in Roman Asia.

Now just at that time there arose no small commotion 23 about the Way. For there was a certain Demetrius, a silver- 24 smith, who made miniature silver shrines of Artemis, a business which brought great profit to the craftsmen in his employ. He called his men together, and others who were 25 engaged in similar trades, and said to them,

"You men well know that our prosperity depends on this business of ours; and you see and hear that, not in Ephesus 26 only but throughout almost the whole province of Asia, this fellow Paul has led away a vast number of people by asserting that those are not gods at all that are made by men's hands. There is danger, therefore, not only that this our trade 27 will become of no account, but also that the temple of the great goddess Artemis will fall into utter disrepute, and that before long she will be actually deposed from her majestic rank—she who is now worshiped by the whole province of Asia; nay, by the whole world."

After listening to this harangue [a long speech of 28 accusation], they became furiously angry and began shouting,

"Great is Artemis of Ephesus!"

The riot and uproar spread through the whole city, till at 29 last with one accord they rushed into the theater, dragging with them Gaius and Aristarchus, two Macedonians who were fellow travelers with Paul. Then Paul would have liked 30 to go in and address the people, but the disciples would not let him do so. A few of the public officials, too, who were 31 friendly to him, sent repeated messages entreating him not to venture into the theater. The people, meanwhile, kept 32 shouting, some one thing and some another; for the assembly was all uproar and confusion, and the greater part had no idea why they had come together. Then some of the people 33 crowded round Alexander, whom the Jews had pushed forward; and Alexander, motioning with his hand to get silence, was prepared to make a defense to the people. No sooner, 34 however, did they see that he was a Jew, than there arose from them all one roar of shouting, lasting about two hours.

"Great is Artemis of Ephesus," they said.

At length the recorder quieted them down. 35

"Men of Ephesus," he said, "who in the world, pray, needs to be told that the city of Ephesus is the guardian of the temple of the great Artemis and of the image which fell down from heaven? These facts, then, being unquestioned, it becomes you 36 to maintain your self-control and not act recklessly. For you 37 have brought these men here, who are neither robbers of temples nor blasphemers of our goddess. If, however, Demetrius 38 and the craftsmen who support his contention have a grievance against any one, there are assize-days [days designated for court sessions] and there are proconsuls [Roman governing officials or provincial governors]: let them bring their charges. But if you desire anything further, it will have to be settled in the 39 regular assembly. For in connection with to-day's proceedings 40 there is danger of our being charged with attempted insurrection, there having been no real reason for this riot; nor shall we be able to justify the behavior of this disorderly mob."

With these words he dismissed the assembly. 41

20 When the uproar had ceased, Paul sent for the 1 disciples; and, after speaking words of encouragement to them, he took his leave, and started for Macedonia. Passing through those districts he greatly encouraged the 2 disciples, and then came into Greece, and spent three 3 months there. The Jews having planned to waylay him whenever he might be on the point of taking ship for Syria, he decided to travel back by way of Macedonia. He was 4 accompanied as far as the province of Asia by Sopater of Beroea, the son of Pyrrhus; by Aristarchus and Secundus of Thessalonica; by Gaius of Derbe, and Timothy; and by Tychicus and Trophimus, men of Asia. These brethren had 5 gone on and were waiting for us in Troas. But we ourselves 6 sailed from Philippi after the days of Unleavened Bread, and five days later joined them in Troas, where we remained for a week.

On the first day of the week, when we had met to break 7 bread, Paul, who was going away the next morning, was preaching to them, and prolonged his discourse till midnight. Now there were a good many lights in the room 8 upstairs where we all were, and a youth of the name of 9 Eutychus was sitting at the window. This lad, gradually sinking into deep sleep while Paul preached at unusual length, overcome at last by sleep, fell from the third story and was taken up dead. Paul, however, went down, threw himself 10 upon him, and folding him in his arms said,

"Cease your wailing; his life is still in him."

Then he went upstairs again, broke the bread, and took 11 some food; and after a long conversation which was continued till daybreak, at last he parted from them. They had 12 taken the lad home alive, and were greatly comforted.

The rest of us had already embarked, and we set sail for 13 Assos, intending to take Paul on board there; for so he had arranged, he himself intending to go by land. Accordingly, 14 when he met us at Assos, we took him on board and came to Mitylene. Sailing from there, we arrived the next day off 15 Chios. On the next we touched at Samos; and on the day following reached Miletus. For Paul's plan was to sail past 16 Ephesus, so as not to spend much time in the province of Asia; since he was very desirous of being in Jerusalem, if possible, on the day of Pentecost.

From Miletus he sent to Ephesus for the elders of the 17 church to come to him. Upon their arrival he said to them, 18

"You elders well know, from the first day of my setting foot in the province of Asia, the kind of life I lived among you the whole time, serving the Lord in all humility, and 19 with tears, and amid trials which came upon me through the plotting of the Jews—and that I never shrank from 20 declaring to you anything that was profitable, or from teaching you in public and in your homes, bearing witness 21 to both Jews and Greeks of their need of conversion to God and of belief in Jesus our Lord.

"And now, under spiritual constraint, I am on my way to 22 Jerusalem, not knowing what will happen to me there, except that the Holy Spirit, at town after town, testifies to me 23 that imprisonment and suffering are awaiting me. But even 24 the sacrifice of my life I count as nothing, if only I may perfect my earthly course, and be faithful to the duty which the Lord Jesus has entrusted to me of bearing witness to the gospel of God's grace.

"And now, I know that none of you among whom I have 25 gone in and out proclaiming the Kingdom will any longer see my face. Therefore I solemnly affirm to you to-day that, 26 should any of you perish, the responsibility is not mine. For 27 I have not shrunk from declaring to you God's whole plan.

"Take heed to yourselves and to all the flock among which 28 the Holy Spirit has placed you as overseers and shepherds to the Church of God, which He has bought with His own blood. I know that, when I am gone, cruel wolves will come 29 among you and will not spare the flock; and that from 30 among your own selves men will rise up who will seek with their perverse talk to draw away the disciples after them. Therefore be on the alert; and remember that, night and 31 day, for three years, I never ceased admonishing every one, even with tears.

"And now I commend you to God and to the word of His 32 grace. He is able to build you up and to give you your inheritance among the saints. No one's silver or gold or clothing 33 have I coveted. You yourselves know that these hands of 34 mine have provided for my own necessities and for the people with me. In every way I have shown you how, by 35 working as I do, you ought to help the weak, and to bear in mind the words of the Lord Jesus, how He Himself said,

"'It is more blessed to give than to receive.'"

Having spoken thus, Paul knelt down and prayed with 36 them all; and with loud lamentation they all threw their arms 37 round his neck, and kissed him lovingly, grieved above all 38 things at his having told them that they were never to behold his face again. And they went with him to the ship.

21 When, at last, we had torn ourselves away and had set 1 sail, we ran in a straight course to Cos; the next day to Rhodes, and from there to Patara. Finding a ship bound for 2 Phoenicia, we went on board and put to sea. After sighting 3 Cyprus and leaving it on our left, we continued our voyage to Syria and put in at Tyre; for there the ship was to unload her cargo. Having searched for the disciples and found them, we 4 stayed at Tyre for seven days. These disciples, taught by the

Spirit, warned Paul not to proceed to Jerusalem. When, how- 5
ever, our time was up, we went on our way, escorted by all the
disciples with their wives and children, till we were out of the
city. Then, after kneeling down on the beach and praying, we 6
took leave of one another; and we went on board, while they
returned home.

Our voyage was over when having sailed from Tyre we 7
reached Ptolemais. Here we inquired after the welfare of
the brethren, and remained a day with them. We left on the 8
morrow and went on to Caesarea, where we entered the
house of Philip the Evangelist, who was one of the seven, and
stayed with him. Philip had four unmarried daughters who 9
were prophetesses.

Now during our somewhat lengthy stay a prophet of the 10
name of Agabus came down from Judaea. When he came to 11
us, he took Paul's girdle, and bound his own feet and arms
with it, and he said,

"Thus says the Holy Spirit, 'So will the Jews in Jerusalem
bind the owner of this girdle, and will hand him over to
the Gentiles.'"

As soon as we heard these words, both we and the 12
brethren at Caesarea entreated Paul not to go up to
Jerusalem. His reply was, 13

"What can you mean by thus unmanning [unnerving]
me with your weeping? Why, I am ready not only to go to
Jerusalem and be put in chains, but even to die there for the
sake of the Lord Jesus."

So when he was not to be dissuaded, we ceased 14
remonstrating [pleading in protest] with him and said,

"The Lord's will be done!"

A few days afterwards we packed our baggage and contin- 15
ued our journey to Jerusalem. Some of the disciples from 16
Caesarea also joined our party, and brought with them

Mnason, a man from Cyprus, one of the early disciples, at whose house we were to lodge. We reached Jerusalem, and there the brethren gave us a hearty welcome. 17

Paul in Jerusalem

On the following day we went with Paul to call on James, 18 and all the elders of the church came also. After exchanging 19 greetings, Paul told in detail all that God had done among the Gentiles by his ministry. And they, when they had heard 20 his statement, gave glory to God.

Then they said,

"You see, brother, how many tens of thousands among the Jews there are of those who have accepted the faith, and they are all zealous upholders of the Law. Now what they have been 21 told about you is that you teach all the Jews among the Gentiles to abandon Moses, telling them not to circumcise their children or observe old-established customs. What, then, 22 ought you to do? They are sure to hear of your arrival; so do 23 what we now tell you. We have four men here who are under a vow. Associate with these men and purify yourself with them, 24 and pay their expenses so that they can shave their heads. Then everybody will know that there is no truth in these stories about you, but that in your own actions you yourself obey the Law. As for the Gentiles who have accepted the faith, we have 25 communicated to them our decision that they are carefully to abstain from anything sacrificed to an idol, from blood, from what is strangled, and from fornication."

So Paul associated with the men; and the next day, having 26 purified himself with them, he went into the Temple, giving notice when the days of their purification would be finished, and there he remained until the sacrifice for each of them was offered.

But, when the seven days were nearly over, the Jews from 27
the province of Asia, seeing Paul in the Temple, stirred up all
the people against him. They laid hands on him, crying out, 28
"Men of Israel, help! This is the man who goes everywhere preaching to everybody against the Jewish people
and the Law and this place. And besides, he has even
brought Gentiles into the Temple and has desecrated this
holy place."

For they had previously seen Trophimus the Ephesian 29
with him in the city, and imagined that Paul had brought
him into the Temple. The excitement spread through the 30
whole city, and the people rushed up in a crowd and laid
hold of Paul and proceeded to drag him out of the Temple;
and the Temple gates were immediately closed.

But while they were trying to kill Paul, word was taken up 31
to the tribune [magistrate] in command of the battalion, that
all Jerusalem was in a ferment. He instantly sent for a few 32
soldiers and their officers, and came down among the
people with all speed. At the sight of the tribune [magistrate]
and the troops they ceased beating Paul. Then the tribune 33
[magistrate], making his way to him, arrested him, and, having ordered him to be secured with two chains, asked who he
was and what he had been doing. Some of the crowd 34
shouted one accusation against Paul and some another,
until, as the uproar made it impossible for the truth to be
ascertained, the tribune [magistrate] ordered him to be
brought into the barracks. When Paul was at the steps, he 35
had to be carried by the soldiers because of the violence of
the mob; for the whole mass of the people pressed on in the 36
rear, shouting, "Away with him!"

When he was about to be taken into the barracks, Paul said 37
to the tribune [magistrate],

"May I speak to you?"

"Do you know Greek?" the tribune [magistrate] asked. "Are you not the Egyptian who some years ago excited the 38 riot of the four thousand cut-throats, and led them out into the desert?"

"I am a Jew," replied Paul, "belonging to Tarsus in Cilicia, 39 and am a citizen of no unimportant city. Give me leave, I pray you, to speak to the people."

So with his permission Paul stood on the steps and 40 motioned to the people to be quiet; and when there was silence he addressed them in Hebrew.

22 "Brethren and fathers," he said, "listen to my defense 1 which I now make before you."

And on hearing him address them in Hebrew, they kept all 2 the more quiet; and he said,

"I am a Jew, born at Tarsus in Cilicia, but brought up in this 3 city. I was carefully trained at the feet of Gamaliel in the Law of our forefathers, and, like all of you to-day, was zealous for God. I persecuted to death this Way, continually binding 4 both men and women and throwing them into prison; as the 5 high priest also and all the elders can bear me witness. It was, too, from them that I received letters to the brethren in Damascus, and I was already on my way to Damascus, intending to bring those also who had fled there, in chains to Jerusalem, to be punished.

"But on my way, when I was now not far from Damascus, 6 about noon a sudden blaze of light from heaven shone round me. I fell to the ground and heard a voice say to me, 7

"'Saul, Saul, why are you persecuting me?'

"'Who art thou, Lord?' I asked. 8

"'I am Jesus, the Nazarene,' He replied, 'whom you are persecuting.'

"Now the men who were with me, though they saw the 9
light, did not hear the words of Him who spoke to me. And 10
I asked,

"'What am I to do, Lord?'

"And the Lord said to me,

"'Rise, and go into Damascus. There you shall be told of all
that has been appointed for you to do.'

"And as I could not see, because the light had been so 11
dazzling, those who were with me had to lead me by the
arm, and so I came to Damascus.

"And a certain Ananias, a pious man who obeyed the 12
Law and bore a good character with all the Jews of the city,
came to me and standing at my side said, 13

"'Brother Saul, recover your sight.'

"I instantly regained my sight and looked up at him.
Then he said, 'The God of our fathers has appointed you to 14
know His will, and to see the righteous One and hear Him
speak. For you shall be a witness for Him, to all men, 15
of what you have seen and heard. And now why delay? 16
Rise, be baptized, and wash away your sins, calling upon
His name.'

"After my return to Jerusalem, and while praying in the 17
Temple, I fell into a trance; and I saw Him, and He said to me, 18

"'Make haste and leave Jerusalem quickly, because they
will not accept your testimony about Me.'

"'Lord,' I replied, 'they themselves well know how active I 19
was in imprisoning, and in flogging in synagogue after
synagogue those who believe in Thee; and when they were 20
shedding the blood of Stephen, Thy witness, I was standing
by, fully approving of it, and I guarded the clothes of those
who were killing him.'

"'Go,' He replied; 'I will send you to nations far away.'" 21

Until they heard this last statement the people listened to 22

Paul, but now with a roar of disapproval they cried out,

"Away with such a fellow from the earth! He ought not to have been allowed to live."

And when they continued their furious shouts, throwing 23 their clothes into the air and flinging dust about, the tribune 24 [magistrate] ordered him to be brought into the barracks, and be examined by flogging, in order to ascertain the reason why they thus cried out against him. But, when they had tied him 25 up with the straps, Paul said to the captain who stood by,

"Does the law permit you to flog a Roman citizen, one too who is uncondemned?"

On hearing this question, the captain went to report the 26 matter to the tribune [magistrate].

"What are you intending to do?" he said. "This man is a Roman citizen."

So the tribune [magistrate] came to Paul and asked him, 27 "Tell me, are you a Roman citizen?"

"Yes," he said.

"I paid a large sum for this citizenship," said the tribune 28 [magistrate].

"But I was born free," said Paul.

So the men who had been on the point of judicially examining him immediately left him. And the tribune 29 [magistrate], too, was frightened when be learned that Paul was a Roman citizen, for he had had him bound.

The next day, wishing to know exactly what charge was being brought against him by the Jews, the tribune [magistrate] 30 ordered his chains to be removed; and, having sent word to the high priests and all the Sanhedrin to assemble, he brought Paul down and made him stand before them.

23 Then Paul, fixing a steady gaze on the Sanhedrin, said, 1 "Brethren, I have lived with a perfectly clear conscience before God up to this day."

On hearing this the high priest Ananias ordered those who 2 were standing near Paul to strike him on the mouth.

"God will strike you, you white-washed wall!" exclaimed 3 Paul. "Are you sitting there to judge me in accordance with the Law, and you yourself break the Law by ordering me to be struck!"

"Do you rail at God's high priest?" cried the men who 4 stood by him.

"I did not know, brethren," replied Paul, "that he was the 5 high priest; for it is written, 'THOU SHALT NOT SPEAK EVIL OF A RULER OF THY PEOPLE'" (Exodus 22:28).

Noticing, however, that the Sanhedrin consisted partly of 6 Sadducees and partly of Pharisees, he called out loudly among them,

"Brethren, I am a Pharisee, the son of Pharisees. It is because of my hope of a resurrection of the dead that I am on my trial."

These words of his caused an angry dispute between 7 the Pharisees and the Sadducees, and the assembly took different sides. For the Sadducees maintain that there is no 8 resurrection, and neither angel nor spirit; but the Pharisees acknowledge them all. So there arose a great uproar; and 9 some of the scribes belonging to the sect of the Pharisees sprang to their feet and fiercely contended, saying,

"We find no harm in the man. What if a spirit has spoken to him, or an angel—!"

But when the struggle was becoming violent, the tribune 10 [magistrate], fearing that Paul would be torn to pieces by the people, ordered the troops to go down and take him from among them by force and bring him into the barracks.

The following night the Lord came and stood at Paul's side, 11
and said,

"Be of good courage, for as you have borne faithful witness about me in Jerusalem, so you must also bear witness
in Rome."

Now when daylight came, the Jews formed a conspiracy 12
and solemnly swore not to eat or drink till they had killed
Paul. There were more than forty of them who bound 13
themselves by this oath. These went to the high priests and 14
elders and said to them,

"We have bound ourselves under a heavy curse to take no
food till we have killed Paul. Now therefore do you and the 15
Sanhedrin make representations to the tribune [magistrate]
for him to bring him down to you, as if you intended to
inquire more minutely about him; and we are prepared to
assassinate him before he comes near the place."

But Paul's nephew heard of the intended attack upon him. 16
So he came and entered the barracks and told Paul about it;
and Paul called one of the captains, and said, 17

"Take this young man to the tribune [magistrate], for he
has information to give him."

So he took him and brought him to the tribune 18
[magistrate], and said,

"Paul, the prisoner, called me to him and begged me to bring
this youth to you, because he has something to say to you."

Then the tribune [magistrate], taking him by the arm, 19
withdrew out of the hearing of others and asked him,

"What have you to tell me?"

"The Jews," he replied, "have agreed to request you to 20
bring Paul down to the Sanhedrin to-morrow for the purpose of making yourself more accurately acquainted with
the case. I beg you not to comply; for more than forty men 21
among them are lying in wait for him, who have solemnly

vowed that they will neither eat nor drink till they have assassinated him; and even now they are ready, awaiting that promise from you."

So the tribune [magistrate] sent the youth home, caution- 22 ing him.

"Do not let any one know that you have given me this information," he said.

Then, calling to him two of the captains, he gave his orders. 23

"Get ready two hundred men," he said, "to march to Caesarea, with seventy cavalry and two hundred light infantry, starting at nine o'clock to-night."

He further told them to provide horses to mount Paul on, 24 so as to bring him safely to Felix the Governor. He also wrote 25 a letter of which these were the contents:

"Claudius Lysias to his Excellency, Felix the Governor: 26 greetings. This man Paul had been seized by the Jews, and 27 was on the point of being killed by them, when I came upon them with the troops and rescued him, for I had been informed that he was a Roman citizen. Wishing to know with 28 certainty the offense of which they were accusing him, I brought him down into their Sanhedrin, and I discovered 29 that the charge had to do with questions of their Law, but that he was accused of nothing for which he deserves death or imprisonment. But now that I have received information 30 of a plot against the man, I immediately send him to you, directing his accusers also to state before you the case they have against him."

So, in obedience to their orders, the soldiers took Paul and 31 brought him by night as far as Antipatris. The next day the 32 infantry returned to the barracks, leaving the cavalry to pro- ceed with him; and the cavalry, having reached Caesarea, 33 delivered the letter to the Governor, and brought Paul also to him. Felix, after reading the letter, inquired from what 34 province he was; and being told "from Cilicia," he said, 35

"I will hear all you have to say, when your accusers also have come."

And he ordered him to be detained in custody in Herod's palace.

24 Five days after this, Ananias the high priest came 1 down to Caesarea with a number of elders and a pleader [one who presents a case in court] called Tertullus. They stated to the governor the case against Paul. So Paul 2 was sent for, and Tertullus began to impeach him as follows:

"Indebted as we are," he said, "to you, most noble Felix, for the perfect peace which we enjoy, and for reforms which your wisdom has conferred upon this nation in every way and in every place, we accept them with profound gratitude. 3 But—not to detain you too long—I beg you in your forbear- 4 ance to listen to a brief statement from us. We have found 5 this man Paul a source of mischief and a disturber of the peace among all the Jews throughout the Empire, and a ring- leader in the sect of the Nazarenes. He even attempted to 6 profane the Temple, but we arrested him. You, however, by 8 examining him, will yourself be able to learn the truth as to all this which we allege against him."

The Jews also joined in the charge, maintaining that these 9 were facts.

Then, at a sign from the governor, Paul answered, 10

"Knowing that for many years you have administered justice to this nation, I cheerfully make my defense. For you 11 have it in your power to ascertain that it is not more than twelve days ago that I went up to worship in Jerusalem; and 12 that neither in the Temple nor in the synagogues, nor anywhere in the city, did they find me disputing with any

opponent or collecting a crowd about me. Nor can they 13
prove the charges which they are now bringing against me.
But this I confess to you—that in the way which they style a 14
sect, I worship the God of our fathers, believing everything
that is taught in the Law or is written in the prophets, and 15
having a hope in God, which my accusers themselves also
entertain, that there will be a resurrection both of the righteous and of the unrighteous. This too is my own earnest 16
endeavour—always to have a clear conscience in relation to
God and man.

"Now after several years' absence I came to bring a sum of 17
money to my countrymen, and to offer sacrifices. While I 18
was busy about these, they found me in the Temple purified,
with no crowd around me and no uproar. But there were
certain Jews from the province of Asia, who ought to have 19
been here before you, and to have been my prosecutors, if
they have any charge to bring against me. Or let these men 20
themselves say what misdemeanor they found me guilty of
when I stood before the Sanhedrin, unless it was that one 21
expression which I made use of when I shouted out as I
stood among them,

"'The resurrection of the dead is the thing about which I
am on my trial before you to-day.'"

At this point Felix, who was fairly well informed about the 22
new faith, adjourned the trial, saying to the Jews,

"When the tribune [magistrate] Lysias comes down, I
will decide your case."

And he gave orders to the captain that Paul was to be kept 23
in custody, but be treated with indulgence, and that his
personal friends were not to be prevented from showing
him kindness.

Not long after this, Felix came with Drusilla his wife, a 24
Jewess, and, sending for Paul, listened to him as he spoke

about faith in Christ Jesus. But when he reasoned about 25 justice, self-control, and the future judgment, Felix became alarmed and said,

"For the present leave me, and when I can find an opportunity I will send for you."

At the same time he hoped that Paul would give him 26 money; and for this reason he sent for him the oftener to converse with him. But after the lapse of two years Felix was 27 succeeded by Porcius Festus; and, being desirous of gratifying the Jews, Felix left Paul still in prison.

25 Festus, having entered on his duties as governor of 1 the province, three days later went up from Caesarea to Jerusalem; whereupon the high priests and the leading 2 men among the Jews immediately made representations to him against Paul, and begged him—asking it as a favor, to 3 Paul's prejudice—to have him brought to Jerusalem. They were planning an ambush to kill him on the way. Festus, 4 however, replied that Paul was in custody in Caesarea, and that he was himself going there very soon.

"Therefore let those of you," he said, "who have influence 5 go down with me, and impeach the man, if there is anything amiss in him."

After a stay of eight or ten days in Jerusalem—not more— 6 he went down to Caesarea; and the next day, taking his seat on the tribunal [court], he ordered Paul to be brought in. Upon Paul's arrival, the Jews who had come down from 7 Jerusalem stood round him, and brought many grave charges against him which they were unable to substantiate. In reply, Paul said, 8

"Neither against the Jewish Law, nor against the Temple, nor against Caesar, have I committed any offense whatever."

Then Festus, being anxious to gratify the Jews, asked Paul, 9
"Are you willing to go up to Jerusalem, and there stand your trial before me on these charges?"

"I am standing before Caesar's tribunal [court]," replied 10 Paul, "where alone I ought to be tried. I have done the Jews no injury of any sort, as you indeed know well enough. If, 11 however, I have done wrong and have committed any offense for which I deserve to die, I do not ask to be excused that penalty. But if there is no truth in what these men allege against me, no one has the right to give me up to them as a favor. I appeal to Caesar."

Then, after conferring with the Council, Festus replied, 12 "To Caesar you have appealed: to Caesar you shall go."

A short time after this, Agrippa the king and Bernice came 13 to Caesarea to pay a complimentary visit to Festus; and, 14 during their rather long stay, Festus laid Paul's case before the king.

"There is a man here," he said, "whom Felix left a prisoner, about whom, when I went to Jerusalem, the high priests and 15 the elders of the Jews made representations to me, begging that sentence might be pronounced against him. My reply 16 was that it is not the custom among the Romans to give up any one for punishment before the accused has had his accusers face to face, and has had an opportunity of defending himself against the charge which has been brought against him.

"When, therefore, a number of them came here, the next 17 day I took my seat on the tribunal [court], without any loss of time, and ordered the man to be brought in. But, when his 18 accusers stood up, they did not charge him with misdemeanors such as I had expected. But they quarreled with 19 him about certain matters connected with their own religion, and about a certain Jesus who had died, but—so Paul

maintained—is now alive. I was at a loss how to investigate 20
such questions, and asked Paul whether he would care to go
to Jerusalem and there stand his trial on these matters. But 21
when Paul appealed to have his case kept for the emperor's
decision, I ordered him to be kept in prison until I could
send him up to Caesar."

"I should like to hear the man myself," said Agrippa. 22

"To-morrow," replied Festus, "you shall."

Accordingly, on the next day Agrippa and Bernice came in 23
state [an imposing, ceremonious display] and took their seats
in the audience hall, attended by the tribunes [magistrates]
and the men of high rank in the city; and, at the command of
Festus, Paul was brought in. Then Festus said, 24

"King Agrippa, and all who are present with us, you see
here the man about whom the whole nation of the Jews
made suit to me, both in Jerusalem and here, crying out
that he ought not to live any longer. I could not discover 25
that he had done anything for which he deserved to die; but
as he has himself appealed to the emperor, I have decided
to send him to Rome. I have nothing very definite, however, 26
to tell our sovereign about him. So I have brought the man
before you all—and especially before you, King Agrippa—
that after he has been examined I may find something
which I can put into writing. For, when sending a prisoner 27
to Rome, it seems to me to be absurd not to state the
charges against him."

26

Then Agrippa said to Paul, 1
"You have permission to speak for yourself."

So Paul, with outstretched arm, proceeded to make his
defense.

"As regards all the accusations brought against me by the 2

Jews," he said, "I think myself fortunate, King Agrippa, in being about to defend myself to-day before you, who are so familiar 3 with all the customs and questions that prevail among the Jews; and for this reason, I pray you, give me a patient hearing.

"The kind of life I have lived from my youth upwards, as 4 exemplified in my early days among my nation and in Jerusalem, is known to all the Jews. For they all know me of 5 old—if they would but testify to the fact—how, being an adherent of the strictest sect of our religion, my life was that of a Pharisee. And now I stand here impeached because of 6 my hope in the promise made by God to our fathers—the 7 promise which our twelve tribes, worshiping day and night with intense devoutness, hope to have made good to them. It is on the subject of this hope, O king, that I am accused by the Jews. Why is it deemed with all of you a thing past belief 8 if God raises the dead to life?

"I myself, however, thought it a duty to be active in hostil- 9 ity to the name of Jesus, the Nazarene. I was so in Jerusalem: 10 armed with authority received from the high priests I shut up many of the saints in various prisons, and when it was a question of putting them to death I gave my vote against them. In all the synagogues also I often punished them and 11 tried to make them blaspheme; and in my wild fury I chased them even to foreign towns.

"While thus engaged, I was traveling one day to 12 Damascus, armed with authority and a commission from the high priests, and on the journey, at noon, O king, I saw a 13 light from heaven—brighter than the brightness of the sun— shining around me and around those who were traveling with me. We all fell to the ground; and I heard a voice which 14 said to me in Hebrew,

"'Saul, Saul, why are you persecuting me? You are finding it painful to kick against the ox-goad.'

"'Who art thou, Lord?' I asked.   15

"'I am Jesus whom you are persecuting,' the Lord replied.
'But rise, and stand on your feet; for I have appeared to you   16
for the very purpose of appointing you my servant and my
witness both as to the things you have already seen and as to
those in which I will appear to you. I will save you from the   17
Jewish people and from the Gentiles, to whom I send you to
open their eyes, that they may turn from darkness to light   18
and from Satan's authority to God, in order to receive forgiveness of sins and an inheritance among those who are
sanctified through faith in me.'

"Therefore, King Agrippa, I was not disobedient to the   19
heavenly vision; but I proceeded to preach first to the people   20
in Damascus, and then to those in Jerusalem and in all
Judaea, and to the Gentiles, that they must repent and turn
to God, and live lives consistent with such repentance.

"It was on this account that the Jews seized me in the   21
Temple and tried to kill me. Having, however, obtained the   22
help which comes from God, I have stood firm until now,
and have solemnly exhorted small and great alike, saying
nothing except what the prophets and Moses predicted, how   23
that the Christ was to be a suffering Christ, and being the
first to rise from the dead He was to proclaim a message of
light both to the Jewish people and to the Gentiles."

As Paul thus made his defense, Festus exclaimed in a   24
loud voice,

"You are mad, Paul; your great learning is turning
your brain."

"I am not mad, most noble Festus," replied Paul; "I am   25
speaking words of sober truth. The king, to whom I speak   26
freely, knows about these matters. I do not believe that any
detail of them has escaped his notice; for all this has not

been done in a corner. King Agrippa, do you believe the 27
prophets? I know that you believe them."

Agrippa answered, 28

"In brief, you are confident that you can make me
a Christian!"

"My prayer to God, whether in brief or at length," replied 29
Paul, "would be that not only you, but all who are my hearers
to-day, might become such as I am—except these chains."

So the king rose, and the governor, and Bernice, and those 30
who were sitting with them; and they retired and conversed 31
together and said,

"This man does nothing for which he deserves death
or imprisonment."

And Agrippa said to Festus, 32

"He might have been set at liberty, if he had not appealed
to Caesar."

Paul's Voyage to Italy

27 Now when it was decided that we should sail for 1
Italy, they handed over Paul and a few other prisoners into the custody of Julius, an officer of the Augustan battalion; and going on board a ship of Adramyttium which was 2
about to sail to the ports of the province of Asia, we put to
sea; Aristarchus, the Macedonian, from Thessalonica, being
one of our party. The next day we put in at Sidon. There Julius 3
treated Paul with thoughtful kindness and allowed him to
visit his friends and enjoy their care.

Putting to sea again, we sailed under the lee [a place 4
sheltered from the wind] of Cyprus, because the winds were
against us; and, sailing the whole length of the sea that lies 5
off Cilicia and Pamphylia, we reached Myra in Lycia. There 6

Julius found an Alexandrian ship bound for Italy, and put us on board of her. It took several days of slow and difficult 7 sailing for us to come off Cnidus; from which point, as the wind did not allow us to get on by the direct course, we ran under the lee [a place sheltered from the wind] of Crete off Salmone. Then, coasting along with difficulty, we reached a 8 place called "Fair Havens," near the town of Lasea.

Our voyage thus far had occupied a long time, and the 9 navigation being now unsafe because the Fast was already over, Paul warned them.

"Sirs," he said, "I perceive that the voyage will be attended 10 with danger and heavy loss, not only to the cargo and the ship but to our own lives also."

But Julius let himself be persuaded by the pilot and by the 11 owner rather than by Paul's arguments; and as the harbor 12 was inconvenient for wintering in, the majority were in favor of putting out to sea, to try whether they could get to Phoenix—a harbor on the coast of Crete facing north-east and south-east—to winter there. And a light breeze from the 13 south sprang up, so that they supposed they were now sure of their purpose. So weighing anchor they ran along the coast of Crete, keeping close inshore.

But it was not long before a furious north-east wind, coming 14 down from the mountains, burst upon us and carried the ship out of her course. She was unable to make headway against 15 the gale; so we gave up and let her drive. Then we ran under 16 the lee [a place sheltered from the wind] of a little island called Cauda, where we managed with great difficulty to secure the boat; and, after hoisting it on board, they used frapping-cables 17 [cables wound around to strengthen/support] to undergird the ship and, as they were afraid of being driven on the Syrtis quicksands, they lowered the gear [rigging] and lay to [to hold a ship stationary with the bow to the wind]. But, as the storm 18 was still violent, the next day they began to lighten the ship; and, on the third day, with their own hands they threw the 19 ship's spare gear overboard. Then, when for several days nei- 20 ther sun nor stars were seen and the terrific gale still harassed us, the last ray of hope was now vanishing.

When for a long time they had taken but little food, Paul, 21 standing up among them, said,

"Sirs, you ought to have listened to me and not have sailed from Crete. You would then have escaped this suffering and loss. But now take courage, for there will be no loss of life 22 among you, but of the ship only. For there stood by my side, 23 last night, an angel of the God to whom I belong, and whom also I worship, and he said, 24

"'Dismiss all fear, Paul, for you must stand before Caesar; and note this—God has granted you the lives of all who are sailing with you.'

"Therefore, Sirs, take courage; for I believe God, and am 25 convinced that things will happen exactly as I have been told. But we are to be stranded on a certain island." 26

It was now the fourteenth night, and we were drifting 27 through the Sea of Adria, when, about midnight, the sailors suspected that land was close at hand. So they hove [heaved] 28 the lead [a lead weight for measuring depth of water] and found twenty fathoms of water; and after a short time they hove [heaved] again and found fifteen fathoms. Then for fear 29 of possibly running on rocks, they threw out four anchors from the stern and longed for daylight. The sailors, however, 30 wanted to make their escape from the ship, and had lowered the boat into the sea, pretending that they were going to lay out anchors from the bow. But Paul, addressing Julius and 31 the soldiers, said,

"Your lives will be sacrificed, unless these men remain on board."

Then the soldiers cut the ropes of the ship's boat and let 32
her fall off.

And as day was dawning Paul urged all on board to take 33
some food.

"This is the fourteenth day," he said, "that you have been
on the strain, and have fasted, eating little or nothing. I 34
therefore strongly advise you to take some food. This is
essential for your safety. For not a hair will perish from the
head of any one of you."

Having said this he took some bread, and, after giving 35
thanks to God for it before them all, he broke it in pieces and
began to eat it. This raised the spirits of all, and they too took 36
food. There were two hundred and seventy-six of us, crew 37
and passengers, all told. After eating a hearty meal they light- 38
ened the ship by throwing the wheat overboard.

When daylight came, they could not recognize the coast, 39
But they noticed an inlet with a sandy beach, and now their
object was, if possible, to run the ship aground in this inlet.
So they cut away the anchors and left them in the sea, 40
unloosing at the same time the bands which secured the
paddle-rudders. Then, hoisting the foresail to the wind, they
made for the beach. But coming to a place where two seas 41
met, they stranded the ship, and her bow sticking fast
remained immovable, while the stern began to go to pieces
under the heavy hammering of the sea.

Now the soldiers recommended that the prisoners should 42
be killed, for fear some one of them might swim ashore and
effect his escape. But their captain, bent on securing Paul's 43
safety, kept them from their purpose, and gave orders that
those who could swim should first jump overboard and get
to land, and that the rest should follow, some on planks, and 44
others on various things from the ship. In this way they all
got safely to land.

28

Our lives having been thus preserved, we discovered 1 that the island was called Malta. The natives showed 2 us remarkable kindness, for they lit a fire and made us all welcome because of the pelting rain and the cold. Now, 3 when Paul had gathered a bundle of sticks and had thrown them on the fire, a viper, driven by the heat, came out and fastened itself on his hand. When the natives saw the creature hanging from his hand, they said to one another, 4

"Beyond doubt this man is a murderer, for, though saved from the sea, Justice has not permitted him to live."

He, however, shook the reptile off into the fire and was 5 unhurt. They expected him soon to swell with inflammation 6 or suddenly fall down dead; but, after waiting a long time and seeing no harm come to him, they changed their minds and said that he was a god.

Now in the same part of the island there were lands 7 belonging to the governor, whose name was Publius. He welcomed us to his house, and for three days generously made us his guests. It happened, however, that his father was lying 8 ill of dysentery and attacks of fever; so Paul went to see him, and, after praying, laid his hands on him and cured him. After this, all the other sick people in the island came and 9 were cured. They also loaded us with honors, and when at 10 last we sailed they put supplies on board for us.

Three months passed before we set sail in an Alexandrian 11 vessel, called the "Twin Brothers," which had wintered at the island. At Syracuse we put in and stayed for three days. From 12 there we worked round and reached Rhegium; and a day later, a 13 south wind sprang up which brought us the next day to Puteoli. Here we found brethren, who urged us to remain with them for 14 a week; and so we reached Rome. Meanwhile the brethren 15 there, hearing of our movements, came as far as Appii Forum and Tres Tabernae to meet us; and when Paul saw them he

thanked God and took courage. Upon our arrival in Rome, Paul 16
received permission to live by himself, guarded by a soldier.

Paul in Rome

After three days he invited the leading men among the 17
Jews to meet him; and, when they were come together, he
said to them,

"Although, brethren, I had done nothing prejudicial to our
people or contrary to the customs of our forefathers, I was
handed over as a prisoner from Jerusalem into the power of
the Romans; who, after they had sharply questioned me, 18
were willing to set me at liberty, because they found no
offense in me for which I deserve to die. But owing to the 19
opposition of the Jews I was compelled to appeal to Caesar;
not, however, that I had any charge to bring against my
nation. For these reasons, then, I have invited you here, that 20
I might see you and speak to you; for it is for the hope of
Israel that I wear this chain."

"For our part," they replied, "we have not received any let- 21
ters from Judaea about you, nor have any of our countrymen
come here and reported or stated anything to your disadvantage. But we should be glad to hear from you what it 22
is that you believe; for as for this sect all we know is that it is
everywhere spoken against."

So they arranged a day with him and came to him to his 23
lodgings in considerable numbers. And then he solemnly
explained to them the Kingdom of God, endeavoring from
morning till evening to convince them about Jesus, both
from the Law of Moses and from the prophets. Some were 24
convinced; others refused to believe. Unable to agree among 25
themselves, they at last left him, but not before Paul had
spoken a parting word to them, saying,

"Right well did the Holy Spirit say to your fathers through the prophet Isaiah:

"'GO TO THIS PEOPLE AND TELL THEM,   26

YOU WILL HEAR AND HEAR, AND BY NO MEANS UNDERSTAND;

AND WILL LOOK AND LOOK, AND BY NO MEANS SEE.

FOR THIS PEOPLE'S MIND HAS GROWN CALLOUS,   27

THEIR HEARING HAS BECOME DULL,

AND THEIR EYES THEY HAVE CLOSED;

LEST THEY SHOULD SEE WITH THEIR EYES,

OR HEAR WITH THEIR EARS,

OR UNDERSTAND WITH THEIR MINDS,

AND TURN BACK,

THAT I MIGHT CURE THEM' (Isaiah 6:9-10).

"Be assured, therefore, that this salvation—God's salvation—   28 has been sent to the Gentiles: they, at any rate, will give heed."

After this Paul lived for fully two years in private hired   30 rooms, receiving all who came to see him. He preached the   31 Kingdom of God and the gospel of the Lord Jesus Christ without let [obstacle] or hindrance.

THE EPISTLE OF PAUL
TO THE ROMANS

Introduction

1 Paul, a servant of Jesus Christ, called to be an apostle, 1
set apart to proclaim God's gospel, which He promised 2
through His prophets in holy writ concerning His son, who, 3
by human descent, belonged to the family of David, but by 4
His Spirit of holiness was miraculously marked out as Son
of God by resurrection of the dead, Jesus Christ our Lord,
through whom I have received grace and a commission for 5
His Name's sake to win men to the obedience that springs
from faith among all the Gentiles, among whom you too are 6
called to belong to Jesus Christ; to all of you in Rome who are 7
loved by God, and called to be saints: grace to you and peace
from God our Father and the Lord Jesus Christ.

First of all I thank my God through Jesus Christ for you 8
all, because the report of your faith is spreading through
the whole world. I call God to witness—to whom I render 9
priestly and spiritual service by preaching the gospel of His
Son—how constantly I make mention of you in my
prayers, ever asking that now at length, if such be His will, 10
the way may by some means be made clear for me to come
to you. For I am longing to see you in order to impart to 11
you some spiritual help, so that you may be strengthened;
in other words, that while I am among you, you and I may 12
be mutually encouraged by one another's faith. And I want 13
you to know, brethren, that I have many a time intended to
come to you—though until now I have been prevented—in

order that I might gather some fruit from my labors, among you, as well as among the other Gentiles. To Greek 14 and non-Greek, to wise and foolish alike, I have a duty to perform: so for my part I am eager to preach the gospel to 15 you in Rome also.

The Main Subject of the Letter

For I am not ashamed of the gospel. It is God's power 16 working for salvation for every one who believes, Jew first, and then Greek. For in the gospel a righteousness which 17 comes from God is revealed, alike depending on faith and leading to faith; as the scripture has it,

"THE RIGHTEOUS MAN SHALL LIVE BY FAITH" (Habakkuk 2:4).

For God's wrath is revealed from heaven against all the 18 impiety and the wickedness of men who through their wickedness suppress the truth; because what may be known 19 of God is plain to their minds; for God has made it plain to them. From the very creation of the world, His invisible per- 20 fections—namely, His eternal power and divine nature—have been perceptible and clearly visible from His works, so that they are without excuse. For though they knew God they have 21 not glorified Him as God, nor rendered Him thanks, but have become absorbed in useless discussions, and their senseless minds darkened. While boasting of their wisdom they are 22 fools; and they have exchanged the glory of the immortal God 23 for images of mortal man, or of birds, beasts, or reptiles.

For this reason, through the lust of their hearts, God has 24 given them up to impurity to dishonor themselves, since 25 they have exchanged God's truth for what is false, and have offered worship and service to the creature rather than to the Creator ever blessed! Amen.

This is why God has given them up to vile passions. Not 26
only have their women exchanged their natural functions for
unnatural ones, but the men also, in the same way, neglect- 27
ing sexual intercourse with women, have burned fiercely in
their lust for one another, men practicing shameful vice with
men, and receiving in themselves the fitting retribution for
their misconduct.

And just as they did not think fit to retain knowledge of 28
God, so God left them with the minds of reprobates to do
unseemly things; with hearts filled with all sorts of dishon- 29
esty, mischief, greed, and malice; full of envy and blood-
thirstiness, quarrelsome, crafty, spiteful, secret backbiters,
open slanderers; hateful to God, insolent, haughty, ostenta- 30
tious; inventors of mischief, disobedient to parents, destitute 31
of sense, faithless, without affection, and without pity. In 32
short, though knowing well the sentence which God pronounces against such deeds as deserving death, they not only
do them, but applaud others who practice them.

2 You are therefore without excuse, whoever you are 1
who pass judgment upon others. In passing judgment
on your neighbor you condemn yourself; for you who pass
judgment commit the same misdeeds; and we know that 2
God's judgment falls rightly upon those who commit such
sins. And you who judge those who commit such sins and 3
yet do the same yourself—do you imagine that you yourself will escape God's judgment? Or is it that you think 4
lightly of the wealth of His goodness, forbearance, and
patience, unaware that the goodness of God is drawing
you to repentance?

In the stubbornness of your impenitent heart you are 5
treasuring up for yourself wrath on the day of Wrath when

God's righteous judgment will stand revealed. TO EACH 6
MAN HE WILL MAKE AN AWARD ACCORDING TO HIS
DEEDS (Psalm 62:12; Proverbs 24:12); to those who, by lives 7
of persistent right-doing, strive for glory, honor, and
immortality, eternal life; while on the self-willed who yield 8
not to the truth but yield to iniquity there will fall wrath and
affliction and anguish upon every human soul who does 9
wrong—upon the Jew first, and then upon the Greek; but 10
glory, honor, and peace for every one who does what is
good—the Jew first and then the Greek. For God pays no 11
attention to this world's distinctions.

All who sin outside the Law will also perish outside the 12
Law, and all who sin while subject to the Law will be judged
by the Law. For it is not those who hear the Law read who 13
are righteous in the sight of God, but it is those who obey
the Law who will be pronounced righteous. When Gentiles 14
who have no law obey by instinct the commands of the Law,
they, without having a law, are a law to themselves; since 15
they exhibit engraved on their hearts the action of the Law,
while their conscience at the same time bears witness to the
Law, and their moral judgments alternately accuse or perhaps defend them—on the day when, according to the 16
gospel I preach, God will judge the secrets of men's lives by
Jesus Christ.

Suppose you claim the name of Jew, find rest in the Law, 17
pride yourself in God, know the Will, are instructed by the 18
Law to appreciate distinctions, and have persuaded yourself 19
that you are a guide to the blind, a light to those in darkness,
a schoolmaster for the foolish, a teacher of novices, because 20
in the Law you possess the actual form of knowledge and
of truth; you, then, who teach your fellow man, do you refuse 21
to teach yourself? You who cry out against stealing, do you
steal? You who forbid adultery, do you commit adultery? 22

You who loathe idols, do you plunder temples? You who 23
pride yourself in the Law, do you violate the Law and so dishonor God? Why, THE NAME OF GOD IS BLASPHEMED 24
AMONG THE GENTILES BECAUSE OF YOU, as holy writ
declares (Isaiah 52:5).

Circumcision does indeed profit, if you obey the Law; but 25
if you are a law-breaker your circumcision counts for nothing. In the same way if an uncircumcised man observes the 26
requirements of the Law, shall not his uncircumcision be
reckoned circumcision, and if he in his natural state of 27
uncircumcision carries out the Law, shall he not judge you
who, for all your written Law and circumcision, are yet a law-
breaker? For the true Jew is not the man who is outwardly a 28
Jew, and true circumcision is not that which is outward and
bodily. But the true Jew is one inwardly, and true circumci- 29
sion is heart-circumcision—not literal, but spiritual. Such a
man receives praise not from men, but from God.

3 What special privilege, then, has a Jew? Or what is the 1
benefit of circumcision? Great in every way. First, the 2
fact that the Jews were entrusted with God's oracles. What if 3
some Jews have proved unfaithful? Shall their faithlessness
nullify God's faithfulness? God forbid! Let God be true, 4
though every man be false. As it stands written,

"THAT THOU MAYEST PROVE RIGHT IN THY
CONTENTIONS,
AND SUCCEED IN THY CAUSE" (Psalm 51:4).

But if our wickedness sets God's righteousness in a clearer 5
light, what shall we say? (Is God unrighteous—I use a human
analogy—when He inflicts punishment? God forbid! For in 6
that case how shall He judge all mankind?) But if my false- 7
hood has brought out God's truthfulness, redounding

[resulting] to His glory, why am I still judged as a sinner? And 8
why not say—as some people wickedly assert that we do
say—"Let us do evil that good may come"? The condemnation of such men is just.

What then? Are we Jews at a disadvantage? Not in the least; 9
for we have already charged all Jews and Gentiles alike with
being in thralldom [slavery] to sin. Thus it stands written, 10

"THERE IS NOT A SINGLE RIGHTEOUS MAN:

THERE IS NOT ONE INTELLIGENT, NOT ONE A SEEKER 11
AFTER GOD.

ALL HAVE TURNED ASIDE; 12

THEY HAVE ALIKE BECOME WORTHLESS;

THERE IS NO ONE WHO DOES GOOD—NO, NOT ONE"
(Psalm 14:1-3).

"THEIR THROAT IS AN OPENED GRAVE; 13

WITH THEIR TONGUE THEY HAVE TALKED DECEIT-
FULLY" (Psalm 5:9).

"THE VENOM OF VIPERS LIES BEHIND THEIR LIPS"
(Psalm 140:3).

"THEIR MOUTH IS FULL OF CURSING AND BITTER- 14
NESS" (Psalm 10:7).

"THEIR FEET MOVE SWIFTLY TO SHED BLOOD. 15

RUIN AND MISERY MARK THEIR PATH; 16

AND THE WAY TO PEACE THEY KNOW NOT" 17
(Isaiah 59:7-8).

"THERE IS NO FEAR OF GOD BEFORE THEIR EYES" 18
(Psalm 36:1).

But we know that all that the Law says is addressed to 19
those who are living subject to the Law, in order that every
mouth may be silenced, and that the whole world may await
sentence from God. For no man living will be declared right- 20
eous before Him on the ground of obedience to Law. Law
simply brings a knowledge of sin.

But now a righteousness of God has been brought to light 21
apart from any Law, both Law and prophets bearing witness
to it—a righteousness of God conditional on faith in Jesus 22
Christ for all who believe. No distinction is made; for all alike 23
have sinned, and consciously fall short of the glory of God,
but are acquitted freely by His grace through the ransom 24
given in Christ Jesus, whom God put forward as an expiation 25
[atonement] available to faith in virtue of His blood. It was
to demonstrate God's justice, in view of the condoning by
His forbearance of sins previously committed—that is, to 26
demonstrate His justice at the present time, that He may be
shown to be just Himself, and the justifier of the man who
believes in Jesus.

Where, then, is there room for boasting? It is shut out. On 27
what principle? On that of merit? No, but on the principle of
faith. For we deem that a man is accounted righteous by 28
faith, apart from fulfillment of the Law.

Is God simply the God of Jews, and not of Gentiles also? 29
Yes, He is the God of Gentiles also, if indeed it is one and the 30
same God who will acquit the circumcised on the ground of
faith, and the uncircumcised through the same faith. Do we 31
then by means of this faith abolish the Law? God forbid! We
confirm the Law.

4 What, then, shall we say of Abraham, our natural fore- 1
father? For if he was held to be righteous on the ground 2
of his actions, he has something to boast of; yes, but not in
the presence of God. For what says the scripture? "ABRAHAM 3
BELIEVED GOD, AND THIS WAS CREDITED TO HIM AS
RIGHTEOUSNESS" (Genesis 15:6). But in the case of a man 4
who works, pay is not reckoned as a favor but as something
due; whereas in the case of a man who in place of working 5

believes in Him who acquits the ungodly, his faith is credited to him as righteousness. In this way David also tells of the blessedness of the man whom God credits with righteousness apart from his actions. 6

"BLESSED," he says, "ARE THOSE WHOSE INIQUITIES ARE FORGIVEN, AND WHOSE SINS ARE COVERED. 7

BLESSED IS THE MAN OF WHOSE SIN THE LORD WILL NOT TAKE ACCOUNT" (Psalm 32:1-2). 8

Is this declaration of blessedness, then, for the circumcised, or for the uncircumcised as well? FOR ABRAHAM'S FAITH— so we affirm—WAS CREDITED TO HIM AS RIGHTEOUSNESS (Genesis 15:6). In what circumstances, then? Was it after he had been circumcised or before? Before, not after. And he received circumcision as a sign, a seal attesting the righteousness which was his by faith while still uncircumcised, that he might be the father of all those who believe even though uncircumcised—in order that this righteousness might be credited to them; and also the father of the circumcised, namely, of those who not merely are circumcised, but also walk in the steps of the faith which our father Abraham had while he was as yet uncircumcised. Again, the promise that he should inherit the world did not come to Abraham or his posterity through Law, but through righteousness depending on faith. For if it is those who rely on Law who are heirs, then faith is useless and the promise counts for nothing. For the effect of the Law is wrath; but where no Law exists, there can be no transgression. All depends on faith for this reason—that righteousness may be by grace, so that the promise should be made sure to all his posterity; not merely to those who rely on the Law, but also to those who rely on a faith like Abraham's. For in the sight of God in whom he believed, who gives life to the dead and speaks of things non-existent as though existing, Abraham is the father of all of us. As it is written, 9 10 11 12 13 14 15 16 17

"I HAVE MADE YOU FATHER OF MANY NATIONS" (Genesis 17:5).

He believed, hoping against hope, so that he might 18 become the father of many nations, in accordance with the words "SO NUMEROUS SHALL YOUR POSTERITY BE" (Genesis 15:5). And without growing weak in faith, he could 19 note his own vital powers now decayed—for he was about a hundred years old—and Sarah's barrenness. Nor did he in 20 unbelief stagger at God's promise, but had intense faith, giving glory to God, and being absolutely certain that whatever 21 He has promised He can also carry out. For this reason 22 also his faith WAS CREDITED TO HIM AS RIGHTEOUSNESS (Genesis 15:6).

Nor was the fact of its being credited to him recorded for 23 his sake only, but for our sakes too. Faith is going to be cred- 24 ited to us who believe in Him who raised Jesus, our Lord, from the dead, who was delivered up because of our of- 25 fenses, and was raised to life for our acquittal.

5 Acquitted, then, as the result of faith, let us enjoy peace 1 with God through our Lord Jesus Christ, through whom 2 we have been brought by our faith into the position of favor in which we stand, and we exult in hope of seeing God's glory. And not only so: we also exult in our afflictions, know- 3 ing as we do that affliction produces endurance; endurance, 4 ripeness of character; and ripeness of character, hope; and 5 that this hope never disappoints, because God's love for us floods our hearts through the Holy Spirit who has been given to us.

For already, while we were still helpless, Christ at the fit- 6 ting time died for the ungodly. Why, it is scarcely conceivable 7 that any one would die for a just man, although for a good man perhaps some one might have the courage even to die. But God gives proof of His love to us in Christ's dying for us 8 while we were still sinners.

Much more, then, now that we have been acquitted by 9 His blood, shall we be delivered from God's anger through Him. For if while we were hostile we were reconciled to 10 Him through the death of His Son, the more certainly, after being reconciled, shall we obtain salvation through Christ's life. And not only so, but we also exult in God through our 11 Lord Jesus Christ, through whom we have now obtained our reconciliation.

Therefore as through one man sin entered into the world, 12 and through sin, death, and so death passed to all mankind, in that all sinned—(For before the Law sin was already in the 13 world; only sin is not entered in the account when no law exists. Yet death reigned from Adam to Moses, even over 14 those who had not sinned in the manner of Adam's transgression. In Adam we have a type of Him who was to come.

But it is not the same with the transgression as with 15 God's free gift.) For if through the transgression of one single man the mass of mankind have died, all the more has God's grace, and the gift made through the grace of the one man Jesus Christ, been abundant for the mass of mankind. And the gift is not comparable with the results of 16 one man's sinning; for the judgment upon that one man's sin led to condemnation, whereas the free gift after many transgressions leads to acquittal. For if, through the trans- 17 gression of one, death entered on his reign by means of one man, all the more shall those who receive God's over-flowing grace and gift of righteousness reign in life through the One—Jesus Christ.

Well, then, just as the result of a single transgression is 18 condemnation for all mankind, so also the result of a single deed of righteousness is a life-giving acquittal for all mankind. For as through the disobedience of one individual 19 the mass of mankind were made sinners, so also through the obedience of One the mass of mankind will be made right-eous. Law crept in later on, so that transgression might 20 increase. But where sin increased, all the more was grace abundant; in order that as sin has reigned and brought 21 death, so grace, too, may reign by means of righteousness leading to eternal life through Jesus Christ our Lord.

A New Life and Character
Result From Acceptance With God

6 What shall we say, then? Are we to persist in sinning in 1 order that God's grace may be the greater? God forbid! 2 How can we who have died to sin, live in it any longer? Or do 3 you not know that all of us who were baptized into Christ Jesus were baptized into His death? Well, then, by our bap- 4 tism we were buried with Him in death, in order that, just as Christ was raised from the dead by the Father's glorious power, we also should live an entirely new life. For if we have 5 become one with Him by sharing in His death, we shall also be one with Him by sharing in His resurrection. This we 6 know—that our old self was nailed to the cross with Him, in order that our sinful nature might be neutralized, so that we should no longer be the slaves of sin; for he who has died is 7 absolved from his sin.

But if we have died with Christ, we believe that we shall 8 also live with Him; because we know that Christ, once raised 9 from the dead, is no longer liable to die. Death has no longer any power over Him. For the death that He died, He died 10 once for all to sin; but the life that He lives, He lives to God.

So too do you regard yourselves as dead to sin, but as alive in 11
Christ Jesus to God.

Let not sin, then, reign in your mortal bodies, causing you 12
to be subject to their passions; and no longer offer your 13
faculties as instruments of wickedness for sin to use. But
rather offer yourselves to God as living men risen from the
dead, and your faculties to God as instruments of righteousness. For sin shall not be lord over you, since you are sub- 14
jects, not of law, but of grace.

Are we therefore to sin because we are no longer under the 15
authority of law, but under grace? God forbid! Do you not 16
know that you are the servants of the man at whose disposal
you put yourselves, to obey him—it may be servants of sin,
which leads to death, or of duty, which leads to righteousness? But thanks be to God that though you were once in 17
thralldom [slavery] to sin, you have now yielded a hearty
obedience to that kind of teaching to which you were committed. You were set free from the tyranny of sin, and 18
became the servants of righteousness—the infirmity of your 19
natures leads me to employ these familiar metaphors—
but just as you once put your faculties at the service of
impurity and of ever-increasing disregard of law, so you
must now put them at the service of righteousness, with
holiness as your goal. For when you were the servants of sin, 20
you were independent of righteousness. Well, what benefit 21
did you get then from conduct which you now regard with
shame? Why, such things finally issue in death. But now, 22
emancipated from sin and become servants of God, you
have your reward in holiness, and eternal life as the result.
For sin's wages are death; but God's free gift is eternal life in 23
Christ Jesus our Lord.

Christ Frees Us From Mere Outward Rules

7 Brethren, do you not know—for I am speaking to peo- 1
ple acquainted with law—that it is during our lifetime
that we are subject to the law? A wife, for instance, while her 2
husband is living is bound to him by law; but if her husband
dies, she is released from the law regarding her husband.
Consequently, if during her husband's life she unites herself 3
to another man, she will get the name of an adulteress; but
if her husband is dead she is free from that law, so that
though she marries again, she is not an adulteress.

So, my brethren, you also became dead to the Law through 4
the body of Christ, that you might belong to another,
namely to Him who rose from the dead that we might yield
fruit to God. For while we obeyed our lower natures, sinful 5
passions—evoked by the Law—were always at work in the
organs of our bodies, to fructify [bear fruit] and result in
death. But we are released by death from the Law by which 6
we were restrained, so that we render a service which is new
and spiritual, not old and ceremonial.

What follows? Is the Law itself a sinful thing? God forbid! 7
On the contrary, except through the Law I should have
known nothing of sin as sin. For instance, I should not have
known what covetousness is, if the Law did not say "THOU
SHALT NOT COVET" (Exodus 20:17; Deuteronomy 5:21). Sin 8
took advantage of this, and by means of the commandment
roused within me every kind of coveting; for apart from law
sin would be dead. Once I was living apart from law, but 9
when the commandment came, sin sprang into life, and I
died. The commandment designed to bring me life, brought 10
me death. For sin seized the advantage and by means of the 11
commandment beguiled me, and also put me to death. So 12
that the Law was holy, and the commandment holy, just, and

good. Did, then, this good thing become death to me? God 13
forbid! But sin did; so that it might be seen in its true light as
sin: it utilized what was good to bring about my death, that
by means of the commandment the unspeakable sinfulness
of sin might be plainly shown.

We know, indeed, that the Law is spiritual; but I am un- 14
spiritual, sold to sin. For I do not recognize what I am doing. 15
I do not act as I would, but I do what I loathe. But if I do 16
what I do not desire, I admit the excellence of the Law; and 17
now it is no longer I that do it, but the sin which has its
home within me. For I know that in me, that is, in my lower 18
self, nothing good has its home; for the wish to do right is
there, but not the power. What I do is not the good deed I 19
desire, but the evil deed I do not desire. But if I do what I do 20
not desire, it is no longer I who do it, but sin which has its
home within me.

I find therefore this rule, that when I desire to do what is 21
right, evil is there with me. In my inmost self all my sympa- 22
thy is with the law of God; but I discover in my faculties a 23
different law, at war with the law of my understanding, and
leading me captive to the law which is in my faculties—the
law of sin.

Unhappy man that I am! who will rescue me from this 24
body of death? God! to whom be thanks through Jesus Christ 25
our Lord! So then I myself serve with my understanding the
law of God, but with my lower nature the law of sin.

Christ Frees Us From Sin and Death

8 There is therefore now no condemnation for those who 1
are in Christ Jesus; for the Spirit's law—life in Christ 2
Jesus—has set me free from the law of sin and death. For 3

what was impossible to the Law—thwarted as it was by human frailty—God effected. Sending His own Son in the form of sinful humanity to deal with sin, God pronounced sentence upon sin in human nature; in order that in our case 4 the requirements of the Law might be fully met. For our lives are ruled not by our lower, but by our spiritual natures.

If men comply with their lower nature, their thoughts are 5 shaped by the lower nature; if with their spiritual nature, by the spiritual. Thoughts shaped by the lower nature mean 6 death; thoughts shaped by the spiritual mean life and peace. For thoughts shaped by the lower nature mean a state of 7 enmity to God. They do not submit to God's law, and indeed cannot. Those who obey the lower nature cannot please God. 8

You, however, are not absorbed in such things, but in 9 things spiritual, if the Spirit of God is dwelling in you; whereas if any man has not the Spirit of Christ, he does not belong to Him. But if Christ is in you, though your body is 10 dead because of sin, yet your spirit has life because of right-eousness. And if the Spirit of Him who raised up Jesus from 11 the dead is dwelling in you, He who raised up Christ from the dead will give life also to your mortal bodies through His Spirit dwelling in you.

Therefore, brethren, it is not to our lower nature that we 12 are under obligation, to live by its rule. If you so live you are 13 on your way to death; but if, by the power of the spirit, you put your merely bodily habits to death, you will live.

For all who are led by God's Spirit are God's sons. You did 14 not receive the spirit of slavery again, inspiring terror; but you 15 did receive the spirit of adopted sons—in which spirit we cry "Abba! Father!" The Spirit Himself bears witness with our own 16 spirits that we are children of God; and if children, then heirs 17 too—heirs of God and co-heirs with Christ; if indeed we share Christ's sufferings, in order to share also His glory.

Why, the sufferings of the present I deem not worth con- 18
sidering compared with the glory soon to be disclosed to us.
All creation is yearning, longing to see the manifestation of 19
the sons of God. For the creation was made subject to futility 20
not of its own choice, but by the will of Him who so subjected
it; yet with the hope that at last the creation itself would 21
be set free from the thralldom [slavery] of decay to enjoy the
liberty that comes with the glory of the children of God.

For we know that the whole of creation is moaning in the 22
pangs of childbirth until this hour. And more than that, we 23
ourselves, though we possess the Spirit as a foretaste of bliss,
yet, we ourselves inwardly moan as we wait for full sonship
in the redemption of our bodies. It is by hope that we have 24
been saved. But an object of hope is such no longer when it
is seen: for why should a man hope for what he already sees?
But if we hope for something we do not see, then we stead- 25
fastly wait for it. In the same way the Spirit also helps us in 26
our weakness; for we know not how to pray as we ought. But
the Spirit Himself pleads for us in yearnings that can find no
words, and the Searcher of hearts knows what the Spirit's 27
meaning is, because His intercessions for the saints are in
harmony with God's will.

Now we know that for those who love God He makes all 28
things work together for good, for those who are called
according to the Divine purpose. Those whom He has fore- 29
known He also has predestined to share the likeness of His
Son, that He might be the Eldest in a vast family of brothers;
and those whom He has predestined He has also called; and 30
those whom He has called He has also acquitted; and those
whom He has acquitted He has also glorified.

What, then, shall we say to this? If God is for us, who can 31
be against us? He who did not withhold even His own Son, 32
but gave Him up for all of us, will He not also with Him freely

give us all things? Who shall impeach those whom God has 33
chosen? Will God, who acquits them? Who is there to con- 34
demn them? Will Christ Jesus, who died, or rather who rose
to life again, who is also at the right hand of God, who moreover is interceding for us? Who shall separate us from Christ's 35
love? Shall affliction or distress, persecution or hunger,
nakedness or danger or the sword? As it is written, 36

"FOR THY SAKE WE ARE BEING KILLED ALL DAY LONG.

WE ARE COUNTED AS SHEEP FOR SLAUGHTER" (Psalm
44:22). Yet in all these things we are more than conquerors 37
through Him who has loved us. For I am convinced that 38
neither death nor life, nor angels nor sovereignties, nor
things present nor things future, nor powers nor height nor 39
depth, nor any other created thing, shall be able to separate
us from the love of God which is in Christ Jesus our Lord.

The Unbelief of the Jews

9 I am telling you the truth as a Christian—it is no false- 1
hood, for my inspired conscience bears me out—when 2
I declare that I have deep grief and unceasing anguish of
heart. For I could pray to be myself accursed from Christ for 3
the sake of my brethren, my natural kinsfolk, who are
Israelites; to whom belong adoption by God, His glorious 4
Presence, the covenants, the giving of the Law, the Temple
service, and the promises. To them the patriarchs belong, 5
and from them in respect of His human lineage came the
Christ, who is exalted above all, God blessed throughout the
ages. Amen.

Not, however, that God's word has failed; for not all who 6
have sprung from Israel count as Israel, nor because they 7
spring from Abraham are they all his. No! "THROUGH ISAAC

SHALL YOUR POSTERITY BE RECKONED" (Genesis 21:12).
In other words, it is not the children by natural descent who 8
are God's children, but the children made such by the
promise are regarded as Abraham's posterity. For the words 9
of the promise were, "ABOUT THIS SEASON I WILL COME,
AND SARAH SHALL HAVE A SON" (Genesis 18:10). Nor is 10
that all: there is Rebecca too. When she was with child by her
husband, our father Isaac, even then, though they were not 11
then born and had not done anything either good or evil, yet
in order that God's electing purpose might stand, based not
on their actions but on His calling them, she was told, "THE 12
ELDER WILL BE SERVANT TO THE YOUNGER" (Genesis
25:23). This agrees with another passage, "JACOB I HAVE 13
LOVED, BUT ESAU I HAVE HATED" (Malachi 1:2-3).

What, then, are we to say? That there is injustice in God? 14
God forbid! His words to Moses are, "I WILL BE MERCIFUL 15
TO WHOM I WILL, AND SHOW COMPASSION ON WHOM I
WILL"(Exodus 33:19).

From this we learn that it is not a matter of man's will 16
or endeavor, but of God's mercy. For the scripture says 17
to Pharaoh,

"IT IS FOR THIS VERY PURPOSE THAT I HAVE LIFTED
YOU SO HIGH—THAT I MAY MAKE MANIFEST IN YOU MY
POWER, AND THAT MY NAME MAY BE PROCLAIMED FAR
AND WIDE IN ALL THE EARTH" (Exodus 9:16).

This means that He has mercy on whom He will, and hard- 18
ens whom He will.

"Why, then, does God still find fault?" you will ask; "for 19
who is resisting His will?"

Nay, but who are you, a mere man, to cavil [quibble] 20
against God?

SHALL THE THING MOLDED SAY TO HIM WHO MOLDED
IT, "WHY HAVE YOU MADE ME THUS?" (Isaiah 29:16). Or 21

has not the potter rightful power over the clay, to make out of the same lump one vessel for a noble and another for an ignoble use? And what if God, while having the will to make manifest His anger and to show His power, has yet borne with great patience with the vessels of His anger who stand ready for destruction, in order to make known the wealth of His glory towards the vessels of His mercy whom He has prepared beforehand for glory, even towards us whom He has called not only from the Jews but also from the Gentiles? 22 23 24

So also in Hosea He says, 25
"I WILL CALL THAT NATION MY PEOPLE WHICH WAS NOT MY PEOPLE,
AND HER BELOVED WHO WAS NOT BELOVED.
AND IN THE PLACE WHERE IT WAS SAID TO THEM, 'YOU ARE NOT MY PEOPLE,' 26
THERE SHALL THEY BE CALLED SONS OF THE LIVING GOD" (Hosea 2:23).

And Isaiah cries concerning Israel, 27
"THOUGH THE NUMBER OF THE SONS OF ISRAEL BE LIKE THE SANDS OF THE SEA, ONLY A REMNANT SHALL BE SAVED; FOR THE LORD WILL HOLD A FINAL AND SUMMARY RECKONING UPON THE EARTH" (Isaiah 10:22, 28:22). 28

Even as Isaiah says in an earlier place, 29
"WERE IT NOT THAT THE LORD, THE GOD OF HOSTS, HAD LEFT US SOME SURVIVORS, WE SHOULD HAVE BEEN AS SODOM, AND HAVE BECOME LIKE GOMORRAH" (Isaiah 1:9).

To what conclusion does this bring us? Why, that the Gentiles, who were not in pursuit of righteousness, have grasped it—a righteousness dependent on faith; while Israel, who was in pursuit of a law that could give righteousness, has not attained to one. And why? Because it was not a righteousness based on faith, but on their deeds. They stumbled 30 31 32 at the stone of stumbling, as scripture says,   33

"SEE, I AM PLACING ON ZION A STONE TO STUMBLE AT,
A ROCK TO TRIP OVER, YET HE WHOSE FAITH RESTS UPON
IT SHALL NEVER BE DISAPPOINTED" (Isaiah 8:14, 28:16).

10 Brethren, my heart's longing, and my prayer to God is 1
for my countrymen's salvation. I bear witness that 2
they possess an enthusiasm for God, but it is an unenlight-
ened one. Ignorant of the righteousness provided by God 3
and seeking to establish their own, they have refused sub-
mission to God's righteousness. For the consummation of 4
law is Christ, to bring righteousness to every believer.

Moses writes that he who performs the righteousness 5
required by the Law shall live by that righteousness. But the 6
righteousness based on faith speaks thus:

"Say not in your heart, 'WHO SHALL ASCEND TO
HEAVEN?'"—that is, to bring Christ down; "nor 'Who shall go 7
down into the abyss?'"—that is, to bring Christ up from the
grave. But what does it say?   8

"THE WORD IS CLOSE TO YOU, IN YOUR MOUTH AND
IN YOUR HEART" (Deuteronomy 30:12-14); that is, the word
which we are publishing about the faith—that if with your 9
mouth you confess Jesus as Lord and in your heart believe
that God raised Him from the dead, you shall be saved. For 10
with the heart men believe and obtain righteousness, and
with the mouth they make confession and obtain salvation.

The scripture says, "NO ONE WHO BELIEVES IN HIM 11
SHALL BE DISAPPOINTED" (Isaiah 28:16). Jew and Greek 12
are on the same footing; the same Lord is Lord over all, rich
in blessing to all who call upon Him. For "EVERY ONE WHO 13
CALLS ON THE NAME OF THE LORD SHALL BE SAVED"
(Joel 2:32).

But how are they to call on One in whom they have not 14
believed? How are they to believe in One whose voice they
have never heard? How are they to hear without a preacher?
And how are men to preach unless they are sent? As it is 15
written, "HOW BEAUTIFUL ARE THE FEET OF THOSE WHO
BRING GOOD TIDINGS!" (Isaiah 52:7).

But, some will say, they have not all hearkened to the 16
gospel. No, for Isaiah asks, "LORD, WHO HAS BELIEVED
OUR MESSAGE?" (Isaiah 53:1). Faith, then, comes from a 17
message heard, and the message from the lips of Christ. But, 18
I ask, have they not heard? Yes, indeed:

"TO THE WHOLE WORLD THEIR VOICE HAS SOUNDED
FORTH,
AND THEIR WORDS TO THE BOUNDS OF THE EARTH"
(Psalm 19:4).

But again, did Israel fail to understand? Listen to Moses 19
first. He says,

"I WILL FIRE YOU WITH JEALOUSY AGAINST A NATION
WHICH IS NO NATION,
AND WITH FURY AGAINST A NATION DEVOID OF
UNDERSTANDING" (Deuteronomy 32:21).

And Isaiah, with strange boldness, exclaims, 20
"I HAVE BEEN FOUND BY THOSE WHO WERE NOT
LOOKING FOR ME,
I HAVE REVEALED MYSELF TO THOSE WHO WERE NOT
INQUIRING OF ME" (Isaiah 65:1).

While as to Israel he says, 21
"ALL DAY LONG I HAVE STRETCHED OUT MY HANDS
TO A SELF-WILLED AND FAULT-FINDING PEOPLE"
(Isaiah 65:2).

11 I ask, then, has God cast off His People? God forbid! 1 Why, I myself am an Israelite, of the posterity of Abraham and of the tribe of Benjamin. God has not cast off His 2 people whom He foreknew. Do you not know what scripture says in the case of Elijah—how he pleads with God against Israel, saying, "LORD, THEY HAVE PUT THY PROPHETS TO 3 DEATH, AND HAVE OVERTHROWN THINE ALTARS; AND, NOW THAT I ALONE REMAIN, THEY ARE SEEKING MY LIFE" (1 Kings 19:10)? But what is the Divine response? "I HAVE 4 RESERVED FOR MYSELF SEVEN THOUSAND MEN WHO HAVE NOT BENT KNEE TO BAAL" (1 Kings 19:18). So also at 5 the present time there has come to be a remnant—a selection by grace. But if it is by grace, it is no longer on the basis of men's 6 deeds; else grace were no longer grace.

Well, then: what Israel is pursuing it has not obtained: but 7 the elect have obtained it, and the rest have become callous. And so scripture says, 8

"GOD HAS GIVEN THEM A SPIRIT OF STUPOR—EYES TO SEE NOTHING and EARS TO HEAR NOTHING—EVEN UNTIL NOW" (Isaiah 29:10; Deuteronomy 29:4).

And David says, 9

"BE THEIR BANQUETS A SNARE AND A TRAP TO THEM,
A STUMBLING-BLOCK AND A RETRIBUTION.
BE THEIR EYES DARKENED THAT THEY SEE NOT, 10
MAKE THEIR BACKS STOOP FOR EVER" (Psalm 69:22-23).

I ask next, 11

"Have they stumbled irretrievably?" God forbid! But by their lapse salvation has come to the Gentiles so as to arouse their jealousy; and if their lapse is the enrichment of the 12 world, and their defeat the enrichment of the Gentiles, what an enrichment will follow their reinstatement!

But I speak to you who are Gentiles. Inasmuch, then, as I 13 am an apostle to Gentiles, I take pride in my ministry, trying 14

whether I can perhaps rouse my fellow Jews to jealousy and
save some of them. For if their rejection means the recon- 15
ciliation of the world, what will their reception be but life
from the dead?

Now if the first piece is holy, so also is the whole lump 16
(Numbers 15:19-21); and if the root is holy, so also are the
branches. And if some of the branches have been pruned 17
away, and you, although a wild olive, have been grafted in
among them and have become a sharer in the rich sap of the
olive root, beware of glorying over the natural branches. Or if 18
you glory, do not forget that it is not you who uphold the
root: the root upholds you.

"Branches have been lopped off," you will say, "for me to 19
be grafted in." True; for their unbelief they were lopped off, 20
and you stand only through your faith. Do not be conceited.
Tremble rather—for if God did not spare the natural 21
branches, neither will He spare you. Notice therefore God's 22
kindness and His severity: on those who have fallen His
severity comes, but upon you His kindness, provided that
you continue responsive to that kindness. Otherwise you
will be cut off also. Moreover, if they do not persist in their 23
unbelief, they too will be grafted in. For God is able to graft
them in again; and if you were cut from that which by nature 24
is a wild olive and contrary to nature were grafted into the
good olive-tree, how much more readily shall these natural
branches be grafted on their own olive-tree?

There is a secret, brethren, of which I do not wish to leave 25
you in ignorance, for fear you should be conceited, namely,
that partial blindness has fallen upon Israel until the great
mass of the Gentiles has come in; and so all Israel will be 26
saved, as is declared in scripture,

"FROM MOUNT ZION A DELIVERER WILL COME:
HE WILL REMOVE ALL UNGODLINESS FROM JACOB;

AND THIS IS THE COVENANT I WILL GRANT THEM 27
(Isaiah 59:20-21);
WHEN I HAVE TAKEN AWAY THEIR SINS" (Isaiah 27:9).

In regard to the gospel they are God's enemies for your 28
sakes; but in regard to God's election they are beloved for
their fathers' sakes. For never does God repent of His free 29
gifts or of His call. Just as you were formerly disobedient to 30
Him, but now have received mercy when they are disobedient, so they also now have been disobedient when you are 31
receiving mercy; so that they too may now receive mercy. For 32
God has imprisoned all in disobedience, that upon all alike
He may have mercy.

Oh the depth of the wealth both of the wisdom and knowl- 33
edge of God! How inscrutable His judgments, how trackless
His footsteps!

"WHO HAS KNOWN THE MIND OF THE LORD, OR 34
SHARED HIS COUNSELS?" (Isaiah 40:13-14).

"WHO HAS FIRST GIVEN GOD ANYTHING, AND THUS 35
EARNED A RECOMPENSE?" (Job 35:7, 41:11).

For all proceeds from Him, and exists by Him and for Him. 36
To Him be the glory for ever! Amen.

Practical Exhortations

12 I plead with you therefore, brethren, by the compas- 1
sion of God, to present all your faculties to Him as a
living and holy sacrifice acceptable to Him—a spiritual
mode of worship. And do not conform to the present age, 2
but be transformed by the entire renewal of your minds, so
that you may learn by experience what God's will is, namely,
all that is good and acceptable to Him and perfect.

Through the grace given me I warn every man among you 3

not to value himself unduly, but to make a sober estimate in accordance with the degree of faith God has allotted to each one. Just as we have in the one body many organs, and these 4 organs have not all the same function; so collectively we 5 form one body in Christ, while individually we serve as organs for one another. But since we have special gifts which 6 differ according to the grace bestowed upon us, if it is prophecy, let it be in exact proportion to our faith; if admin- 7 istration, let our hearts be in our ministry; the teacher's in his teaching; and the pastor's in his exhortation. One who gives 8 should be liberal; one who presides should be zealous; and one who gives help should do it cheerfully.

Let your love be sincere. Regard evil with horror; cling to 9 the right. Let your love of the brethren be true mutual affec- 10 tion; in point of precedence defer to one another. Let not 11 your zeal slacken. Have your spirits aglow as the Lord's own 12 servants, full of joyful hope, steadfast under affliction, per- sistent in prayer. Relieve the necessities of the saints; always 13 practice hospitality. Invoke blessings on your persecutors— 14 blessings, not curses. Rejoice with those who rejoice; weep 15 with those who weep. Have full sympathy with one another. 16 Do not let your thoughts be highflown [high-sounding], but accommodate yourselves to humble ways. DO NOT BE SELF-OPINIONATED (Proverbs 3:7).

Pay back to no man evil for evil. "TAKE THOUGHT FOR 17 WHAT IS RIGHT IN EVERY ONE'S ESTEEM"(Proverbs 3:4, LXX). If you can, so far as it depends on you, live at peace 18 with all the world. Never take revenge, my friends, but leave 19 it to God's wrath; for it is written, "'REVENGE BELONGS TO ME: I WILL REPAY,' says the Lord" (Deuteronomy 32:35). On 20 the contrary, "IF YOUR ENEMY IS HUNGRY, GIVE HIM FOOD; IF HE IS THIRSTY, GIVE HIM DRINK. FOR BY DOING THIS YOU WILL BE HEAPING BURNING COALS

UPON HIS HEAD" (Proverbs 25:21-22). Do not be overcome 21
by evil, but overcome evil by goodness.

13 Let every subject be obedient to the ruling authori- 1
ties, for there is no authority not under God's control,
and under His control the existing authorities have been
constituted. Therefore the man who rebels against such 2
authority is resisting God's appointment; and those who
thus resist will incur sentence. Judges and magistrates are no 3
terror to right-doers but to wrong-doers. You desire—do you
not?—to have no reason to fear your ruler. Well, do what is
right, and he will commend you. He is God's servant for your 4
benefit. But if you do what is wrong, be afraid. He does not
wear the sword to no purpose: he is God's servant—an
avenger to inflict punishment upon the wrong-doer. We 5
must obey therefore, not only for fear of punishment, but
also for conscience' sake.

This indeed is the reason you pay taxes: tax-gatherers are 6
ministers of God, devoting their energies to this very work.
Pay to all men what is due to them: tax to whom tax is due, 7
toll to whom toll, respect to whom respect, and honor to
whom honor.

Leave no debt unpaid except the standing debt of mutual 8
love; for he who loves his fellow man has fulfilled the law.
For the commandments, "THOU SHALT NOT COMMIT 9
ADULTERY," "THOU SHALT DO NO MURDER," "THOU SHALT
NOT STEAL," "THOU SHALT NOT COVET" (Exodus 20:13-17;
Deuteronomy 5:17-21), and all other commandments, are
summed up in this, "THOU SHALT LOVE THY NEIGHBOR AS
THYSELF" (Leviticus 19:18). Love avoids wronging one's neigh- 10
bor, and is therefore the fulfillment of the law.

Live thus, realizing the situation, that it is now high time to 11 rouse yourselves from sleep; for our salvation is now nearer than when we first became believers. The night is far 12 advanced; day is about to dawn. Let us therefore lay aside the deeds of darkness, and put on the armor of light. As in the 13 daytime, let us behave becomingly, not indulging in revelry and drunkenness, nor in lust and debauchery [extreme indulgence of sensual appetites], nor in quarreling and jealousy. But put on as your armor the Lord Jesus Christ, and 14 make no provision for the passions of your lower nature.

14

I now pass to another subject. Welcome among you a 1 man whose faith is weak, but not in order to pass judgment on his doubts. One man's faith allows him to eat 2 anything, while a man of weaker faith eats only vegetables. Let not the eater belittle the abstainer, nor the abstainer 3 censure [condemn] the eater, for God has accepted him. Who are you to find fault with another man's servant? 4 Whether he stands or falls is his own master's concern. But stand he will; for the Master can give him the power. One 5 man esteems one day more highly than another; another esteems all days alike. Let every one be convinced in his own mind. He who observes the day observes it for the Lord's 6 sake; and he who eats eats for the Lord's sake, for he gives thanks to God; and the abstainer abstains for the Lord's sake, and he also gives thanks to God.

For not one of us lives for himself, not one dies for himself. 7 If we live, we live for the Lord: if we die, we die for the Lord, 8 so whether we live or die we are the Lord's. For this was the 9 purpose of Christ's dying and coming to life, to be Lord both of dead and of living.

But you, why do you find fault with your brother? Or you, 10 why do you look down upon your brother? We shall all stand at the bar of God; for it is written, 11

"'AS I LIVE,' says the Lord, 'TO ME EVERY KNEE SHALL BOW, AND EVERY TONGUE SHALL GIVE PRAISE TO GOD'" (Isaiah 45:23).

Therefore every one of us will give account of himself to God. 12

Therefore let us no longer censure [condemn] one another, but rather do you come to this decision, not to put any obstacle or stumbling-block in your brother's path. I know and feel assured in the Lord Jesus that in itself nothing is "impure"; but if any one regards anything as impure, to him it is so. 13 14

Still, if your brother is pained by the food you are eating, you are no longer following the guidance of love. Do not by your food ruin a man for whom Christ died. Therefore do not let what is a boon [blessing] to you and others bring reproach. For the Kingdom of God does not consist in eating and drinking, but in uprightness, peace, and joy in the Holy Spirit; and whoever in this way serves Christ pleases God and is approved by men. 15 16 17 18

Therefore let us aim at whatever makes for peace and the spiritual upbuilding of one another. Do not for food's sake be throwing down God's work. All food is pure; but a man is in the wrong if his food is a stumbling-block to others. The right course is to forgo eating meat or drinking wine or doing anything that tends to your brother's fall. 19 20 21

As to your faith, keep it to yourself and to God. Happy the man who does not censure [condemn] himself in the deeds he approves. But one who has misgivings stands self-condemned if he eats, because his act is not based on faith; for all action not so based is sin. 22 23

15 Our duty if we are strong is to bear with the weaknesses of those who are not strong, and not seek our own pleasure. Let each of us endeavor to please his neighbor, aiming at his spiritual upbuilding. For indeed Christ did not seek His own pleasure, but exemplified that scripture, "THE REPROACHES OF THOSE THAT REPROACH THEE HAVE FALLEN ON ME" (Psalm 69:9). All that was written of old has been written for our instruction, that with steadfastness and the comfort derived from the scriptures we may sustain our hope. And may the God of steadfastness and of comfort grant you full sympathy with one another after the example of Christ Jesus, that with oneness of heart and voice you may glorify the God and Father of your Lord Jesus Christ.

Therefore welcome one another, just as Christ has welcomed you, to promote the glory of God. My meaning is that Christ has become a servant to the circumcised in vindication of God's truthfulness—to fulfill the promises made to our forefathers—and to make the Gentiles glorify God for His mercy. So it is written,

"FOR THIS REASON I WILL PRAISE THEE AMONG
THE GENTILES AND SING PSALMS TO THY NAME"
(Psalm 18:49).
And again the Psalmist says,

"BE GLAD, YE GENTILES, IN COMPANY WITH HIS
PEOPLE" (Deuteronomy 32:43).
And again,

"PRAISE THE LORD, ALL YE GENTILES,
AND LET ALL THE NATIONS EXTOL HIM" (Psalm 117:1).
And again Isaiah says,

"THERE SHALL COME THE OFFSPRING OF JESSE,
ONE WHO RISES UP TO RULE THE GENTILES.
ON HIM SHALL THE GENTILES BUILD THEIR HOPES"
(Isaiah 11:1, 10).

May God, the giver of hope, fill you with all joy and peace 13
because you trust in Him—so that you may be overflowing
with hope through the power of the Holy Spirit.

Personal Explanations

But as to you, brethren, I am in my very heart convinced 14
that you yourselves are full of goodness, and equipped with
all knowledge and competent to advise one another. But my 15
letter is at times rather bold, by way of stimulating your own
recollection, because of God's grant to me in His grace, that 16
I should be a minister of Christ Jesus to the Gentiles, doing a
priest's service to God's gospel, that the Gentiles consecrated
by the Holy Spirit may prove an acceptable offering to Him.
I have therefore my reason to boast of my relation to God in 17
Christ Jesus.

For I will not venture to say a word of what Christ has done 18
through me in converting the Gentiles, by word and by deed,
with power manifested in signs and marvels, with the power 19
of the Holy Spirit; so that, beginning from Jerusalem and the
surrounding districts, I have preached without reserve even
as far as Illyricum the gospel of Christ. Herein I made it my 20
aim not to preach the gospel where Christ's name was
already known, for fear I should be building on another
man's foundation. As scripture says, 21

"THOSE WHO HAVE NOT BEEN TOLD ABOUT HIM
SHALL SEE,
AND THOSE WHO HAVE NOT HEARD SHALL UNDER-
STAND" (Isaiah 52:15).

And it is really this which has again and again prevented 22
my coming to you. But now, as there is no more opening in 23
this part of the world, and I have for years past been eager to
pay you a visit, I hope, when I am on my way to Spain, to see 24

you in passing and be helped forward by you, when I have first enjoyed being with you for a time.

But at present I am going to Jerusalem to serve the saints, 25 for Macedonia and Greece have thought it good to con- 26 tribute a certain sum in relief of the poor among the saints in Jerusalem. Yes, they have thought it good, and in fact it was a 27 debt they owed them. For seeing that the Gentiles have been admitted into partnership in their spiritual blessings, they in turn are bound to serve them with material benefits. So after 28 discharging this duty, and making sure that these gifts reach their destination, I shall start for Spain, visiting you on my way; and I know that when I come to you it will be with rich 29 blessing from Christ.

But I entreat you, brethren, in the name of our Lord Jesus 30 Christ and by the love which His Spirit inspires, to join with me in very earnest prayer to God on my behalf, that I may 31 escape unhurt from the unbelievers in Judaea, and that my service to Jerusalem may be well received by the saints there, in order that if God be willing I may come to you with a glad 32 heart, and may enjoy a time of rest with you. May the God of 33 peace be with you all! Amen.

Conclusion

16 Herewith I introduce to you our sister Phoebe, who is 1 a servant of the Church at Cenchreae, that you may 2 receive her in the Lord's name in a manner worthy of saints, and may assist her in any matter in which she may need help. For she has indeed befriended many, including myself.

Greetings to Prisca and Aquila, my fellow laborers in 3 Christ Jesus—friends who have endangered their own lives 4 for mine. I am grateful to them, and not I alone, but all the

Gentile churches also. Greetings, too, to the church that meets at their house. 5

Greetings to my dear Epaenetus, who was the earliest convert to Christ in the province of Asia; to Mary who has labored 6 strenuously for you; and to Andronicus and Junias, my 7 countrymen, who once shared my imprisonment. They are of note among the apostles, and have been Christians longer than I myself. Greetings to Ampliatus, dear to me in the Lord; 8 to Urban, our fellow laborer in Christ, and to my dear Stachys. 9 Greetings to Apelles—that veteran believer—and to the 10 members of the household of Aristobulus. Greetings to my 11 countryman, Herodion; and to the believing members of the household of Narcissus. Greetings to those Christian workers, 12 Tryphaena and Tryphosa; also to dear Persis, who has labored strenuously in the Lord's work. Greetings to Rufus, who is the 13 Lord's elect; and to his mother, who has also been a mother to me. Greetings to Asyncritus, Phlegon, Hermes, Patrobas, 14 Hermas, and to the brethren associated with them; to 15 Philologus and Julia, Nereus and his sister and Olympas, and to all the saints associated with them.

Salute one another with a holy kiss. 16

All the churches of Christ send greetings to you.

But I beseech you, brethren, to keep a watch on those who 17 are causing divisions and occasions of stumbling among you, in defiance of the instruction which you have received; and to shun them. For men of that stamp are not servants of 18 our Lord, but of their own appetites; and by their plausible words and their flattery they deceive simple minds. Your 19 fidelity to the truth is everywhere known. I rejoice over you, therefore, but I wish you to be wise in what is good, and innocent in what is evil. And, before long, the God of peace 20 will crush Satan under your feet. The grace of our Lord Jesus Christ be with you!

Timothy, my fellow worker, sends you greetings, and so do 21
my countrymen Lucius, Jason, and Sosipater. I, Tertius, who 22
write this letter, greet you in the Lord. Gaius, my host, who is 23
also the host of the whole Church, greets you. So do Erastus,
the treasurer of the city, and Quartus our brother.

To Him who is able to make you strong, according to the 25
gospel I preach, and the proclamation concerning Jesus
Christ, in harmony with the unveiling of the mystery
shrouded in silence in past ages, but now brought to light, 26
and by the command of the eternal God made known
through the writings of the prophets among all the Gentiles
to win them to obedience to the faith—to God, the only wise, 27
through Jesus Christ, even to Him be the glory through all
the ages. Amen.

THE FIRST EPISTLE OF PAUL
TO THE CORINTHIANS

Introduction

1 Paul, called to be an apostle of Christ Jesus by the will of 1
God, and our brother Sosthenes, to the church of God in 2
Corinth, men and women consecrated in Christ Jesus, called
to be saints, with all in any place who call on the name of our
Lord Jesus Christ—their Lord as well as ours: grace and peace 3
be to you from God our Father and the Lord Jesus Christ.

I thank my God continually for the grace of God bestowed 4
on you in Christ Jesus—that in Him you have been enriched 5
with everything, with readiness of speech and fullness of
knowledge. Thus my testimony to Christ has been con- 6
firmed in your case, so that there is no special gift in which 7
you come short while waiting for the revealing of our Lord
Jesus Christ. He will also confirm you to the end, so that you 8
may be free from reproach on the day of our Lord Jesus
Christ. God is ever faithful, and by Him you were called into 9
fellowship with His Son Jesus Christ, our Lord.

The Divisions in the Corinthian Church

I entreat you all, brethren, in the name of our Lord Jesus 10
Christ, to avoid disputes and divisions, and to be in perfect
harmony in your minds and judgments. For I have been 11
informed, my brethren, by Chloe's people, that there are dis-
sensions among you. What I mean is that each of you says, "I 12
am a follower of Paul"; "I of Apollos"; "I of Cephas"; "I of

Christ." Is Christ split up? Was Paul crucified for you? Or were 13
you baptized into the name of Paul? I thank God that I did 14
not baptize any of you except Crispus and Gaius—for fear 15
people should say that you were baptized into my name. I 16
did, however, baptize Stephanas's household as well: but I do
not know that I baptized any one else.

Christ did not send me to baptize, but to preach the 17
gospel; and not with merely clever words—lest the cross of
Christ should be frustrated. For the story of the cross is fool- 18
ishness to those who are on the way to perdition, but it is the
power of God to those whom He is saving. For so it is written, 19
"I WILL BAFFLE THE WISDOM OF THE WISE, AND THE
ACUTENESS OF THE ACUTE I WILL THWART" (Isaiah
29:14). Where is your wise man? Where your scholar? Where 20
your disputant of this present age? Has not God stultified
[made to seem foolish] the world's wisdom?

For when by God's wise ordinance the world by its wisdom 21
had failed to gain the knowledge of God, God was pleased, by
the foolishness of the preaching, to save those who believe;
seeing that Jews demand miracles, and Greeks pursue 22
wisdom, while we proclaim a crucified Christ—to Jews a 23
stumbling-block, to Gentiles foolishness, but to those who are 24
called, whether Jews or Greeks, Christ the power of God and
the wisdom of God. Because the foolishness of God is wiser 25
than men, and the weakness of God is stronger than men.

For consider, brethren, your own calling. Not many 26
worldly-wise, not many influential, not many of noble
birth have been called. But God has chosen the foolish 27
things of the world in order to shame its wise men; and God
has chosen the weak things of the world in order to shame
what is strong; and the mean and despised things of the 28
world—things that are nothing—God has chosen in order
to bring to nothing things that are; to prevent any mortal 29

man from boasting before God. But thanks to Him you are in 30
Christ Jesus: He has become our wisdom from God, which
is righteousness and sanctification and redemption; that 31
it may be as scripture says, "HE WHO BOASTS—LET HIS
BOAST BE IN THE LORD" (Jeremiah 9:24).

2 For my part, brethren, when I came to you, it was not 1
with superiority of speech or wisdom that I came,
announcing to you the testimony of God. For I determined 2
not to know anything when among you except Jesus Christ,
and a crucified Jesus Christ. It was in weakness and fear and 3
great trepidation that I was among you. And my language 4
and my preaching were not armed with persuasive words of
wisdom, but with the convincing power of the Spirit; so that 5
your trust might rest not on the wisdom of man, but on the
power of God.

Yet there is a wisdom that we utter among the mature; a 6
wisdom, however, not deriving from the present age nor
from the powers who are in control of this age—though
their days are numbered. We speak God's wisdom in a 7
mystery—that hidden wisdom which, before the world
began, God purposed for our glory; a wisdom which not 8
one of the powers who control the present age has learned;
for if they had learned it, they would not have crucified the
Lord of glory. But we speak—to use the words of scripture— 9
of THINGS WHICH EYE HAS NOT SEEN NOR EAR HEARD,
and which have not entered the heart of man: ALL THAT
GOD HAS IN READINESS FOR THEM THAT LOVE HIM
(Isaiah 64:4). For to us God has revealed them through the 10
Spirit; for the Spirit searches everything, including the
deeps of God.

For who among men knows a man's thoughts, except the 11

man's own spirit within him? In the same way also only God's Spirit is acquainted with God's thoughts. But we have not 12 received the spirit of the world, but the Spirit which comes from God, that we may know what is freely given us by God. This we also utter, not in language which man's wisdom 13 teaches us, but in that which the Spirit teaches, adapting spiritual words to spiritual truths. The unspiritual man 14 rejects the teachings of the Spirit of God; to him they are folly, and he cannot learn them, because they are spiritually appraised. But the spiritual man appraises everything, 15 although he is himself appraised by no one. For WHO HAS 16 LEARNED THE MIND OF THE LORD, SO AS TO INSTRUCT HIM? (Isaiah 40:13). But we have the mind of Christ.

3 And I myself, brethren, could not speak to you as to 1 spiritual men: it had to be as to worldlings [worldly persons]—mere babes in Christ. I fed you with milk and not 2 with solid food, since for this you were not yet strong enough. Why, even now you are not strong enough: you are still un- 3 spiritual. For so long as there are jealousy and strife among you, are you not unspiritual and behaving like mere men? For when one says, "I am for Paul," and another, "I am for 4 Apollos," are you not mere men?

What, then, is Apollos? And what is Paul? Men through 5 whose ministry, and as the Lord granted power to each, you came to believe. I planted, Apollos watered; but it was God 6 who caused the growth. So that neither the planter nor the 7 waterer is anything, but God who causes the growth. Now 8 in effect the planter and the waterer are one; and yet each will receive his own reward, answering to his own work. We 9 are fellow workers in God's service, you are God's field— God's building.

In exercise of the grace given me by God, I, like a competent master-builder, have laid a foundation, and others are building upon it. But let every one be careful how he builds. For no one can lay any foundation other than that which is already laid, namely, Jesus Christ. And whether the building which any one erects on that foundation be of gold or silver or costly stones, or of timber or hay or straw—the character of each man's work will appear. For the Day will disclose it, because that Day is to reveal itself in fire, and it is the fire which shall test the quality of every one's work. If the work which any one has erected stands the test, he shall be rewarded. If any one's work is burned up, he will suffer loss; he will himself be rescued, but only, as it were, by escaping through the fire.

Do you not know that you are God's sanctuary, and that the Spirit of God dwells within you? If any one destroys the sanctuary of God, God will destroy him; for the sanctuary of God is sacred, and this sanctuary you are.

Let no one deceive himself. If any man among you imagines that he is wise with the wisdom of the present age, let him become "foolish" so that he may be wise. This world's wisdom is foolishness to God; for it is written, "HE SNARES THE WISE WITH THEIR OWN CUNNING" (Job 5:13). And again, "THE LORD KNOWS THAT THE REASONINGS OF THE WISE ARE USELESS" (Psalm 94:11). Therefore let no one boast about men. For everything is yours—be it Paul, be it Apollos, be it Cephas, be it the world, be it life, be it death, be it the present, be it the future—everything is yours; and you are Christ's and Christ is God's.

4 This is how men should think of us—we are Christ's servants, and stewards of God's secret truths. In this

connection further what is required in stewards is to prove faithful. I, however, am very little concerned at undergoing 3 your scrutiny, or that of any human tribunal [court]; in fact I do not even scrutinize myself. Though I am not conscious of any 4 fault, yet I am not thereby acquitted; but He who scrutinizes me is the Lord. Therefore form no premature judgments, but 5 wait until the Lord comes. He will both bring to light the secrets of darkness and will disclose the motives that have been in people's hearts; and then each man's praise will come to him from God.

Now these considerations, brethren, I have specially 6 applied to Apollos and myself, for your sakes, in order to teach you by our example the maxim [principle] not to exceed what is written; so that you may not be arrogant champions of one teacher against another.

Why, who gives you your superiority, my brother? Or what 7 have you that you did not receive? And if you did receive it, why boast as if you had not?

You all have already all you can wish; already you have 8 grown rich; without us, you have ascended the throne! Ay [Yes], would to God that you had ascended the throne, that we also might reign with you! It seems to me that God 9 has exhibited us apostles last of all, like men condemned to death; for we have become a spectacle to all creation—alike to angels and to men. We rank as fools for Christ's sake: you 10 are shrewd men in Christ. We are weaklings: you are strong. You are in high repute: we are outcasts. To this very moment 11 we endure both hunger and thirst; we are barely clad and roughly handled. Homes we have none. We tire ourselves out 12 working with our own hands. When reviled, we bless; when persecuted, we bear it patiently; when slandered, we try to 13 conciliate [reconcile]. We are regarded as the scum of the earth—the dregs of the world, even to this hour.

I am not writing this to shame you, but to advise you as my 14
beloved children. For even if you were to have ten thousand 15
tutors in Christ, yet you would not have several fathers. It is
I who in Christ Jesus became your father through the gospel.
I entreat you therefore to become like me. For this reason I 16
have sent Timothy to you. He is my beloved and faithful 17
child in the Lord. He will remind you of my conduct as a
Christian teacher—the manner in which I teach everywhere
in every Church.

But some of you have grown arrogant, as though I were 18
not coming to you. But I shall come to you soon if the Lord 19
wills, and I shall discover not the fine speeches of these arrogant people, but their power. For God's Kingdom is not a 20
thing of words, but of power. What will you have? Shall I 21
come to you with a rod, or in a loving and tender spirit?

A Stern Rebuke

5 It is actually reported that there is licentiousness 1
among you, and of a kind unheard of even among the
Gentiles—a man has his father's wife! And you, instead of 2
mourning and removing from among you the man who has
done this deed, are self-complacent! I for my part, present 3
with you in spirit although absent in body, have already, as
though I were present, judged him who has so acted. In the 4
name of our Lord Jesus, assembled in spirit with you, along
with the power of our Lord Jesus, I have handed over such a 5
man to Satan for the destruction of his body, that his spirit
may be saved on the day of the Lord Jesus.

It is no good thing—this boast of yours. Do you not know 6
that a little leaven leavens the whole of the dough? Clear out 7
the old leaven so that you may be a new dough; for in fact you

are free from that leaven. For our Passover lamb has been sacrificed—Christ! Therefore let us keep our festival, not with old 8
leaven nor with the leaven of villainy and mischief, but with
bread free from leaven—the bread of sincerity and of truth.

I wrote to you in that letter not to be associated with licen- 9
tious people; not meaning that you must wholly avoid the 10
licentious of this world, or the avaricious and grasping, or
idolaters. For then you would have to go out of the world
altogether. But what I actually meant was that you are not to 11
be associated with any one bearing the name of "brother," if
he is licentious or avaricious or idolatrous or scurrilous
[using coarse language] or drunken or grasping. With such a
man you ought not even to eat. Is it my business to judge 12
outsiders? Is it not those who are within the Church whom
you are to judge? Those who are outside God will judge. 13
"REMOVE THE WICKED MAN FROM AMONG YOU"
(Deuteronomy 22:24).

Litigation at Corinth

6 If one of you has a grievance against an opponent, does 1
he dare to go to law before wicked men and not before
the saints? Do you not know that the saints shall judge the 2
world? And if you are the court before which the world is
judged, are you unequal to these pettiest cases? Do you not 3
know that we are to judge angels, not to mention matters of
this life? If therefore you have matters of this life to be de- 4
cided, is it men who have no standing at all in the Church
whom you make your judges? I say this to your shame. Is 5
there not then among you a single wise man competent to
decide between brethren, but brother goes to law with 6
brother, and that before unbelievers?

Even now it is altogether a token of your defeat that 7
you have lawsuits with one another. Why not rather be
wronged? Why not rather be defrauded? On the contrary, 8
you yourselves inflict wrong and fraud, and upon brethren
too. Do you not know that wicked men will not inherit 9
God's Kingdom?

Make no mistake. Neither the licentious, nor idolaters, nor
adulterers, nor men guilty of unnatural crime, nor thieves, 10
nor avaricious, nor drunken nor scurrilous [using coarse
language] nor grasping people shall inherit God's Kingdom.
And such were some of you. But you have washed, you have 11
been consecrated, you have been acquitted, in the name of
our Lord Jesus Christ and through the Spirit of our God.

"Everything is allowable to me," but not everything is prof- 12
itable. "Everything is allowable to me," but to nothing will I
become enslaved. "Food is for the stomach, and the stomach 13
is for food," and God will bring both of them to nothing. The
body is not for licentiousness, but for the Lord, and the Lord
is for the body; and as God by His power raised the Lord, so 14
He will also raise us.

Do you not know that your bodies are members of Christ? 15
Shall I, then, take the members of Christ and make them
members of a harlot? God forbid! Or do you not know that a 16
man who is tied to a harlot is one with her in body? For God
says, "THE TWO SHALL BECOME ONE" (Genesis 2:24). But 17
he who is tied to the Lord is one with Him in spirit. Flee from 18
licentiousness. Any other sin that a man commits is outside
the body; but the licentious man sins against his own body.
Or do you not know that your body is a sanctuary of the Holy 19
Spirit within you—the Spirit whom you have from God? And
you are not your own, for you have been bought at a price. 20
Glorify God, then, in your bodies.

The Subject of Marriage

7 Now as to the topics of your letter. It is better for a man to abstain from marriage. There is, however, so much licentiousness that every man should have a wife of his own, and every woman should have a husband of her own. Let the husband pay his wife her due, and let a woman also pay her husband his. A wife has not the control of her own person, but her husband has. In the same way a husband has not the control of his own person, but his wife has. Do not deprive one another—unless by mutual consent for a time, so that you may devote yourselves to prayer and then associate again; otherwise Satan may tempt you because of your lack of self-control.

I say this by way of concession, not of command. Yet I would have everybody be as I am; but each of us has his own special gift from God—one of one kind and another of another.

But I say to the unmarried, and to widows, that it is well for them to remain as I am. If, however, they cannot control themselves, let them marry; for marriage is better than the fever of passion. But to those already married my instructions—yet not mine, but the Lord's—are, that a wife is not to be separated from her husband; or if she is separated, let her either remain unmarried or be reconciled to him; and that a husband is not to put away his wife.

To the rest it is I who speak—not the Lord. If a brother has a wife who is an unbeliever, and she consents to live with him, let him not put her away. And a woman who has an unbelieving husband—if he consents to live with her, let her not put him away. For the unbelieving husband is hallowed by union with a Christian woman, and the unbelieving wife is hallowed by union with a Christian brother. Otherwise your children would be unholy, but in reality they are holy. If, 15 however, the unbeliever is determined to separate, let him do so. In such circumstances the Christian man or woman is no slave; God has called us to be at peace. For how do you 16 know, O woman, if you will save your husband? Or how do you know, O man, if you will save your wife?

Only, whatever the condition which the Lord has assigned 17 to each one—and whatever his condition when God called him—in that let him continue. This is what I enjoin in all the churches. Was any one already circumcised when he 18 was called? Let him not try to disguise it. Was any one uncircumcised when called? Let him remain uncircumcised. Circumcision is nothing, and uncircumcision is nothing: 19 obedience to God's commandments is everything. Let each 20 man remain in the condition in which he was called. Were 21 you a slave when God called you? Never mind. (And yet if you can get your freedom, you had better take it.) For a slave 22 who has received his calling in the Lord is the Lord's freedman, and in the same way a free man, if called, is the slave of Christ. You have been bought at a price: do not become 23 slaves to men. Where each one was when he was called, 24 there, brethren, let him still stand—close to God.

Concerning unmarried women I have no order from the 25 Lord; but I give an opinion, as one who through the Lord's mercy is trustworthy. I think, then, that, in view of the imminent distress, it is well for a man to remain as he is. Are you 27 bound to a wife? Do not seek to become free. Are you free from a wife? Do not seek for a wife. Yet if you get married, you 28 have not sinned; and if a maiden gets married, she has not sinned. Such people, however, will have outward trouble. But I am for sparing you.

Yet this I tell you, brethren: the time has been shortened: 29 for the future let those who have wives be as though they had

none, those who weep as though they did not weep, those 30
who rejoice as though they did not rejoice, those who buy as
though they did not keep, and those who use the world as 31
though not using it to the full. For the form of this world is
passing away. But I would have you free from anxiety. An 32
unmarried man's anxiety is about the Lord's business—how
to please the Lord; but a married man is anxious about the 33
concerns of the world—how to please his wife, and he is
drawn two ways. And the unmarried woman or maid is anx- 34
ious about the Lord's business—to be holy both in body and
in spirit; but the married woman is anxious about the concerns of the world—how to please her husband. This I say in 35
your own interest; not to put shackles on you, but to promote seemliness and undistracted devotion to the Lord.

If, however, any one thinks that he is acting unfairly 36
towards his betrothed, if his passions are strong and necessity urges, let him do as he pleases; there is no sin; let them
marry. But the man who is steadfast in his resolve, who is not 37
driven by necessity, but has control where his will is concerned, and has determined to keep his betrothed as she is,
will do well. So, then, he who marries his betrothed does 38
well, and yet he who does not marry will do better.

A woman is bound to her husband as long as he lives; but 39
if he dies, she is free to marry whom she will, only in the
Lord. But in my judgment, she is happier if she remains as 40
she is; and I think that I also have the Spirit of God.

Idol Sacrifices

8 Now as to things that have been sacrificed to idols. We 1
are aware that "we all have knowledge." "Knowledge"
puffs up; but love builds up. If any one imagines that he has 2

any knowledge, he never yet came to know as he ought to know; but if any one loves God, that man is known by God. 3 Well now, as to eating things which have been sacrificed to 4 idols, we are aware that an idol is nothing whatever, and that there is no God but One. If, indeed, there are so-called gods, 5 either in heaven or on earth—and in fact there are gods many and lords many—yet for us there is but one God, the 6 Father, who is the source of all things, and for whom we exist, and but one Lord, Jesus Christ, through whom we and all things exist.

But not every one has this knowledge. Some, through 7 being accustomed to idols hitherto [until now], eat idol sacrifices as such; and their consciences, being but weak, are polluted. It is true that food will not bring us near to God; we 8 neither lose if we abstain, nor gain if we eat. But take care lest 9 this liberty of yours should prove any obstacle to the weak. For if any one sees you, who have that knowledge, reclining 10 at table in an idol's temple, will not his conscience (supposing him to be weak) be emboldened [given courage] to eat the food which has been sacrificed to the idol? Why, your 11 knowledge is the ruin of the weak believer—your brother, for whom Christ died! Besides, when you thus sin against the 12 brethren and wound their weak consciences, you are sinning against Christ. Therefore if food is the cause of my brother's 13 fall, I will eat no flesh as long as I live, for fear I should cause my brother's fall.

9 Am I not free? Am I not an apostle? Have I not seen 1 Jesus, our Lord? Are you not yourselves the evidence of my work in the Lord? If to other men I am not an apostle, yet 2 at least I am to you; for your conversion is the seal on my apostleship. That is how I vindicate myself to my critics. 3

Have we not a right to food and drink? Have we not a right 4
to take a Christian wife about with us, as the rest of the apos- 5
tles do—and the Lord's brothers and Cephas? Or again, is it 6
only Barnabas and myself who have no right to give up
working for our living? What soldier ever serves at his own 7
cost? Who plants a vineyard and yet does not eat the grapes?
Or who tends a flock and yet does not taste their milk?

Am I saying merely what men say? Does not the Law say 8
the same? For in the law of Moses it is written, 9

"THOU SHALT NOT MUZZLE AN OX WHILE IT IS
TREADING OUT THE GRAIN" (Deuteronomy 25:4).

Is God thinking about oxen? Or is it in our interest that He 10
speaks? Of course, it was written in our interest, because the
plowman is meant to plow, and the thresher to thresh, in the
hope of sharing in the produce.

If we sowed the spiritual grain in you, is it a great thing that 11
we should reap a temporal harvest from you? If other teach- 12
ers share that right over you, do not we possess it much
more? Yet we have not availed ourselves of the right, but we
endure everything patiently rather than cause the least
impediment to the gospel of Christ. Do you not know that 13
those who perform the sacred rites have their food from
the sacred place, and that those who serve at the altar have
their share of the altar-gifts? In the same way the Lord also 14
directed those who proclaim the gospel to get their living by
the gospel.

But I have not taken advantage of any of these rights. Nor 15
do I now write with that object so far as I am concerned, for
I would rather die than have anybody make this boast of
mine an empty one. If I preach the gospel, that is nothing for 16
me to boast of; for I feel compelled to do so; alas for me, if I
fail to preach it! And if I do it voluntarily, I have my reward; 17
but if against my will, a stewardship has nevertheless been

entrusted to me. What is my reward, then? To make the 18
gospel free of charge when I preach, so that I do not exhaust
my privileges as a Christian preacher.

Though free from all men, I have made myself the slave of 19
all, in the hope of winning as many converts as possible. To 20
the Jews I have become like a Jew in order to win Jews; to
men under the Law as if I were under the Law—although I
myself am not—in order to win those who are under the
Law; to men without Law as if I were without Law—although 21
I am not without God's Law—being subject to Christ's law—
in order to win those who are without Law. To the weak I 22
have become weak so as to gain the weak. To all men I have
become all things, in the hope that by all possible means I
may save some. And all I do is for the sake of the gospel, that 23
I may get my share in it.

Do you not know that in the foot-race, while the runners all 24
run, only one gets the prize? Run so as to win. But every man 25
in training is temperate in all things. They indeed do this to
win a fading wreath, but we an unfading one. I, then, so run, 26
as with no uncertain aim. I am a boxer who does not beat the
air; I bruise my body and make it my slave, lest possibly, after 27
being a herald to others, I myself should be rejected.

10 For I would have you know, brethren, that our fore- 1
fathers were all of them under the cloud, and all got
through the sea. All were pledged to Moses by baptism in the 2
cloud and the sea. All ate the same spiritual food, and all 3
drank the same spiritual drink; for they drank from the spir- 4
itual rock that went with them—and that rock was Christ.
But with most of them God was not well pleased; for they 5
were laid low in the desert.

And this serves as a warning to us, not to hanker as they 6

did after evil. And you must not be idolaters, as some of 7
them were, as it is written,

"THE PEOPLE SAT DOWN TO EAT AND DRINK, AND
STOOD UP TO PLAY" (Exodus 32:6).

Nor may we be licentious, as some of them were, and on a 8
single day twenty-three thousand of them fell. And let us not 9
try the Lord's forbearance, as some of them did, and they
were destroyed by serpents. And do not grumble, as some 10
of them did, and they were destroyed by the Destroyer.
All this happened to them by way of warning; but it was re- 11
corded by way of admonition to us who live in the last days
of the world.

So, then, let the man who thinks he stands secure beware 12
of falling. No temptation has overtaken you but such as is 13
common to men; and God is faithful and will not allow you
to be tempted beyond your strength; but when the temptation comes, He will also provide the way out, so that you may
be able to bear it.

Therefore, my dear friends, keep clear of idolatry. I speak 14
as to men of sense; judge for yourselves what I say. The cup 15
of blessing which we bless, does it not mean participation in 16
the blood of Christ? The bread which we break, does it not
mean participation in the body of Christ?

Since there is one bread, we, many as we are, are one body; 17
we all of us share in that one bread. Look at Israel—the 18
nation. Are not those who eat the sacrifices partakers in the
altar? Do I mean that a thing sacrificed to an idol is anything, 19
or that an idol is anything? No, but what men sacrifice, they 20
sacrifice to demons, not to God; and I would not have you
prove partakers with demons. You cannot drink the Lord's 21
cup and the cup of demons: you cannot be partakers both in
the table of the Lord and in the table of demons. Or are we 22
arousing the Lord to jealousy? Are we stronger than He is?

"Everything is allowable," but not everything is profitable. 23
"Everything is allowable," but everything does not edify.
Let no one seek his own good, but let each seek that of his 24
fellow man.

Anything that is sold in the market eat, and ask no ques- 25
tions for conscience' sake; for THE EARTH IS THE LORD'S, 26
AND ALL THAT IT CONTAINS (Psalm 24:1). If an unbeliever 27
invites you and you consent to go, eat whatever is put before
you, and ask no questions for conscience' sake. But if any one 28
tells you, "This food has been offered in sacrifice," abstain
from eating it for the sake of him who warned you, and for
conscience' sake—I mean his conscience, not your own. For 29
why is my personal freedom to be decided by another man's
conscience? If I partake with a grateful heart, why am I to be 30
maligned in regard to a thing for which I give thanks?

Whether, then, you eat or drink, or whatever you do, let 31
everything be done to the glory of God.

Do not be causes of stumbling either to Jews or to Greeks 32
or to the church of God. That is how I too seek in everything 33
the approval of all men, not aiming at my own profit, but at
that of the many, in the hope that they may be saved.

11 Be imitators of me, as I myself am an imitator of Christ. 1
Now I commend you for remembering me in every- 2
thing, and for keeping my instructions just as I delivered
them to you. I would have you know, however, that of every 3
man Christ is the head, that the head of a woman is her husband, and that the head of Christ is God. A man who wears a 4
veil when praying or prophesying dishonors his head; but a 5
woman who prays or prophesies with her head uncovered
dishonors her head, for she is exactly the same as a woman
who is shorn.

If a woman will not wear a veil, let her also cut off her hair. 6
But since it is a dishonor to a woman to have her hair cut off
or to be shaved, let her wear a veil. For a man ought not to 7
have a veil on his head, since he is the image and glory of
God; while woman is the glory of man. Man does not origi- 8
nate from woman, but woman from man. For man was not 9
created for woman's sake, but woman for man's. That is why 10
a woman ought to have on her head a symbol of subjection,
because of the angels. Yet, in the Lord, woman is not inde- 11
pendent of man nor man of woman. For just as woman 12
originates from man, so also man has his birth through
woman; but everything comes ultimately from God.

Judge for yourselves: is it seemly for a woman to pray 13
unveiled to God? Does not nature itself teach you that if a 14
man has long hair, it is a dishonor to him; but that if a 15
woman has long hair, it is her glory, because her hair was
given her for a covering? But if any one is inclined to be con- 16
tentious on the point, we have no such custom, nor have the
churches of God.

Matters Relating to Christian Worship

But while giving you this injunction I cannot praise you, in 17
that you meet together not for the better but for the worse.
In the first place, I hear that when you meet as a church there 18
are divisions among you; and I partly believe it. For there 19
must necessarily be differences of opinion among you, in
order to show who are the men of worth among you.

When, however, you meet together, there is no eating the 20
Supper of the Lord; for every one seizes first his own supper, 21
and one remains hungry, while another drinks to excess.
Why, have you no homes in which to eat and drink? Or 22
would you show your contempt for the church of God and

shame those who are poor? What shall I say to you? Shall I praise you? In this matter I do not praise you.

For it was from the Lord that I received what in turn I 23 handed on to you—that the Lord Jesus, on the night He was betrayed, took bread, and after giving thanks, He broke it 24 and said,

"This is my body which is broken for you. Do this in memory of me."

In the same way when the meal was over, He also took 25 the cup.

"This cup," He said, "is the new covenant as sealed with my blood. Do this, every time that you drink it, in memory of me."

For every time that you eat this bread and drink from the 26 cup, you proclaim the Lord's death—until He comes. Whoever, therefore, eats the bread or drinks from the cup of 27 the Lord in an unworthy manner sins against the body and blood of the Lord. Let a man examine himself, and having 28 done that, let him eat the bread and drink from the cup. For 29 any one who eats and drinks, if he fails to understand the body, eats and drinks to his own condemnation. That is why 30 many among you are sickly and out of health, and why not a few die. If, however, we understood ourselves aright, we 31 should not be judged. But when we are judged by the Lord, 32 chastisement follows, to save us from being condemned along with the world.

So then, brethren, when you come together for this meal, 33 wait for one another. If any one is hungry, let him eat at home; 34 so that your coming together may not lead to judgment.

The other matters I will deal with when I come.

12

Now about spiritual gifts, brethren, I would not have 1
you ignorant. You know that when you were hea- 2
thens you went astray after dumb idols, wherever you might
be led. For this reason I inform you that no one speaking 3
under the influence of the Spirit of God says, "Jesus is
accursed," and that no one is able to say, "Jesus is Lord,"
except under the influence of the Holy Spirit.

Now there are various kinds of gifts, but there is the same 4
Spirit; various kinds of official service, and yet the same 5
Lord; various kinds of effects, and yet the same God who 6
produces all the effects in each person. But to each a mani- 7
festation of the Spirit has been granted for the common
good. To one the word of wisdom has been granted through 8
the Spirit; to another the word of knowledge by the will of
the same Spirit; to one, in the same Spirit, special faith; to 9
another various gifts of healing, in the one Spirit; to another 10
the exercise of miraculous powers; to another the gift of
prophecy; to another the power of discriminating between
spirits; to one varieties of the gift of "tongues"; to another the
interpretation of tongues. But all these results are brought 11
about by one and the same Spirit, allotting them to each
individually as He pleases.

For just as the body is one and yet has many parts, and all 12
its parts, many as they are, constitute but one body, so it is
with Christ. In fact, in one Spirit all of us—whether Jews or 13
Greeks, slaves or free men—were baptized to form one body;
and we were all imbued [filled/saturated] with one Spirit.

The body does not consist of one part, but of many. Were 14
the foot to say, "Because I am not a hand, I am not a part of 15
the body," that would not make it any the less a part of the
body. Or were the ear to say, "Because I am not an eye, I am 16
not a part of the body," that would not make it any the less a
part of the body. If the whole body were an eye, where would 17

the hearing be? If the whole body were an ear, where would the smelling be? But, as it is, God has arranged the parts in the body—every one of them—as He has seen fit. If they were all one part, where would the body be? But, in fact, there are many parts and but one body. 18 19 20

It is also impossible for the eye to say to the hand, "I do not need you"; or again for the head to say to the feet, "I do not need you." So far from that, even those parts of the body which seem somewhat feeble are yet indispensable; and those which we deem less honorable we clothe with additional honor; and so our ungraceful parts come to have additional grace, while our graceful parts have no need of it. No, God in building up the body has bestowed additional honor on the part that came short, that there might be no disunion in the body, but that all the members might entertain the same anxiety for one another. And if one part suffers, every other part suffers with it, or if one part is honored, every other part shares in the joy. 21 22 23 24 25 26

Now, you are the body of Christ, and individually members of it. And by God's appointment there are in the church, first apostles, secondly prophets, thirdly teachers. Then come miraculous powers, and then ability to cure diseases or render assistance, or powers of organization, or varieties of the gift of tongues. Are all apostles? Are all prophets? Are all teachers? Have all miraculous powers? Have all ability to cure diseases? Do all speak in tongues? Do all interpret? But ever seek to excel in the greater gifts. 27 28 29 30 31

And still I have to show you a more excellent way.

13 If I can speak with the tongues of men and of angels, but have not love, I am a blaring trumpet or a clanging cymbal. Or if I can prophesy and am versed in all mysteries 1 2 and all knowledge, and have such absolute faith that I can remove mountains, but have not love, I am nothing. And if I 3 use all I have to feed the poor, and give up my body to be burned, but have not love, it profits me nothing.

Love is forbearing and kind. Love knows no jealousy. Love 4 does not brag; is not conceited. She is not unmannerly, nor 5 selfish, nor irritable, nor mindful of wrongs. She does not 6 rejoice in injustice, but joyfully sides with the truth. She can 7 overlook faults. She is full of trust, full of hope, full of endurance.

Love never fails. But if there are prophecies, they will come 8 to an end; if there are tongues, they will cease; if there is knowledge, it will come to an end. For our knowledge is par- 9 tial, and so is our prophesying; but when that which is 10 perfect is come, all that is partial will come to an end. When 11 I was a child, I talked like a child, thought like a child, reasoned like a child: now that I have become a man, I have put an end to childish ways. For at present we see things as 12 in a mirror, obscurely; but then we shall see face to face. At present I gain but partial knowledge, but then I shall know fully, even as I am fully known. And so there remain faith, 13 hope, love—these three; but of these the greatest is love.

14 Make love your quest, and be eager for spiritual gifts, 1 but chiefly for prophecy. For he who speaks in a 2 tongue is not speaking to men, but to God; for no one understands him; but in the Spirit he speaks divine secrets. But he 3 who prophesies speaks to men words of edification, encouragement, and comfort. He who speaks in a tongue edifies 4 himself, but he who prophesies edifies the Church. I should 5 like you all to speak in tongues, but yet more that you should prophesy. The man who prophesies is superior to him who

speaks in tongues, except when the latter interprets in order that the Church may receive edification. But as things are, 6 brethren, if I come to you speaking in tongues, what good shall I do you, unless I address you with a revelation or knowledge or prophecy or teaching?

If inanimate things—flutes or harps, for instance—though 7 they yield a sound, yet make no distinction in the notes, how shall the tune which is played on the flute or the harp be known? If the bugle, again, gives an uncertain sound, who 8 will prepare for battle? And so with you; if with the tongue 9 you fail to utter intelligible words, how will people know what you are saying? You will be talking to the winds.

There are, we will suppose, so many languages in the 10 world, and none without a meaning. If, then, I do not know 11 the meaning of the language, I shall seem to the speaker, and he to me, to be a foreigner. Therefore, seeing that you are 12 ambitious for spiritual gifts, seek to excel in them, so as to edify the Church.

So let a man who has the gift of tongues pray for the power 13 of interpreting them. For if I pray in a tongue, my spirit prays, 14 but my understanding is barren. What then follows? I will 15 pray with my spirit, and I will pray with my understanding also. I will sing praise with my spirit, and I will sing praise with my understanding also. Otherwise, if you bless God in 16 spirit only, how shall any one who lacks the gift say "Amen" to your thanksgiving when he does not know what you mean? You are giving thanks rightly enough, and yet your 17 neighbor is not edified. I speak in tongues, thank God, more 18 than all of you; but in the church I would rather speak five 19 words with my understanding, so as to instruct others also, than ten thousand words in a tongue.

Brethren, do not be mentally children. As regards evil 20 indeed be babes, but in intelligence be mature. In the Law it 21

is written, "'BY MEN OF OTHER TONGUES AND BY THE
LIPS OF OTHERS WILL I SPEAK TO THIS PEOPLE, BUT EVEN
THEN THEY WILL NOT LISTEN TO ME'" (Isaiah 28:11-12),
says the Lord. This shows that the gift of tongues is intended 22
as a sign not to those who believe but to unbelievers, whereas
prophecy is intended not for unbelievers but for those who
believe. Accordingly, if the whole church has assembled 23
together and all are speaking in tongues, and there come in
some who lack the gift, or unbelievers, will they not say that
you are mad? If, on the other hand, every one is prophesying, 24
and an unbeliever or one who lacks the gift comes in, he is
convicted by all; he is sifted by all, and the secrets of his heart 25
are brought to light. And thus he will fall on his face and worship God, pronouncing that truly God is among you.

What then, brethren? Whenever you assemble, there is not 26
one of you who is not ready either with a song of praise, a
sermon, a revelation, a tongue, or an interpretation. Let
everything be done with a view to edification. If there is 27
speaking in a tongue, only two or at the most three should
speak, one at a time, and one should interpret; or if there is 28
no interpreter, let the speaker be silent in the church, speaking to himself and to God. Let two or three prophets speak, 29
and let the rest judge. And if anything is revealed to some 30
one else who is seated, let the first be silent. For you can all 31
prophesy one by one, so that all may learn and all be encouraged: the spirits of prophets are under their own control. For 32
God is not a God of disorder, but of peace, as He is in all the 33
churches of the saints.

Let women be silent in the churches, for they are not per- 34
mitted to speak. They must be subordinate, as the Law also
says; and if they wish to learn anything, they should ask their 35
own husbands at home. For it is disgraceful for a woman to
speak in church.

Was it from you that God's word first went forth, or is it to 36
you only that it has come?

If any one reckons himself a prophet or a man with spirit- 37
ual gifts, let him recognize as the Lord's command what I
am now writing to you. But if any one is ignorant, let him 38
be ignorant.

In conclusion, my brethren, be eager to prophesy, and do 39
not check speaking with tongues; only let everything be 40
done in a becoming and orderly manner.

The Resurrection of the Dead

15 Now let me recall to you, brethren, the gospel which 1
I preached to you, which you accepted, and in
which you stand; through which also you are saved, if you 2
hold to the substance of my preaching—unless indeed your
faith was mere caprice [a sudden, impulsive change]. I 3
transmitted to you before all else what had also been transmitted to me, that Christ died for our sins in accordance
with the scriptures; that He was buried; that He rose on the 4
third day in accordance with the scriptures, and was seen 5
by Cephas, and then by the Twelve. Afterwards He was seen 6
by more then five hundred brethren at once, most of whom
are still alive, although some of them have died. Afterwards 7
He was seen by James, and then by all the apostles. And last 8
of all He appeared to me also, to this abortion, so to speak,
of an apostle.

For I am the least of the apostles, and am not fit to be 9
called an apostle, because I persecuted the church of God.
But by the grace of God I am what I am, and the grace He 10
bestowed upon me did not prove ineffectual. I labored more
strenuously than all of them: yet it was not I, but God's grace

helping me. Whether, then, it is I or they, this is the way we   11
preach and the way that you came to believe.

But if we preach that Christ rose from the dead, how is it   12
that some of you say that there is no such thing as a resurrection of the dead? If there is no such thing as a resurrection   13
of the dead, not even Christ has risen. And if Christ has not   14
risen, then our preaching is in vain, and your faith also is in
vain. Further, we are shown to be bearing false witness about   15
God, because we have testified that God raised Christ, whom
He did not raise, if in fact dead men do not rise. For if dead   16
men do not rise, then Christ has not risen; and if Christ has   17
not risen, your faith is of no avail: you are still in your sins. It   18
follows also that those who have fallen asleep in Christ have
perished. If we have had our hope in Christ in this life, and   19
nothing more, we are the most pitiable of all men.

But, in reality, Christ has risen from the dead—the first of   20
those who are asleep. For seeing that death came through   21
man, through man comes also the resurrection of the dead.
Just as in Adam all die, so also in Christ all will be made alive   22
again. But each in his own order—Christ first, and after-   23
wards Christ's people at His return. After that comes the end,   24
when He is to surrender the kingship to God the Father,
when He has abolished all other government and all other
authority and power. For He must be King until He has put   25
all His enemies under His feet (Psalms 8:6, 110:1). The last   26
enemy that is to be abolished is death; for God has put all   27
things under His feet. And when He says, "All things are
put under," obviously this does not include Him who has
put them all under Him. But when all things have been put   28
under Him, then the Son Himself will also come under Him
who has put all things under Him, in order that GOD may
be all in all.

Otherwise what will those do who are baptized for the   29

dead? If the dead do not rise at all, why are they baptized for them? Why also do we apostles take such risks every hour? I 30 risk death day by day. I affirm this, brethren, by my glorying 31 in you, as I justly do, in Christ Jesus our Lord. If from merely 32 human motives I have fought with wild beasts in Ephesus, what profit is it to me? If the dead do not rise, let us eat and drink, for to-morrow we are to die (Isaiah 22:13). Do not 33 deceive yourselves:

"Bad companionships spoil good morals."

Return to a truly sober mind, and cease to sin; for some 34 have no knowledge of God. I say this to your shame.

But some one will say, "How do the dead rise? And with 35 what kind of body do they come back?" Foolish man! the 36 seed you yourself sow does not come to life unless it dies; and what you sow is not the body which is to be, but a bare 37 grain of wheat (it may be) or of something else, and God 38 gives it a body as He pleases, and to each kind of seed a body of its own. All flesh is not the same: there is human flesh, 39 and flesh of cattle, of birds, and of fishes. There are celestial 40 bodies and also earthly bodies, but the glory of the celestial is one thing, and that of the earthly is another. There is one 41 glory of the sun, another of the moon, and another of the stars: star differs from star in glory.

It is the same with the resurrection of the dead. The body 42 is sown perishable, it rises imperishable; it is sown in dis- 43 honor, it rises in glory; it is sown in weakness, it rises in power; it is sown an animal body, it is raised a spiritual body. 44 Just as there is an animal body, so there is also a spiritual body. Thus too it is written, "THE FIRST MAN ADAM 45 BECAME A LIVING BEING" (Genesis 2:7); the last Adam a life-giving Spirit. Yet it is not the spiritual that comes first, 46 but the animal; then the spiritual. The first man is a man of 47 earth, of dust; the second man is from heaven. What the man 48 of dust is, that also are those who are of dust; and what the heavenly One is, that also are those who are heavenly. As we 49 have worn the likeness of the man of dust, we shall also wear the likeness of the heavenly One.

But this I tell you, brethren, flesh and blood cannot inherit 50 the Kingdom of God, nor shall the perishable inherit the imperishable. See, I will tell you a secret: we shall not all 51 sleep, but we shall all be changed, in a moment, in the twin- 52 kling of an eye, at the last trumpet call; for the trumpet will sound, and the dead will rise imperishable, and we shall be changed. For this perishable nature must clothe itself with 53 the imperishable, and this mortality must clothe itself with immortality. Now when this perishable nature has put on the 54 imperishable, and this mortality has put on immortality, then shall the words of scripture be fulfilled, "DEATH HAS BEEN SWALLOWED UP IN VICTORY" (Isaiah 25:8). "WHERE, O DEATH, IS THY VICTORY? WHERE, O DEATH, IS THY 55 STING?" (Hosea 13:14). Now sin is the sting of death, and the 56 Law is the stronghold of sin; but God be thanked who gives 57 us the victory through our Lord Jesus Christ! Therefore, my 58 beloved brethren, be firm, immovable, abounding at all times in the work of the Lord, knowing that your toil is not fruitless in the Lord.

The Poor in Jerusalem

16 As to the collection for the saints, what I have directed 1 the churches of Galatia to do, you must do also. On 2 the first day of the week, let each of you put by and keep any profit he may have made; so that there may be no col- lections made after I have come. And when I arrive, whatever 3 brethren you approve I will send with letters to carry your

kind gift to Jerusalem. And if it is worth while for me also to 4
go, they shall go with me.

Personal Matters, and Farewell

I shall come to you after passing through Macedonia; for I am 5
going to pass through Macedonia; and I shall make some stay 6
perhaps, or even spend the winter with you, in order that you
may help me forward, whichever way I travel. For I do not wish 7
to see you just now merely in passing; if the Lord permits, I hope
to remain some time with you. I shall remain in Ephesus, how- 8
ever, until Pentecost, for a door that offers wide and effective 9
service stands open before me, and there are many opponents.

If Timothy comes, see that his intercourse with you may 10
be free from fear; for he is engaged in the Master's work just
as I am. Therefore let no one slight him, but do you help him 11
forward in peace to join me; for I am waiting for him with
others of the brethren.

As for our brother Apollos, I have repeatedly urged him to 12
accompany the brethren who are coming to you; but he is
quite resolved not to do so at present. He will come, however, when he has a good opportunity.

Be alert; stand firm in the faith; acquit yourselves like men; 13
be strong. Let all that you do be done from love. 14

I beseech you, brethren—you know the household of 15
Stephanas, how they were the earliest Greek converts, and
have devoted themselves to the service of the saints—do 16
you show deference [respect] to such men, and to every one
who shares their work and toils hard. It is joy to me that 17
Stephanas, Fortunatus, and Achaicus have arrived, because
they have supplied what was wanting on your part. They 18
have refreshed my spirit, and yours. Acknowledge the worth
of such men as these.

The churches of Asia send you greetings; and Aquila and 19
Prisca send you hearty greetings in the Lord, together with
the church which meets at their house. The brethren all send 20
greetings to you. Greet one another with a holy kiss.

The greeting of me—Paul—with my own hand. If any one 21
does not love the Lord, let him be accursed. Maranatha 22
(OUR LORD, COME!). The grace of the Lord Jesus be with 23
you. My love be with you all in Christ Jesus. 24

THE SECOND EPISTLE OF PAUL
TO THE CORINTHIANS

The Apostle and His Readers

1 Paul, an apostle of Christ Jesus by the will of God—and 1
our brother Timothy, to the church of God in Corinth,
with all the saints throughout Greece: grace and peace to 2
you from God our Father and the Lord Jesus Christ.

Blessed be the God and Father of our Lord Jesus Christ, the 3
Father of mercies and God of all comfort. He comforts us in 4
all our affliction so that we may be able to comfort those who
are in any kind of affliction by the comfort with which we ourselves are comforted by God. For as we have more than our 5
share of suffering for Christ, so also through Christ we have
more than our share of comfort. But if we endure affliction, it 6
is for your comfort and salvation; and if we receive comfort, it
is for your comfort—the feeling you acquire when you steadfastly endure the same sufferings as we also endure. And our 7
hope for you is firm; for we know that as you are sharers in the
sufferings, so you are also sharers in the comfort.

About our affliction which came upon us in the province of 8
Asia, we would have you know, brethren, that we were exceedingly depressed, quite beyond endurance, so that we re-
nounced all hope even of life. Nay, we had the presentiment 9
[foreboding] of death within ourselves, in order that our confidence may repose, not on ourselves, but on God who raises
the dead. He rescued us from so imminent a death, and will 10
do so again; and we have a firm hope in Him that He will still
rescue us, while you lend us your aid by entreaty for us, so that 11

thanksgivings may rise from many on our behalf for the boon [blessing] granted to us at the intercession of many.

The reason of our boasting is this—the witness of our own 12 conscience that it has been in holiness and with pure motives before God, not with worldly wisdom but by the grace of God, that we have conducted ourselves in the world, and above all in our relations with you. We write to you noth- 13 ing different from what you read, or indeed recognize as true, and will, I trust, recognize to the end; just as you have 14 partly recognized that we are your reason for boasting, as you will be ours, on the day of Jesus our Lord.

It was with this confidence that I intended to visit you 15 first—so that you might receive a twofold joy—and to come 16 your way into Macedonia and to return from Macedonia to you, and so be helped forward by you to Judaea. Well, did I 17 show any levity in this? Or the plans which I form—do I form them on worldly principles, so that it should be, "Yes, yes," and then "No, no" with me?

As certainly as God is faithful, our language to you is not 18 "yes" and "no." For the Son of God, Jesus Christ, who was 19 proclaimed among you by us, by Silvanus and Timothy and myself—did not show Himself "yes" and "no": it is always "yes" with Him. For all the promises of God have their "yes" 20 in Him; and therefore through Him also we utter the "Amen" to the glory of God. But He who confirms us as well as you in 21 union with Christ, and has anointed us, is God, and He has 22 also set His seal upon us, and has put His Spirit into our hearts as a guarantee.

But I call God as my soul's witness that it was to spare you 23 that I gave up my visit to Corinth. Not that we would domi- 24 neer over your faith; we would rather assist your joy; for as to your faith you stand firm.

2 But I have resolved not to make a painful visit to you 1 again. For if I give you pain, who then is there to glad- 2 den me, but the persons to whom I give pain? And I wrote 3 that in order that when I came I might not suffer pain from those who ought to give me joy, confident in all of you that my joy is the joy of you all. For with many tears I wrote to 4 you, in deep affliction and anguish of spirit, not in order to pain you, but in the hope of showing you how brimful [full to the brim] my heart is with love for you.

Now if any one has given pain, he has given it not so much 5 to me, as, in some degree—I have no wish to exaggerate—to all of you. For such a person the punishment inflicted by the 6 majority is enough. So that you may now take the opposite 7 course and forgive and comfort him, lest perhaps he be driven to despair by his excess of grief. I beg you therefore 8 fully to reinstate him in your love. For I wrote with this object 9 in view—to test whether you were obedient in every respect. When you forgive a man an offense I also forgive it; for in fact 10 what I have forgiven, if I have forgiven anything, has been for your sakes, in the presence of Christ, for fear Satan 11 should gain an advantage over us. For we are not ignorant of his devices.

Now when I came to Troas to spread the gospel of Christ, 12 even though in the Lord's providence a door stood open before me, yet I had no relief for my spirit, because I did not 13 find my brother Titus, so I bade them farewell and went on into Macedonia. But to God be the thanks who in Christ ever 14 leads us in His triumphal procession, displaying everywhere through us the sweetness of the knowledge of Him. For we 15 are a fragrance of Christ grateful to God in those being saved and in those perishing; to the one an odor of death that leads 16 to death, and to others an odor of life that leads to life. And for such service as this who is competent? Unlike most 17 teachers, we do not hawk God's word for gain; but with sincerity, as sent by God, in God's presence we speak in Christ.

3 Do you say that we are beginning to commend 1
ourselves once more? Or do we need, as some do, letters of recommendation to you or from you? Our letter is 2 yourselves—written on our hearts and known and read by all men. For you show that you are a letter of Christ penned by 3 us, written not with ink, but with the Spirit of the living God, not on tablets of stone, but on human hearts as tablets.

Such is the confidence which we have through Christ 4 toward God; not that of ourselves we are competent to 5 decide anything of our own judgment, but our competency comes from God. He has also made us competent servants 6 of a new covenant, which is not a written code but a Spirit; for the written code kills, but the Spirit gives life.

But if the service that brings death—its code being 7 engraved in writing upon stones—came with glory, so that the children of Israel could not look steadily on the face of Moses because of the brightness of his face—a transient luster; will not the service of the Spirit be far more glorious? 8 For if the service which pronounces doom had glory, far 9 more glorious still is the service which offers righteousness. For, in fact, that which was so glorious (Exodus 34:30, LXX) 10 has no glory at all in comparison with the surpassing glory. For if that which was to be abolished came with glory, much 11 more is that which is permanent arrayed in glory.

With such a hope as this, then, we speak without reserve, 12 unlike Moses, who used to throw a veil over his face to hide 13 from the gaze of the children of Israel the passing away of what was but transitory. But indeed their minds had grown 14 dense; for to this day during the reading of the Old Testament the same veil remains unlifted, because it is in Christ that it is to be abolished. Yes, to this day, whenever Moses is read, a 15 veil lies upon their hearts. But whenever they return to the 16 Lord, the veil is withdrawn (Exodus 34:34, LXX).

Now the Lord means the Spirit; and where the Spirit of the 17 Lord is, freedom is. But all of us, as with unveiled faces we 18 mirror the glory of the Lord, are transformed into the same likeness, from glory to glory, even as derived from the Lord the Spirit.

4 Therefore, while engaged in this service, as we have ex- 1 perienced mercy we do not lose heart. We have re- 2 nounced the secrecy which means shame. We do not deal in cunning, nor do we adulterate God's word; but by clear statement of the truth we commend ourselves to every human conscience before God. If, indeed, our gospel is 3 veiled, the veil is on the heart of those who are perishing, in 4 whom the god of this world has blinded their unbelieving minds so as to shut out the radiance of the gospel of the glory of Christ, who is the image of God. (For we do not pro- 5 claim ourselves, but Christ Jesus as Lord, and ourselves as your servants for the sake of Jesus.) For the God who said, 6 "Out of darkness light shall shine," is He who has shone in our hearts to give the light of the knowledge of the glory of God in the face of Jesus Christ.

But we have this treasure in fragile earthen pots, in order 7 that the surpassing greatness of the power may be seen to be God's and not to come from us. At all points we are hard 8 pressed, yet not hemmed in; perplexed, yet not at our wits' end; pursued, yet not forsaken; struck down, yet not 9 destroyed; always carrying about in our bodies the putting to 10 death of Jesus, so that in our bodies the life of Jesus also may

be manifest. For we, alive though we are, are continually sur- 11
rendering ourselves to death for the sake of Jesus, so that in
our mortal nature the life of Jesus also may be manifest.
Thus death is at work in us, but life in you. 12

But as we have that same Spirit of faith of which it is 13
written, "I BELIEVED, AND THEREFORE I SPOKE" (Psalm
116:10), we too believe; therefore we also speak. For we know 14
that He who raised the Lord Jesus will raise us also with
Jesus, and will set us with you in His presence. For every- 15
thing is for your sakes, in order that grace may increase with
the increased number of its recipients, and so provoke abundant thanksgiving to the glory of God.

Therefore we do not lose heart. But, even though our 16
outward man does waste away, yet our inward man is renewed day by day. For our light and transitory affliction is 17
achieving for us, beyond all proportion, an eternal weight of
glory—if we look not at the seen, but at the unseen; for the 18
seen is temporary, but the unseen is eternal.

5 For we know that if the mere tent, which is our earthly 1
house, is taken down, we have in heaven a building
from God, a house not made by human hands, but eternal.
In this one, indeed, we sigh, because we long to put on over 2
it our dwelling which comes from heaven—sure that, when 3
we have put it on we shall not be found unclothed. Yes, we 4
who are in this tent do sigh under our burdens, not that we
wish to lay aside our tent, but rather to put the other over it,
so that our mortality may be absorbed in life. And He who 5
formed us for this very purpose is God, who has given us His
Spirit as guarantee.

We have therefore an unfailing confidence. We know that 6
while we are at home in the body we are away from the Lord;

for we guide ourselves by faith and not by external appearance. So we have confidence, and we should be better pleased to leave our home in the body and make our home with the Lord. For this reason also we make it our aim, whether in our home or away, to please Him. For we must all of us appear before Christ's judgment-seat in our true light, in order that each may receive an award for his actions in this life, in accordance with what he has done, whether it be good or bad. 7 8 9 10

Knowing, then, what the fear of the Lord means, we endeavor to win men, and to God our motives are clear, and I hope clear also to you in your own consciences. We are not commending ourselves again to you, but are furnishing you with a ground of boasting on our behalf, so that you may have a reply ready for those who boast openly but yet insincerely. For if we have been beside ourselves, it has been towards God; or if we are in our senses, it is for your good. For the love of Christ overmasters us, since we are convinced of this, that One died for all, hence they all died, and that He died for all in order that the living may no longer live to themselves, but to Him who for them died and rose again. 11 12 13 14 15

Therefore for the future we know no one simply as a man. Even if we have known Christ simply as a man, yet now we do so no longer. So if any one is in Christ, he is a new creature: the old state of things has passed away; a new has come. And all this is from God, who has reconciled us to Himself through Christ, and has appointed us ministers of this reconciliation, to tell how in Christ God was reconciling the world to Himself, not charging men's transgressions to their account, and how He has deposited with us the message of this reconciliation. 16 17 18 19

As Christ's ambassadors, therefore, we speak, seeing that God is making entreaty through us: we entreat you on 20

Christ's behalf, be reconciled to God. He has made Him who 21
knew nothing of sin to be sin for us, in order that in Him we
may become the righteousness of God.

6 And as God's fellow workers, we entreat also that 1
God's grace be not received in vain by you. For He says, 2
"AT AN ACCEPTABLE TIME I HAVE LISTENED TO YOU, AND
ON A DAY OF SALVATION I HAVE SUCCOURED YOU"
(Isaiah 49:8). See, now is the acceptable time! Now is the day
of salvation!

We give no cause for stumbling of any sort, lest our min- 3
istry should incur discredit. On the contrary, we seek to com- 4
mend ourselves as God's servants in every way—by great
endurance, by afflictions, distresses, anguish; in floggings, 5
imprisonments, tumults; by toil, sleeplessness, hunger and
thirst; by purity, knowledge, patience, kindness, by the Holy 6
Spirit, by sincere love; by truthful speech, by the power of 7
God; by the weapons of righteousness in right hand and left;
through honor and ignominy [dishonor], through calumny 8
[slander] and praise: regarded as impostors, and yet true
men; as unknown, yet well known; as dying, and behold we 9
are yet alive; as chastised, but not done to death; as grieved, 10
but always joyful; as poor, but enriching many; as having
nothing, yet possessing everything.

To you, Corinthians, we speak frankly: we have opened 11
our hearts to you. There is no lack of room for you in us; the 12
lack of room is in your own affection. Then as a fair return— 13
I speak as to my children—let your hearts be opened also.

{Avoid unsuitable connections with unbelievers. For what is 14
there in common between righteousness and lawlessness? Or
what partnership has light with darkness? What harmony can 15

exist between Christ and Belial? Or what participation has a believer with an unbeliever? And what compact has the temple 16 of God with idols? For we are the temple of the living God; as God has said, "I WILL DWELL AMONG THEM, AND HOLD INTERCOURSE WITH THEM; AND WILL BE THEIR GOD, AND THEY SHALL BE MY PEOPLE" (Leviticus 26:12; Ezekiel 37:27).

Therefore, 17

"'COME OUT FROM AMONG THEM AND SEPARATE YOURSELVES,' SAYS THE LORD, 'AND TOUCH NOTHING UNCLEAN; AND I WILL RECEIVE YOU, AND WILL BE A 18 FATHER TO YOU, AND YOU SHALL BE MY SONS AND DAUGHTERS,' SAYS THE LORD ALMIGHTY" (Isaiah 52:11; Hosea 1:10; Isaiah 43:6).

7 Having therefore these promises, beloved, let us 1 cleanse ourselves from all defilement of body and of spirit, and attain to holiness through the fear of God.}

Make room for us in your hearts. We have wronged no one, 2 we have ruined no one, we have overreached no one. I do 3 not say this as blaming you, for, as I have already said, you have such a place in our hearts that we would die with you or live with you. I have great confidence in you: loudly do I 4 boast of you. I am filled with comfort: my heart overflows with joy amid all our affliction.

For even after our arrival in Macedonia we could get 5 no relief for body or mind. We were greatly harassed; there were conflicts without and fears within. But God, who comforts the 6 downcast, comforted us by the coming of Titus, and not by his 7 coming only but also by the comfort he had on your account, as he reported to us your eager affection, your grief, and your jealousy on my behalf, so that I rejoiced more than ever.

For if I did give you pain by my letter, I do not regret it; if I 8
did regret it (for I see that that letter, if only for a time, gave you
pain), now I rejoice, not in your pain, but because the pain led 9
to repentance; for your pain was such as God accepts, so that
you received no injury from us in any respect. For the pain 10
God accepts produces repentance not to be regretted, leading
to salvation; but the pain of the world finally produces death.
For mark this very pain that God accepts, what earnestness it 11
has called forth in you, what self-defense, what indignation,
what alarm, what longing affection, what jealousy, what
requital [return or repayment] of wrong! You have completely
wiped away reproach from yourselves in the matter. So then, 12
though I wrote to you, it was not because of him who did the
wrong, nor him who suffered it, but in order to make clear
among you your earnest care for us in the sight of God.

For this reason we feel comforted; and—in addition to 13
our own comfort—we have been filled with all the deeper
joy at the joy of Titus, because his spirit has been set at rest
by you all. For however I may have boasted to him about 14
you, I have not been shamed; but as all we have said to you
is true, so also our boasting before Titus about you has
proved true. And his affection is all the more drawn to you 15
when he calls to mind the obedience of you all, how with
fear and trembling you received him. I rejoice that I have 16
complete confidence in you.

Help for the Poor in Jerusalem

8 But, brethren, we desire to let you know of the grace of 1
God which has been bestowed on the churches of
Macedonia; how, amid a trial of great affliction, their abun- 2
dant joy even in their deep poverty has overflowed in the

wealth of their liberality. I testify that to the extent of their 3
power, and even beyond their power, they have of their own
choice given help. With earnest entreaty they begged from us 4
the favor of sharing in this service to the saints. They indeed 5
exceeded our expectations. First of all they gave themselves to
the Lord and to us as God willed. This led us to urge Titus that, 6
as he had been the one who began the work, so he should
complete among you this act of beneficence [charity] also.
Well, as you are eminent in everything, in faith and speech 7
and knowledge and all zeal, and in your love for us, see that
this beneficent [charitable] spirit also flourishes in you.

I am not saying this by way of command, but to test by 8
other men's earnestness the genuineness of your love also.
For you know the grace of our Lord Jesus Christ—how for 9
your sakes He became poor, though He was rich, in order
that you through His poverty might become rich. But in this 10
matter I give my opinion; for this is to your advantage, seeing that you were the first, not merely to act, but even to form
the purpose a year ago.

And now complete the act also, in order that your readi- 11
ness of will may be matched by execution in proportion to
your means. For if the readiness is forthcoming, the gift is 12
acceptable according to what a man has, and not what he
has not. Not that others are to have relief while you are hard 13
pressed, but that by way of reciprocity your surplus should at 14
the present juncture contribute to their deficiency, in order
that their surplus may in turn contribute to your deficiency,
so that there may be reciprocity. As it is written, "HE WHO 15
GATHERED MUCH HAD NOT TOO MUCH, AND HE WHO
GATHERED LITTLE HAD NOT TOO LITTLE" (Exodus 16:18).

But thanks be to God that He inspires the heart of Titus 16
with the same interest in you; he welcomed our request, and 17
being in very earnest comes to you of his own choice. And we 18

send with him the brother whose praises for his preaching the gospel are sounded throughout all the churches. And 19 more than that, he was chosen by the vote of the churches to travel with us, in our administration of this generous gift, to promote the Lord's glory and gratify our own desire. For we 20 are taking steps to prevent any one from blaming us in respect to these liberal contributions which we are administering. We aim at appearing honorable in the sight not only 21 of God, but also of men.

And we send with them our brother, whom we have often 22 in many matters proved to be zealous, and now far more zealous through the strong confidence which he has in you.

As for Titus, he is my partner and comrade in my labors for 23 you. And as for our brethren, they are apostles of churches, and are the glory of Christ. Exhibit therefore to the churches 24 an evidence of your love and a vindication of our boasting to these brethren about you.

9 As to this service to the saints, it is really unnecessary for 1 me to write to you. For I know your readiness, of which 2 I boast of you to the Macedonians, pointing out that for a whole year Greece has been ready; and your ardor has stimulated the majority of them. Still, I send the brethren in 3 order that in this matter our boast about you may not prove hollow; so that, as I told them, you may be ready; for fear that 4 if any Macedonians come with me and find you unprepared, we—not to say yourselves—should be put to shame by this confidence of ours. I have thought it necessary therefore to 5 request these brethren to visit you first, and to make sure beforehand that your promised benefaction [charitable offering] may be ready as a benefaction, and not as something extorted from you.

But note this: he who sows thinly will also reap thinly, and 6
he who sows bountifully will also reap bountifully. Let each 7
contribute as he has decided in his own mind, and not with
pain or constraint, "IT IS A CHEERFUL GIVER THAT GOD
LOVES" (Proverbs 22:8, LXX). And God is able to bestow 8
every blessing on you in abundance, so that having in every
case all sufficiency at all times, you may have ample means
for all good works. As it is written, 9

"HE HAS SCATTERED ABROAD,
HE HAS GIVEN TO THE POOR,
HIS RIGHTEOUSNESS REMAINS FOR EVER" (Psalm 112:9).

And God, who supplies SEED FOR THE SOWER AND 10
BREAD FOR EATING (Isaiah 55:10), will supply you with
seed and multiply it, and will increase the benefits wrought
by your almsgiving. You will thus be enriched in every way so 11
as to show all liberality, such as through our instrumentality
evokes thanksgiving to God. For the service rendered in this 12
ministry not only helps to relieve the wants of the saints, but
it also has an overflow in many thanksgivings to God. By the 13
evidence of this service, you bring glory to God for your loyalty to your profession of the gospel of Christ, and for the liberality of your contributions for them and for all, while they 14
themselves also in prayer on your behalf yearn towards you
because of the surpassing grace of God which rests upon
you. Thanks be to God for His unspeakable gift! 15

Paul's Vindication of His Apostleship

10 Now I, Paul, entreat you by the gentleness and rea- 1
sonableness of Christ—I who (as you say) when
present am humble among you, but when absent am bold
towards you. I beg that you will not force me, when I do 2

come, to show my courage by the confidence with which I reckon I shall be bold, against some who reckon that we are guided by worldly motives. For though we live in the world, it is no worldly warfare that we are waging. The weapons of our warfare are not of this world, but are mighty before God for overthrowing fortresses. For we overthrow reasonings and everything raised aloft against the knowledge of God; and we lead every thought captive and bring it into obedience to Christ; while we hold ourselves in readiness to punish all disobedience, as soon as you have fully shown your obedience.

Open your eyes to what is before your face. If any man is sure of himself that he belongs to Christ, let him consider again that, just as he belongs to Christ, so also do we. If, indeed, I were to boast somewhat loudly of our authority, which the Lord has given that we may build you up, not cast you down I should not be ashamed. Let it not seem as if I wanted to frighten you by my letters. For they say, "His letters are weighty and forcible, but his personal presence is feeble, and his speech is contemptible." Let such people take account of this, that whatever we are in word by our letters when absent, the same are we also in act when present.

We do not venture to rank or compare ourselves with certain persons who recommend themselves. Yet they are not wise in measuring and comparing themselves with one another. We, however, will not boast beyond our due limits, but will keep within the limit of the sphere which God has assigned to us as a limit, which reaches even to you. There is no straining of authority on our part, as though it did not extend to you. For we were the first to come to you with the gospel of Christ. We do not boast beyond our due limits, nor of other men's labors; but we entertain the hope that, as your faith grows, our field of activity among you may be enlarged

till it goes beyond you, and we may preach the gospel in the 16
districts beyond you, not boasting in another man's field
about work already done by him.

But "WHOEVER BOASTS, LET HIS BOAST BE IN THE 17
LORD" (Jeremiah 9:24). It is not the man who commends 18
himself that is accepted, but the one whom the Lord
commends.

11 I wish you could have borne with a little folly on my 1
part: nay, do bear with me. I am jealous over you with 2
God's own jealousy. For I have betrothed you to Christ to present you like a faithful bride to her one husband. But I am 3
afraid that, as the serpent in his craftiness deceived Eve, so
your thoughts may be perverted from their simplicity and
their fidelity to Christ. If indeed a chance-comer proclaims 4
another Jesus whom we did not proclaim, or if you receive a
spirit different from the one you have received, or a gospel
different from that which you have welcomed, your tolera-
tion is admirable indeed! Why, I reckon myself in no respect 5
inferior to those pre-eminent apostles. And if in speech I am 6
no orator, yet in knowledge I am not deficient. Nay, we have
in every way made that evident to you.

Did I sin in abasing myself that you might be exalted, in that 7
I proclaimed God's gospel to you without reward? Other 8
churches I robbed, receiving pay from them in order to do you
service. And when I was with you and my resources failed, I 9
was a dead-weight on no one; for the brethren, when they
came from Macedonia, fully supplied my wants—and I kept
myself from being in the least a burden to you, and will do so
still. It is Christ's truth on my lips when I say that I will not be 10
stopped from boasting of this anywhere in Greece. And why? 11
Because I do not love you? God knows that I do. What I am 12

doing I will still do, to cut the ground from under the feet of those who desire ground for being recognized as equal with us in the matters they boast about. Men of this stamp are 13 sham apostles, dishonest workmen, assuming the garb of apostles of Christ. And no wonder! Satan himself assumes the 14 garb of an angel of light. It is therefore no great thing for his 15 servants also to assume the garb of servants of righteousness. Their end will be in accordance with their deeds.

Again I say, let no one think that I am a fool. Or if you must, 16 make allowance for me even as a fool, in order that I, too, may boast a little. What I am now saying, I do not say by the 17 Lord's command, but as a fool in his folly in this confident boasting. Since many boast for merely human reasons, I too 18 will boast. Wise as you are, you find pleasure in tolerating 19 fools. For you tolerate it if any one makes a slave of you, lives 20 at your expense, makes off with your property, gives himself airs, or strikes you on the face!

I speak in self-disparagement as though admitting our 21 feebleness. Yet let who will be "courageous"—I speak in folly—I too am courageous. Are they Hebrews? So am I. Are 22 they Israelites? So am I. Are they descendants of Abraham? So am I. Are they servants of Christ? (I speak as if I were out 23 of my senses.) Much more I; exceeding them in labors, exceeding them in imprisonments, quite surpassing them in floggings, with risk of life many a time. From the Jews 24 I have five times received forty lashes all but one. Thrice I 25 have been beaten with rods, once I have been stoned, thrice I have been shipwrecked, a whole night and day I have passed in the deep. I have traveled much, amid dangers 26 from rivers, dangers from robbers, dangers from my own people, dangers from Gentiles; dangers in the city, dangers in the desert, dangers by sea, dangers among false brethren; in labor and toil, with many a sleepless night, in hunger and 27

thirst, in frequent fastings, in cold and lack of clothing. And 28
apart from all else, there is that which presses on me daily—
my anxiety for all the churches. Who is weak, and I not 29
weak? Who is led astray, and I not fired with anger?

If boast I must, it shall be of things which display my 30
weakness. The God and Father of our Lord Jesus Christ— 31
who is blessed for ever—knows that I am speaking the truth.

In Damascus the governor under King Aretas had the city 32
watched, in order to arrest me, but I was let down in a basket 33
through a window in the wall, and so escaped his hands.

12 I am obliged to boast. It is not profitable, but I will 1
proceed to visions and revelations of the Lord. I 2
know a man in Christ who fourteen years ago—whether in
the body or out of the body I know not; God knows—was
caught up, this man, even to the third heaven. And I know 3
that this man—whether in the body or apart from the body I
do not know; God knows—was caught up into Paradise and 4
heard unspeakable things which no human being is permitted to repeat. Of such a one I will boast; but of myself I will 5
not boast, except in my weaknesses. If indeed I should 6
choose to boast, I should not be a fool, for I should be speaking the truth. But I forbear, lest any one should esteem me
more highly than by what he sees of me or hears from my
lips. And because the revelations were of such surpassing 7
grandeur—therefore, lest I should be over-elated there was
given me a thorn in the flesh, Satan's angel to torture me, lest
I should be over-elated. Concerning this, three times have I 8
besought the Lord that he might leave me; but He has said to 9
me, "My grace suffices for you, for power is perfected in
weakness." Most gladly therefore will I rather glory in my
infirmities in order that the power of Christ may overshadow

me. Hence I take delight in infirmities, in insults, in dis- 10
tresses, in persecutions, in grievous difficulties—for Christ's
sake; for when I am weak, then am I strong.

I have descended to folly, but you have compelled me. 11
Why, you ought to have been my vindicators; for in no
respect have I been inferior to the pre-eminent apostles,
even though I am nothing. The signs that mark the apostle 12
have been done among you, in unwearied persistence,
with signs and marvels and mighty works. In what respect 13
have you been worse used than other churches, except
that I myself was not a dead-weight upon you? Forgive
this injustice!

See, I am now for the third time prepared to visit you, and 14
I will not be a dead-weight on you. I desire not your money,
but yourselves; for children ought not to put by [save up] for
their parents, but parents for their children. And I will most 15
gladly spend and be utterly spent for the good of your souls.
If I love you so intensely, am I the less to be loved? Be that as 16
it may, I was not a burden to you.

But I was cunning and entrapped you, they say! Is there 17
one of these I have sent to you by whom I overreached you?
I begged Titus to visit you, and sent our brother with him. 18
Did Titus overreach you at all? Were we not guided by the
same Spirit, and did we not walk in the same steps?

You are thinking all this time that we are making our 19
defense to you. Really it is before God in Christ that we
speak. But, beloved, it is all with a view to your upbuilding.
For I am afraid that perhaps when I come I may not find you 20
what I desire, and that you may find me what you do not
desire; that perhaps there may be contention, jealousy,
anger, party spirit, calumny [slander], backbiting, and arro-
gance; and that upon revisiting you I may be humbled by my 21
God in your presence, and may have to mourn over many

who formerly sinned, and who have not repented of the uncleanness, licentiousness, and sensuality which they have practiced.

13 This is my third visit to you. "ON THE EVIDENCE OF TWO OR THREE WITNESSES EVERY WORD SHALL BE CONFIRMED" (Deuteronomy 19:15). Those who sinned formerly, and indeed the rest of you, I have forewarned and still forewarn, as when I was with you the second time, and now in my absence, that, when I come again, I shall not spare you; since you want a proof that Christ speaks by my lips. Christ is not feeble towards you, but powerful among you. Though He was crucified through weakness, yet He lives through the power of God. And though we share His weakness, yet with Him we shall live to deal with you through the power of God.

It is your own selves you must test to discover whether you are true believers: examine yourselves. Or do you not know that Jesus Christ is within you—unless you cannot stand the test? But I trust that you will recognize that we can stand the test. And our prayer to God is that you may do nothing wrong; not in order that we may be shown to stand the test, but that you may do what is right, even though we may seem not to stand the test. For we have no power against the truth, but only for the truth; and we rejoice when we are feeble but you are strong. This we also pray for—your perfection. For this reason I write thus while absent, that when present I may not have to act severely in the exercise of that authority which the Lord has given me for building up, and not for pulling down.

Finally, brethren, farewell; seek perfection, take comfort, be of the same spirit, live in peace. And the God of love and peace shall be with you.

Salute one another with a holy kiss. All the saints sa- 12
lute you. 13

The grace of the Lord Jesus Christ, the love of God, and the 14
fellowship of the Holy Spirit be with you all.

THE EPISTLE OF PAUL
TO THE GALATIANS

Introduction

1 Paul, an apostle—sent not from men nor through any
man, but through Jesus Christ and God the Father who
raised Him from the dead—and all the brethren who are
with me: to the churches of Galatia. Grace to you and peace
from God the Father, and from our Lord Jesus Christ, who
gave Himself for our sins in order to rescue us from the present wicked world in accordance with the will of our God
and Father. To Him be the glory for ever and ever! Amen.

Paul Vindicates His Apostolic Authority

I am amazed that you are so readily deserting for a different gospel Him who called you by the grace of Christ. For
other gospel there is none; but there are some persons who
are troubling you, and seeking to distort the gospel of Christ.
But even if we or an angel from heaven should preach you a
gospel contrary to that which we have preached to you, let
him be accursed. What I have said I say again: if any one
preaches to you a gospel contrary to that which you have
received, let him be accursed. Is it man's favor or God's that I
try to gain? Or am I seeking to please men? If I were still a
man-pleaser, I should not be Christ's servant.

I must tell you, brethren, that the gospel which I preach
bears no human impress. For indeed it was not from man
that I received or learned it, but by a revelation from Jesus

Christ. You have heard of my early career in Judaism—how 13
furiously I persecuted the church of God, and made havoc of
it; and how in devotion to Judaism I outstripped many men 14
of my own age among my people, being far more zealous
than they for the traditions of my forefathers. But when He 15
who set me apart even from my birth, and called me by His
grace, saw fit to reveal His Son within me, in order that I 16
might preach Him among the Gentiles, I did not confer with
any human being, nor did I go up to Jerusalem to those who 17
were apostles before me, but I went away at once into
Arabia, and afterwards came back to Damascus.

Then, three years later, I went up to Jerusalem to visit 18
Cephas, and I spent a fortnight with him. I saw none of the 19
other apostles, except James, the Lord's brother. Be sure 20
that in writing this to you I am speaking the truth, as in the
sight of God. Afterwards I visited the districts of Syria and 21
Cilicia. But to the Christian churches in Judaea I was per- 22
sonally unknown. They only heard it said, "He who was 23
once our persecutor is now preaching the faith on account
of which he formerly made havoc." And they gave glory to 24
God on my account.

2 Then, after an interval of fourteen years I again went up 1
to Jerusalem with Barnabas, taking Titus also with me. I 2
went up in obedience to a revelation, and I put before them
the gospel which I proclaim among the Gentiles. I did this
in private to the leaders of the church, for fear that I was
running or should have run in vain. But although my com- 3
panion Titus was a Greek, not even he was compelled to be
circumcised. My action was on account of the false brethren 4
secretly introduced, who had stolen in to spy out the freedom which is ours in Christ Jesus, in order to enslave us

again. Not for an hour did we give way and submit to these, 5
that the gospel might continue with you in its purity. Further, 6
from the reputed leaders (whether they were men of importance or not matters nothing to me: God recognizes no
external distinctions)—from these reputed leaders I received
no new suggestions. So far from that, when they saw that I 7
was entrusted with the preaching of the gospel to the
Gentiles as Peter had been with that to the Jews—for He who 8
had been at work in Peter for an apostleship to the Jews had
also been at work in me for the Gentiles—and when they 9
perceived the grace which was granted to me, the reputed
pillars of the church, James, Cephas, and John, welcomed
Barnabas and me to their fellowship, on the understanding
that we were to go to the Gentiles and they to the Jews. Only 10
they urged that we should remember their poor—a thing
which I myself was even eager to do.

But when Peter visited Antioch, I opposed him to his face, 11
because his conduct condemned him. For until certain per- 12
sons came from James he would eat with Gentiles; but when
they came, he withdrew and separated himself for fear of the
circumcision party. And along with him the other Jews also 13
concealed their real opinions, so that even Barnabas was
carried away by their dissimulation [hiding one's feelings,
motives by pretense]. As soon as I saw that they were not 14
keeping to the true line of the gospel, I said to Cephas, before
them all,

"If you, though a Jew, live as a Gentile does, and not as a
Jew, how can you make the Gentiles live like Jews?"

We, though we are Jews by birth and not Gentile sinners, 15
know that a man is justified, not by keeping the Law, but only 16
through faith in Jesus Christ. So we too have believed in
Christ Jesus, that we might be justified through faith
in Christ, and not through keeping the Law. For through

keeping the Law no human being shall be justified. But if 17
while we are seeking in Christ acquittal from guilt we ourselves are convicted of sin, is Christ then an agent of sin?
God forbid! Why, if I rebuild that which I had demolished, I 18
thereby constitute myself a transgressor; for by the Law I 19
died to the Law in order that I might live for God. I have been 20
crucified with Christ, and it is no longer I that live, but Christ
lives in me; and the life which I now live in the body I live by
faith in the Son of God who loved me and gave Himself up
for me. I do not nullify the grace of God; for if acquittal from 21
guilt comes through the Law, then Christ died in vain.

The Jewish Law Far Inferior to the Christian Faith

3 You foolish Galatians! who has bewitched you—before 1
whose very eyes was portrayed Jesus Christ crucified!
This one question I would ask you: 2

Is it on the ground of obeying the Law that you received
the Spirit, or is it because you heard and believed?

Are you so foolish? Having begun by the spiritual, are you 3
now going to reach perfection by the external? Have you 4
experienced so much to no purpose—if indeed it has been to
no purpose? He who gives you His Spirit and works miracles 5
among you—is it on the ground of your doing the Law, or of
your having heard and believed? Even as ABRAHAM 6
BELIEVED GOD, AND IT WAS PLACED TO HIS ACCOUNT
AS RIGHTEOUSNESS (Genesis 15:6).

You see, then, that those who rest on faith are the true sons 7
of Abraham. And the scripture, foreseeing that in conse- 8
quence of faith God would justify the Gentiles, foretold the
gospel to Abraham, saying, "IN YOU ALL THE NATIONS
SHALL BE BLESSED" (Genesis 12:3, 18:18). So we see that 9

those who rest on faith are blessed with believing Abraham. All who depend upon obedience to the Law are under a **10** curse; for it is written, "CURSED IS EVERY ONE WHO DOES NOT ABIDE BY ALL THE PRECEPTS OF THE LAW AND PRACTICE THEM" (Deuteronomy 27:26).

It is evident, too, that no one can be put right with God by **11** Law, because "THE RIGHTEOUS SHALL LIVE BY FAITH" (Habakkuk 2:4), and the Law has nothing to do with faith. It **12** teaches that "HE WHO DOES THESE THINGS SHALL LIVE BY THEM" (Leviticus 18:5). Christ purchased our freedom **13** from the curse of the Law by becoming accursed for us (for scripture says, "CURSED IS EVERY ONE WHO HANGS UPON A TREE" {Deuteronomy 21:23}), in order that in **14** Christ Jesus the blessing of Abraham might come upon the Gentiles, so that through faith we might receive the promised Spirit.

Brethren, I will take an illustration from current life. Even **15** a human covenant, when once ratified, no one can set aside or amplify. Now the promises were given to Abraham and to **16** his seed. It does not say "and to seeds" referring to many, but "AND TO YOUR SEED" (Genesis 12:7) referring to one—and this is Christ. I mean that the covenant which God had rati- **17** fied is not abrogated [abolished] by the Law which was given four hundred and thirty years later—so as to annul the promise. For if the inheritance comes from Law, it no longer **18** comes from a promise. But God has granted it to Abraham by promise.

Why, then, the Law? It was imposed later on with a view **19** to transgressions, until the seed should come to whom the promise had been made, and it was arranged by angels through the hand of a mediator. But there cannot be a **20** mediator for only one. God, however, is only one. Is the Law **21** then opposed to the promises of God? God forbid! for if a

law had been given which could have conferred life, right- 22
eousness would certainly have come by the law. But scripture has imprisoned all under sin, in order that the promise
depending on faith in Jesus Christ may be given to those
who believe.

Before this faith came, we were imprisoned under the Law, 23
waiting in custody for the faith which was to be revealed. So 24
that the Law has proved a tutor to discipline us for Christ,
that through faith we may be justified. But now that this faith 25
has come, we are no longer under a tutor. You are all sons of 26
God through faith in Christ Jesus; for all of you who have 27
been baptized into Christ have clothed yourselves with
Christ. There cannot be Jew and Greek, slave and free man, 28
male and female; you are all one in Christ Jesus. And if you 29
belong to Christ, then you are indeed Abraham's offspring,
and are heirs in accordance with the promise.

4 Now I say that so long as an heir is a child, he in no way 1
differs from a slave, although he is the owner of everything, but he is under guardians and trustees until the time 2
his father has appointed. So we also, when we were minors, 3
were kept like slaves under the world's rudimentary notions.
But, when the time was fully come, God sent forth His Son, 4
born of a woman, born subject to Law, in order to ransom 5
those who were subject to Law, so that we might receive
recognition as sons. And because you are sons, God has sent 6
out the Spirit of His Son to enter your hearts and cry "Abba!
Father!" Therefore you are no longer a slave, but a son; and 7
if a son, then an heir also through God's own act.

But at one time, you, having no knowledge of God, were 8
slaves to gods which were no gods at all. Now, however, 9
when you have come to know God—or rather to be known

by Him—how is it you are turning back again to the weak and worthless rudimentary notions to which you are once more willing to be enslaved? You observe days and months, 10 special seasons, and years. I am alarmed about you, that I 11 have perhaps bestowed labor upon you to no purpose.

Brethren, become as I am, I beseech you; for I also became 12 like you. I do not imply that you have done me any wrong. As 13 you know, in former days it was on account of bodily infirmity that I proclaimed the gospel to you, and yet the physi- 14 cal condition which was such a trial to you, you did not regard with contempt or loathing, but you received me as an angel of God or Christ Jesus Himself! What, then, has 15 become of that self-congratulation of yours? For I bear you witness that had it been possible you would have torn out your own eyes and have given them to me. Can it be that I 16 have become your enemy by speaking the truth to you?

These men pay court [pay flattering attention] to you, but 17 not honorably. They want to isolate you, so that you may pay court to them. To be paid court to in an honorable cause is 18 an honorable thing always, and not only when I am with you, my children—you for whom I am again in birth-pangs, 19 until Christ is formed within you. Would that I were with you 20 just now and could change my tone, for I am perplexed about you.

Tell me—you who want to be subject to Law—will you not 21 listen to the Law? It is written that Abraham had two sons, 22 one by the slave-woman and one by the free woman. But 23 whereas the child of the slave-woman had an ordinary birth, the child of the free woman was born in fulfillment of God's promise. All this is allegorical; for the women represent two 24 covenants. One originates on Mount Sinai, and bears children destined for slavery. This is Hagar: for the name Hagar 25 stands for Mount Sinai in Arabia, and corresponds to the present Jerusalem, which is in bondage together with her children. But the Jerusalem which is above is free, and she is 26 our mother. For it is written, 27

"REJOICE, THOU BARREN WOMAN THAT BEAREST NOT, BREAK FORTH INTO A JOYFUL CRY, THOU THAT DOST NOT TRAVAIL.
FOR THE DESOLATE WOMAN HAS MANY CHILDREN— MORE THAN SHE WHO HAS A HUSBAND" (Isaiah 54:1).

But you, brethren, like Isaac, are the children of a promise. 28 Yet just as, at that time, the child of ordinary birth persecuted 29 the one born according to the word of the Spirit, so it is now. But what says the scripture? "SEND AWAY THE SLAVE- 30 WOMAN AND HER SON, FOR NEVER SHALL THE SLAVE-WOMAN'S SON SHARE THE INHERITANCE WITH THE SON OF THE FREE WOMAN" (Genesis 21:10). Therefore, 31 brethren, we are not the children of a slave-woman, but of the free woman.

5 For freedom Christ has made us free; stand fast, then, 1 and do not again be hampered with the yoke of slavery.

Mark [look/take note], it is I Paul who tell you that if you 2 receive circumcision Christ will avail you nothing. I once 3 more protest to every man who receives circumcision that he is under obligation to keep the whole of the Law. You have 4 lost the good of union with Christ if you seek acquittal by Law: you have fallen from grace. For in spirit and owing to 5 our faith we wait in hope of acceptance. In Christ Jesus nei- 6 ther circumcision nor uncircumcision is of any avail; but only faith working through love.

You were running the race nobly! Who has interfered to 7 stop your obeying the truth? Such ill persuasion is not from 8 Him who calls you. A little leaven leavens the whole mass. 9

For my part I am convinced about you in the Lord that you 10
will adopt no new views. But the man—be he who he may—
who is troubling you, will have to bear his sentence. As for 11
me, brethren, if I am still a preacher of circumcision, why am
I still suffering persecution? Then the Cross has ceased to be
a stumbling-block! Would to God that those who are unset- 12
tling you would even mutilate themselves.

Moral and Spiritual Exhortations

You indeed, brethren, were called to freedom. Only do not 13
make your freedom an incentive to your lower nature; but
serve one another in love. For the entire Law is summed up 14
in the one precept, "YOU ARE TO LOVE YOUR NEIGHBOR
AS YOURSELF" (Leviticus 19:18). But if you bite and devour 15
one another, beware lest you are destroyed by one another.

I say, then, let your lives be guided by the Spirit, and then 16
you will not fulfill the cravings of your lower nature. For the 17
cravings of the lower nature are opposed to the Spirit, and the
Spirit is opposed to the lower nature, because these are antag-
onistic to each other, so that you cannot do as you would wish.
But if guided by the Spirit, you are not subject to Law. 18

Now the doings of the lower nature are familiar to you, 19
namely, licentiousness, impurity, indecency, idol-worship, 20
magic, animosity, strife, jealousy, ill temper, intrigues, dissen-
sions, factions, envy, drunkenness, carousing, and the like. I 21
forewarn you, as I have already forewarned you, that those
who practice such things will not inherit the Kingdom of
God. The Spirit, on the other hand, brings a harvest of love, 22
joy, peace; forbearance, kindness, benevolence; good faith,
meekness, self-restraint. Against such things there is no law. 23
Now those who belong to Christ Jesus have crucified the 24
lower nature with its passions and appetites. If we live by the 25

Spirit, by the Spirit also let us be guided. Let us not become 26 vain-glorious, challenging one another, envying one another.

6 Brethren, if anybody be overtaken in any misconduct, 1 you who are spiritual should restore such a one in a spirit of meekness. And let each of you keep an eye on himself, lest he also fall into temptation. Carry one another's 2 burdens, and so fulfill the law of Christ. For if any one thinks 3 himself to be somebody when he is nobody, he is deluding himself. But let every man scrutinize his own conduct, and 4 then he will have his reason for boasting, not by comparison with another but in regard to himself. For every man will 5 have to shoulder his own load.

Let those who receive instruction in the word share with 6 their instructors all temporal blessings. Do not deceive your- 7 selves. God is not to be mocked. For whatever a man sows, that he will also reap. He who sows for his lower nature will 8 from that nature reap destruction; but he who sows for the Spirit will from that Spirit reap the life eternal. Let us not lose 9 heart in doing what is right; for in due time we shall reap a harvest, if we do not faint. So then, as we have opportunity, let 10 us do good to all, and especially to the household of the faith.

See in what large letters I am writing to you with my own 11 hand. All who desire to make a good show outwardly try to 12 compel you to receive circumcision, simply that they may escape being persecuted for the cross of Christ. For the cir- 13 cumcised themselves do not really keep the Law, but they would have you circumcised in order that they may glory in your subjection to external rites. But God forbid that I 14 should glory in anything except in the cross of our Lord Jesus Christ, by which the world is crucified to me, and I to the world. For neither circumcision nor uncircumcision is 15

of any importance, but only a new nature. And all who will 16
regulate their lives by this principle—may peace and mercy
be upon them—and on the true Israel of God.

From this time onward let no one trouble me; for I bear on 17
my body the brand-marks of Jesus.

The grace of our Lord Jesus Christ be with your spirits, 18
brethren. Amen.

THE EPISTLE OF PAUL
TO THE EPHESIANS

1 Paul, an apostle of Christ Jesus by the will of God, to the saints {who are in Ephesus} faithful in Christ Jesus: may grace and peace be granted to you from God our Father and the Lord Jesus Christ.

Blessed be the God and Father of our Lord Jesus Christ, who has crowned us with every spiritual blessing in the heavenly realms in Christ; even as, in His love, He chose us as His own in Christ before the creation of the world, that we might be holy and without blemish in His presence. For He predestined us to be adopted by Himself as sons through Jesus Christ—such being His gracious will and pleasure—to the praise of the splendor of His grace with which He has enriched us in the beloved One.

It is in Him, and through the shedding of His blood, that we have our deliverance—the forgiveness of our offenses— so abundant was God's grace, the grace which He, the possessor of all wisdom and understanding, lavished upon us, when He made known to us the secret of His will. And this is in harmony with God's merciful purpose for the government of the world when the times are ripe for it—the purpose which He has cherished in His own mind of restoring the whole creation to find its one Head in Christ; yes, things in heaven and things on earth, to find their one Head in Him.

In Him, too, we have been made heirs, having been chosen beforehand in accordance with the intention of Him whose might carries out in everything the design of His own will, so that we should be devoted to the extolling of His glorious attributes—we who were the first to fix our hopes on Christ. And in Him you also, after listening to the word of 13 the truth, the gospel of your salvation—having believed in Him—were sealed with the promised Holy Spirit; that Spirit 14 being a pledge and foretaste of our inheritance, in anticipation of its full redemption—the inheritance which He has purchased to be specially His for the extolling of His glory.

For this reason I too, having heard of the faith in the Lord 15 Jesus which prevails among you, and of your love for all the saints, offer never-ceasing thanks on your behalf while I make 16 mention of you in my prayers. For I always beseech the God of 17 our Lord Jesus Christ—the Father most glorious—to give you a spirit of wisdom and of insight into mysteries through knowledge of Him, the eyes of your heart being enlightened 18 so that you may know what is the hope which His call to you inspires, what the wealth of the glory of His inheritance in the saints, and what the transcendent greatness of His power in 19 us believers as seen in the working of His infinite might when 20 He displayed it in Christ by raising Him from the dead, and seating Him at His own right hand in the heavenly realms, high above all other government and authority and power 21 and dominion, and every title of sovereignty used either in this age or in the age to come. God has put all things under His 22 feet, and has appointed Him universal and supreme Head of the Church, which is His Body, the completeness of Him who 23 everywhere fills the universe with Himself.

2 To you also, who were dead through your offenses and 1 sins, which were once habitual to you while you walked 2 in the ways of this world and obeyed the prince of the powers of the air, the spirits that are now at work in the hearts of the disobedient—to you God has given life.

Among them we too once all passed our lives, governed by 3 the inclinations of our lower nature, indulging the cravings of that nature and of our thoughts, and were in our original state deserving of anger like all others. But God, being rich in 4 mercy, because of the intense love which He bestowed on us caused us, dead though we were through our offenses, to live 5 with Christ—it is by grace that you have been saved—raised 6 us with Him from the dead, and enthroned us with Him in the heavenly realms as being in Christ Jesus, in order that, by 7 His goodness to us in Christ Jesus, He might display in the ages to come the transcendent riches of His grace. For it is by 8 grace that you have been saved through faith; and that not of yourselves. It is God's gift, and is not on the ground of 9 merit—so that it may be impossible for any one to boast. For 10 we are God's own handiwork, created in Christ Jesus for good works which He has predestined us to practice.

Therefore, do not forget that formerly you were Gentiles as 11 to your bodily condition. You were called "the Uncircumcision" by those who style themselves the Circumcised—a circumcision in the body made by hands. At that time you 12 were living apart from Christ, estranged from the commonwealth of Israel, with no share by birth in the covenants which are based on the promises, and you had no hope and no God, in all the world. But now in Christ Jesus you who 13 once were so far away have been brought near through the blood of Christ.

For He is our peace—He who has made Jew and Gentile 14 one, and in His own human nature has broken down the hostile dividing wall, by setting aside the Law with its com- 15 mandments, expressed, as they were, in definite decrees. His design was to unite the two sections of humanity in Himself so as to form one new man, thus effecting peace, and to rec- 16 oncile Jew and Gentile in one body to God, by means of His

cross—slaying by it their mutual enmity. So He came and 17
proclaimed the gospel of peace to you who were so far away,
and peace to those who were near; because it is through Him 18
that Jew and Gentile alike have access through one Spirit to
the Father.

You are therefore no longer mere foreigners or persons 19
excluded from civil rights. On the contrary, you share citizenship with the saints and are members of His family. You 20
are a building which has been reared on the foundation of
the apostles and prophets, the cornerstone being Christ
Jesus Himself, in union with whom the whole fabric, truly 21
bonded together, is rising so as to form a holy sanctuary in
the Lord; in whom you also are being built up together to 22
become a fixed abode for God through the Spirit.

3 For this reason I Paul, the prisoner of Christ Jesus on 1
behalf of you Gentiles—if, that is, you have heard of my 2
ministry of that grace of God which was given me for your
benefit, in that by a revelation the truth hitherto [until now] 3
kept secret was made known to me, as I have already briefly
explained to you. By means of that explanation, as you read it, 4
you can judge of my insight into the truth of Christ which in 5
earlier ages was not made known to the human race, as it has
now been revealed to His holy apostles and prophets through
the Spirit—I mean the truth that the Gentiles are joint heirs 6
with us Jews, and that they form one body with us, and have
the same interest as we have in the promise which has been
made good in Christ Jesus through the gospel. Of this gospel I 7
have been appointed a minister by the gift of the grace of God,
which in the exercise of His power He has bestowed on me.

To me who am less than the least of all the saints has this 8
work been graciously entrusted—to proclaim to the Gentiles

the gospel of the exhaustless wealth of Christ, and to show all 9
men in a clear light what my stewardship is. It is the stewardship of the truth which from all the ages lay concealed in
the mind of God, the Creator of all things—concealed in 10
order that the Church might now be used to display to the
powers and authorities in the heavenly realms the innumer-
able aspects of God's wisdom. Such was the eternal purpose 11
which He had formed in Christ Jesus our Lord, in whom we 12
have this bold and confident access through our faith in
Him. Therefore I entreat you not to lose heart in the midst of 13
my sufferings on your behalf, for they bring you glory.

For this reason, on bended knee I beseech the Father, 14
from whom the whole family in heaven and on earth 15
derives its name, to grant you—in accordance with the 16
wealth of His glorious perfections—to be strengthened by
His Spirit with power permeating your inmost being. I pray 17
that Christ may make His home in your hearts through your
faith; so that having your roots deep and your foundations
strong in love, you may become mighty to grasp the idea, 18
as it is grasped by all the saints, of the breadth and length,
the height and depth—yes, to know the love of Christ that 19
surpasses knowledge, so that you may be filled up to all the
fullness of God.

Now to Him who, in the exercise of His power that is at 20
work within us, is able to do infinitely beyond all our highest
prayers or thoughts—to Him be the glory in the Church and 21
in Christ Jesus to all generations, world without end! Amen.

4 I, then, the prisoner for the Lord's sake, entreat you to 1
live and act as becomes those who have received the
call that you have received—with all lowliness of mind and 2
unselfishness, and with patience, bearing with one another

lovingly, and earnestly striving to maintain, in the uniting 3
bond of peace, the unity given by the Spirit. There is but one 4
body and but one Spirit, as also when you were called you
had one and the same hope held out to you. There is but one 5
Lord, one faith, one baptism, and one God and Father of all, 6
who rules over all, acts through all, and dwells in all.

Yet to each of us individually His grace was given, meas- 7
ured out with the munificence [generosity] of Christ. For this 8
reason scripture says:

"HE ASCENDED ON HIGH,

HE LED CAPTIVE A HOST OF CAPTIVES,

AND GAVE GIFTS TO MEN" (Psalm 68:18).

(Now this "ascended"—what does it mean but that He had 9
first descended into the lower regions of the earth? He who 10
descended is the same as He who ascended again, far above
all the heavens, in order to fill the universe.)

And He Himself appointed some to be apostles, some to 11
be prophets, some to be evangelists, some to be pastors and
teachers, in order fully to equip His people for the work of 12
serving—for the building up of Christ's body—till we all of us 13
arrive at oneness in faith and in the knowledge of the Son of
God, and at mature manhood and the stature of full-grown
men in Christ. So we shall no longer be babes, nor shall we 14
resemble mariners tossed on the waves and carried about
with every changing wind of doctrine, according to men's
cleverness and unscrupulous cunning, that makes use of
every shifting device to mislead. But we shall lovingly hold to 15
the truth, and shall in all respects grow up into union with
Him who is our Head, even Christ. Dependent on Him, the 16
whole body—its various parts closely fitting and firmly
adhering to one another—grows by the aid of every contrib-
utory ligament, with power proportioned to the need of each
individual part, so as to build itself up in a spirit of love.

Therefore I warn you, and I implore you in the name of the 17
Lord, no longer to live as the Gentiles in their perverseness
live, with darkened understandings, having by reason of the 18
ignorance which is deep-seated in them and the insensibil-
ity of their moral nature no share in the life which God gives.
Such men being past feeling have abandoned themselves to 19
impurity, greedily indulging in every kind of profligacy
[shameless immorality].

But these are not the lessons which you have learned from 20
Christ; if at least you have heard His voice and in Him have 21
been taught—and this is true Christian teaching—to put 22
away your original evil nature, as displayed in your former
mode of life, a nature which is doomed to perish as befits its
misleading impulses, and to get yourselves renewed in the 23
temper of your minds and to clothe yourselves with that new 24
and better self which has been created to resemble God in
the righteousness and holiness of the truth.

For this reason, laying aside falsehood, every one of you 25
should speak the truth to his fellow man; for we are, as it
were, parts of one another. If angry, beware of sinning. Let 26
not your irritation last until the sun goes down; and do not 27
leave room for the devil. He who has been a thief must steal 28
no more, but, instead of that, should work with his own
hands in honest industry, so that he may have something of
which he can give the needy a share. Let no unwholesome 29
words ever pass your lips, but let all your words be good for
benefiting others according to the need of the moment, so
that they may be a means of blessing to the hearers. And 30
beware of grieving the Holy Spirit of God, in whom you have
been sealed in preparation for the day of redemption. Let all 31
bitterness and all passionate feeling, all anger and loud
insulting language, be unknown among you—and also every
kind of malice. On the contrary, learn to be kind to one 32

another, tenderhearted, forgiving one another, just as God in Christ has also forgiven you.

5 Therefore be imitators of God, as His dear children. And 1 live and act lovingly, as Christ also loved you and gave 2 Himself up to death on our behalf as an offering and sacrifice to God, yielding a fragrant odor.

But fornication and every kind of impurity, or covetousness, let them not even be mentioned among you, for they 3 ought not to be named among the saints. Avoid shameful and 4 foolish talk and low jesting—they are all alike discreditable— and in place of these give thanks. For be well assured that no 5 fornicator or immoral person and no profligate—or in other words idol-worshiper—has any share awaiting him in the Kingdom of Christ and of God.

Let no one deceive you with empty words, for it is on 6 account of these very sins that God's anger is coming upon the disobedient. Therefore do not become sharers with them. 7

There was a time when you were nothing but darkness. 8 Now, as Christians, you are light itself. Live and act as sons of light—for the effect of the light is seen in every kind of good- 9 ness, uprightness, and truth—and learn in your own experi- 10 ences what is fully pleasing to the Lord. Have nothing to do 11 with the barren unprofitable deeds of darkness, but, instead of that, set your faces against them; for the things which are 12 done by these people in secret it is disgraceful even to speak of. But everything can be tested by the light and thus be 13 shown in its true colors; for whatever shines of itself is light. For this reason it is said, 14

"Rise, sleeper;
Rise from among the dead,
And Christ will shed light upon you."

Therefore be very careful how you live and act. Let it not 15
be as unwise men, but as wise. Buy up your opportunities, 16
for these are evil times. On this account do not prove your- 17
selves wanting in sense, but try to understand what the
Lord's will is.

Do not indulge in much wine—a thing in which excess is 18
so easy—but drink deeply of God's Spirit. Speak to one 19
another with psalms and hymns and spiritual songs. Sing
and offer praise in your hearts to the Lord. Always and for 20
everything let your thanks to God the Father be presented in
the name of our Lord Jesus Christ; and submit to one 21
another out of reverence for Christ.

Married women, submit to your own husbands as if to the 22
Lord; because a husband is the head of his wife, as Christ 23
also is the Head of the Church, Himself the Savior of the Body.
And just as the Church submits to Christ, so also married 24
women should be entirely submissive to their husbands.

Married men, love your wives, as Christ also loved the 25
Church and gave Himself up to death for her, in order to 26
make her holy, cleansing her with the baptismal water by
the word, that He might present the church to Himself a glo- 27
rious bride, without spot or wrinkle or any other defect—
holy and unblemished. So, too, married men ought to love 28
their wives as much as they love themselves. He who loves
his wife loves himself. For never yet has a man hated his 29
own body. On the contrary, he feeds and cherishes it, just as
Christ feeds and cherishes the Church; because we are, as it 30
were, parts of His Body.

"FOR THIS REASON A MAN IS TO LEAVE HIS FATHER 31
AND HIS MOTHER AND CLING TO HIS WIFE, AND THE
TWO SHALL BE AS ONE FLESH" (Genesis 2:24).

That is a great truth hitherto [until now] kept secret: I 32
mean the truth concerning Christ and the Church. Yet I insist 33

that among you also, each man is to love his own wife as much as he loves himself, and let a married woman see to it that she treats her husband with respect.

6 Children, be obedient to your parents as a Christian 1 duty, for this is right. "HONOR YOUR FATHER AND 2 YOUR MOTHER"—this is the first commandment which has a promise added to it—"SO THAT IT MAY BE WELL WITH 3 YOU, AND THAT YOU MAY LIVE LONG ON THE EARTH" (Exodus 20:12). And you, fathers, do not irritate your chil- 4 dren, but bring them up tenderly in the instruction and admonition of the Lord.

Slaves, be obedient to your earthly masters, with respect 5 and eager anxiety to please and with simplicity of motive as if you were obeying Christ. Let it not be in acts of eye-service 6 as if you had but to please men, but as Christ's bondservants who are doing God's will from the heart. With right good will 7 be faithful to your duty, as service rendered to the Lord and not to man. You well know that for whatever right thing any 8 one does he will receive a requital [return or repayment] from the Lord, whether he is a slave or a free man.

And you masters, act towards your slaves on the same 9 principles, and refrain from threats. For you know that in heaven there is One who is your Master as well as theirs, and that of merely earthly distinctions there are none with Him.

In conclusion, strengthen yourselves in the Lord and in 10 the power which His supreme might imparts. Put on the 11 complete armor of God, so as to be able to stand firm against all the stratagems of the devil. For ours is not a conflict with 12 mere flesh and blood, but with the despotisms, the empires, the forces that control and govern this dark world—the spiritual hosts of evil arrayed against us in the heavenly warfare.

Therefore put on the complete armor of God, so that you 13
may be able to stand your ground in the evil day, and, having
fought to the end, to remain victors on the field. Stand there- 14
fore, first fastening round you the girdle of truth and putting
on the breastplate of uprightness as well as the shoes of the 15
gospel of peace—a firm foundation for your feet. And 16
besides all these take the great shield of faith, on which you
will be able to quench all the flaming darts of the Wicked
One; and receive the helmet of salvation, and the sword of 17
the Spirit which is the word of God. Pray with unceasing 18
prayer and entreaty at all times in the Spirit, and be always
on the alert to seize opportunities for doing so, with unwearied persistence and entreaty on behalf of all the saints, and 19
ask on my behalf that words may be given to me so that, outspoken and fearless, I may make known the truths (hitherto
[until now] kept secret) of the gospel—to spread which I am 20
an ambassador in chains—so that when telling them I may
speak out boldly as I ought.

But in order that you also may know how I am doing, 21
Tychicus our dearly-loved brother and faithful helper in the
Lord's service will tell you everything. I have sent him to you 22
for the very purpose—that you may know about us and that
he may encourage you.

Peace be to the brethren and love combined with faith, 23
from God the Father and the Lord Jesus Christ. May grace be 24
with all who love our Lord Jesus Christ with perfect sincerity.

THE EPISTLE OF PAUL
TO THE PHILIPPIANS

1 Paul and Timothy, bondservants of Christ Jesus, to all 1
the saints in Christ Jesus who are at Philippi, with the
ministers of the church and their assistants: grace and peace 2
to you from God our Father and the Lord Jesus Christ.

I thank my God at my every remembrance of you—always 3
when offering any prayer on behalf of you all, finding a joy in 4
offering it. I thank my God, I say, for your co-operation in 5
spreading the gospel, from the time it first came to you even
until now. For of this I am confident, that He who has begun 6
a good work within you will go on to perfect it in preparation
for the day of Jesus Christ. And I am justified in having this 7
confidence about you all, because, both during my imprisonment and when I stand up in defense of the gospel or to
confirm its truth, I have you in my heart, sharers as you all
are in the same grace as myself. For God is my witness how I 8
yearn over all of you with tender Christian affection.

And it is my prayer that your love may be more and more 9
accompanied by clear knowledge and keen perception for testing things that differ, so that you may be men of transparent 10
character, and may be blameless, in preparation for the day of
Christ, being filled with those fruits of righteousness which 11
come through Jesus Christ—to the glory and praise of God.

Now I would have you know, brethren, that what I have 12
gone through has turned out to the furtherance of the gospel
rather than otherwise. And thus it has become notorious 13
among all the imperial guards and the people generally that
it is for the sake of Christ that I am a prisoner; and the greater 14

part of the brethren, made confident in the Lord through my imprisonment, now declare God's word without fear, more boldly than ever.

Some indeed actually preach Christ out of envy and contentiousness, but there are also others who do it from good will. These latter preach Him from love to me, knowing that I am here for the defense of the gospel; while the others proclaim Him from motives of rivalry, and insincerely, supposing that by this they are embittering my imprisonment. 15 16 17

What does it matter, however? In any case Christ is preached—either perversely or in honest truth; and in that I rejoice, yes, and will rejoice. For I know that it will result in my salvation through your prayers and a bountiful supply of the Spirit of Jesus Christ, in fulfillment of my eager expectation and hope that I shall never have reason to feel ashamed, but that by my perfect freedom of speech Christ will be glorified in me, now as always, either by my life or by my death. 18 19 20

For, with me, to live is Christ and to die is gain. But since to live means a longer stay on earth, that implies more labor for me—and not unsuccessful labor; and which I am to choose I cannot tell. I am in a dilemma, my earnest desire being to depart and be with Christ, for that is far, far better. But for your sakes it is more important that I should still remain in the body. I am convinced of this, and I know that I shall remain, and shall go on working side by side with you all, to promote your progress and joy in the faith; so that in Christ Jesus you may have additional reason for glorying about me as the result of my being with you again. 21 22 23 24 25 26

Only let the lives you live be worthy of the gospel of the Christ, in order that, whether I come and see you or, being absent, only hear of you, I may know that you are standing fast in one spirit and with one mind, fighting shoulder to shoulder for the faith of the gospel. Never for a moment 27 28 quail [draw back in fear] before your antagonists. Your fear-lessness will be to them a sure token of impending destruc-tion, but to you it will be a sure token of your salvation—a token coming from God. For you have had the privilege 29 granted you on behalf of Christ—not only to believe in Him, but also to suffer on His behalf; maintaining, as you do, the 30 same kind of conflict that you once saw in me and which you still hear that I am engaged in.

2 If, then, I can appeal to you as the followers of Christ, if 1 there is any persuasive power in love and any common sharing of the Spirit, or if any tender-heartedness and compas-sion, make my joy complete by being of one mind, united in 2 mutual love, with harmony of feeling giving your minds to one and the same object. Do nothing in a spirit of factiousness or of 3 vainglory, but with humility let every one regard the rest as being of more account than himself; each fixing his attention, 4 not simply on his own interests, but also on those of others.

Let the very spirit which was in Christ Jesus be in you also. 5 From the beginning He had the nature of God. Yet He did not 6 regard equality with God as something at which He should grasp. Nay, He stripped Himself of His glory, and took on 7 Him the nature of a bondservant by becoming a man like other men. And being recognized as truly human, He hum- 8 bled Himself and even stooped to die; and that, too, a death on the cross. It is because of this also that God has so highly 9 exalted Him, and has conferred on Him the Name which is supreme above every other name, in order that in the Name 10 of JESUS every knee should bow, of beings in the highest heavens, of those on the earth, and of those in the under-world, and that every tongue should confess that JESUS 11 CHRIST is LORD, to the glory of God the Father.

Therefore, my dearly-loved friends, as I have always found 12
you obedient, labor earnestly with fear and trembling—not
merely as though I were present with you, but much more
now since I am absent from you—labor earnestly, I say, to
make sure of your own salvation. For it is God Himself whose 13
power creates within you both the desire and the power to
execute His gracious will.

Be ever on your guard against a grudging and contentious 14
spirit, so that you may always prove yourselves to be blameless 15
and spotless—irreproachable children of God in the midst of
a crooked and perverse generation, among whom you are
seen as heavenly lights in the world, holding out to them the 16
word of life. It will then be my glory on the day of Christ that
I did not run my race in vain nor toil in vain. Nay, even if my 17
life is being poured as a libation upon the sacrificial offering
of your faith, I rejoice, and I congratulate you all. And I bid 18
you also share my gladness, and congratulate me.

But, if the Lord Jesus permits it, I hope before long to send 19
Timothy to you that I, in turn, may be cheered by getting
news of you. For I have no one like-minded who will cherish 20
a genuine care for you: everybody concerns himself about 21
his own interests, not about those of Jesus Christ. But you 22
know Timothy's approved worth—how, like a child working
with his father, he has served with me in furtherance of the
gospel. So he it is that I hope to send as soon as ever I see 23
how things go with me; but trusting, as I do, in the Lord, I 24
believe that I shall myself also come to you before long.

Yet I deem it important to send Epaphroditus to you now: 25
he is my brother and comrade both in labor and in arms, and
is your messenger who has ministered to my needs. I send 26
him because he is longing for you all, and is distressed at
your having heard of his illness. For it is true that he has been 27
ill, and was apparently at the point of death; but God had

pity on him, and not only on him, but also on me, to save me from having sorrow upon sorrow. I am therefore all the more 28 eager to send him, in the hope that when you see him again you may be glad and I may have the less sorrow. Receive 29 him, therefore, with all joy, and hold in honor men like him; because it was for the sake of Christ's work that he came so 30 near death, hazarding, as he did, his very life in endeavoring to make good any deficiency that there might be in your service to me.

3 Moreover, my brethren, be joyful in the Lord. For me to 1 write to you the same things as before is not irksome to me, while so far as you are concerned it is a safe precaution. Beware of "the dogs," the dishonest workmen, the self- 2 mutilators. For we are the true circumcision—we who render 3 to God a spiritual worship and make our boast in Christ Jesus and have no confidence in outward ceremonies; although I 4 myself might have some excuse for confidence in outward ceremonies. If any one else claims a right to trust in them, far more may I—circumcised, as I was, on the eighth day, a 5 member of the race of Israel and of the tribe of Benjamin, a Hebrew sprung from Hebrews; as to the Law, a Pharisee; as to 6 zeal, a persecutor of the Church; as to the righteousness which comes through Law, blameless.

Yet all that was gain to me, for Christ's sake I have reckoned 7 as loss. Nay, I even reckon all things as pure loss because of 8 the priceless privilege of knowing Christ Jesus my Lord. For His sake I have suffered the loss of everything, and reckon it all as mere refuse, in order that I may win Christ and be found 9 in Him, not having a righteousness of my own, derived from the Law, but that which arises from faith in Christ—the righteousness which comes from God through faith. I long to 10 know Christ and the power which is in His resurrection, and to share in His sufferings and die even as He died; in the hope that I may attain to the resurrection from the dead. 11

I do not say that I have already gained this knowledge or already reached perfection. But I press on, striving to lay hold of that for which I was also laid hold of by Christ Jesus. Brethren, I do not imagine that I have yet laid hold of it. But this one thing I do—forgetting everything which is past and stretching forward to what lies in front of me, with my eyes fixed on the goal I push on to secure the prize of God's heavenward call in Christ Jesus. Therefore let all of us who are mature believers cherish these thoughts; and if in any respect you think differently, that also God will make clear to you. But whatever be the point that we have already reached, let us persevere in the same course. 12 13 14 15 16

Brethren, vie with one another in imitating me, and carefully observe those who follow the example which we have set you. For there are many whom I have often described to you, and I now even with tears describe them, as being enemies to the cross of Christ. Their end is destruction, their bellies are their god, their glory is in their shame, and their minds are devoted to earthly things. We, however, are free citizens of heaven, and we are waiting with longing expectation for the coming from heaven of a Savior, the Lord Jesus Christ, who, in the exercise of the power which He has even to subject all things to Himself, will transform this body of our humiliation until it resembles the body of His glory. 17 18 19 20 21

4 Therefore, my brethren, dearly loved and longed for, my joy and crown, so stand firm in the Lord, my dearly-loved ones. 1

I entreat Euodia, and I entreat Syntyche, to be of one 2

mind, as sisters in Christ. Yes, and I beg you also, my true 3 yoke-fellow, to help these women, for they shared my toil in connection with the gospel, together with Clement and the rest of my fellow laborers, whose names are recorded in the Book of Life.

Always rejoice in the Lord: I will repeat it, rejoice. Let your 4 forbearing spirit be known to every one: the Lord is near. Do 5 not be anxious about anything, but by prayer and earnest 6 pleading together with thanksgiving let your requests be unreservedly made known before God. So will the peace of 7 God, which surpasses all power of thought, be a garrison to guard your hearts and minds in Christ Jesus.

Finally, brethren, whatever is true, whatever wins respect, 8 whatever is just, whatever is pure, whatever is lovable, whatever is of good repute—if there is any virtue or anything deemed worthy of praise—cherish the thought of these things. Let all that you learned and received and heard and 9 saw in me fashion your conduct; and the God of peace will be with you.

But I rejoice in the Lord greatly that now at length you 10 have revived your thoughtfulness for my welfare. Indeed you have always been thoughtful for me, although opportunity failed you. I do not refer to this through fear of privation, for 11 I indeed have learned, whatever be my outward experiences, to be content. I know both how to live in straitened circum- 12 stances and how to live amid abundance. I am fully initiated into all the secrets both of fullness and of hunger, of abundance and of want. I have strength for anything through Him 13 who gives me power.

Yet I thank you for taking your share in my troubles. And 14 you men and women of Philippi also know that at the first 15 preaching of the gospel, when I had left Macedonia, no other church except yourselves held communication with me

about giving and receiving; because even in Thessalonica 16
you sent several times to minister to my needs. Not that I 17
crave for gifts from you, but I do want to see a rich harvest of
service placed to your account. I have enough of every- 18
thing—and more than enough. My wants are fully satisfied
now that I have received from the hands of Epaphroditus the
generous gifts which you sent me: they are a fragrant odor,
an acceptable sacrifice, truly pleasing to God. But my God— 19
so great is His wealth of glory in Christ Jesus—will fully supply every need of yours. And to our God and Father be the 20
glory for ever and ever! Amen.

My greetings in Christ to every saint. The brethren who are 21
with me send their greetings. All the saints here greet you— 22
especially the members of Caesar's household.

The grace of our Lord Jesus Christ be with your spirit. 23

THE EPISTLE OF PAUL TO THE COLOSSIANS

1 Paul, by the will of God an apostle of Christ Jesus, and Timothy our brother, to the saints and the believing brethren at Colossae who are in Christ: may grace and peace be granted to you from God our Father.

We give thanks to God, the Father of our Lord Jesus Christ, constantly praying for you as we do, because we have heard of your faith in Christ Jesus, and of the love which you cherish towards all the saints on account of the hope treasured up for you in heaven. Of this hope you have already heard in the word of the truth of the gospel. For it has reached you, and remains with you, just as it has also spread through the whole world, yielding fruit there and increasing. It has done so among you from the day when first you heard it and came really to know the grace of God, as you learned it from Epaphras our dearly-loved fellow servant. He is to you a faithful minister of Christ in our stead, and moreover he has informed us of your love, which is inspired by the Spirit.

For this reason we also, from the day we first received these tidings, have never ceased to pray for you and to entreat that you may be filled with a clear knowledge of His will accompanied by thorough wisdom and discernment in spiritual things; so that your lives may be worthy of the Lord and perfectly pleasing to Him, while you bear fruit in every good work, and increase in the knowledge of God. Since His power is so glorious, may you be strengthened with strength of every kind, and be prepared for cheerfully enduring all things with fortitude and patience; and may you give thanks to the Father who has made us fit to receive our share of the inheritance of the saints in Light.

It is God who has delivered us out of the dominion of 13 darkness, and has transferred us into the Kingdom of His dearly-loved Son, in whom we have our redemption—the 14 forgiveness of our sins. Christ is the visible representation of 15 the invisible God, the firstborn of all creation. For in Him 16 was created the universe of things in heaven and on earth, things seen and things unseen, thrones, dominions, prince-doms, powers—all were created, and exist, through and for Him. And HE IS before all things, and in and through Him 17 the universe is one harmonious whole.

Moreover He is the head of His Body, the Church. He is the 18 beginning, the firstborn from among the dead, in order that He Himself may in all things occupy the foremost place. For 19 it was the Father's gracious will that the whole of the divine perfections should dwell in Him. And God purposed 20 through Him to reconcile the universe to Himself, making peace through His blood, which was shed upon the cross— to reconcile to Himself through Him, I say, things on earth and things in heaven.

And you, estranged as you once were and even hostile in 21 your minds amidst your evil deeds, He has now, in His 22 human body, reconciled to God by His death, to bring you, holy and faultless and irreproachable, into His presence; if, 23 indeed, you are still firmly holding to faith as your founda-tion, without ever shifting from your hope that rests on the gospel that you have heard, which has been proclaimed among the whole creation under heaven, of which I Paul became a minister.

Now I can find joy amid my sufferings for you, and I fill up 24 in my own person whatever is lacking in Christ's afflictions on behalf of His Body, the Church, I have been appointed to 25 serve the Church in the position of responsibility entrusted to me by God for your benefit, so that I may fully deliver God's word—the truth which has been kept secret from all 26 ages and generations, but has now been revealed to His saints, to whom it was His will to make known how vast 27 a wealth of glory for the Gentile world is implied in this truth—the truth that Christ is in you, the hope of glory. Him 28 we preach, admonishing every one and instructing every one, as wisely as we can, so that we may bring every one into God's presence, made perfect through Christ. To this end, 29 like an eager wrestler, I exert all my strength in reliance upon the power of Him who is mightily at work within me.

2 For I would have you know in how severe a struggle I am 1 engaged on behalf of you and the brethren in Laodicea and of all who have not known me personally, in order that 2 their hearts may be cheered, they themselves being welded together in love and advancing towards an abounding wealth of understanding, even to the knowledge of the secret of God. In Him all the treasures of wisdom and knowledge 3 are stored up, hidden from view.

I say this to prevent your being misled by any one's plausi- 4 ble sophistry [unsound, misleading reasoning]. For although 5 I am absent from you in body, yet in spirit I am present with you, and am delighted to witness your good discipline and the solid front presented by your faith in Christ.

As therefore you have received the Christ, even Jesus our 6 Lord, live and act in vital union with Him; having the roots of 7 your being firmly planted in Him, and continually building yourselves up in Him, and always being increasingly confirmed in the faith as you were taught it, and abounding in it with thanksgiving.

Take care lest there be any one who leads you away as 8
prisoners by means of his philosophy and idle fancies, following human traditions and the world's crude notions
instead of following Christ. For it is in Christ that the full- 9
ness of God's nature dwells embodied, and in Him you are 10
made complete, and He is the Lord of all princes and rulers.
In Him also you were circumcised with a circumcision not 11
performed by hand, when you threw off your sinful nature
in the circumcision of Christ; having been buried with Him 12
in your baptism, in which you were also raised with Him
through faith produced within you by God, who raised
Him from among the dead.

And to you—dead as you once were in your transgressions 13
and in the uncircumcision of your natural state—He has
nevertheless given you life with Him, having forgiven us all
our transgressions. The bond, with its requirements, which 14
was in force against us and was hostile to us, He canceled
and cleared it out of the way, nailing it to His cross. And the 15
hostile princes and rulers He stripped off from Himself, and
boldly displayed them as His conquests, when by the cross
He triumphed over them.

Therefore suffer no one to sit in judgment on you as to eat- 16
ing or drinking or with regard to a festival, a new moon, or a
sabbath. These were a shadow of things that were to come, 17
but the substance belongs to Christ. Let no one defraud you 18
of your prize, priding himself on his humility and on his worship of the angels, and taking his stand on the visions he has
seen, and idly puffed up with his unspiritual thoughts. Such 19
a one does not keep his hold upon Christ, the Head, from
whom the Body, in all its parts nourished and strengthened
by its points of contact and its connections, grows with a
divine growth.

If you have died with Christ and have escaped from the 20

world's rudimentary notions, why, as though your life still belonged to the world, do you submit to such precepts as, "Do not handle this"; "Do not taste that"; "Do not touch that 21 other thing"—referring to things which are all intended to be 22 used up and to perish—in obedience to mere human injunctions and teachings? These rules have indeed an appearance 23 of wisdom, where there is self-imposed worship and an affectation of humility and an ascetic severity. But not one of them is of any value in combating the indulgence of our lower natures.

3 If, however, you have risen with Christ, seek the things 1 that are above, where Christ is, enthroned at God's right hand. Give your minds to the things that are above, not to 2 the things that are on the earth. For you have died, and your 3 life is hidden with Christ in God. When Christ appears—He 4 is our true life—then you also will appear with Him in glory.

Therefore put to death your earthward inclinations— 5 fornication, impurity, sensual passion, unholy desire, and all greed, for that is a form of idolatry. It is on account of these 6 very sins that God's wrath is coming, and you also were once 7 addicted to them, while you were living under their power.

But now you must rid yourselves of every kind of sin— 8 angry and passionate outbreaks, ill-will, evil speaking, foulmouthed abuse—so that these may never soil your lips. Do 9 not lie to one another, for you have stripped off the old self with its doings, and have clothed yourselves with the new 10 self, which is being remolded into full knowledge so as to become like Him who created it. In that new creation there 11 can be neither Greek nor Jew, circumcision nor uncircumcision, barbarian, Scythian, slave nor free man, but Christ is all and in all.

Clothe yourselves therefore, as saints holy and dearly 12
loved, with tender-heartedness, kindness, lowliness of mind,
meekness and long-suffering; bearing with one another, and 13
readily forgiving each other, if any one has a grievance
against another. Just as the Lord has forgiven you, you also
must forgive. And over all these put on love, which is the per- 14
fect bond of union; and let the peace which Christ gives set- 15
tle all questionings in your hearts, to which peace indeed you
were called as belonging to His one Body; and be thankful.

Let the word of Christ remain as a rich treasure in your 16
hearts. In all wisdom teach and admonish one another with
psalms, hymns, and spiritual songs, and sing with grace in
your hearts to God. And whatever you do, in word or in deed, 17
do everything in the name of the Lord Jesus, and through
Him give thanks to God the Father.

Married women, be submissive to your husbands, as is fit- 18
ting in the Lord. Married men, be affectionate to your wives, 19
and do not treat them harshly. Children, be obedient to your 20
parents in everything; for that is well-pleasing in the Lord.
Fathers, do not fret and harass your children, or you may 21
make them sullen and morose. Slaves, be obedient in every- 22
thing to your earthly masters; not with acts of eye-service, as
aiming only to please men, but with simplicity of purpose,
because you fear the Lord. Whatever you are doing, let your 23
hearts be in your work, as a thing done for the Lord and not
for men. For you know that it is from the Lord you will 24
receive the inheritance as your reward. Christ is the Master
whose bondservants you are. The man who perpetrates a 25
wrong will find the wrong repaid to him: with God there are
no merely earthly distinctions.

4 Masters, deal justly and equitably with your slaves, 1 knowing that you too have a master in heaven.

Be earnest and unwearied in prayer, being intent on it and 2 on your giving of thanks. And pray at the same time for us 3 also, that God may open for us a door for preaching, for us to tell the truth concerning Christ for the sake of which I am even a prisoner. Then I shall proclaim it fully, as it is my duty 4 to do. Behave wisely in relation to the outside world, seizing 5 your opportunities. Let your language be always seasoned 6 with the salt of grace, so that you may know how to give every man a fitting answer.

Tychicus, our much-loved brother, a trusty assistant and 7 fellow servant with us in the Lord's work, will give you every information about me. And for this very purpose I send him 8 to you that you may know how we are faring; and that he may cheer your hearts. And with him I send our dear and 9 trusty brother Onesimus, who is one of yourselves. They will inform you of everything here.

Aristarchus my fellow prisoner sends greeting to you, and 10 so does Mark the cousin of Barnabas. You have received instructions about him; if he comes to you, give him a welcome. Jesus, called Justus, also sends greeting. These three 11 are Jewish converts. They alone among such have worked loyally with me for the Kingdom of God: they are men who have been a comfort to me.

Epaphras, who is one of yourselves, a bondservant of Jesus 12 Christ, sends greeting to you, always wrestling on your behalf in his prayers, that you may stand firm, as men of ripe character and of clear conviction as to everything which is God's will. For I can bear witness to the deep interest he takes 13 in you and in the brethren at Laodicea and in those at Hierapolis. Luke, the dearly-loved physician, salutes you, 14 and so does Demas.

Greetings to the breth[...] Laodicea, especially to 15
Nymphas, and to the chu[...]at meets at their house. And 16
when this letter has bee[...]d among you, let it be read also
in the church of the L[...]ceans, and you in turn must read
the one I am sending[...]Laodicea. And tell Archippus to dis- 17
charge carefully the[...]ties devolving upon [being passed on
to] him as a serva[...]of the Lord.

I Paul add with my own hand this final greeting. Be mind- 18
ful of me in my imprisonment. Grace be with you.

THE FIRST EPISTLE OF PAUL TO THE THESSALONIANS

Introduction

1 Paul, Silvanus, and Timothy, to the church of the 1
Thessalonians which is in God the Father and the Lord
Jesus Christ: grace to you and peace.

We give thanks to God continually because of you all, 2
while we make mention of you in our prayers. For we never 3
fail to remember your works of faith and labors of love
and steadfast hope in our Lord Jesus Christ as before our
God and Father; knowing as we do, brethren beloved by 4
God, that He has chosen you, since our gospel did not come 5
to you in words only, but also with power and with the Holy
Spirit and with great conviction. You know indeed the sort
of men we became among you for your sakes. And you fol- 6
lowed our example and the Lord's, after receiving the word
amid severe affliction with the joy which the Holy Spirit
gives, so that you became a pattern to all the believers in 7
Macedonia and Greece.

For from you the word of the Lord has sounded forth not 8
only in Macedonia and Greece; but everywhere your faith in
God has become known, so that we have no need to say one
word. Of their own accord people report the visit we made to 9
you, and how you turned from your idols to God, to serve a
living and true God, and to await the return from heaven of 10
His Son, whom He raised from the dead—Jesus, our
deliverer from God's coming wrath.

...d Their Converts

The Apos...

2 You yourselves, ...en, know that our visit to you did 1
not prove usel...ut, as you are aware, after we had 2
already met with s...ng and outrage at Philippi, we found
courage in our G...to tell you amid much opposition the
gospel of God. O...appeal does not rest on delusion, nor on 3
uncleanness, ...d does not deal in fraud. But as God 4
approved us t...entrust us with the gospel, so in what we say
we seek to pl...ase not men but God, who tests our hearts.

As you know, we have never used the language of flattery 5
or pretexts for enriching ourselves: God is our witness. Nor 6
did we seek glory from men either from you or any other,
although we might have stood on our dignity as apostles of
Christ. Rather we showed ourselves gentle when among you 7
as a nursing mother cherishing her own children. With this 8
tender regard for you, we were ready to impart to you not
only the gospel of God, but our very lives also, because you
had become very dear to us.

For you remember, brethren, our labor and toil: how work- 9
ing night and day so as not to become a burden to any
of you, we proclaimed to you the gospel of God. You are 10
witnesses—and God is witness—how holy and upright and
blameless our dealings with you believers were. For you 11
know that we acted towards every one of you as a father
towards his own children, encouraging and cheering you,
and adjuring you to live lives worthy of the God who invites 12
you to share His own Kingdom and glory.

For this reason we too render unceasing thanks to God, 13
that, when you received the word of God which you heard
from us, you embraced it, not as men's word, but as—what it
really is—God's word, which also is at work in you who
believe. For you, brethren, followed the example of the 14

churches of God in Christ Jesus which are in Judaea; seeing that you endured the same ill-treatment from your own countrymen as they did from the Jews, who killed both the 15 Lord Jesus and the prophets, and drove us out; these men are displeasing to God, and enemies of all mankind; for they try 16 to prevent our preaching to the Gentiles that they may be saved. They thus continually fill up the measure of their sins, and God's anger has overtaken them to the utmost.

But we brethren, having been for a short time taken from 17 you—in person, not in spirit—endeavored all the more with intense longing to see you face to face. And so we wanted to 18 come to you—I Paul again and again—but Satan hindered us. For what is our hope or joy, or the crown of which we 19 boast? Is it not you yourselves in the presence of our Lord Jesus at His coming? Yes, you are our glory and our joy. 20

3 So when we could endure it no longer, we decided to 1 remain behind in Athens alone; and we sent Timothy 2 our brother and God's minister in Christ's gospel, that he might strengthen you and encourage you in your faith; so 3 that none of you might be perturbed by these trials: for you yourselves know that they are our appointed lot. Even when 4 we were with you, we forewarned you that we were soon to suffer affliction; and this has actually happened, as you know. For this reason I too, when I could no longer endure it, 5 sent to learn about your faith, lest perhaps the Tempter had tempted you, and our labor should prove to no purpose.

But now that Timothy has come back to us from you, and 6 has brought us the good news of your faith and love, and that you cherish a constant and affectionate recollection of us, longing to see us as we also long to see you—for this reason 7 in all our distress and trial we have been comforted about

you, brethren; through your faith. For now we live indeed, if 8
you stand fast in the Lord.

What thanksgiving indeed can we offer to God on your 9
behalf in return for all the joy which we feel before our God
for you, while night and day with intense earnestness we 10
pray that we may see your faces, and make good whatever
may be lacking in your faith?

But may our God and Father Himself and our Lord Jesus 11
guide our way to you; and may the Lord make you increase 12
and overflow in love to one another and to all men, as we do
to you. Thus He will confirm your hearts blameless in holi- 13
ness in the presence of our God and Father at the coming of
our Lord Jesus with all His holy ones.

Practical Exhortations

4 Further, brethren, we beg and exhort you in the name of 1
the Lord Jesus, as you learned from us how you ought to
live so as to please God, as indeed you do live, so to do even
more thoroughly. For you know the commands which we 2
gave you by the authority of the Lord Jesus.

It is God's will that you be pure, that you abstain from for- 3
nication; that each of you shall know how to procure himself 4
a wife in purity and honor, not in lustful passion like the 5
Gentiles who have no knowledge of God; and that in this 6
matter there be no trespass on a brother's rights and no over-
reaching him. For the Lord is an avenger in all such cases, as
we have already taught you and solemnly warned you. God 7
has not called us to uncleanness, but to purity. Therefore he 8
who disregards this disregards not man but God, who puts
His Holy Spirit into your hearts.

But about love for the brotherhood it is unnecessary to 9

write to you, for you yourselves have been taught by God to love one another; and indeed you do love all the brethren 10 throughout Macedonia. We exhort you, brethren, to do so more and more, and make a quiet life your aim, and to mind 11 your own business and work with your hands, as we bade you to do; so as to bear yourselves becomingly towards out- 12 siders, and to be independent.

The Re-appearing of the Lord Jesus

Now, concerning those who fall asleep we would not have 13 you ignorant, brethren, lest you should mourn, as do the rest who have no hope. For if we believe that Jesus died and rose 14 again, in the same way also through Jesus God will bring with Him those who have fallen asleep.

And this we declare to you on the Lord's own word—that 15 we who are alive and survive until the coming of the Lord will have no advantage over those who have fallen asleep. For the Lord Himself will come down from heaven with a 16 loud summons, with the voice of an archangel, and with the trumpet of God, and the dead in Christ will rise first. Afterwards we who are alive and survive will be caught up 17 along with them in the clouds to meet the Lord in the air. And so we shall be with the Lord for ever. Therefore encour- 18 age one another with these words.

5 But as for times and dates it is unnecessary that any- 1 thing be written to you. For you yourselves know per- 2 fectly well that the day of the Lord comes like a thief in the night. While they are saying "Peace and safety," then, in a 3 moment, destruction falls upon them, like birth-pains on a woman who is with child; and escape there is none. But you, 4

brethren, are not in darkness, that the day should surprise you like a thief; for all of you are sons of light and sons of day. We belong neither to night nor to darkness. 5

So, then, let us not sleep like the rest, but let us keep awake and be sober. For those who sleep, sleep at night, and those who get drunk, are drunk at night. But let us, since we belong to the day, be sober, putting on the breastplate of faith and love, and for a helmet the hope of salvation. God has not destined us to incur His anger, but to obtain salvation through our Lord Jesus Christ; who died for us, so that whether we are awake or sleeping we may share His life. Therefore encourage one another, building each other up, as in fact you do. 6 7 8 9 10 11

Conclusion

Now we beg you, brethren, to respect those who labor among you and preside over you in the Lord and counsel you, and to hold them in the most affectionate esteem for their work's sake. Be at peace among yourselves. 12 13

And we exhort you, brethren, admonish the idle, encourage the faint-hearted, sustain the weak, and keep your temper with all men. 14

See to it that no one repays another with evil for evil; but always aim at doing good both to one another and to all the world. 15

Be always joyful. Be unceasing in prayer. Always be thankful; for this is God's will concerning you in Christ Jesus. Do not quench the Spirit. Do not depreciate prophetic revelations; but test them all, and hold fast to the good. Keep yourselves aloof from every form of evil. 16– 18 19– 21 22

And may the God of peace Himself make you entirely holy; and may your spirits, souls, and bodies be preserved 23

complete and be found blan.
Jesus Christ. Faithful is He wh., coming of our Lord
accomplish it.   1, and He will also   24

Brethren, pray for us. Greet all
kiss. I charge you in the Lord's name, ren with a holy   25–
to all the brethren.   this letter read   27

The grace of our Lord Jesus Christ be v.   28
                                        1.

Introduction

1 Paul, Silvanus, and Timothy, to the church of the 1
Thessalonians in God our Father and the Lord Jesus
Christ: grace to you and peace from God our Father and the 2
Lord Jesus Christ.

We owe unceasing thanks to God on your behalf, brethren. 3
They are due because your faith grows beyond measure, and
the love of all of you, without exception, one to another goes
on increasing, so that we ourselves make you our boast 4
among the churches of God because of your endurance and
faith amid all the persecutions and afflictions which you are
suffering. For these are a plain token of God's righteous judg- 5
ment, which designs that you should be found worthy of the
Kingdom of God, for the sake of which, indeed, you are suf-
ferers; since it is a righteous thing for Him to requite [repay] 6
with affliction those who afflict you; and to recompense with 7
rest you who suffer affliction—rest with us at the revelation
of the Lord Jesus from heaven with the angels of His power.
He will come in flames of fire to take vengeance on those 8
who do not acknowledge God and do not obey the gospel of
our Lord Jesus. They will pay the penalty of eternal destruc- 9
tion, away from the presence of the Lord and from the glory
of His might, when He comes to be glorified in His saints and 10
to be wondered at in all who have believed (for our testimony to you was believed) on that day.

It is with this in view also that we continually pray for you, 11

that our God will count you w
power accomplish every desire for His call, and by His
of faith; in order that the name oness and every work
glorified in you, and you in Him, accord Jesus may be 12
our God and the Lord Jesus Christ! g to the grace of

The Re-appearing of the Lord Jesus

2 Now with respect to the coming of our Lord Jesus Christ 1
and our gathering to meet Him, we ent at you,
brethren, not readily to become unsettled in mind r trou- 2
bled, either by any spiritual revelation or by any word or letter alleged to come through us, to the effect that the day of
the Lord is already here. Let no one in any way deceive you, 3
for it cannot come unless the apostasy comes first, and the
appearing of the man of sin, the son of perdition, who sets 4
himself against and exalts himself above every so-called god
or object of worship, and goes the length of taking his seat in
the temple of God, giving it out that he himself is God.

Do you not remember that while I was still with you, I told 5
you this? And now you know what restrains him, that he may 6
be revealed only at his appointed time. For lawlessness is 7
already at work in secret; but in secret only until the man
who now restrains it is removed, and then the lawless one 8
will be revealed, whom the Lord Jesus will slay with the
breath of His mouth, and overwhelm by the manifestation of
His Presence.

The appearing of the lawless one will be attended by all 9
sorts of miracles and signs and delusive marvels—for so
Satan works—and by every kind of wicked deception for 10
those who, because they did not entertain the love of the
truth so that they might be saved, are on the way to perdition.

And for this reason ...nds them a fatal delusion that 11
they may believe th... order that all may be judged who 12
have refused to b... the truth and have taken pleasure
in unrighteousne... in unrighteousne...

...nksgiving and Exhortations

But from u... ...anks are always due to God on your behalf, 13
brethren who... the Lord loves, because God from the beginning has chos... you for salvation through the Spirit's sanctifying influe... ...e and your belief in the truth. To this He has 14
called yo... your gospel, so that you may attain to the glory
of our Lord Jesus Christ.

So then, brethren, stand firm, and hold fast to the teach- 15
ings which you have received from us, whether by word of
mouth or by letter. And may our Lord Jesus Christ Himself, 16
and God our Father who has loved us and has given us in His
grace eternal consolation and good hope, comfort your 17
hearts and make you steadfast in every good work and word.

3 Moreover, brethren, pray for us, that the Lord's word 1
may spread rapidly and be extolled, as it was among
you; and that we may be delivered from perverse and wicked 2
men. It is not everybody who has faith; but the Lord is faith- 3
ful, and He will confirm and will guard you from the Evil
One. And we have confidence in you in the Lord, that you are 4
doing and will do what we command. And may the Lord 5
guide your hearts into the love of God and into the steadfastness of Christ!

But in the name of the Lord we command you, brethren, to 6
stand aloof [withdraw] from every brother who is living an idle
life [not supporting himself] not in accordance with the

teaching which you received from us. You yourselves know 7
that it is your duty to follow our example. There was no idle-
ness in our life among you, nor did we get bread to eat from 8
any one without paying for it, but by labor and toil, working
night and day in order not to be a burden to any of you. Not 9
that we have not a right to such support, but it was in order to
set you an example—for you to imitate us. Even when we were 10
with you, we gave you this injunction: "If a man refuses to
work, neither shall he eat."

For we hear that there are some of you who live idle lives 11
and are mere idle busybodies. Persons of that sort we call 12
upon and command in the Lord Jesus Christ to work quietly
and eat their own bread.

But you, brethren, must not grow weary in doing right. If 13
any one refuses to obey these our written instructions, mark 14
that man and hold no communication with him; so that he
may be ashamed. And yet do not regard him as an enemy, 15
but caution him as a brother. And may the Lord of peace 16
Himself continually grant you peace in every way. The Lord
be with you all.

Conclusion

I Paul add a greeting with my own hand, which is the cre- 17
dential in every letter of mine. This is my handwriting. The 18
grace of our Lord Jesus Christ be with you all.

THE FIRST EPISTLE OF PAUL
TO TIMOTHY

1 Paul, an apostle of Christ Jesus by command of God our 1
Savior and Christ Jesus our hope, to Timothy, my true 2
son in the faith: grace, mercy, and peace from God the Father
and Christ Jesus our Lord.

When I was on my journey to Macedonia I begged you to 3
remain on in Ephesus that you might caution certain persons against erroneous teaching and attention to mere 4
fables and endless genealogies, such as foster discussions
rather than acceptance in faith of God's provision for salvation. Do so still.

The object to be secured by such caution is the love which 5
springs from a pure heart, a clear conscience, and a sincere
faith. From these some have deviated, and have lost their way in 6
empty reasoning. They are ambitious to be teachers of the Law, 7
although they do not understand either their own words or the
things about which they make their confident assertions.

Now we know that the Law is good, if a man uses it in a 8
lawful way, and remembers that a law is not enacted for a 9
righteous man, but for the lawless and rebellious, the irreligious and sinful, the godless and profane—for those who
strike their fathers or their mothers, for murderers, the licen- 10
tious, sodomites, kidnappers, liars, and false witnesses; and
for whatever else is opposed to the wholesome teaching of 11
the glorious gospel of the blessed God with which I have
been entrusted.

I am thankful to Christ Jesus our Lord who gave me the 12
needful strength—because He has judged me faithful and

has put me into His service, though I was previously guilty of 13
blasphemy and persecution and wanton outrage. Yet mercy
was shown me, because I had acted ignorantly, in unbelief;
and the grace of our Lord was more than abundant, evoking 14
faith and the love which centers in Christ Jesus.

True is the saying, and deserving of universal acceptance, 15
that Christ Jesus came into the world to save sinners; among
whom I am foremost. But mercy was shown me in order that 16
in me as the foremost Christ Jesus might display the fullness
of His patience as a striking example for those who would
afterwards rest their faith on Him with a view to eternal life.

Now to the immortal, invisible and eternal King, who 17
alone is God, be honor and glory for ever and ever! Amen.

This is the charge which I entrust to you, my son Timothy, 18
in accordance with the prophecies formerly uttered concerning you, that being equipped with them you may fight
the good fight, holding fast to faith and a clear conscience.
This some have cast aside and have made shipwreck of 19
their faith: among these are Hymenaeus and Alexander, 20
whom I have delivered to Satan that they may be taught not
to blaspheme.

2 I exhort, then, first of all, that supplications, prayers, 1
petitions, and thanksgivings be offered on behalf of all
men; including kings and all who are in high station, that we 2
may live peaceful and tranquil lives with all godliness and
in good repute. This is right and pleasing in the sight of God 3
our Savior, who wishes all mankind to be saved and to come 4
to a knowledge of the truth. For there is one God and one 5
Mediator between God and men—Christ Jesus, Himself
man; who gave Himself as a ransom for all—a fact testified to 6
at its own appointed time. Of this fact I have been made a 7

herald and an apostle (I speak the truth: it is not fiction), a teacher of the Gentiles in faith and truth.

So, then, I would have the men in every place of worship 8 pray, lifting to God holy hands without anger or strife; and 9 I would have the women dress becomingly, with modesty and sobriety, not with plaited hair or gold or pearls or costly clothes, but—as befits women making a claim to godliness— 10 with the ornament of good works.

A woman should learn in silence with entire submissive- 11 ness. I do not permit a woman to teach, nor to have authority 12 over a man, but she must remain silent. For Adam was formed 13 first and then Eve; Adam was not deceived, but his wife was 14 thoroughly deceived, and became involved in transgression. Yet a woman will be saved through child-bearing if they 15 continue in faith and love and holiness, with self-restraint.

3 True is the saying, "If any one is eager for the office of 1 bishop [minister], he desires a noble work." A bishop, 2 then, must be irreproachable, the husband of one wife, temperate, sober-minded, well-behaved, hospitable, and with a gift for teaching; not a hard drinker nor given to blows 3 [physically striking another], but gentle, not pugnacious [quarrelsome]; nor fond of money; one who manages his own 4 household well, keeping his children under control with true dignity. If a man does not know how to manage his own house- 5 hold, how shall he take care of the church of God? He ought not 6 to be a new convert, for fear he should be blinded with pride and come under the same condemnation as the devil. It is 7 needful also that he bear a good character with people outside the church, lest he fall into reproach or a snare of the devil.

Deacons, in the same way, must be men of serious 8 demeanor, not double-tongued, nor addicted to much wine, nor greedy of base gain, but holding the mysterious truths of the faith with a clear conscience. And these, too, must undergo probation, and then, if they are of unblemished character, let them serve as deacons. Women, in the same way, must be serious-minded, not slanderers, but in every way temperate and trustworthy.

Let a deacon be the husband of one wife, and rule his children and his own household well. For those who have filled the deacon's office well gain for themselves an honorable standing, and acquire great boldness of speech in their faith in Christ Jesus.

All this I write to you, though I am hoping before long to come to see you. But, for fear I may be hindered, I now write, so that you may know how to behave in God's household, which is the church of the living God, the pillar and buttress of the truth. And beyond controversy, great is the mystery of our religion—He who

Was revealed in the flesh,
  And proved righteous by the Spirit;
Was seen by angels,
  And proclaimed among Gentile nations;
Was believed on in the world,
  And received up into glory.

4 Now the Spirit expressly declares that in later times some will fall away from the faith, giving heed to deceiving spirits and the teachings of demons; and this through the hypocrisy of men who teach falsely and have their own consciences seared as with a hot iron, forbidding people to marry, and insisting on abstinence from foods which God has created to be partaken of with thankfulness by those who believe and know the truth. For everything that

God has created is good; and nothing is to be rejected, if only it is received with thanksgiving: it is made holy by the word 5 of God and by prayer.

If you put this to the brethren, you will be a good servant of 6 Christ Jesus, nourished on the lessons of the faith and of the good teaching which you have faithfully followed. But pro- 7 fane stories, fit only for old women, have nothing to do with.

Train yourself for godliness. Exercise for the body is not 8 useless, but godliness is useful in every respect, possessing the promise of the present and the future life. Faithful is this 9 saying and deserving of universal acceptance: and this is the 10 motive of our toiling and wrestling, that we have our hopes fixed on the living God, who is the Savior of all mankind and especially of believers.

Command this and teach this. Let no one treat you slight- 11 ingly because you are a young man; but in speech, conduct, 12 love, faith, and purity, be an example to your fellow Christians. Till I come, pay attention to public reading, 13 exhortation, and teaching. Do not neglect the gifts with 14 which you are endowed, which were conferred on you by prophetic indication when the hands of the elders were placed upon you. Practice these duties and be absorbed in 15 them; so that your progress in them may be evident to all. Take pains with yourself and your teaching. Persevere in 16 these things; for by doing this you will secure your own and your hearers' salvation.

5 Never administer a sharp reprimand to an older man, 1 but entreat him as if he were your father, and the younger men as brothers; the elder women, too, as mothers, 2 and the younger women as sisters, with perfect modesty.

Relieve widows who are really in need. But if a widow has 3

children or grandchildren, let these learn first to show their 4
filial [as coming from a son or daughter] piety at home and
to make requital [return or repayment] to their parents; for
this is acceptable in the sight of God. A widow who is really 5
such, even though desolate, has her hopes fixed on God, and
continues at her supplications and prayers night and day;
but a pleasure-loving widow is dead even while still alive. 6
Press these facts upon them, so that they may live lives free 7
from reproach. If a man makes no provision for his own rela- 8
tions, and especially for his own household, he has disowned the faith and is behaving worse than an unbeliever.

No widow is to be put on the roll who is under sixty years 9
of age. She must have been the wife of but one man, and well 10
reported of for good deeds, as having brought up children,
exercised hospitality, washed the feet of the saints, given
relief to the distressed, and devoted herself to good works of
every kind.

But younger widows you must not enroll; for as soon as 11
their affections stray wantonly from Christ, they want to 12
marry, and they incur the censure [condemnation] of having
broken their first plighted faith. And at the same time they 13
also learn to be idle as they go around from house to house;
and they are not only idle, but are gossips also and busybodies, speaking of things that ought not to be spoken of.

I would therefore have the younger women marry, bear 14
children, manage the house, and furnish the adversary with
no excuse for slander. For already some of them have gone 15
astray, following Satan. If a believing woman has widows 16
dependent on her, she should relieve them, and save the
church from being burdened—so that the church may
relieve the widows who are really in need.

Let the elders who preside well be held worthy of double 17
honor, especially those who labor in preaching and teaching.

For the scripture says, "YOU ARE NOT TO MUZZLE 18
THE OX WHILE IT IS TREADING OUT THE GRAIN"
(Deuteronomy 25:4); and the workman deserves his pay.

Never entertain an accusation against an elder except on 19
the evidence of two or three witnesses. Those who persist in 20
sin rebuke in the presence of all, so that the rest also may be
afraid to sin.

I solemnly call upon you, in the presence of God and of 21
Christ Jesus and of the elect angels, to carry out these
instructions without prejudice, and to do nothing from partiality. Do not lay hands upon any one hastily; and do not be 22
a partaker in the sins of others; keep yourself pure. (No 23
longer be a water-drinker; but take a little wine for the sake
of your stomach and your frequent ailments.)

The sins of some men are obvious, going before them to 24
judgment, but the sins of others follow after them. So also 25
the right actions of some are obvious, and those that are not
cannot remain for ever hidden.

6 Let all who are under the yoke of slavery hold their own 1
masters to be deserving of all honor, so that the name of
God and the teaching may not be spoken against. And those 2
who have believing masters should not be wanting in
respect towards them because they are brethren, but should
serve them all the more, because those who profit by the
service are believers and beloved.

Thus teach and exhort. If any one teaches differently, and 3
refuses assent to the wholesome instructions of our Lord
Jesus Christ and the teaching that harmonizes with true godliness, he is blinded with conceit and really knows nothing, 4
but is crazy with discussions and controversies about words
which give rise to envy, quarrelings, revilings, ill-natured 5

suspicions, and persistent wranglings on the part of people perverted in mind and so deprived of the truth, who imagine that godliness means gain.

Godliness is indeed great gain when accompanied by contentment; for we brought nothing into the world, nor can we carry anything out of it; and if we have food and clothing, with these we should be satisfied. But people who want to be rich fall into temptation and a snare, and into many unwise and pernicious cravings, which sink mankind in destruction and ruin. From love of money all sorts of evils arise; and some have so hankered after money that they have gone astray from the faith and have caused themselves many pangs of sorrow.

But you, O man of God, must flee from these things, and strive for uprightness, godliness, faith, love, fortitude, and gentleness. Struggle your hardest in the good contest for the faith; seize hold of eternal life, to which you were called; you made the good confession before many witnesses. I charge you—in the presence of God who gives life to all, and of Christ Jesus who at the bar of Pontius Pilate made the noble confession—that you keep God's commandment stainlessly and without reproach till the appearing of our Lord Jesus Christ: this will be brought about at its appointed time by the blessed and only Sovereign, the King of kings and Lord of lords; who alone possesses immortality, and who dwells in unapproachable light, and whom no man has seen or can see. To Him be eternal honor and dominion! Amen.

Impress on those who are rich in the present world that they must not be haughty or set their hopes on an uncertain thing like riches, but on God who provides us richly with all things for our enjoyment. They must be beneficent [charitable], rich in good deeds, openhanded, and liberal; storing up for themselves what shall form a solid

6
7
8
9

10

11
12

13

14

15

16

17

18

19

foundation for the future, that they may lay hold of the life which is life indeed.

O Timothy, guard the truths entrusted to you, shunning 20 irreligious and frivolous talk, and objections from what is falsely called "knowledge"; which some have claimed to pos- 21 sess and they have missed the true faith.

Grace be with you all.

THE SECOND EPISTLE OF PAUL TO TIMOTHY

1 Paul, by the will of God an apostle of Christ Jesus, to proclaim the promise of the Life which is in Christ Jesus, to Timothy my beloved child: grace, mercy, and peace from God the Father and Christ Jesus our Lord.

I thank God, whom I serve with a pure conscience, as my fathers did, that night and day I unceasingly remember you in my prayers, and, ever mindful of your tears, I long to see you, that I may be filled with joy. For I recall the sincere faith which is in you—a faith which dwelt first in your grandmother Lois and your mother Eunice, and, I am convinced, dwells in you also.

For this reason let me remind you to rekindle God's gift, which is yours through the laying on of my hands. For the spirit which God has given us is not a spirit of cowardice, but one of power and of love and of self-discipline.

Do not be ashamed, then, of witnessing for our Lord or of me His prisoner; but rather share suffering with me for the gospel, in reliance on the power of God. For He saved us and called us with a holy call, not in accordance with our deserts [deserved reward or punishment], but in accordance with His own purpose and the grace which He bestowed on us in Christ Jesus from all eternity, but which has now been revealed through the appearing of our Savior, Christ Jesus. He has put an end to death and has brought life and immortality to light through the gospel, for which I have been appointed a preacher, apostle, and teacher. That indeed is the reason why I suffer as I do. But I am not ashamed, for I know in whom I have trusted, and I am confident that He is able to keep what I have entrusted to Him until that Day.

Keep to the example of the sound teaching which you 13 have heard from me, in the faith and love which are in Christ Jesus. That precious truth which is entrusted to you guard 14 through the Holy Spirit who has His home in our hearts.

Of this you are aware, that all the Christians in Asia have 15 deserted me: and among them Phygelus and Hermogenes. May the Lord show mercy to the household of Onesiphorus; 16 for many a time he gave me fresh vigor and he was not ashamed of my chain. Nay, when he was here in Rome, he 17 took great pains to inquire for me, and he found me. (The 18 Lord grant that he may obtain mercy at His hands on that Day!) And you yourself well know all the services which he rendered me in Ephesus.

2 You then, my son, must grow strong in the grace that is 1 in Christ Jesus. What you have been taught by me in the 2 hearing of many witnesses, you must hand on to trusty men, who shall be competent to instruct others also.

As a good soldier of Christ Jesus accept your share of suf- 3 fering. Every one who serves as a soldier avoids becoming 4 entangled in the affairs of civil life, so that he may satisfy the officer who enlisted him. And if any one takes part in an 5 athletic contest, he gets no prize unless he obeys the rules. The harvestman who labors must be the first to get a share 6 of the crop. Reflect on what I am saying: the Lord will give 7 you understanding in everything.

Never forget Jesus Christ risen from the dead, a descend- 8 ant of David, as is declared in the gospel which I preach. For this I suffer, and am even put in chains, as if I were a 9

criminal: yet the word of God is not chained. And so I endure 10
all things for the sake of the elect; so that they also may
obtain the salvation which is in Christ Jesus—and with it
eternal glory.

True is the saying: 11

If we died with Him, we shall also live with Him;

If we endure, we shall also reign with Him; 12

If we disown Him, He will also disown us;

If we are faithless, He remains faithful—He cannot dis- 13
own Himself.

Bring this to men's remembrances, solemnly charging 14
them in the presence of God not to wrangle about words,
which is altogether unprofitable and tends only to the ruin of
the hearers.

Earnestly seek to commend yourself to God as a workman 15
who, because of his straightforward dealing with the word of
truth, has no reason to feel any shame. But from irreligious 16
and frivolous talk hold aloof, for those who indulge in it will
proceed from bad to worse in impiety, and their teaching 17
will spread like a running sore. Hymenaeus and Philetus are
men of that stamp. As for finding the truth, they have gone 18
astray, saying that the resurrection is already past, and they
are upsetting the faith of some.

Yet God's solid foundation stands unmoved, bearing 19
this guarantee,

"THE LORD KNOWS THOSE WHO BELONG TO HIM"
(Numbers 16:5).

And this also,

"LET EVERY ONE WHO NAMES THE NAME OF THE
LORD RENOUNCE WICKEDNESS" (Isaiah 26:13).

Now in a great house there are articles not only of gold and 20
silver, but also of wood and of earthenware; and some are for
honorable, and others for common use. If, therefore, a man 21

keeps himself clear of these, he will be for honorable use, consecrated, fit for the Master's service, and equipped for every good work.

Curb the cravings of youth; and strive for integrity, faith, 22 love, peace, in company with all who pray to the Lord with pure hearts. But decline foolish discussions with ignorant 23 men, knowing that these lead to quarrels; and a servant of 24 the Lord must not quarrel, but must be inoffensive towards all men, a skillful teacher, and patient under wrongs. He 25 must instruct his opponents with gentleness, in the hope that God will some day grant them repentance, leading to knowledge of the truth, and that they may return from the 26 devil's delusion to a sober mind, though they are now entrapped by him to do his will.

3 But of this be assured: in the last days grievous times 1 will set in. For men will be lovers of self, lovers of money 2 boastful, haughty, profane. They will be disobedient to parents, thankless, irreligious, hard-hearted, unforgiving, 3 slanderers. They will have no self-control, but will be brutal, opposed to goodness, treacherous, headstrong, self- 4 important. They will love pleasure instead of loving God, and 5 will keep up a make-believe of piety and yet exclude its power. Turn away from people of this sort.

Among them are included the men who make their way 6 into private houses and captivate weak women—women who, weighed down by the burden of their sins, are led by ever-changing caprice [whims], and are always learning, and 7 yet never able to arrive at knowledge of the truth.

Just as Jannes and Jambres withstood Moses, so also these 8 withstand the truth—being men of debased mind, and reprobates so far as faith is concerned. But they will have no 9 further success; for their folly will be manifest to all men, just as that of the opponents of Moses came to be. But you have 10 faithfully followed my teaching, life, aims, faith, patience, love, fortitude, persecutions and sufferings, all the things 11 which happened to me in Antioch, Iconium, and Lystra, the persecutions I endured, and how the Lord delivered me out of them all. And indeed every one who is determined to 12 live a godly life in Christ Jesus will be persecuted. Bad men 13 and impostors will go from bad to worse, misleading and being misled.

But do you cling to the truths which you have learned and 14 of which you are convinced, knowing who your teachers were, and that from infancy you have known the sacred writ- 15 ings which are able to make you wise to obtain salvation through faith in Christ Jesus. Every scripture is inspired by 16 God and is useful for teaching, for reproof, for correction and for instruction in right doing; so that the man of God may be 17 complete, perfectly equipped for every good work.

4 I adjure you, in the presence of God and of Christ Jesus 1 who is to judge the living and the dead, and by His appearing and His Kingdom: preach the word, be zealous in 2 season and out of season; reprove, rebuke, encourage, with the utmost patience and instruction. For a time is coming 3 when men will not tolerate wholesome instruction, but, wanting to have their ears tickled, they will find a multitude of teachers to satisfy their own fancies, and will close their 4 ears to the truth and will turn away to fables.

But do you be circumspect in all matters, and ready to 5 suffer; do the duty of an evangelist and fully discharge the obligations of your office.

I am a drink-offering already being poured out; and the 6

time for my departure is close at hand. I have fought the 7
good fight; I have run the race; I have kept the faith.
Hereafter there is reserved for me the crown of righteousness 8
which the Lord, the righteous Judge, will award to me on that
day, and not only to me, but also to all who have loved the
thought of His appearing.

Make an effort to come to me speedily; for Demas has 9
deserted me—loving the present world—and has gone to 10
Thessalonica; Crescens has gone to Galatia, and Titus to
Dalmatia. Luke alone is with me. Call for Mark and bring him 11
with you, for he is a great help to me in my ministry. Tychicus 12
I have sent to Ephesus.

When you come, bring the cloak which I left behind 13
at Troas at the house of Carpus, and the books, especially
the parchments.

Alexander the smith did me much mischief: the Lord will 14
requite [repay] him according to his doings. You also should 15
beware of him; for he has violently opposed our words.

At my first defense I had no one at my side; all deserted 16
me: may it not be laid to their charge! The Lord, however, 17
stood by me and filled me with strength that through me the
message might be fully proclaimed and that all the Gentiles
might hear it; and I was rescued from the lion's jaws. The 18
Lord will deliver me from every malicious attack and will
bring me safe to His heavenly Kingdom. To Him be the glory
for ever and ever! Amen.

Greet Prisca and Aquila, and the household of Onesiphorus. 19
Erastus stayed in Corinth; Trophimus I left behind me 20
at Miletus, ill. Make an effort to come before winter. 21
Eubulus greets you, and so do Pudens, Linus, Claudia, and
all the brethren.

The Lord be with your spirit. Grace be with you all. 22

THE EPISTLE OF PAUL
TO TITUS

1 Paul, a servant of God and an apostle of Jesus Christ 1
for furthering the faith of God's elect and a knowledge of
the truths of religion, in hope of eternal life, which God, who 2
never deceives, promised from all eternity; and at 3
the appointed time He made known His word by the preaching with which I was entrusted by the command of God our
Savior, to Titus my own true child in our common faith: grace 4
and peace from God the Father and Christ Jesus our Savior.

I have left you behind in Crete that you may set right the 5
things still requiring attention, and may appoint elders in
every town, as I directed you; namely, wherever there is a 6
man of blameless life, the husband of one wife, having children who are believers and are free from every reproach of
profligacy [shameless immorality] or of disorderliness. For, 7
as God's steward, a bishop [minister] must be blameless, not
self-willed, not quick-tempered or a hard drinker, not given
to blows [physically striking another] or greedy of gain; but 8
hospitable, a lover of goodness, sober-minded, upright,
saintly, self-controlled; holding fast to the trustworthy word 9
as he has learned it, so that he may be able both to encourage others with sound teaching and to refute opponents.

For there are many disorderly persons given to idle and 10
misleading talk, who, for the most part, are of the Jewish
party. You must stop the mouths of such men, for they upset 11
whole families, teaching what they ought not for the sake of
making money. One of themselves—a prophet of their 12
own—has said,

"Cretans are always liars, noxious [morally injurious] beasts, idle gluttons."

This testimony is true. Therefore sternly reprove them, 13 that they may keep sound in their faith, and not give atten- 14 tion to Jewish legends and the maxims [principles] of men who turn their backs on the truth. To the pure everything is 15 pure. But to the polluted and unbelieving nothing is pure; on the contrary, their very minds and consciences are polluted: they profess to know God, but in their actions they disown 16 Him; for they are detestable, disobedient men, for any good work useless.

2 But do you speak in a manner that befits wholesome 1 teaching. Exhort aged men to be temperate, grave, 2 sober-minded, and sound in their faith, their love, and their endurance. In the same way exhort aged women to be rever- 3 ent in bearing [behavior], not slanderers nor enslaved to wine. As patterns of virtue they should give good advice, and school the young women to be affectionate to their husbands 4 and children, to be sober-minded, chaste, domesticated 5 [keepers at home], kind, and submissive to their husbands, so that the word of God may not be exposed to reproach.

In the same way exhort the younger men to be self- 6 restrained. And above all exhibit in your own life a pattern of 7 right conduct, in your teaching sincerity and seriousness and 8 wholesome language which no one can censure [condemn], so that our opponents may feel ashamed at having nothing evil to say against us. Exhort slaves to be obedient to their own- 9 ers and to give them satisfaction, not contradicting and not 10 pilfering [stealing], but manifesting perfect good faith, in order to do credit to the teaching of our Savior, God, in all things.

For the grace of God has displayed itself with saving power 11

to all mankind, training us to renounce ungodliness and 12
worldly desires, and to live sober, upright, and pious lives in
the present world, awaiting fulfillment of our blessed hope— 13
the appearing in glory of our great God and Savior Jesus
Christ; who gave Himself for us to purchase our freedom 14
from all iniquity, and purify for Himself a people who should
be His own, zealous for good works.

Thus speak, exhort, reprove, with all impressiveness. Let 15
no one make light of you.

3 Remind your hearers that they must submit to the 1
rulers who are in authority, and obey their regulations;
they must be ready to undertake any good work, not speak 2
evil of any one, nor be contentious, but be yielding and constantly manifesting a gentle spirit towards all men.

There was a time when we also were unintelligent, obsti- 3
nate, deluded, the slaves of various cravings and pleasures,
spending our lives in malice and envy, deserving hatred ourselves and hating one another. But when the goodness of God 4
our Savior and His love to man came to light, not in virtue of 5
any righteous deeds which we had done, but in His own
mercy, He saved us by means of the bath of regeneration and
renewal by the Holy Spirit, which He poured out on us richly 6
through Jesus Christ our Savior; in order that having been 7
acknowledged righteous through His grace we might become
heirs to eternal life in fulfillment of our hopes. These words 8
are trustworthy.

And on these points I would have you insist strenuously, in
order that those who have their faith fixed on God may take
care to be foremost in all right actions; for these are not only
right in themselves, but are also useful to mankind.

But hold yourself aloof from foolish disputes and genealo- 9
gies and quarrels and wrangling about the Law, for they are
useless and vain.

After a first and second admonition, have nothing further 10
to do with a man who causes divisions; for, as you know, a 11
person of that sort has gone astray and is a sinner self-
condemned.

After I have sent Artemas or Tychicus to you, lose no time 12
in joining me at Nicopolis, for I have decided to pass the
winter there. Help Zenas the lawyer on his journey with 13
especial care, and Apollos, so that nothing may be wanting
to them. And let our people, too, learn to follow honest 14
occupations [work] for the supply of their necessities, so
that they may not live useless lives.

Every one here sends you greeting. Greet the believers 15
who hold us dear.

May grace be with you all.

THE LETTER OF PAUL
TO PHILEMON

Paul, a prisoner for Christ Jesus, and Timothy our brother, 1
to Philemon our dearly-loved fellow laborer—and to our 2
sister Apphia and our comrade Archippus—as well as to the
church in your house: grace to you all, and peace, from God 3
our Father and the Lord Jesus Christ.

I give continual thanks to my God while making mention 4
of you, my brother, in my prayers, because I hear of your love 5
and of the faith which you have towards the Lord Jesus and
which you manifest towards all the saints; praying as I do, 6
that their participation in your faith may result in the full
recognition of all the right affection that is in us toward
Christ. For I have found great joy and comfort in your love, 7
because the hearts of the saints have been, and are,
refreshed through you, my brother.

Therefore, though I might with Christ's authority speak 8
very freely and order you to do what is fitting, it is for love's 9
sake that—instead of that—although I am none other than
Paul the aged, and now also a prisoner for Christ Jesus, I 10
entreat you on behalf of my own child whose father I have
become while in my chains—I mean, Onesimus. Formerly 11
he was useless to you but now—true to his name—he is of
great use to you and to me.

I am sending him back to you, though in so doing I send 12
part of myself. It was my wish to keep him at my side for him 13
to attend to my wants, as your representative, during my
imprisonment for the gospel. Only I wished to do nothing 14
without your consent, so that this kind action of yours might

not be done under pressure, but might be of your own free will. For perhaps it was for this reason he was parted from 15 you for a time, that you might receive him back wholly and for ever yours; no longer as a slave, but as something better 16 than a slave—a brother peculiarly dear to me, and even dearer to you, both as a servant and as a fellow Christian. If, 17 therefore, you regard me as a comrade, receive him as if he were I myself.

And if he was ever dishonest or is in your debt, debit me 18 with the amount. I Paul write this with my own hand—I will 19 pay you in full. (I say nothing of the fact that you owe me even your own self.) Yes, brother, do me this favor for the 20 Lord's sake. Refresh my heart in Christ.

I write to you in the full confidence that you will meet my 21 wishes, for I know you will do even more than I say. And at 22 the same time provide a lodging for me; for I hope that through your prayers I shall be permitted to come to you.

Greetings to you, my brother, from Epaphras my fellow 23 prisoner for the sake of Christ Jesus; and from Mark, 24 Aristarchus, Demas, and Luke, my fellow workers.

May the grace of our Lord Jesus Christ be with the spirit of 25 every one of you.

THE EPISTLE TO THE HEBREWS

Introduction. Christ's Superiority to Prophets and Angels

1 God, who of old spoke to our forefathers in many frag- 1
ments and by various methods through the prophets, has 2
at the end of these days spoken to us through a Son, who is the
predestined Lord of the universe, and through whom He
made the world. He brightly reflects God's glory and is the 3
exact representation of His being, and upholds the universe
by His all-powerful word. After securing man's purification
from sin He took His seat at the right hand of the Majesty on
high, having become as far superior to the angels as the Name 4
He possesses by inheritance is more excellent than theirs.

For to which of the angels did God ever say, 5
"MY SON ART THOU:
I HAVE THIS DAY BECOME THY FATHER" (Psalm 2:7);
and again,
"I WILL BE A FATHER TO HIM,
AND HE SHALL BE MY SON"? (2 Samuel 7:14).
And again when He brings His Firstborn into the world, 6
He says,
"AND LET ALL GOD'S ANGELS WORSHIP HIM"
(Deuteronomy 32:43, LXX; Psalm 97:7, LXX).
Moreover of the angels He says, 7
"HE CHANGES HIS ANGELS INTO WINDS,
AND HIS MINISTERING SERVANTS INTO A FLAME OF
FIRE" (Psalm 104:4).
But of His Son, He says, 8
"THY THRONE, O GOD, IS FOR EVER AND EVER,

AND THE SCEPTER OF THY KINGDOM IS A SCEPTER
OF ABSOLUTE JUSTICE.

THOU HAST LOVED RIGHTEOUSNESS AND HATED 9
LAWLESSNESS;

THEREFORE GOD, THY GOD, HAS ANOINTED THEE

WITH THE OIL OF GLADNESS BEYOND THY FELLOWS"
(Psalm 45:6-7).

It is also of His Son that God says, 10

"THOU, O LORD, IN THE BEGINNING DIDST LAY THE
FOUNDATIONS OF THE EARTH,

AND THE HEAVENS ARE THE WORK OF THY HANDS.

THE HEAVENS WILL PERISH, BUT THOU REMAINEST; 11

AND THEY WILL GROW OLD LIKE A GARMENT,

AND AS A MANTLE THOU WILT ROLL THEM UP; 12

YES, LIKE A GARMENT, AND THEY WILL UNDERGO
CHANGE.

BUT THOU ART THE SAME,

AND THY YEARS WILL NEVER COME TO AN END"
(Psalm 102:25-27).

To which of the angels has He ever said, 13

"SIT AT MY RIGHT HAND

TILL I MAKE THY FOES A FOOTSTOOL FOR THY FEET"?
(Psalm 110:1).

Are not all angels spirits that serve Him—whom He sends 14
out to render service for the benefit of those who are to
inherit salvation?

2 For this reason we ought to pay the more earnest heed 1
to the things which we have heard, for fear we should
drift away from them. For if the message delivered through 2
angels proved to be true, and every transgression and act of
disobedience met with just retribution, how shall we 3

escape if we neglect a salvation as great as that now offered to us? This, after having first of all been announced by the Lord Himself, had its truth made sure to us by those who heard Him, while God corroborated their testimony by 4 signs and marvels and various mighty works, and by gifts of the Holy Spirit distributed in accordance with His own will.

It is not to angels that God has assigned the sovereignty of 5 that coming world of which we speak. But, as we know, a 6 psalmist has exclaimed,

"HOW POOR A CREATURE IS MAN, AND YET THOU DOST REMEMBER HIM,
AND A SON OF MAN, AND YET THOU DOST COME TO HIM!
THOU HAST MADE HIM FOR A LITTLE WHILE LOWER 7 THAN THE ANGELS;
WITH GLORY AND HONOR THOU HAST CROWNED HIM,
AND HAST SET HIM OVER THE WORKS OF THY HANDS.
THOU HAST PUT EVERYTHING IN SUBJECTION UNDER 8 HIS FEET" (Psalm 8:4-6).

For this subjecting of the universe to man implies the leaving nothing not subject to him. But we do not as yet see the universe subject to him. But we do see Him who was made 9 for a little while lower than the angels—even Jesus—because of His suffering of death crowned with glory and honor, that by God's grace He might taste death for every man.

For it was fitting that He for whom and through whom all 10 things exist, in bringing many sons to glory, should perfect by suffering the Prince Leader of their salvation. For both He 11 who sanctifies and those whom He is sanctifying have all one Father; and for this reason He is not ashamed to speak of them as His brothers; as when He says: 12

"I WILL PROCLAIM THY NAME TO MY BROTHERS:
IN THE MIDST OF THE CONGREGATION I WILL HYMN THY PRAISES" (Psalm 22:22);

and again, 13

"I WILL BE ONE WHOSE TRUST REPOSES IN GOD" (Psalm 18:2; Isaiah 12:2);

and again,

"HERE AM I, AND HERE ARE THE CHILDREN GOD HAS GIVEN ME" (Isaiah 8:18).

Since, then, the children referred to are all alike sharers in 14 perishable human nature, He Himself also, in the same way, took on Him a share of it, in order that through death He might render powerless him who had authority over death, that is, the devil, and might set at liberty all those who 15 through fear of death had been subject to lifelong slavery. For 16 assuredly it is not to angels that He reaches a helping hand, but it is to the descendants of Abraham. And for this purpose 17 it was necessary that in all respects He should be made to resemble His brothers, so that He might prove Himself a compassionate and faithful High Priest in things relating to God, in order to atone for the sins of the people. For inas- 18 much as He has Himself felt the pain of temptation and trial, He is also able to help those who are tempted and tried.

3 Therefore, holy brethren, sharers with others in a heav- 1 enly calling, fix your thoughts on Jesus, the Apostle and High Priest whose followers we profess to be. How faithful 2 He was to Him who appointed Him, just as Moses also was faithful in all God's house! For Jesus has been counted wor- 3 thy of greater glory than Moses, in so far as he who has built a house has higher honor than the house itself. For every 4 house has a builder, the Builder of all things being God.

Moreover, Moses was faithful in all God's house as a serv- 5 ant in delivering the message given him to speak; but Christ 6 was faithful as a Son having authority over God's house, and we are that house, if we hold firm to the end the boldness and the hope which we boast of as ours.

For this reason—as the Holy Spirit warns us, 7
"TO-DAY, IF YOU SHOULD HEAR HIS VOICE,
DO NOT HARDEN YOUR HEARTS AS IN THE TIME OF 8
THE PROVOCATION
ON THE DAY OF THE TEMPTATION IN THE DESERT,
WHERE YOUR FATHERS TEMPTED AND TESTED ME 9
AND THEY SAW ALL THAT I DID
DURING FORTY YEARS. THEREFORE I WAS GREATLY 10
GRIEVED WITH THAT GENERATION,
AND I SAID, 'IN THEIR HEARTS THEY ARE EVER ASTRAY,
THEY HAVE NOT LEARNED TO KNOW MY PATHS.'
WHILE I SWORE IN MY ANGER, 11
THEY SHALL NOT BE ADMITTED TO MY REST" (Psalm 95:7-11)—see to it, brethren, that there is never in any one of 12 you—as perhaps there may be—a sinful and unbelieving heart, manifesting itself in revolt from the ever-living God.

On the contrary encourage one another, day after day, so 13 long as "to-day" lasts, so that not one of you may be hardened through the deceitful character of sin. For we have, all alike, 14 become sharers with Christ, if we really hold our first confidence firm to the end; seeing that the warning still comes to us, 15
"TO-DAY, IF YOU SHOULD HEAR HIS VOICE,
DO NOT HARDEN YOUR HEARTS AS YOUR FORE-
FATHERS DID IN THE TIME OF THE PROVOCATION"
(Psalm 95:7-8).

For who were they that heard, and yet provoked God? Was it 16 not the whole of the people who had come out of Egypt under the leadership of Moses? And with whom was God so greatly 17 grieved for forty years? Was it not with those who had sinned, and whose dead bodies fell in the desert? And to whom did He 18 swear that they should not be admitted to His rest, if it was not

to those who were disobedient? And so we see that it was 19
owing to lack of faith that they could not be admitted.

4 Therefore let us be on our guard lest perhaps, while He 1
still leaves us a promise of entering into His rest, any
one of you should be found to have failed to obtain it. For a 2
gospel has been brought to us as truly as to them; but the
word they heard failed to benefit them, because they were
not united by faith with those who gave heed to it. We who 3
have believed are to be admitted to that rest; as He has said,

"WHILE I SWORE IN MY ANGER,

THEY SHALL NOT BE ADMITTED TO MY REST" (Psalm
95:11); although God's works were completed from the
creation of the world. For, as we know, when speaking of the 4
seventh day He has used the words, "AND GOD RESTED ON
THE SEVENTH DAY FROM ALL HIS WORKS" (Genesis 2:2);
and He has also declared, "THEY SHALL NOT BE ADMIT- 5
TED TO MY REST" (Psalm 95:11).

Since, then, it is still true that some will be admitted to it, 6
and that because of disobedience those who formerly had
the gospel proclaimed to them were not admitted, He again 7
definitely mentions a certain day, "to-day," saying long afterwards, by David's lips, in the words already quoted,

"TO-DAY, IF YOU SHOULD HEAR HIS VOICE,

DO NOT HARDEN YOUR HEARTS" (Psalm 95:7-8).

For if Joshua had given them rest, God would not have 8
continued to speak later about another still future day. It fol- 9
lows that there still remains a sabbath-rest for the people of
God. For whoever has been admitted to his rest, has rested 10
from his works as God did from His.

Let it, then, be our earnest endeavor to be admitted to that 11
rest, so that no one may perish through following the same

example of disobedience. For the word of God is full of life 12
and power, and is keener than the sharpest two-edged
sword. It pierces even to the severance of soul from spirit,
and penetrates between the joints and the marrow, and it
can discern the secret thoughts and purposes of the heart.
And no created thing is able to escape its scrutiny; but every- 13
thing lies bare and completely exposed before the eyes of
Him with whom we have to do.

Inasmuch, then, as we have in Jesus, the Son of God, a 14
great High Priest who has passed into heaven itself, let us
hold firmly to our profession of faith. For we have not a High 15
Priest who is unable to feel for us in our weaknesses, but one
who was tempted in every respect, just as we are tempted,
and yet did not sin. Therefore let us come boldly to the 16
throne of grace, that we may receive mercy and find grace to
help us in our time of need.

5 For every high priest, chosen as he is from among men, 1
is appointed to act on behalf of men in matters relating
to God, in order to offer both gifts and sin-offerings, and he 2
must be one who is able to bear patiently with the ignorant
and erring, because he himself also is beset with infirmity.
And for this reason he is required to offer sin-offerings not 3
only for the people but also for himself.

And no one takes this honorable office upon himself, but 4
only accepts it when called to it by God, as Aaron was. So 5
Christ also did not claim for Himself the honor of being
made High Priest, but was appointed to it by Him who said
to Him,

"MY SON ART THOU:

I HAVE THIS DAY BECOME THY FATHER" (Psalm 2:7);
as also in another passage He says, 6

"THOU ART A PRIEST FOR EVER,
BELONGING TO THE ORDER OF MELCHIZEDEK"
(Psalm 110:4).

For Jesus during His earthly life offered up prayers and 7
entreaties, crying aloud and weeping as He pleaded with
Him who was able to save Him from death, and He was
heard for His godly fear. Although He was God's Son, yet He 8
learned obedience from the sufferings which He endured;
and so, having been made perfect, He became to all who 9
obey Him the source and giver of eternal salvation. For God 10
Himself addresses Him as a High Priest for ever, belonging to
the order of Melchizedek.

Of this we have much to say, and much that it would be 11
difficult to make clear to you, since you have become so dull
of apprehension. For although, considering the long time 12
you have been believers, you ought now to be teachers of
others, you really need some one to teach you over again the
very rudiments of the truths of God, and you have come to
require milk instead of solid food. By people who live on 13
milk I mean those who are imperfectly acquainted with the
doctrine of righteousness. Such persons are mere babes. But 14
solid food is for adults—that is, for those who through constant practice have their spiritual faculties carefully trained
to distinguish good from evil.

6 Therefore leaving elementary instruction about the 1
Christ, let us advance to mature manhood, and not be
continually relaying a foundation of repentance from lifeless
works and of faith in God, or teaching about ceremonial 2
washings, the laying on of hands, the resurrection of the
dead, and the last judgment. And advance we will, if God 3
permits us to do so.

For it is impossible, in the case of those who have once for 4 all been enlightened, and have tasted the sweetness of the heavenly gift, and have been made partakers of the Holy Spirit, and have realized how good the word of God is and how 5 mighty are the powers of the coming age, and then fall away— 6 it is impossible, I say, to bring them back to a new repentance, since, to their own undoing, they are crucifying the Son of God afresh and exposing Him to open shame. For land which 7 has drunk in the rain that often falls upon it, and brings forth vegetation useful to those for whose sakes it is tilled, has a share in God's blessing. But if it yields only a mass of thorns 8 and thistles, it is considered worthless, and is in danger of being cursed, and in the end will be destroyed by fire.

But we, even while we speak in this tone, have a happier 9 conviction concerning you, my dearly-loved friends—a conviction of things which point towards salvation. For God is 10 not unjust so as to be unmindful of your labor and of the love which you have manifested towards Himself in having rendered services to His people and in still rendering them. But 11 we long for each of you to continue to show the same earnestness, with a view to your enjoying fullness of hope to the very end; so that you may not become half-hearted, but 12 be imitators of those who through faith and endurance are heirs to the promises.

For when God gave the promise to Abraham, since He had 13 no one greater to swear by, He swore by Himself, saying, 14

"ASSUREDLY I WILL BLESS YOU,

AND I WILL INCREASE YOU" (Genesis 22:16-17).

And so, as the result of patient waiting, our forefather 15 obtained what God had promised. Men swear by what is 16 greater than themselves; and with them an oath in confirmation of a statement always puts an end to a dispute. In the 17 same way, since it was God's desire to prove more convincingly to the heirs of the promise how unchangeable His purpose was, He added an oath, in order that, through two unchangeable things, in which it is impossible for Him to prove false, we may possess mighty encouragement—we who, for safety, have hastened to lay hold of the hope set before us. That hope we have as an anchor of the soul—an anchor that can neither break nor drag. It passes in behind the veil, where Jesus has entered as a forerunner on our behalf, having become, like Melchizedek, a high priest for ever. 18 19 20

7 This Melchizedek, king of Salem, priest of the Most High God, who met Abraham as he was returning from the slaughter of the kings and blessed him, to whom also Abraham assigned a tenth part of all the spoil, was in the first place, as his name means, king of righteousness, and besides that, king of Salem, that is, king of peace. Being without father or mother or ancestry, having neither beginning of days nor end of life, but made like to the Son of God, he remains a priest in perpetuity (Genesis 14:18-20; Psalm 110:4). 1 2 3

Now think how great this man must have been, to whom Abraham, the patriarch, gave a tenth part of the best of the spoil. Those of the descendants of Levi who receive the priesthood are indeed authorized by the Law to take tithes from the people, that is, from their brethren, though these have sprung from Abraham. But, in this instance, one who does not trace his origin from them takes tithes from Abraham, and blesses him to whom the promises belong! And beyond all dispute it is always the inferior who is blessed by the superior. 4 5 6 7

Moreover, here mortal men receive tithes: there one receives them about whom it is witnessed that he lives. And even Levi—if I may so speak—pays tithes through Abraham: 8 9

for Levi was yet in the loins of his forefather when 10
Melchizedek met Abraham.

If, then, perfection was attainable by means of the 11
Levitical priesthood—for on this basis the people received
the Law—what further need was there for a priest of a different kind to be raised up belonging to the order of
Melchizedek instead of being said to belong to the order
of Aaron? For when the priesthood changes, a change of law 12
also of necessity takes place.

He of whom all this is said is connected with a different 13
tribe, not one man of which has anything to do with the altar.
For it is undeniable that our Lord sprang from Judah, a tribe 14
concerning which Moses said nothing about priests. And 15
this is still more abundantly clear when we read that it is as
belonging to the order of Melchizedek that a priest of a different kind is to arise, and to hold His office not in obedience 16
to any temporary law, but by virtue of an indestructible Life.
The words indeed are in evidence, 17

"THOU ART A PRIEST FOR EVER, BELONGING TO THE
ORDER OF MELCHIZEDEK" (Psalm 110:4).

On the one hand we have here the abrogation [abolition] 18
of an earlier code because it was weak and ineffective—for 19
the Law made nothing perfect; on the other hand we have
the bringing in of a new and better hope by means of which
we draw near to God.

And since this was effected not without an oath—for those 20
others became priests apart from any oath, but He entered 21
upon an office confirmed by an oath from Him who said to
Him, "THE LORD HAS SWORN AND WILL NOT RECALL HIS
WORDS, THOU ART A PRIEST FOR EVER" (Psalm 110:4)—so 22
much the more also is the covenant of which Jesus has
become the guarantor, a better covenant.

And they have been appointed priests many in number, 23

because death prevents their continuance in office: but He, 24
because He continues for ever, has a priesthood which does
not pass to any successor. Hence, too, He is able to save to 25
the uttermost those who come to God through Him, seeing
that He ever lives to make intercession on their behalf.

Such a high priest as this was exactly suited to our need— 26
holy, guileless, undefiled, far removed from sinful men, and
exalted above the heavens; who, unlike other high priests, is 27
not under the necessity of offering up sacrifices day after
day, first for His own sins, and afterwards for those of the
people; because this He did once for all when He offered up
Himself. For the Law constitutes men—men with all their 28
infirmity—as high priests; but the word of the oath, which
came later than the Law, constitutes as High Priest a Son
who has been made for ever perfect.

Christ's High Priesthood, and the New Covenant

8 Now of what we have been saying the main point is this. 1
We have a High Priest who has taken His seat at the
right hand of the throne of God's Majesty in the heavens, and 2
ministers in the holy place and in the true tabernacle built by
the Lord and not by man.

Every high priest, however, is appointed to offer both 3
bloodless gifts and sacrifices. Therefore this High Priest also
must have some offering to present. If, then, He were still on 4
earth, He would not be a priest at all, since there are already
those who present the offerings in obedience to the Law, and 5
do service to a copy and type of things heavenly, just as
Moses was divinely instructed when about to build the
tabernacle. God said, "SEE THAT YOU MAKE EVERYTHING
AFTER THE PATTERN SHOWN YOU ON THE MOUNTAIN"

(Exodus 25:40). But, as a matter of fact, the ministry which 6
Christ has obtained is all the nobler a ministry, in that He is
at the same time the negotiator of a sublimer covenant,
based upon sublimer promises.

For if that first covenant had been free from imperfection, 7
there would have been no occasion to introduce a second.
But scripture says that God was dissatisfied with His people: 8

"'THERE ARE DAYS COMING,' SAYS THE LORD,
'WHEN I WILL ESTABLISH WITH THE HOUSE OF ISRAEL
AND WITH THE HOUSE OF JUDAH A NEW COVENANT—
A COVENANT UNLIKE THE ONE WHICH I MADE WITH 9
THEIR FATHERS
ON THE DAY WHEN I TOOK THEM BY THE HAND TO
LEAD THEM OUT FROM THE LAND OF EGYPT;
FOR THEY WOULD NOT REMAIN FAITHFUL TO MY
COVENANT,
SO I TURNED FROM THEM,' SAYS THE LORD.
'BUT THIS IS THE COVENANT THAT I WILL MAKE WITH 10
THE HOUSE OF ISRAEL
AFTER THOSE DAYS,' SAYS THE LORD:
'I WILL PUT MY LAWS INTO THEIR MINDS
AND WILL WRITE THEM UPON THEIR HEARTS.
AND I WILL INDEED BE THEIR GOD
AND THEY SHALL BE MY PEOPLE.
AND THERE SHALL BE NO NEED FOR THEM TO TEACH 11
EACH ONE HIS FELLOW CITIZEN
AND EACH ONE HIS BROTHER, SAYING, KNOW THE
LORD.
FOR ALL WILL KNOW ME
FROM THE LEAST OF THEM TO THE GREATEST;
BECAUSE I WILL BE MERCIFUL TO THEIR WRONGDOINGS, 12
AND THEIR SINS I WILL REMEMBER NO LONGER'"
(Jeremiah 31:31-34).

By using the words, "a new covenant," He has made the first one obsolete. But whatever is decaying and showing signs of old age is not far from disappearing altogether. 13

9 Now even the first covenant had regulations for divine worship, and had also its sanctuary—a sanctuary belonging to this material world. A sacred tent was constructed—the outer one, in which were the lamp and the table and the presented loaves; and this is called the Holy Place. And behind the second veil was a sacred tent called the Holy of Holies. This had a golden altar of incense, and the ark of the covenant completely covered with gold, and in it there were a gold vase holding the manna, and Aaron's rod which budded, and the tables of the covenant. And above the ark were the Cherubim of the glory over-shadowing the mercy-seat. But I cannot now speak about all these in detail. 1 2 3 4 5

These arrangements having been completed, the priests, when conducting the divine services, continually enter the outer tent. But into the second the high priest goes on only one day of the year, and goes alone, taking with him blood, which he offers both on his own behalf and on account of the sins which the people have ignorantly committed. The lesson which the Holy Spirit teaches is this—that the way into the true Holy Place is not yet open so long as the outer tent still stands. And this for this present time is symbolic. According to that symbol both gifts and sacrifices are offered, unable though they are to give complete freedom from sin to him who worships. For reliance is placed only on meats and drinks and various washings—regulations for the body, imposed until a time of reformation. 6 7 8 9 10

But when Christ appeared as a High Priest of the blessings 11 that are to come, He entered through the greater and more perfect tabernacle (a tent not built with hands—that is to say, which does not belong to this material creation); and by 12 means of His own blood, not the blood of goats and calves, He once for all entered the Holy Place; thus securing an eternal redemption.

For if the blood of goats and bulls and the ashes of a heifer 13 sprinkling those who have contracted defilement make them holy so as to bring about ceremonial purity, how much more 14 certainly shall the blood of Christ, who through the eternal Spirit offered Himself to God, free from blemish, purify your consciences from lifeless works to serve the living God?

And because of this He is the mediator of a new covenant, 15 in order that, since a life has been given in deliverance from the offenses committed under the first covenant, those who have been called may receive the eternal inheritance which has been promised to them. For where there is a legal "will," 16 there must also be a death brought forward in evidence—the death of him who made it. And a will is only of force in the 17 case of a deceased person, being never of any avail so long as he who made it lives.

Accordingly we find that the first covenant was not inau- 18 gurated without blood. Thus when Moses had proclaimed to 19 all the people every commandment contained in the Law, he took the blood of the calves and of the goats and with them water, scarlet wool and hyssop, and sprinkled both the book itself and the people generally, saying, 20

"THIS IS THE BLOOD WHICH CONFIRMS THE COV-ENANT THAT GOD HAS MADE BINDING UPON YOU" (Exodus 24:8).

In the same way he also sprinkled blood upon the tent of 21 worship and upon all the vessels used in the ministry. Indeed 22 we may almost say that in obedience to the Law everything is sprinkled with blood, and that apart from the shedding of blood there is no remission of sins.

It was needful, therefore, that the copies of the things in 23 heaven should be cleansed in this way, but that the heavenly things themselves should be cleansed with more costly sacrifices. For not into a holy place built by men's hands—a 24 mere copy of the reality—did Christ enter, but He entered heaven itself, now to appear in the presence of God on our behalf. Nor was it for the purpose of many times offering 25 Himself in sacrifice, as the high priest enters the Holy Place, year after year, taking with him blood not his own. In that 26 case Christ would have needed to suffer many times, from the creation of the world onwards; but, as a matter of fact, He has appeared once for all, at the close of the ages, in order to do away with sin by the sacrifice of Himself.

And since it is reserved for all mankind once to die, and 27 afterwards to be judged; so the Christ also, having been 28 once offered in sacrifice in order that He might bear the sins of many, will appear a second time, separated from sin, to those who are eagerly expecting Him, to make their salvation complete.

10 Now, since the Law exhibits only an outline of the 1 blessings to come and not a perfect representation of the realities, the priests can never, by repeating the same sacrifices which they continually offer year after year, give complete freedom from sin to those who draw near. For then 2 would not the sacrifices have ceased to be offered, because the consciences of the worshipers, in that case cleansed once for all, would no longer be burdened with sins? But in those 3 sacrifices sins are recalled to memory year after year. It is 4 impossible for the blood of bulls and goats to take away sins.

That is why, when He comes into the world, He says, 5
"SACRIFICE AND OFFERING THOU HAST NOT DESIRED,
BUT A BODY THOU HAST PREPARED FOR ME.
IN WHOLE BURNT-OFFERINGS AND IN SIN-OFFERINGS 6
THOU HAST TAKEN NO PLEASURE.
THEN I SAID, 'I AM COME—IN THE ROLL OF THE BOOK 7
IT IS WRITTEN CONCERNING ME—
TO DO THY WILL, O GOD'" (Psalm 40:6-8).

After saying the words I have just quoted, "SACRIFICES 8
AND OFFERINGS or WHOLE BURNT-OFFERINGS AND
SIN-OFFERINGS THOU HAST NOT DESIRED OR TAKEN
PLEASURE IN" (all such being offered in obedience to the
Law), He then adds, "I AM COME TO DO THY WILL." He 9
does away with the first in order to establish the second. It 10
is through that divine will that we have been set free from
sin, through the offering of Jesus Christ as our sacrifice once
for all.

And while every priest stands ministering, day after day, 11
and constantly offering the same sacrifices—though these
can never rid us of our sins—this Priest, on the contrary, 12
after offering for sins a single sacrifice of perpetual efficacy
[effectiveness], took His seat at God's right hand, waiting 13
from that time onward until His enemies be put as a footstool under His feet. By one single offering He has for ever 14
perfected the sanctified.

And the Holy Spirit also gives us His testimony; for when 15
He had said,

"'THIS IS THE COVENANT THAT I WILL MAKE WITH 16
THEM
AFTER THOSE DAYS,' SAYS THE LORD:
'I WILL PUT MY LAWS UPON THEIR HEARTS
AND WILL WRITE THEM ON THEIR MINDS;'"
He adds, 17

"AND THEIR SINS AND OFFENSES I WILL REMEMBER NO LONGER" (Jeremiah 31:33-34).

But where these have been forgiven no further offering for 18 sin is required.

Exhortations Based on the New Covenant

Since then, brethren, we have free access to the holy place 19 through the blood of Jesus, by the new and living way which 20 He opened up for us through the veil—that is to say, His flesh—and since we have a great Priest who has authority 21 over the house of God, let us draw near with sincerity 22 and unfaltering faith, our hearts sprinkled clean from consciences oppressed with sin, and our bodies bathed in pure water. Let us hold firmly to an unflinching avowal of our 23 hope, for He is faithful who gave us the promises. And let us 24 bestow thought on one another with a view to arousing one another to brotherly love and right conduct; not neglecting— 25 as some habitually do—to meet together, but encouraging one another, and doing this all the more since you can see the Day of Christ drawing near.

For if we willfully persist in sin after having received the 26 knowledge of the truth, there no longer remains in reserve any other sacrifice for sins. There remains nothing but a certain 27 awful expectation of judgment, and the fury of a fire which is to consume the enemies of God. Any one who bids defiance 28 to the Law of Moses is put to death without mercy on the testimony of two or three witnesses. How much severer 29 punishment, think you, will he be held to deserve who has trampled under foot the Son of God, has not regarded as holy that covenant-blood with which he was set free from sin, and has insulted the Spirit from whom comes grace? For we know 30 who it is that has said, "VENGEANCE BELONGS TO ME: I

WILL PAY BACK" (Deuteronomy 32:35); and again, "THE LORD WILL BE HIS PEOPLE'S JUDGE" (Deuteronomy 32:36). It is an awful thing to fall into the hands of the living God. 31

But recall to mind the days now past, when on being first 32 enlightened you went through a great conflict and many sufferings. This was partly through allowing yourselves to be 33 made a public spectacle amid reproaches and persecutions, and partly through coming forward to share the sufferings of those who were thus treated. For you not only showed sym- 34 pathy with those who were imprisoned, but you even submitted with joy when your property was taken from you, being well aware that you have in your own selves a more valuable possession and one which will remain.

Therefore do not cast from you your confident hope, for it 35 will receive a vast reward. You have need of endurance, so 36 that, as the result of having done the will of God, you may receive the promised blessing. There is still but a short time, 37 and then

"THE COMING ONE WILL COME AND WILL NOT DELAY.
BUT IT IS BY FAITH THAT MY RIGHTEOUS SERVANT 38
SHALL LIVE;
AND IF HE SHRINKS BACK, MY SOUL TAKES NO PLEAS-
URE IN HIM" (Habakkuk 2:3-4, LXX).

We, however, are not the ones to shrink back and perish, but 39 are of those who believe and so win possession of their souls.

Faith and Its Ancient Heroes

11 Now faith is a confident assurance of that for which 1 we hope, a conviction of the reality of things which we do not see. By it the saints of old won God's approval. 2 Through faith we understand that the world came into being 3

by the command of God, so that what is seen does not owe its existence to that which is visible (Genesis 1:1).

Through faith Abel offered to God a more acceptable 4 sacrifice than Cain, and through this faith he had witness borne to him that he was righteous, God bearing witness by accepting his gifts (Genesis 4:4); and through his faith, though he is dead, he still speaks.

Through faith Enoch was taken from the earth so that he 5 did not see death, and he could not be found, because God took him; for before he was taken he had witness borne to him that he pleased God (Genesis 5:22, 24). Where there is no 6 faith it is impossible truly to please Him; for the man who draws near to God must believe that there is a God, and that He proves Himself a rewarder of those who seek after Him.

Through faith Noah, being divinely warned about things 7 as yet unseen, reverently gave heed and built an ark for the safety of his family (Genesis 6:13-22); and by this act he condemned the world, and became an heir of the righteousness which depends on faith.

Through faith Abraham, called to leave home and go into 8 a land which he was to receive for an inheritance, obeyed; and he went out, not knowing where he was going (Genesis 12:1, 4). Through faith he came and made his home for a 9 time in a land which had been promised to him, as if in a foreign country, living in tents together with Isaac and Jacob, sharers with him in the same promise; for he was looking 10 forward to the city which has the foundations, whose architect and builder is God.

Through faith even Sarah herself received strength to 11 become a mother—although she was past the time of life for this—because she judged Him faithful who had given the promise (Genesis 21:1-2). And thus there sprang from one 12 man, one practically dead, a nation like the stars of the sky in number, and like the sands on the sea-shore which cannot be counted.

All these died sustained by faith. They had not received the 13 promised blessings, but had seen them from a distance and had greeted them, and had acknowledged themselves to be foreigners and strangers here on earth: men who acknowledge 14 this make it manifest that they are seeking elsewhere a country of their own. If they had cherished the remembrance of the 15 country they had left, they would have found an opportunity to return; but, as it is, we see them eager for a better land, that 16 is to say, a heavenly one. For this reason God is not ashamed to be called their God, for He has prepared a city for them.

Through faith Abraham, when he was being put to the 17 test, offered up Isaac (Genesis 22). Yes, he who had joyfully welcomed the promises was ready to sacrifice his only son with regard to whom he had been told, "IT IS THROUGH 18 ISAAC THAT YOUR POSTERITY SHALL BE TRACED" (Genesis 21:12). For he reckoned that God is even able to 19 raise a man up from the dead, and, figuratively speaking, it was from the dead that he received Isaac back again.

Through faith Isaac blessed Jacob and Esau, even as to 20 things yet to come (Genesis 27:27-40). Through faith Jacob, 21 when dying, blessed each of Joseph's sons, and, bowing upon the top of his staff, worshiped God (Genesis 48:8-20). Through faith Joseph, when he was near his end, made men- 22 tion of the exodus of the sons of Israel, and gave orders about his own body (Genesis 50:24-25).

Through faith the child Moses was hid for three months by 23 his parents, because they saw his rare beauty; and the king's edict had no terror for them (Exodus 2:2).

Through faith Moses, when he grew to manhood, refused 24 to be known as Pharaoh's daughter's son, preferring rather to 25 endure ill-treatment along with the people of God than to

enjoy the short-lived pleasures of sin; because he deemed 26
the reproaches which he might meet with in the service of
the Christ to be greater riches than all the treasures of Egypt;
for he fixed his gaze on the coming reward. Through faith he 27
left Egypt, not being afraid of the king's anger; for he held on
his course as seeing the unseen One (Exodus 2:14-15).
Through faith he instituted the Passover and the sprinkling 28
of the blood so that the destroyer of the firstborn might not
touch the Israelites (Exodus 12:21-22).

Through faith they passed through the Red Sea as though 29
they were passing over dry land, but the Egyptians, when they
tried to do the same, were swallowed up (Exodus 14:22-28).

Through faith the walls of Jericho fell to the ground after 30
being surrounded for seven days (Joshua 6:20).

Through faith Rahab the harlot did not perish along with 31
the disobedient, because she had welcomed the spies and
had sheltered them (Joshua 2:1, 6:23).

And why need I say more? For time will fail me if I tell the 32
story of Gideon, Barak, Samson, Jephthah, and of David and
Samuel and the prophets; men who, through faith, con- 33
quered whole kingdoms, executed true justice, obtained
promises, shut the mouths of lions (Daniel 6:22), quenched 34
the power of fire (Daniel 3), escaped the edge of the sword,
out of weakness were made strong, became mighty in war,
put to flight foreign armies. Women received back their dear 35
ones alive from the dead (1 Kings 17:23; 2 Kings 4:37); and
others were put to death with torture, refusing the deliverance offered to them—that they might secure a better resurrection. Others, again, were tested by cruel mockery and by 36
scourging; yes, and by chains and imprisonment. They were 37
stoned (2 Chronicles 24:20-21), they were sawn asunder,
they were tried by temptation, they were killed with the
sword (1 Kings 19:14; Jeremiah 26:20-23). They went from

place to place in sheepskins or goatskins, enduring want, oppression, and cruelty—men of whom the world was not 38 worthy: they wandered across deserts and mountains, or hid themselves in caves and in holes in the ground.

And although by their faith they all won God's approval, 39 none of them received the fulfillment of His promise; because God had provided for us something better, so that 40 apart from us they were not to be perfected.

Renewed Exhortations

12 Therefore, surrounded as we are by such a vast cloud 1 of witnesses, let us fling aside every encumbrance and the sin that so readily entangles our feet. And let us run with endurance the race that lies before us, simply fixing our 2 gaze upon Jesus, the Leader and Perfecter of faith. He, for the sake of the joy which lay before Him, patiently endured the cross, looking with contempt upon its shame, and is now seated at the right hand of the throne of God.

Therefore, if you would escape becoming weary and faint- 3 hearted, compare your own sufferings with those of Him who endured such hostility directed against Him by sinners. In your struggle against sin you have not yet resisted to the 4 shedding of blood; and you have quite forgotten the encour- 5 aging words which are addressed to you as sons,

"MY SON, DO NOT THINK LIGHTLY OF THE LORD'S DISCIPLINE,

AND DO NOT FAINT WHEN HE CORRECTS YOU;

FOR THOSE WHOM THE LORD LOVES HE DISCIPLINES: 6

AND HE SCOURGES EVERY SON WHOM HE ACCEPTS" (Proverbs 3:11-12; Job 5:17).

The sufferings that you are enduring are for your 7

discipline. God is dealing with you as sons; for what son is there whom his father does not discipline? And if you are 8 left without discipline, of which all have had a share, that shows that you are bastards, and not sons.

Besides this, our earthly fathers used to discipline us and 9 we treated them with respect, and shall we not be still more submissive to the Father of our spirits, and live? They disci- 10 plined us for a few years according as they thought fit; but He does it for our certain good, in order that we may become sharers in His own holy character. Now, at the time, disci- 11 pline seems to be a matter not for joy, but for grief; yet it afterwards yields to those who have passed through its train- ing the peace of a righteous life.

Therefore strengthen the drooping hands and paralyzed 12 knees, and make straight paths for your feet, so that what is 13 lame may not be put entirely out of joint but may rather be restored. Ever strive for peace with all men, and for that 14 sanctification apart from which no one will see the Lord. Carefully see to it that no one fails to avail himself of the 15 grace of God; that no root bearing bitter fruit spring up and cause trouble among you, and through it the whole brother- hood be defiled; and that there be no fornicator, and no 16 ungodly person like Esau, who, in return for a single meal, parted with his birthright. For you know that even after- 17 wards, when he wished to secure the blessing, he was re- jected; he found no opportunity for repentance, though he sought the blessing earnestly with tears.

The Difference Between the Inauguration of the Earthly and Heavenly Kingdoms of God

No, you have not come near to something material all 18 ablaze with fire, and to gloom and darkness and storm and 19 trumpet-blast and the sound of words—a sound such that those who heard it entreated that no further word should be added. For they could not endure the order which had been 20 given, "EVEN A BEAST, IF IT TOUCHES THE MOUNTAIN, SHALL BE STONED TO DEATH" (Exodus 19:12-13); and so 21 terrible was the scene that Moses said, "I TREMBLE WITH FEAR" (Deuteronomy 9:19). No! you have come to Mount 22 Zion, and to the city of the living God, the heavenly Jerusalem, to countless hosts of angels, to the festal gather- 23 ing and Church of the firstborn, whose names are recorded in heaven, and to the God of all as judge, and to the spirits of righteous men made perfect, and to Jesus the mediator of a 24 new covenant, and to the sprinkled blood which speaks in more gracious tones than that of Abel.

See to it that you do not refuse to listen to Him who is 25 speaking to you. For if they of old did not escape unpunished when they refused to listen to Him who spoke on earth, much less shall we escape who turn a deaf ear to Him who now speaks from heaven. His voice then shook the earth, but 26 now we have His promise, "YET AGAIN I WILL, ONCE FOR ALL, CAUSE NOT ONLY THE EARTH TO TREMBLE, BUT HEAVEN ALSO" (Haggai 2:6). Here the words "Yet again, 27 once for all" denote the removal of the things which can be shaken—created things—in order that the things which cannot be shaken may remain.

Therefore, receiving a kingdom which cannot be shaken, 28 let us cherish thankfulness, so that we may offer to God an acceptable service with godly reverence and awe. "FOR OUR 29 GOD IS INDEED A CONSUMING FIRE" (Deuteronomy 4:24).

Final Exhortations

13 Let brotherly love continue. Do not neglect to show hospitality to strangers; for, by being hospitable, some, without knowing it, have had angels as their guests (Genesis 18, 19; Judges 13). Remember prisoners, as if you were in prison with them; and remember those suffering ill-treatment, for you yourselves also are still in the body. Let marriage be held in honor among all, and let the marriage bed be unpolluted; fornicators and adulterers God will judge.

Your lives should be untainted by love for money. Be content with what you have; for God Himself has said,

"I WILL NEVER LET YOU GO:

I WILL NEVER FORSAKE YOU" (Genesis 28:15; Deuteronomy 31:6-8; Joshua 1:5).

So that we fearlessly say,

"THE LORD IS MY HELPER: I WILL NOT BE AFRAID: WHAT CAN MAN DO TO ME?" (Psalm 118:6).

Remember your former leaders—it was they who brought you the word of God. Bear in mind how they ended their lives, and imitate their faith. Jesus Christ is the same yesterday and to-day—yes, and for ever. Do not be drawn aside by all sorts of strange teaching; for it is well to have the heart strengthened by grace and not by meats, from which those who place dependence upon them have derived no benefit.

We Christians have an altar from which those who serve the tabernacle have no right to eat. For the bodies of those animals of which the blood is carried by the high priest into the Holy Place as an offering for sin are burned outside the camp (Leviticus 16). And for this reason Jesus also, in order, by His own blood, to set the people free from sin, suffered outside the gate. Therefore let us go to Him outside the camp, bearing the same reproach as He. For we have no abiding city here, but we seek the city which is to come.

Through Him, then, let us continually lay on the altar a 15 sacrifice of praise to God, that is, the fruit of lips that give thanks to His Name. And do not forget to be kind and liberal; 16 for with sacrifices of that sort God is greatly pleased.

Obey your leaders and be submissive to them, because 17 they are keeping watch over your souls as those who will have to give account; so that they may do this with joy and not with lamentation—for that would be of no advantage to you.

Pray for us; for we are sure that we have clear consciences, 18 and we desire to live honorably in every respect. I specially 19 urge this upon you all the more, that I may the sooner be restored to you.

Now may the God of peace who brought up from the dead 20 the great Shepherd of the sheep with the blood of the eternal covenant, even Jesus our Lord, equip you with every good for 21 the doing of His will, effecting in us that which is pleasing in His sight through Jesus Christ. To Him be the glory for ever and ever. Amen.

Bear with me, brethren, when I thus exhort you; for, in 22 fact, it is but a short letter that I have written to you.

You will rejoice to hear that our brother Timothy has been 23 set at liberty. If he comes soon, I will see you with him. Greet 24 all your leaders and all the saints. The brethren from Italy send you greetings.

Grace be with you all. Amen. 25

THE EPISTLE OF JAMES

1 James, a servant of God and of the Lord Jesus Christ: to 1
the twelve tribes of the Dispersion, greeting.

Reckon it nothing but joy, my brethren, whenever you find 2
yourselves surrounded by various temptations. Be assured 3
that the testing of your faith leads to power of endurance;
only let endurance do its full work so that you may become 4
perfect and complete, deficient in nothing. If any one of you 5
is deficient in wisdom, let him ask God who gives with open
hand to all men and without upbraiding; and it will be given
him. But let him ask in faith and have no doubts; for he who 6
has doubts is like the surge of the sea, driven by the wind and
tossed about. A person of that sort must not expect to receive 7
anything from the Lord, being a man of two minds, unde- 8
cided in every step he takes.

Let a brother in humble life rejoice when he is promoted; but 9
a rich man should rejoice in being brought low, for like flowers 10
of the field he will pass away. The sun rises with his scorching 11
heat and dries up the herbage, so that its flowers drop off and
the beauty of its appearance perishes; and in the same way rich
men in the midst of their occupations will fade away.

Blessed is he who endures trials; for when he has stood 12
the test, he shall gain the crown of life which the Lord has
promised to those who love Him. Let no one say when pass- 13
ing through trial, "My temptation is from God;" for God is
incapable of being tempted by evil, and He Himself tempts
no one. But when a man is tempted, it is his own passions 14
that carry him away and serve as a bait. Then the passion 15
conceives, and becomes the parent of sin; and sin, when
fully matured, gives birth to death.

Do not be deceived, my beloved brethren. Every good gift 16
and every perfect boon [blessing] is from above, and comes 17
down from the Father, who is the source of all Light. In Him
there is no variation nor the shadow of change. In accord- 18
ance with His will He made us His children, through the
word of the truth so that we might, in a sense, be the firstfruits of the things which He has created.

You may be sure of this, my beloved brethren. But let every 19
one be quick to hear, slow to speak, and slow to be angry. A 20
man's anger does not accomplish God's righteousness.
Ridding yourselves, therefore, of all that is vile and of the 21
rank growth of malice, welcome in a humble spirit the word
implanted within you, which is able to save your souls.

But prove yourselves obedient to the word, and do not be 22
mere hearers of it, deluding yourselves. If any one listens 23
but does not obey, he is like a man who carefully looks at his
own face in a mirror; for although he looks carefully at him- 24
self, he goes away and immediately forgets what sort of man
he was. He, however, who looks closely into the perfect law 25
of freedom and continues looking, being not a hearer who
forgets, but an obedient doer, will find blessing in the very
act of obedience.

If a man thinks that he is religious, although he does not 26
curb his tongue but deceives his own heart, his religion is
worthless. The religion which is pure and stainless in the 27
sight of our God and Father is to visit orphans and widows in
their time of trouble, and to keep one's own self unspotted
from the world.

2 My brethren, while holding to your faith in our Lord 1
Jesus Christ who is the Glory, do not show partiality.
Suppose a man comes into one of your meetings wearing 2

gold rings and fine clothes, and there also comes in a poor man wearing shabby clothes, and you pay regard to the one 3 who wears the fine clothes, and say, "Sit here; this is a good place"; while to the poor man you say, "Stand there, or sit on the floor at my feet"—is it not plain that in your hearts you 4 have little faith, seeing that you have become judges full of wrong thoughts?

Listen, my beloved brethren. Has not God chosen those 5 whom the world regards as poor to be rich in faith and heirs of the Kingdom which He has promised to those that love Him? But you have put dishonor upon the poor man. 6 Yet is it not the rich who grind you down? Are not they the people who drag you into the law courts? the people who 7 speak evil of the noble Name by which you are called? If, 8 however, you perform the royal law, in obedience to the scripture, "YOU ARE TO LOVE YOUR NEIGHBOR AS YOU LOVE YOURSELF"(Leviticus 19:18), you act rightly. But if 9 you show partiality you commit sin, and are convicted by the Law as offenders.

A man who keeps the Law as a whole, but fails in a single 10 point, has become guilty of violating all. For He who said, 11 "DO NOT COMMIT ADULTERY," also said, "DO NOT COMMIT MURDER" (Exodus 20:13-14; Deuteronomy 5:17-18); and if you are a murderer, although not an adulterer, you have become an offender against the Law. Speak and act as 12 those should who are to be judged by the law of freedom. For 13 he who shows no mercy will incur judgment without mercy; but mercy triumphs over judgment.

What good is it, my brethren, if a man professes to have 14 faith, and yet his actions do not correspond? Can such faith save him? Suppose a brother and a sister are poorly clad or 15 lack daily food, and one of you says to them, "Fare you well; 16 keep yourselves warm and well fed," and yet you do not

supply their bodily needs; what is the use of that? So also 17
faith, if it is unaccompanied by obedience, is dead in itself.

Nay, some one will say, "You have faith, I have actions: 18
prove to me your faith apart from corresponding actions and
I will prove mine to you by my actions. You believe that God 19
is one, and you are quite right: evil spirits also believe this,
and shudder."

But, idle boaster, are you willing to be taught that faith 20
apart from obedience is worthless? Was it not because of his 21
actions that Abraham our father was declared to be righteous when he had offered up his son Isaac upon the altar?
You notice that his faith was co-operating with his actions, 22
and that by his actions his faith was perfected; and the scrip- 23
ture was fulfilled which says, "AND ABRAHAM BELIEVED
GOD, AND HIS FAITH WAS CREDITED TO HIM AS RIGHT-
EOUSNESS" (Genesis 15:6), and he received the name of
God's friend (2 Chronicles 20:7; Isaiah 41:8). You see that it is 24
because of actions that a man is pronounced righteous, and
not simply because of faith. In the same way also was not the 25
harlot Rahab declared to be righteous because of her actions
when she welcomed the spies and sent them off another
way? For just as a human body without a spirit is lifeless, so 26
also faith is lifeless without obedience.

3 Not many of you, my brethren, should become teach- 1
ers, knowing as you do that we teachers shall undergo
severer judgment; for all of us often stumble and fall. If any 2
one never stumbles in speech, he is a perfect man, able to
curb even his whole nature. Now if we put the horses' bits 3
into their mouths to make them obey us, we can turn them
wholly round. Look, again, at the ships: great as they are, and 4
driven along by strong gales, yet they can be steered with a

very small rudder in whatever direction the will of the man at the helm determines. In the same way the tongue is an 5 insignificant part of the body, but utters great boasts. Remember how a mere spark may set a vast forest in flames.

And the tongue is a fire. The tongue—that world of 6 wickedness—is that one of our organs which soils our whole nature, and sets the whole course of our lives on fire, being itself set on fire by Gehenna. All kinds of beasts and 7 birds, reptiles and fishes, can be and have been tamed by human nature. But the tongue no man can tame—a restless 8 mischief, full of deadly poison. With it we bless the Lord and 9 Father, and with it we curse men, who are made in God's likeness. Out of the same mouth there proceed blessing and 10 cursing. My brethren, this ought not to be. Does a fountain 11 send forth fresh water and bitter from the some opening? Can a fig-tree, my brethren, yield olives, or a vine yield figs? 12 No; nor can salt water yield sweet water.

Which of you is a wise and well-instructed man? Let 13 him by a right life show his conduct to be guided by a wise gentleness. But if in your hearts you have bitter envy and 14 rivalry, do not speak boastfully and falsely, in defiance of the truth. That is not the wisdom which comes down from 15 above: it belongs to earth, to the unspiritual nature, and to evil spirits. For where envy and rivalry are, there also are 16 unrest and every vile deed. The wisdom from above is first 17 of all pure, then peaceful, courteous, compliant, full of compassion and kind actions, free from vacillation and from insincerity. And righteousness is the fruit of the seed that is 18 sown in peace by the peacemakers.

4 What causes wars and contentions among you? Is it not 1 the passions which are ever at war in your natures? You 2

covet things and cannot get them; you commit murder. You are envious and cannot gain your end; you fight and make war. You have not, because you do not pray; you ask 3 and yet do not receive, because you pray wrongly, your object being to waste on your pleasures what you acquire.

Do you, like wanton women, not know that friendship 4 with the world means enmity to God? Whoever is bent on being friendly with the world makes himself an enemy to God. Do you suppose that it is to no purpose that the scrip- 5 ture says, "He jealously yearns for the spirit which He made to dwell in us"? And He gives more abundant grace. Hence 6 He says, "GOD SETS HIMSELF AGAINST THE HAUGHTY, BUT TO THE LOWLY HE SHOWS GRACE" (Proverbs 3:34). Submit therefore to God: resist the devil, and he will flee 7 from you. Draw near to God, and He will draw near to you. 8 Cleanse your hands, you sinners, and make your hearts pure, you double-minded. Afflict yourselves and mourn and 9 weep; let your laughter be turned into grief, and your gladness into shame. Humble yourselves in the presence of the 10 Lord, and He will exalt you.

Do not speak evil of one another, brethren. The man who 11 speaks evil of a brother or judges his brother speaks evil of the Law and judges the Law. And if you judge the Law, you are no longer one who obeys the Law, but a judge. The only 12 Lawgiver and Judge is He who is able to save or to destroy. Who are you to be judging your neighbor?

Come, you who say, "To-day or to-morrow we will go to 13 this or that city, and spend a year there and carry on a successful business," when you do not know what will happen 14 to-morrow. For what is your life? Why, it is but a mist, which appears for a short time and then disappears. Instead of that 15 you ought to say, "If it is the Lord's will, we shall live and do this or that." But, as it is, you boast in your presumption: all 16

such boasting is evil. If, then, a man knows what is right and 17
does not do it, he commits a sin.

5 Come now, you rich men, weep and howl for the woes 1
which are coming upon you. Your treasures are rot- 2
ten, and your clothes are moth-eaten; your gold and silver 3
are corroded, and their corrosion will give evidence
against you, and will eat your flesh like fire. You have 4
hoarded up wealth in these last days. See, the pay of the
laborers who have reaped your fields—pay which you have
kept back—is crying out; and the outcries of your har-
vesters have entered into the ears of the Lord of the hosts
of heaven. Here on earth you have lived self-indulgent and 5
profligate [shameless, immoral] lives. You have gratified
your appetite (only to be ready) for the day of slaughter!
You have condemned—you have murdered—the right- 6
eous man: he offers no resistance.

Be patient, therefore, brethren, until the coming of the 7
Lord. Notice how a farmer awaits a precious crop! He is
patient over it till it has received the early and the latter
rain. So you also must be patient, keeping up your courage; 8
for the coming of the Lord is at hand. Do not cry out 9
against one another, brethren, lest you come under judgment. See, the Judge is standing at the door. In illustration, 10
brethren, of persecution patiently endured, take the
prophets who have spoken as messengers from the Lord.
Remember that we call those blessed who endured. You 11
have also heard of Job's endurance, and have seen the issue
of the Lord's dealings with him—how full of tenderness
and pity the Lord is.

But above all things, my brethren, do not swear, either by 12
heaven or by the earth, or with any other oath. Let your "yes"

be simply "yes," and your "no" be simply "no"; that you may not come under condemnation.

Is any one of you suffering? Let him pray. Is any one in good spirits? Let him sing praise. Is any one ill? Let him send for the elders of the church, and let them pray over him, after anointing him with oil in the name of the Lord. And the prayer of faith will restore the sick man, and the Lord will raise him up; and if he has committed sins, they shall be forgiven him. 13 14 15

Therefore confess your sins to one another, and pray for one another, so that you may be cured. Powerful is the heart-felt supplication of a righteous man. Elijah was a man with a nature similar to ours, and he earnestly prayed that there might be no rain: and no rain fell on the land for three years and six months. Again he prayed, and the sky gave rain and the land yielded its crops (1 Kings 17, 18). 16 17 18

My brethren, if one of you strays from the truth and some one brings him back, let him know that he who brings a sinner back from his wrong road will save a soul from death and throw a veil over a multitude of sins. 19 20

THE FIRST EPISTLE OF PETER

1 Peter, an apostle of Jesus Christ, to God's elect of the 1
Dispersion in Pontus, Galatia, Cappadocia, Asia, and
Bithynia, chosen in accordance with the foreknowledge of 2
God the Father, through the sanctifying work of the Spirit,
with a view to obedience and to sprinkling with the blood
of Jesus Christ: may more and more grace and peace be
granted to you.

Blessed be the God and Father of our Lord Jesus Christ, 3
who in His great mercy has begotten us anew to a living hope
through the resurrection of Jesus Christ from the dead, to an 4
inheritance imperishable, undefiled, and unfading, reserved
in heaven for you, who are kept by God's power through your 5
faith for a salvation that is ready to be unveiled at the end of
the world. Exult in the prospect of this, even if now, for a 6
short time, you are compelled to sorrow amid various trials.
These happen in order that what is genuine in your faith— 7
being more precious than gold, which perishes but yet is
proved by fire—may be found to result in praise and glory
and honor at the revelation of Jesus Christ. You love Him, 8
though you have never seen Him. In Him, though at present
you do not see Him, you yet trust, and triumph with a joy
unspeakable and crowned with glory, while you are securing 9
as the outcome of your faith the salvation of your souls.

After that salvation prophets made earnest inquiry and 10
search, and they spoke beforehand of the grace which was
to come to you. They investigated the time which the Spirit 11
of Christ within them kept indicating, or its characteristics,
when He solemnly made known beforehand the sufferings
that were destined for Christ and the glories which would

follow. To them it was revealed that they were serving not 12
themselves but you, in predicting the things which have now
been announced to you by those who, through the Holy
Spirit sent from heaven, brought you the gospel. Angels long
to peer into these things.

Therefore prepare your minds, and fix your hopes calmly 13
and unfalteringly upon the boon [blessing] that is soon to be
yours at the revelation of Jesus Christ. And, like obedient 14
children, do not shape your lives by the cravings which were
formerly yours in the time of your ignorance, but, in imita- 15
tion of the holy One who has called you, do you also be holy
in all your behavior; since it is written, "YOU ARE TO BE 16
HOLY, BECAUSE I AM HOLY" (Leviticus 11:44, 19:2).

And if you address as your Father the One who judges 17
impartially in accordance with each man's actions, then
spend in fear the time of your stay on earth, knowing that it 18
was not with perishable wealth, silver or gold, that you were
ransomed from the futile habits of life inherited from your
forefathers, but with the precious blood of Christ—as of an 19
unblemished and spotless lamb. He was predestined indeed 20
to this work, even before the creation of the world, but has
been manifested in these last days for your sakes; through 21
Him you are faithful to God, who raised Him from the dead
and gave Him glory, so that your faith and hope are resting
upon God.

Now that, through your obedience to the truth, you have 22
prepared your souls by purification for sincere brotherly
love, you must love one another heartily and fervently. For 23
you have been begotten again by God's living and enduring
word not from perishable, but imperishable seed. For 24
"ALL MANKIND IS LIKE GRASS,
AND ALL THEIR BEAUTY IS LIKE ITS FLOWERS.
THE GRASS DRIES UP,

AND ITS FLOWERS DROP OFF;

BUT THE WORD OF THE LORD REMAINS FOR EVER" 25
(Isaiah 40:6-8).

And that means the message which has been proclaimed
to you in the gospel.

2 Rid yourselves, therefore, of all ill-will and all deceitful- 1
ness, of insincerity and envy, and of all evil speaking.
Thirst, like newlyborn infants, for pure milk for the soul, that 2
by it you may grow up to salvation; if you have had any taste 3
of the goodness of the Lord.

Come to Him, the living Stone, rejected indeed by men, 4
but in God's esteem chosen and valuable. And yourselves 5
also like living stones be built up into a spiritual house, as a
holy priesthood to offer spiritual sacrifices acceptable to
God through Jesus Christ. For it is contained in scripture, 6

"SEE, I AM PLACING IN ZION A CORNERSTONE, CHO-
SEN AND VALUABLE,

AND HE WHOSE FAITH RESTS ON HIM SHALL NEVER
BE DISAPPOINTED" (Isaiah 28:16).

You believers, therefore, feel His value; but for unbelievers— 7
"A STONE WHICH THE BUILDERS REJECTED HAS BEEN
MADE THE CORNERSTONE" (Psalm 118:22), and "A 8
STONE TO TRIP OVER, AND A ROCK TO STUMBLE AT"
(Isaiah 8:14). They trip over it because they are disobedient to
God's message, and to this they were destined. But you are 9
a chosen race, a royal priesthood, a holy nation, a people
belonging to God, that you may make known the perfections
of Him who called you out of darkness into His marvelous
light. Once you were not a people, but now you are the peo- 10
ple of God. Once you had not found mercy, but now you have.

Beloved, I entreat you as strangers and foreigners to 11

restrain the cravings of your lower natures which wage war upon the soul. Live honorable lives among the Gentiles, in 12 order that, although they speak against you as evil-doers, from your good deeds they may witness your character, and may glorify God on the day of visitation.

Submit, for the Lord's sake, to every authority set up by 13 man, whether it be to the emperor as supreme, or to gover- 14 nors as sent by him for the punishment of evil-doers and the encouragement of well-doers. For it is God's will that by doing 15 well you should thus silence the ignorant talk of foolish persons. Be free men, and yet do not make your freedom a 16 screen for base conduct, but be God's servants. Honor every 17 one. Love the brotherhood, fear God, honor the emperor.

Servants, be submissive to your masters, with the utmost 18 respect—not only if they are kind and thoughtful, but also if they are unreasonable. For it is acceptable with God, if, 19 through consciousness of His presence, a man bears wrong, when treated unjustly. If you do wrong and receive a blow for 20 it, what credit is there in your bearing it patiently? But if when you do right and suffer for it you bear it patiently, this is acceptable with God.

It is to this you were called; because Christ also suffered on 21 your behalf, leaving you an example so that you should follow in His steps. He never sinned, and no guile was ever 22 heard from His mouth. When He was reviled, He did not 23 answer with reviling; when He suffered, He did not threaten, but left His cause in the hands of the righteous Judge. Our 24 sins He Himself bore in His own body on the cross, so that we, being alienated from our sins, may live righteous lives. By His wounds you have been healed. For you were astray 25 like lost sheep, but now you have come back to the Shepherd and Guardian of your souls.

3 Married women, in the same way, be submissive to your 1
husbands, so that even if some of them disbelieve the
word, they may, without a word being spoken, be won over
by the daily life of their wives, after seeing your daily lives so 2
chaste and reverent. Yours ought not to be the outward 3
adornment of plaiting the hair, putting on jewels of gold,
or wearing various dresses, but an inward beauty of nature, 4
the imperishable ornament of a gentle and peaceful spirit,
which is indeed precious in the sight of God. For this is how 5
of old the holy women who set their hopes upon God used to
adorn themselves, being submissive to their husbands. Thus 6
Sarah obeyed Abraham, calling him master. And you have
become Sarah's children if you do right and permit nothing
whatever to terrify you.

Husbands, in the same way, live with your wives with 7
a clear recognition of the fact that they are weaker than
you. Yet, since you are heirs with them of God's free gift of
Life, treat them with honor; so that your prayers may be
unrestrained.

In conclusion, all of you should be harmonious, sympa- 8
thetic, kind to the brethren, tender-hearted, lowly-minded,
not requiting [repaying] evil with evil nor abuse with abuse, 9
but, on the contrary, giving a blessing, because a blessing is
what you have been called by God to inherit. For 10

"HE WHO WISHES TO ENJOY LIFE
AND SEE HAPPY DAYS—
LET HIM RESTRAIN HIS TONGUE FROM EVIL,
AND HIS LIPS FROM DECEITFUL WORDS;
LET HIM TURN FROM EVIL, AND DO GOOD; 11
LET HIM SEEK PEACE AND PURSUE IT.
FOR THE EYES OF THE LORD ARE UPON THE 12
RIGHTEOUS,
AND HIS EARS ARE OPEN TO THEIR SUPPLICATION;

DOERS" (Psalm 34:12-16).

And who will harm you, if you show yourselves zealous for 13
what is good? But even if you suffer for righteousness' sake, 14
you are to be envied. So do not be alarmed by their threats,
nor troubled; but in your hearts consecrate Christ as Lord, 15
being always ready to make your defense to any one who asks
from you a reason for the hope which you cherish. Yet argue
gently and cautiously, keeping your consciences clean, so 16
that, when you are spoken against, those who slander your
good Christian lives may be put to shame.

For it is better that you should suffer for doing right, if 17
such be God's will, than for doing evil; because Christ also 18
once for all died for sins, the innocent One for the guilty
many, in order to bring us to God. He was put to death in the
flesh, but made alive in the spirit, in which He also went and 19
preached to the spirits that were in prison, who in former 20
times had been disobedient, when God's long-suffering
patiently waited in the days of Noah during the building of
the ark, in which a few persons—eight in number—were
brought safely through the water. And, corresponding to that 21
figure, baptism now saves you—not the washing off of material defilement, but the craving of a good conscience after
God—through the resurrection of Jesus Christ, who is at
God's right hand. He has gone into heaven, and angels, 22
authorities, and powers have been made subject to Him.

4 Since, then, Christ has suffered in the flesh, you also 1
must arm yourselves with the same resolve—because
he who has suffered in the flesh has done with sin—that 2
henceforth you may spend the rest of your earthly lives,
governed not by human passions, but by the will of God. For 3

you have given time enough in the past to the things which the Gentiles delight in—pursuing, as you did, a course of license [undisciplined freedom], debauchery [extreme indulgence of sensual appetites], hard drinking, revelry, carousing, and unholy idolatry. In regard to this they are 4 astonished that you do not run into the same excess of profligacy [shameless immorality] as they do; and they abuse you. But they will have to give account to Him who is 5 ready to pronounce judgment on the living and the dead. For it is to this end that the gospel was proclaimed even to 6 dead men, that they may be judged as men in the body, but may live as God lives in the spirit.

But the end of all things is at hand: therefore be sober- 7 minded and temperate, that you may give yourselves to prayer. Above all love one another fervently, for love veils a 8 multitude of faults. Extend ungrudging hospitality towards 9 one another. Whatever be the gifts which each has received, 10 you must use them for one another's benefit, as good stewards of God's manifold kindness. If any one preaches, 11 let it be as uttering God's oracles; if any one renders a serv-ice, let it be in the strength which God supplies; so that in everything glory may be given to God through Jesus Christ, to whom belong the glory and the dominion for ever and ever. Amen.

Beloved, do not be surprised at the fiery ordeal coming 12 among you to put you to the test—as though some excep-tional thing were happening to you. No, in the degree that 13 you share in the sufferings of Christ rejoice, so that at the unveiling of His glory you may also rejoice with exultation. Blessed are you if you are reproached for bearing the name 14 of Christ; for the Spirit of glory—even the Spirit of God—is resting upon you. But let not one of you suffer as a murderer 15 or a thief or an evil-doer, or as a busy-body. If, however, 16 any one suffers because he is a Christian, let him not be ashamed, but let him glorify God for that name.

For the time has come for judgment to begin at the house 17 of God; and if it begins with us, what will be the end of those who reject God's gospel? And if it is difficult for a righteous 18 man to be saved, what will become of irreligious men and sinners?

So then, let those who suffer in accordance with the will 19 of God and are leading a good life entrust their souls to a faithful Creator.

5 Now I exhort the elders among you—I who am their 1 fellow elder and an eye-witness of the sufferings of Christ, and also a sharer in the glory which is to be revealed: be shepherds of God's flock which is among you. Exercise the 2 oversight not reluctantly but voluntarily, in accordance with the will of God; not for base gain but readily; not lording it 3 over your charges but proving yourselves patterns to the flock. And then, when the chief Shepherd appears, you will 4 receive the never-withering wreath of glory.

In the same way you younger men must submit to your 5 elders; and all of you must gird yourselves with humility towards one another, for God sets Himself against the proud, but shows grace to the humble. Humble yourselves, there- 6 fore, under the mighty hand of God, so that at the right time He may set you on high. Throw the whole of your anxiety 7 upon Him, because He cares for you.

Be circumspect, and be on the alert. Your enemy, the devil, 8 is going about like a roaring lion to see whom he can devour. Withstand him, firm in your faith; knowing that the same 9 sufferings are imposed on your brethren in all the world. And the God of all grace, who has called you to share His 10 eternal glory, through Christ, after you have suffered for a short time, will Himself make you perfect, firm, and strong. His is the dominion for ever and ever! Amen.   11

I have written you this short letter by the hand of Silvanus,   12
our faithful brother—for such I regard him—in order to encourage you, and to bear witness that such is the true grace of God. In it stand fast. The church in Babylon, elect   13
like yourselves, sends greetings, and so does Mark my son. Greet one another with a kiss of love. Peace be with all of you   14
who are in Christ.

THE SECOND EPISTLE OF PETER

1 Simon Peter, a servant and apostle of Jesus Christ, to 1
those to whom there has been allotted a faith of equal
privilege with ours through the righteousness of our God
and of our Savior Jesus Christ: may more and more grace 2
and peace be granted to you in the knowledge of God and
of Jesus our Lord, seeing that His divine power has given us 3
all things that are needful for life and godliness, through
the knowledge of Him who called us by His own glory
and perfection.

Thereby He has granted us His exceeding great and pre- 4
cious promises, in order that through them you may
become sharers in the divine nature, having escaped the
corruption which is now in the world by reason of lustful
passions. And for this very cause—adding, besides, all 5
earnestness—with your faith exhibit also a noble character:
with a noble character, knowledge; with knowledge, self- 6
control; with self-control, endurance; with endurance, godliness; with godliness, love to the brethren; and with love to 7
the brethren, love. If these things exist in you, and increase, 8
they prevent your being either idle or unfruitful in advancing towards a full knowledge of our Lord Jesus Christ. For 9
the man in whom they are lacking is blind, short-sighted,
forgetful that he has been cleansed from his old sins.

For this reason, brethren, be all the more in earnest to 10
make certain of your calling and election; for, so long as you
practice these things, you will never stumble. And so a tri- 11
umphant admission into the eternal Kingdom of our Lord
and Savior Jesus Christ shall be accorded to you.

For this reason I shall always persist in reminding you of 12 these things, although you know them and are steadfast believers in the truth which you possess. But I think it right, 13 so long as I sojourn in this body, to arouse you by such reminders. For I know that soon my body must be laid aside, 14 as indeed our Lord Jesus Christ revealed to me. So on every 15 occasion I will also do my best to enable you to recall these things after my departure.

When we made known to you the power and coming of 16 our Lord Jesus Christ, we were not following cleverly devised legends, but we had been eye-witnesses of His majesty. He 17 received honor and glory from God the Father, and out of the wondrous glory words such as these were conveyed to Him, "This is My beloved Son, in whom I take delight." And we 18 ourselves heard these words conveyed from heaven, when we were with Him on the holy mountain.

So we have the word of prophecy confirmed; to which you 19 do well to pay attention—as to a lamp shining in a dark place—until day dawns and the morning star rises in your hearts. But, above all, remember that no prophecy in scrip- 20 ture is a matter of private interpretation; for never did any 21 prophecy come by human will, but men sent by God spoke as they were impelled by the Holy Spirit.

2 But there were also false prophets among the people, 1 as there will be teachers of falsehood among you too, who will cunningly introduce fatal heresies, disowning even the Sovereign who has redeemed them, and bringing on themselves swift destruction. And in their immoral ways 2 they will have many disciples, through whom the true Way will be brought into disrepute. Greedy for riches, they will 3 trade on you with their canting [religious/hypocritical] talk. From of old their condemnation has not been in abeyance [temporary suspension], and their destruction has not been slumbering.

For if God did not spare angels when they had sinned, but 4 hurled them down to Tartarus and consigned them to caves of darkness, keeping them in reserve for judgment; and if He 5 did not spare the ancient world, although He preserved Noah, that herald of righteousness, with seven others, when He brought a deluge on the world of the ungodly; if He 6 reduced to ashes the cities of Sodom and Gomorrah, and condemned them to overthrow, making them an example to people who should thereafter live godless lives, but rescued 7 righteous Lot, who was sore distressed by the dissolute [immoral] conduct of lawless men (for their lawless deeds 8 were torture, day after day, to the righteous soul of that righteous man—all that he saw and heard in their midst), then the Lord knows how to rescue godly men from tempta- 9 tion, and on the other hand how to keep the unrighteous under punishment for the day of judgment, and especially 10 those who are abandoned to sensuality—craving for polluted things, and scorning control.

Audacious [bold or daring] and self-willed, they do not tremble when speaking evil of the angelic Orders; while 11 angels, though greater than they in might and power, do not bring any railing accusation against these in the presence of the Lord. But these men, like brute beasts, born with such 12 natural instincts that they are only to be captured or destroyed, in their ignorance are abusive, and in their cor- ruption they will perish, receiving injury in retribution for 13 the injuries they do. They reckon it pleasure to roll in luxury in broad daylight. They are spots and blemishes, while revel- ing in their deceits, as they banquet with you. Their eyes are 14 full of adultery, eyes such as cannot cease from sin. These men set traps for unsteadfast souls, their own hearts being

trained in covetousness—an accursed race! Forsaking the 15
straight road, they have gone astray, having followed in the
steps of Balaam, the son of Beor, who preferred the wages of
unrighteousness. He, however, was rebuked for his trans- 16
gression: a dumb beast of burden spoke with a human voice
and checked the madness of the prophet.

These people are wells without water, mists driven along 17
by a storm, men for whom the densest darkness has been
reserved. For, while they pour out their frivolous and 18
arrogant talk, they use sensual pleasures—various kinds
of immorality—as a trap for men who are just escaping
from those who live in error. And they promise them free- 19
dom, although they are themselves the slaves of corruption. For a man is the slave of any thing by which he has
been overcome.

For if, after escaping from the pollutions of the world 20
through knowledge of our Lord and Savior Jesus Christ,
people are once more entangled in these pollutions and
are overcome, their last state is worse than their first. It 21
would have been better for them not to have known the way
of righteousness, than, after knowing it, to turn back from
the holy commandment which was delivered to them. Their 22
case is that described in the true proverb, "A DOG RETURNS
TO WHAT HE HAS VOMITED" (Proverbs 26:11), and "A sow
when washed falls to rolling in filth."

3 This is the second letter which I have now written to 1
you, beloved. In both I seek to revive in your sincere
minds certain memories, so that you may recall the words 2
spoken beforehand by the holy prophets, and the commandment of our Lord and Savior given through your apostles.

First remember that, in the last days, men will come 3

with their mockery—men governed by their own passions, and asking, 4

"Where is His promised return? For from the time our fathers fell asleep all things continue as they have been ever since the creation."

They are willfully blind to the fact that there were heavens 5 of old and an earth rising from and extended through water, by the word of God; and that, by means of these, the then 6 existing world was overwhelmed with water and perished. But the present heavens and earth are, by the same word, 7 stored up, reserved for fire against a day of judgment and of destruction for the ungodly.

But this one thing, beloved, you must not forget. With the 8 Lord one day is as a thousand years, and a thousand years are as one day. The Lord is not slow about His promise, as 9 some men count slowness. He bears patiently with you, His desire being that no one should perish but that all should come to repentance. But the day of the Lord will come like a 10 thief, on which the heavens will pass away with a rush and a roar, the elements be destroyed in the fierce heat, and the earth and all its works will vanish.

Since all these things are thus on the verge of dissolution, 11 what sort of men ought you to be in all holy living and godly conduct, expecting and helping to hasten the coming of the 12 day of God, by reason of which the heavens, all ablaze, will be dissolved, and the elements will burn and melt? But in 13 accordance with His promise we expect new heavens and a new earth, in which righteousness dwells.

Therefore, beloved, as you are expecting this, earnestly 14 seek to be found by Him, free from blemish or reproach, in peace. And regard the forbearance of our Lord as salvation, 15 as our beloved brother Paul also has written to you in virtue of the wisdom granted to him. That is what he says in all his 16 letters, when speaking in them of these things. In those letters there are some statements hard to understand, which ill-taught and unstable people pervert, just as they do the rest of the scriptures, to their own ruin.

You, therefore, beloved, being warned beforehand, must be 17 on your guard so as not to be led away by the errors of lawless men nor fall from your own steadfastness. But grow in the 18 grace and knowledge of our Lord and Savior Jesus Christ.

To Him be the glory, both now and to the day of eternity!

THE FIRST EPISTLE OF JOHN

Introduction

1 What was from the beginning, what we have heard, and have seen with our own eyes, what we once beheld and our own hands handled concerning the Word of Life— the Life was manifested, and we have seen and bear witness, and we declare unto you the Life eternal which was with the Father and was manifested to us—what we have seen and heard we announce to you also, in order that you also may have fellowship with us, our fellowship being with the Father and with His Son Jesus Christ. We write these things in order that our joy may be made complete.

Some Vivid Contrasts

This is the message which we have heard from Him and report to you—God is light, and in Him there is no darkness. If, while we are living in darkness, we profess to have fellowship with Him, we speak falsely and do not carry out the truth. But if we live in the light as He is in the light, we have fellowship with one another, and the blood of Jesus, His Son, cleanses us from all sin. If we claim to be free from sin, we deceive ourselves and the truth is not in us. If we confess our sins, He is faithful and just to forgive us our sins and cleanse us from all unrighteousness. If we deny that we have sinned, we make Him a liar, and His word is not in us.

2 My dear children, I write thus to you that you may not 1 sin. If any one does sin, we have an advocate with the Father—Jesus Christ the righteous; and He is Himself the 2 expiation [atonement] for our sins, and not for ours only, but also for the sins of the whole world. And by this we learn that 3 we know Him—if we obey His commands. He who professes 4 to know Him, and does not obey His commands, is a liar, and the truth is not in him. But whoever obeys His word, in him 5 love for God has reached perfection. By this we can learn that we are in Him. The man who professes to continue in 6 Him is himself also bound to live as He lived.

Beloved, it is no new command that I am writing you, but 7 an old command which you have had from the beginning. By the old command I mean the word which you have heard. And yet I am writing you a new command, for such it really 8 is, so far as both He and you are concerned; because the darkness is passing away and the true light is already shining. Any one who professes to be in the light and hates his 9 brother is still in darkness. He who loves his brother contin- 10 ues in the light, and there is no stumbling-block in him. But 11 he who hates his brother is in darkness and walks in darkness; and he does not know where he is going, because the darkness has blinded his eyes.

I am writing to you, dear children, because your sins are 12 forgiven you for His sake. I am writing to you, fathers, be- 13 cause you know Him who has existed from the beginning. I am writing to you, young men, because you have overcome the Evil One.

I have written to you, children, because you know the Father. I have written to you, fathers, because you know Him 14 who has existed from the beginning. I have written to you, young men, because you are strong and God's word continues to be in you, and you have overcome the Evil One.

Love not the world, nor the things in the world. If any one 15
loves the world, there is no love in him for the Father. For all 16
that is in the world—the desire of the flesh, the desire of the
eyes, the show and pride of life—comes not from the Father,
but from the world. And the world, with its desire, is passing 17
away, but he who does God's will continues for ever.

Warnings Against Backsliders and False Teachers

Dear children, the last hour has come; and as you have 18
heard that antichrist is coming, so even now many anti-
christs have appeared. By this we may know that the last
hour has come. They have gone forth from our midst, but 19
they did not belong to us; for had they belonged to us, they
would have remained with us. But they left us that it might
be manifest that none of them belongs to us. As for you, you 20
have an anointing from the holy One and you all have
knowledge. I have written to you, not because you are igno- 21
rant of the truth, but because you do know it, and that no lie
comes from the truth.

Who is the liar but he who denies that Jesus is the Christ? 22
He who disowns the Father and the Son is the antichrist.
No one who disowns the Son has the Father. He who 23
acknowledges the Son has also the Father. For yourselves, 24
let the teaching which you have heard from the beginning
abide within you. If that teaching does abide within
you, you also will abide in the Son and in the Father. And 25
this is the promise which He Himself has given us—the
life eternal.

I have thus written to you concerning those who try to 26
lead you astray. But the anointing which you yourselves 27
received from Him remains within you, and you have no
need for any one to teach you; but as His anointing gives you

instruction in all things—and is true and is no falsehood—you are abiding in Him, even as it has taught you to do.

And now, dear children, abide in Him; so that, when He 28 appears, we may have confidence, and may not shrink away in shame from Him at His coming. Since you know that He is 29 righteous, be assured that every one also who acts righteously is a child of His.

God's Children and the Devil's Children

3 See what love the Father has bestowed upon us, that we 1 should be called God's children: and that is what we are. For this reason the world does not recognize us, because it did not recognize Him. Beloved, we are now God's children, 2 but what we are to be has not yet been manifested. We know that when He appears we shall be like Him, because we shall see Him as He is. And any one who has this hope fixed on 3 Him, purifies himself as He is pure.

Every one who commits sin also commits lawlessness; for 4 sin is lawlessness. And you know that He appeared in order to 5 take away sins; and in Him there is no sin. No one who abides 6 in Him sins: no one who sins has seen Him or knows Him.

Dear children, let no one lead you astray. The man who 7 acts righteously is righteous, just as He is righteous. He who 8 commits sin belongs to the devil, because the devil has been a sinner from the beginning. The Son of God appeared for the purpose of undoing the work of the devil.

No one who is a child of God commits sin. A divine princi- 9 ple remains in him, and he cannot sin—because he is a child of God. By this are distinguished God's children and the 10 devil's children: no one who fails to act righteously is a child of God, nor he who does not love his brother. For this is the 11 message you have heard from the beginning—that we are to love one another. We are not to resemble Cain, who was a 12 child of the Evil One and killed his brother. And why did he kill him? Because his own actions were wicked and his brother's righteous.

Do not be surprised, brethren, if the world hates you. We 13 know that we have passed out of death into life—because we 14 love our brothers. He who does not love abides in death. Every one who hates his brother is a murderer; and you 15 know that no murderer has eternal life abiding in him.

We know what love is because He laid down His life for us; 16 and we ought to lay down our lives for our brethren. But if 17 any one has this world's goods and sees that his brother is in need, and yet closes his heart against him—how can love for God continue in him? Dear children, let us not love in word 18 only and with the lips, but in deed and truth.

In this way we shall come to know that we are loyal to the 19 truth, and shall reassure our hearts in His presence in what- 20 ever matters our hearts condemn us—because God is greater than our hearts and knows everything. Beloved, if our hearts 21 do not condemn us, we address God with confidence; and 22 whatever we ask for we obtain from Him, because we obey His commands and do what is pleasing in His sight. And this 23 is His command—that we are to believe in the name of His Son Jesus Christ and love one another, as He has commanded us to do. The man who obeys His commands abides in God, 24 and God in him; and through His Spirit which He has given us we can know that He abides in us.

The Conflict Between Truth and Falsehood

4 Beloved, do not believe every spirit, but test the spirits to 1 see whether they are from God; for many false prophets have gone out into the world. The test by which you may rec- 2 ognize the Spirit of God is that every spirit which acknowledges that Jesus Christ has come in the flesh is from God, and 3 that no spirit is from God which does not acknowledge this about Jesus. Such is the spirit of the antichrist; you have heard that it is to come, and now it is already in the world.

You, dear children, are God's children, and have overcome 4 them; for greater is He who is in you than he who is in the world. They are the world's children, and so their language is 5 that of the world, and the world listens to them. We are God's 6 children. The man who knows God listens to us, but he who is not a child of God does not listen to us. By this test we can distinguish the spirit of truth from the spirit of error.

The Duty of Brotherly Love

Beloved, let us love one another; for love comes from God, 7 and every one who loves is a child of God and knows God. He 8 who does not love has no knowledge of God; because God is love. God's love for us has been manifested in that God 9 has sent His only Son into the world so that we may have Life through Him. Here is the love—not that we loved God, 10 but that He loved us and sent His Son to be an expiation [atonement] for our sins.

Beloved, if God so loved us, we also ought to love one 11 another. No one has ever seen God. If we love one another, 12 God abides in us, and His love is perfect in us. We can know 13 that we abide in Him and He in us, by the fact that He has given us a portion of His Spirit. And we have seen and bear 14 witness that the Father has sent the Son to be the Savior of the world. Whoever acknowledges that Jesus is the Son of God—God abides in him, and he abides in God. And, we our- selves know and we confide in the love which God has for us.

God is love, and he who abides in love abides in God, and God abides in him. In this will love in its perfection be dis- played in us, in our being fearless on the day of judgment; because what He is, that we also are in this world. Love has in it no fear; but perfect love drives away fear, because fear involves punishment, and if a man fears, there is something imperfect in his love. We love because He first loved us. If any one says that he loves God, while he hates his brother, he is a liar; for he who does not love his brother whom he has seen, cannot love God whom he has not seen. And this com- mand we have from Him, that he who loves God must love his brother also.

5 Every one who believes that Jesus is the Christ is a child of God; and every one who loves the Father loves Him who is the Father's child. The fact that we love God, and obey His commands, is a proof to us that we love God's children. Love for God means obedience to His commands; and His commands are not irksome. For every thing that is born of God overcomes the world; and the victory which has over- come the world is our faith. Who overcomes the world but the man who believes that Jesus is the Son of God?

Jesus Christ is He who came by water and blood; not with the water only, but with the water and with the blood. And it is the Spirit who gives witness—because the Spirit is the truth. For there are three that give witness—the Spirit, the water, and the blood; and the three have the same purport [meaning and intention]. If we accept the witness of men,

God's witness is greater: for God's witness is what He has testified about His Son. He who believes in the Son of God has 10 the witness in himself: he who does not believe God has made Him a liar, in that he has refused to believe the witness which God has given about His Son. And that witness is to 11 the effect that God has given us the eternal life, and that this life is in His Son. He who has the Son has the life: he who has 12 not the Son of God has not the life.

Conclusion

I write all this to you who believe in the name of the Son of 13 God, that you may know for certain that you have eternal life. And this is the confidence which we have in Him, that when- 14 ever we ask anything in accordance with His will, He listens to us. And since we know that He listens to us, whatever we 15 ask, we know that we have the requests which we have asked from Him. If any one sees his brother committing a sin which 16 is not mortal, he shall ask and God shall give him life—for any who do not sin mortally. There is such a thing as mortal sin; for that I do not bid him make request. Any kind of wrong- 17 doing is sin; but there is sin which is not mortal.

We know that no one who is a child of God sins, but He 18 who was born of God keeps him, and the Evil One cannot touch him. We know that we are children of God, and that 19 the whole world lies in the power of the Evil One. And we 20 know that the Son of God has come, and has given us understanding to know the true One, and we are in the true One, in His Son Jesus Christ. This is the true God and eternal life.

Dear children, guard yourselves from idols. 21

THE SECOND EPISTLE OF JOHN

The elder to the elect lady and her children, whom I truly 1
love, and not I alone, but also all who know the truth, for 2
the sake of the truth which abides in us and will be with us
for ever: grace, mercy, and peace will be with us from God 3
the Father, and from Jesus Christ the Son of the Father, in
truth and love.

I am overjoyed to have found some of your children living 4
true lives, in obedience to the command which we have
received from the Father. And now, lady, I pray you—writing 5
to you no new command, but the one which we have had
from the beginning—let us love one another. The love I 6
mean consists in our living in obedience to His commands.
God's command is that you should live in love, as you have
been taught from the beginning. For many deceivers have 7
gone out into the world—men who do not acknowledge
Jesus Christ as coming in the flesh. Such a one is "the de-
ceiver" and "the antichrist."

Look to yourselves, so that you may not lose the result of 8
your deeds, but may receive a full reward. No one has God 9
who, instead of remaining true to the teaching of Christ, goes
beyond it: but he who remains true to that teaching has both
the Father and the Son. If any one who comes to you does not 10
bring this teaching, do not receive him under your roof nor
greet him; for he who greets him is a sharer in his evil deeds. 11

I have a great deal to write to you, but will not write it with 12
paper and ink. I hope to come to see you and speak face to
face, so that your happiness may be complete.

The children of your elect sister send greetings to you. 13

THE THIRD EPISTLE OF JOHN

The elder to his dearly loved Gaius, whom I truly love. 1
Dearly loved one, I pray that you may in all respects pros- 2
per and keep well, as your soul prospers. For I am overjoyed 3
when brethren come and bear witness to your fidelity to the
truth, how you live in obedience to the truth. I have no greater 4
joy than to hear that my children are living in the truth.

Beloved, you are acting faithfully in all your behavior 5
towards the brethren, particularly when they are strangers
to you. They have testified, in the presence of the church, to 6
your love; and you will do well to help them on their journey
in a manner worthy of your fellowship with God. For it is for 7
the Name's sake that they have gone forth, accepting nothing from the Gentiles. It is therefore our duty to entertain 8
such men, so that we may be fellow workers with the truth.

I wrote to the church; but Diotrephes, who loves to have 9
the foremost place among them, refuses to listen to us. For 10
this reason, when I come, I shall call attention to his conduct, his idle and mischievous talk against us. And not
content with this, not only will he himself not receive the
brethren, but those who desire to do this he hinders, and
excludes them from the church.

Dearly loved one, do not copy evil, but good. He who does 11
good is a child of God: he who does evil has not seen God.

Demetrius has a good word from all men, and the witness 12
of the truth itself. We also give our witness, and you know
that our witness is true.

I had a great deal to say to you, but I do not wish to write 13
to you with ink and pen. But I hope to see you very soon, and 14
then we will speak face to face.

Peace be with you. Our friends send greetings to you. Greet our friends one by one.

THE EPISTLE OF JUDE

Jude, a servant of Jesus Christ and a brother of James, to 1
those saints who are beloved as God the Father's, and kept
for Jesus Christ: may mercy, peace, and love be abundantly 2
granted to you.

Beloved ones, while I was eager to write to you on the subject 3
of our common salvation, I find myself constrained to write
and urge you to defend the faith delivered once for all to the
saints. For certain persons have crept in unnoticed—men for 4
whom in ancient writings this condemnation was foretold—
ungodly men, who pervert the grace of our God into immorality, and disown Jesus Christ, our only Sovereign and Lord.

I desire to remind you—although the whole matter is suf- 5
ficiently familiar to you—that the Lord saved a people out of
the land of Egypt, but afterwards destroyed those who had
no faith. And angels who did not keep their own primacy 6
[state of order, rank], but deserted their proper abode, He
reserves in everlasting bonds, in darkness, for the judgment
of the great day. So also Sodom and Gomorrah and the 7
neighboring towns, having in the same manner been guilty
of gross immorality and pursued unnatural vice, are now
before us as an example of eternal fire in the punishment
which they are undergoing. Yet in just the same way these 8
dreamers also pollute the body, while they set authority at
naught and speak evil of the angelic Orders.

But Michael the archangel, when contending with the 9
devil and disputing with him about the body of Moses, did
not dare to pronounce judgment on him in abusive terms,
but said, "The Lord rebuke you." Yet these men are abusive in 10
matters of which they know nothing, and in things which,

like the brutes, they do understand instinctively—in all these they become depraved. Woe to them! for they have followed 11 in the steps of Cain; for the sake of gain they have rushed on headlong in the errors of Balaam, and have perished in the rebellion of Korah.

These are the men who, like sunken rocks in your love- 12 feasts, are not afraid to feast with you, caring only for themselves; clouds without water, driven along by the winds; trees in autumn, fruitless, doubly dead, uprooted; wild waves of 13 the sea, foaming out their own shame; wandering stars, for whom is reserved dense darkness for ever.

It was about these that Enoch, the seventh from Adam, 14 prophesied, saying,

"The Lord comes with myriads of His people, to execute 15 judgment upon all, and to convict all the ungodly of all the ungodly deeds which they have committed, and of all the hard words which they, ungodly sinners, have spoken against Him."

These men are murmurers, complaining of their lot. Their 16 lives are guided by their evil passions, and their mouths are full of big and boastful words, while they defer to persons for the sake of the advantage they may gain.

But do you, beloved, remember the words that before now 17 were spoken by the apostles of our Lord Jesus Christ—how they 18 declared to you, "In the last times there shall be scoffers, obeying only their own ungodly passions." These are those who 19 cause divisions: they are men of the world, devoid of the Spirit.

But do you, beloved, building yourselves up on your most 20 holy faith and praying in the Holy Spirit, keep yourselves in 21 the love of God, waiting for the mercy of our Lord Jesus Christ which issues in eternal life. On some who are in doubt 22 you should have pity; others you must save, snatching them 23 out of the fire; and on others have pity mingled with fear, while you hate even the garment stained by the flesh.

Now to Him who is able to keep you from stumbling, and 24 cause you to stand in the presence of His glory free from blemish and exultant—to the only God our Savior through 25 Jesus Christ our Lord—be glory, majesty, dominion, and authority, before all time, now, and to all time! Amen.

THE REVELATION OF JOHN

Introduction

1 The revelation given by Jesus Christ, which God granted 1
Him, that He might make known to His servants certain
events which must shortly come to pass. He sent His angel
and communicated it to His servant John; who now is mak- 2
ing a faithful record of the word that came from God and the
truth revealed by Jesus Christ and all the things that he saw
in his vision. Blessed is he who reads, and blessed are those 3
who listen to the words of this prophecy and lay to heart
what is written in it; for the time for its fulfillment is now
close at hand.

John sends greetings to the seven churches in the province 4
of Asia. May grace be granted to you, and peace, from Him
who is and was and is to be; and from the seven Spirits which
are before His throne; and from Jesus Christ, the truthful 5
witness, the first of the dead to be born to life, and the Ruler
of the kings of the earth.

To Him who loves us and has freed us from our sins with
His own blood, and has formed us into a kingdom, to be 6
priests to God, His Father—to Him be ascribed the glory
and the dominion for ever and ever. Amen.

Lo, He is coming in the clouds, and every eye will see Him, 7
and so will those who pierced Him; and all the nations of the
earth will gaze on Him and mourn. Even so. Amen.

"I am the Alpha and the Omega," says the Lord God, "He 8
who is and was and is to be—the Ruler of all."

I John, your brother, and a sharer with you in the sorrows 9
and kingdom and endurance of Jesus, found myself in the

island of Patmos, for my loyalty to the word of God and
the truth told us by Jesus. On the Lord's day I was inspired by 10
the Spirit, and I heard behind me a loud voice like the blast
of a trumpet. It said, 11

"Write your vision in a book, and send it to the seven
churches—to Ephesus, Smyrna, Pergamum, Thyatira, Sardis,
Philadelphia, and Laodicea."

I turned to see who it was that was speaking to me; and 12
then I saw seven golden lampstands, and in the center of the 13
lampstands One resembling the Son of Man, clothed in a
robe which reached to His feet, and with a girdle of gold
across His breast. His head and His hair were white, like 14
white wool—as white as snow; and His eyes were like a flame
of fire. His feet were like silver-bronze when it is white-hot in 15
a furnace; and His voice was as the sound of many waters. In 16
His right hand He held seven stars, and a sharp, two-edged
sword was seen coming from His mouth; and His face was
like the sun shining in its full power.

When I saw Him, I fell at His feet as if dead. But He laid His 17
hand upon me and said,

"Do not be afraid: I am the First and the Last, and the ever- 18
living One. I died; but I am now alive for evermore, and I
have the keys of the gates of death and of Hades! Write 19
down, therefore, the things you have just seen—the things
which are and the things which are to be hereafter; the secret 20
meaning of the seven stars which you have seen in My right
hand, and of the seven lampstands of gold. The seven stars
are the angels of the seven churches, and the seven lampstands are the seven churches.

The Letters to the Seven Churches

2 "To the angel of the church in Ephesus write: 1

"'These are the words of Him who holds the seven stars in His right hand and walks to and fro among the seven lamp-stands of gold. I know your doings and your toil and your 2 endurance. And I know that you cannot tolerate wicked men, but have put to the test those who call themselves apostles but are not, and you have found them to be liars. And you endure 3 patiently and have borne burdens for My sake and have never flagged. Yet I have this against you—that you no longer love Me 4 as you did at first. Be mindful, therefore, of the height from 5 which you have fallen. Repent at once, and act as you did at first, or else I will surely come and remove your lampstand out of its place—unless you repent. Yet this you have in your favor: 6 you hate the doings of the Nicolaitans, which I also hate.

"'Let all who have ears give heed to what the Spirit is saying 7 to the churches. To the victor I will give the privilege of eating the fruit of the tree of Life, which is in the paradise of God.'

"To the angel of the church at Smyrna write as follows: 8

"'These are the words of Him who is the First and the Last—who died and has returned to life. Your sufferings I 9 know, and your poverty—but you are rich—and the evil name given you by those who say that they themselves are Jews, and are not, but are Satan's synagogue. Dismiss your 10 fears concerning all that you are about to suffer. I tell you that the devil is about to throw some of you into prison that you may be put to the test, and for ten days you will have to endure persecution. Be faithful, even if you have to die for it, and then I will give you the crown of Life.

"'Let all who have ears give heed to what the Spirit is say- 11 ing to the churches. The victor shall be in no way hurt by the second death.'

"To the angel of the church at Pergamum write as follows : 12

"'These are the words of Him who has the sharp two-edged sword. I know where you dwell. Satan's throne is there; 13 and yet you are true to Me, and did not deny your faith in Me, even in the days of Antipas My faithful witness, who was martyred among you, in the place where Satan dwells. Yet I 14 have a few things against you, because you have with you some that cling to the teaching of Balaam, who taught Balak to put a stumbling-block in the way of the descendants of Israel—to eat what had been sacrificed to idols, and commit fornication. So even you have some that cling in the same 15 way to the teaching of the Nicolaitans. Repent at once; or 16 else I will come to you quickly, and will make war upon them with the sword which is in My mouth.

"'Let all who have ears give heed to what the Spirit is saying to the churches. As for the victor—to him I will give some 17 of the hidden manna, and a white stone with a new name inscribed upon it known only to him who receives it.'

"To the angel of the church at Thyatira write as follows: 18

"'These are the words of the Son of God who has eyes like a flame of fire, and feet resembling silver-bronze. I know 19 your doings, your love, your faith, your service, and your patient endurance; and that of late you have toiled harder than you did at first. Yet I have this against you, that you tol- 20 erate the woman Jezebel, who calls herself a prophetess and by her teaching leads astray My servants, so that they commit fornication and eat what has been sacrificed to idols. I 21 have given her time to repent, but she is determined not to repent of her fornication. I tell you that I am about to cast her 22 upon a bed of sickness, and I will severely afflict those who commit adultery with her, unless they repent of conduct such as hers. Her children too shall surely die; and all the 23 churches shall come to know that I am He who searches into men's inmost thoughts; and I will requite [repay] each of you in accordance with his deeds. But to you, the rest of you in 24 Thyatira, all who do not hold this teaching and have not learned the "deep things," as they call them (the deep things of Satan!)—to you I say that I lay no other burden on you. Only hold fast to what you possess until I come. 25

"'And to the victor, the one who obeys my commands to 26 the very end, I will give authority over the nations. And he 27 shall be their shepherd, ruling them with a rod of iron, just as potter's ware is dashed to atoms; and his power over them shall be like that which I Myself have received from My Father; and I will give him the Morning Star. Let all who have 28 ears give heed to what the Spirit is saying to the churches.' 29

3 "To the angel of the church at Sardis write as follows: 1 "'These are the words of Him who has the seven Spirits of God and the seven stars. I know your doings—you are supposed to be alive, but in reality you are dead. Rouse yourself 2 and keep awake, and strengthen what still remains though it is on the point of death; for I have found no doings of yours perfect in the sight of My God. Be mindful, therefore, of the lessons 3 you have received and heard. Continually lay them to heart, and repent. If, however, you fail to rouse yourself and keep awake, I shall come upon you suddenly like a thief, and you will certainly not know the hour at which I shall come to judge you. Yet you have in Sardis a few who have not soiled their garments; 4 and they shall walk with Me in white; for they are worthy.

"'He who conquers shall thus be clothed in white gar- 5 ments; and never will I erase his name from the Book of Life, but will acknowledge him in the presence of My Father and His angels. Let all who have ears give heed to what the Spirit 6 is saying to the churches.'

"To the angel of the church at Philadelphia write as follows: 7

"'These are the words of Him who is Holy and True—He who has the key of David—He who opens and no one shall shut, and shuts and no one shall open. I know your doings. I 8 have put a door wide open in front of you, which no one can shut; because you have but a little power, and yet you have kept My word and have not disowned Me. I will cause some 9 belonging to Satan's synagogue who say that they themselves are Jews, and are not, but are liars—I will make them come and prostrate themselves before your feet and know for certain that I have loved you. Because you have kept the 10 word for which I suffered, I in turn will keep you from that hour of trial which is soon coming upon the whole world, to put to the test the inhabitants of the earth. I am coming 11 quickly: hold fast to that which you already possess, so that your crown of victory be not taken away from you.

"'As for the victor—I will make him a pillar in the sanctu- 12 ary of My God, and he shall never go out from it again. And I will write on him the name of My God, and the name of the city of My God, the new Jerusalem, which is to come down out of heaven from My God, and My own new name. Let all who have ears give heed to what the Spirit is saying to 13 the churches.'

"And to the angel of the church at Laodicea write 14 as follows:

"'These are the words of Him who is the Amen—the Witness faithful and true, the Beginning of God's creation. I 15 know your doings—you are neither cold nor hot; I would that you were cold or hot! So, because you are lukewarm and 16 neither hot nor cold, before long I will vomit you out of My mouth. You say, I am rich, and have wealth stored up, and I 17 stand in need of nothing; and you do not know that if there is a wretched creature it is you—pitiable, poor, blind, naked.

Therefore I counsel you to buy of Me gold refined in the fire 18
that you may become rich, and white robes to put on to hide
your shameful nakedness, and eye-salve to anoint your eyes
with, so that you may be able to see. All whom I hold dear, I 19
reprove and chastise; therefore be in earnest and repent. See, 20
I am now standing at the door and knocking. If any one listens to My voice and opens the door, I will come in to him,
and feast with him, and he shall feast with Me.

"'To the victor I will give the privilege of sitting down 21
beside Me on My throne, as I also have won the victory and
have sat down beside My Father on His throne. Let all 22
who have ears give heed to what the Spirit is saying to
the churches.'"

A Vision of God on His Throne

4 After all this I looked and saw a door in heaven standing 1
open; and the voice that I had previously heard, like the
blast of a trumpet, again spoke to me and said,

"Come up here, and I will show you things which are to
happen in the future."

Immediately I found myself in the Spirit, and saw a throne 2
in heaven, and One sitting on the throne. The appearance of 3
Him who sat there was like jasper or sardius; and encircling
the throne was a rainbow, in appearance like an emerald.
Surrounding the throne there were also twenty-four other 4
thrones, on which sat twenty-four elders clothed in white
robes, with golden crowns upon their heads.

Out from the throne there came flashes of lightning, and 5
voices, and peals of thunder, while in front of the throne
seven blazing torches were burning, which are the seven
Spirits of God. And in front of the throne there seemed to 6

be a sea of glass, resembling crystal. And round about the throne, between it and the elders, were four living creatures, full of eyes in front and behind. The first living 7 creature resembled a lion, the second an ox, the third had a face like that of a man, and the fourth resembled an eagle flying. And the four living creatures had each of them six 8 wings, and all round their bodies and under their wings they are full of eyes; day after day, and night after night, they never cease saying,

"Holy, holy, holy, Lord God, the Ruler of all, who wast and art and art to be."

And whenever the living creatures give glory and honor 9 and thanks to Him who is seated on the throne and lives for ever and ever, the twenty-four elders fall down before Him 10 who sits on the throne and worship Him who lives for ever and ever, and they cast their crowns down in front of the throne, saying,

"Worthy art Thou, our Lord and God, to receive glory and 11 honor and power,
For Thou didst create all things,
And it was by Thy will that they came into existence, and were created."

The Breaking of the Seven Seals

5 And I saw in the right hand of Him who sat on the 1 throne a book written on both sides of the page and closely sealed with seven seals. And I saw a mighty angel 2 who was exclaiming in a loud voice,

"Who is worthy to open the book and break its seals?"

But no one in heaven, or on earth, or under the earth, was 3 able to open the book or look into it.

And while I was weeping bitterly, because no one was 4
found worthy to open the book or look into it, one of the 5
elders said to me,

"Do not weep. The Lion which belongs to the tribe of
Judah, the Root of David, has won the right to open the book
and break its seven seals."

Then I saw, between the throne (with the four living 6
creatures) and the elders, a Lamb standing, looking as if it
had been slain. And it had seven horns and seven eyes,
which are the seven Spirits of God who have been sent far
and wide into all the earth. And it came and took the book 7
out of the right hand of Him who is seated on the throne.
And when He had taken the book, the four living creatures 8
and the twenty-four elders fell down before the Lamb, having each of them a harp and golden bowls full of incense,
which represent the prayers of the saints. And now they sing 9
a new song, saying,

"Worthy art Thou to take the book
And break its seals;
Because Thou hast been slain,
And hast purchased for God with Thine own blood
Men out of every tribe and tongue and people and nation,
And hast formed them into a Kingdom to be priests to 10
our God,
And they shall reign over the earth."

And I looked, and heard the voices of many angels on 11
every side of the throne, and of the living creatures and the
elders, numbering myriads of myriads and thousands of
thousands, and in loud voices they were singing, 12

"Worthy is the Lamb which has been slain to receive all
power and riches and wisdom and might and honor and
glory and blessing."

And I heard every created thing in heaven and on earth and 13
under the earth and on the sea (and all that is therein) saying,

"To Him who is seated on the throne,
And to the Lamb,
Be ascribed all blessing and honor
And glory and dominion,
For ever and ever!"

Then the four living creatures said "Amen," and the elders 14
fell down and worshiped.

6 And when the Lamb broke one of the seven seals I saw 1
it, and I heard one of the four living creatures say, as if
in a voice of thunder,

"Come."

And I looked, and a white horse appeared, and its rider 2
carried a bow; and a crown was given to him; and he went
out conquering and to conquer.

And when the Lamb broke the second seal, I heard the 3
second living creature say,

"Come."

And out came another horse—a fiery-red one; and power 4
was given to its rider to take peace from the earth, and to
cause men to kill one another; and a great sword was given
to him.

When the Lamb broke the third seal, I heard the third 5
living creature say,

"Come."

I looked, and a black horse appeared, its rider carrying a
balance in his hand. And I heard what seemed to be a voice 6
speaking in the midst of the four living creatures, and saying,

"A whole day's wage for a loaf of bread, a whole day's wage
for three barley cakes, but do not damage the oil or the wine."

When the Lamb broke the fourth seal, I heard the voice of 7
the fourth living creature say,

"Come."

I looked and a pale-colored horse appeared. Its rider's 8
name was Death, and Hades came close behind him; and
authority was given to them over the fourth part of the earth,
to kill with the sword or with famine or pestilence or by
means of the wild beasts of the earth.

When the Lamb broke the fifth seal, I saw at the foot of the 9
altar the souls of those whose lives had been sacrificed
because of the word of God and of the testimony which they
had given. And now in loud voices they cried out, saying, 10

"How long, O Sovereign Lord, the holy One and the true,
dost Thou delay judgment and the taking of vengeance upon
the inhabitants of the earth for our blood?"

And there was given to each of them a long white robe, 11
and they were bidden to wait patiently for a short time
longer, until the full number of their fellow bondservants
should also be complete—namely of their brethren who
were to be killed just as they had been.

When the Lamb broke the sixth seal, I looked, and there 12
was a great earthquake, and the sun became as dark as sackcloth, and the whole disk of the moon became like blood.
The stars in the sky also fell to the earth, as when a fig-tree, 13
shaken by a gale of wind, casts its unripe figs to the ground.
The sky too passed away, as if a scroll were being rolled up, 14
and every mountain and island was removed from its place.
The kings of the earth and the great men, the military chiefs, 15
the wealthy and the powerful—all, whether slaves or free
men—hid themselves in the caves and in the rocks of the
mountains, while they called to the mountains and the 16
rocks, saying,

"Fall on us and hide us from the presence of Him who sits on the throne and from the anger of the Lamb; for the 17 day of His wrath—that great day—has come, and who is able to stand?"

7 After this I saw four angels standing at the four corners 1 of the earth, and holding back the four winds of the earth so that no wind should blow over the earth or the sea or upon any tree. And I saw another angel ascending from 2 the east and carrying a seal belonging to the ever-living God. He called in a loud voice to the four angels whose work it was to injure the earth and the sea.

"Injure neither land nor sea nor trees," he said, "until we have 3 sealed the bondservants of our God upon their foreheads."

When the sealing was finished, I heard how many were 4 sealed out of all the tribes of the descendants of Israel. They were one hundred and forty-four thousand.

Of the tribe of Judah, twelve thousand were sealed; 5
Of the tribe of Reuben, twelve thousand;
Of the tribe of Gad, twelve thousand;
Of the tribe of Asher, twelve thousand; 6
Of the tribe of Naphtali, twelve thousand;
Of the tribe of Manasseh, twelve thousand;
Of the tribe of Symeon, twelve thousand; 7
Of the tribe of Levi, twelve thousand;
Of the tribe of Issachar, twelve thousand;
Of the tribe of Zebulun, twelve thousand; 8
Of the tribe of Joseph, twelve thousand;
Of the tribe of Benjamin, twelve thousand.

After this I looked, and a vast host appeared, which it was 9 impossible for any one to count, gathered out of every nation and from all tribes and peoples and languages, standing before the throne and before the Lamb, clothed in long white robes, and carrying palm-branches in their hands. In loud voices they cried, 10

"To our God seated on the throne, and to the Lamb, we owe our salvation!"

All the angels were standing in a circle round the throne 11 and round the elders and the four living creatures, and they fell on their faces in front of the throne and worshiped God.

"Amen!" they cried: 12

"The blessing and the glory

And the wisdom and the thanks

And the honor and the power and the might

Be ascribed to our God,

For ever and ever!

Amen!"

Then, addressing me, one of the elders said, 13

"Who are these people clothed in the long white robes? And where have they come from?"

"My lord, you know," I replied. 14

"They are those," he said, "who have just come out of the great distress, and have washed their robes and made them white in the blood of the Lamb. For this reason they stand 15 before the very throne of God, and render Him service day and night in His sanctuary, and He who is sitting upon the throne will shelter them in His tent. Nevermore shall they 16 hunger, nevermore shall they thirst, nevermore shall the sun smite them nor any scorching heat. For the Lamb who is 17 before the throne will be their Shepherd, and will guide them to the water-springs of Life, and God will wipe every tear from their eyes."

8 When the Lamb broke the seventh seal, there was 1
silence in heaven for about half an hour.

The Sounding of the Seven Trumpets

Then I saw the seven angels who are in the presence of 2
God, and seven trumpets were given to them. And another 3
angel went and stood close to the altar, carrying a censer of
gold; and abundance of incense was given to him that he
might place it with the prayers of all the saints upon the
golden altar in front of the throne. And the smoke of the 4
incense rose into the presence of God from the angel's hand,
and mingled with the prayers of His people. So the angel 5
took the censer and filled it with fire from the altar and flung
it to the earth; and there followed peals of thunder, and
voices, and flashes of lightning, and an earthquake.

Then the seven angels who had the seven trumpets made 6
preparations for blowing them.

The first blew his trumpet; and there came hail and fire, 7
mixed with blood, falling upon the earth; and a third part
of the earth was burned up, and a third part of the trees and
all the green grass.

The second angel blew his trumpet; and what seemed to 8
be a great mountain, all ablaze with fire, was hurled into the
sea; and a third part of the sea was turned into blood. And a 9
third part of the living creatures that were in the sea died;
and a third part of the ships were destroyed.

The third angel blew his trumpet; and there fell from 10
heaven a great star, blazing like a torch. It fell upon a third
part of the rivers and upon the springs of water. The name of 11
the star is "Wormwood"; and a third part of the waters were
turned into wormwood, and many people died from drinking the water, because it had become bitter.

Then the fourth angel blew his trumpet; and a third part of 12
the sun was smitten, a third part of the moon, and a third
part of the stars, so that a third part of them might be darkened, and for a third of the day, and also of the night, there
might be no light.

Then I looked, and I heard a solitary eagle crying in a 13
loud voice, as it flew across the sky, "Alas, alas, alas, for the
inhabitants of the earth, because of the trumpet blasts which
the three angels are about to blow!"

9 The fifth angel blew his trumpet; and I saw a star which 1
had fallen from heaven to the earth; and to him was
given the key of the depths of the bottomless pit, and he 2
opened the depths of the bottomless pit. And smoke came
up out of the pit like the smoke of a vast furnace, so that the
sun and the air were darkened by the smoke of the pit.

And from the midst of the smoke there came locusts on to 3
the earth, and power was given to them like the power which
earthly scorpions possess. And they were forbidden to injure 4
the herbage of the earth, or any green thing, or any tree. They
were only to injure human beings who have not the seal of
God on their foreheads. Their mission was not to kill, but to 5
cause awful agony for five months; and this agony was like
that which a scorpion inflicts when it stings a man. And at 6
that time people will seek death, but will not find it, and they
will long to die, but death evades them.

The appearance of the locusts was like that of horses 7
equipped for war. On their heads they had a kind of crown
which looked like gold. Their faces seemed human and they 8
had hair like women's hair, but their teeth resembled those
of lions. They had breastplates which seemed to be made of 9
iron; and the noise caused by their wings was like that of a

vast number of horses and chariots hurrying into battle. They had tails like those of scorpions, and also stings; and in their tails lay their power of injuring mankind for five months. 10

The locusts had a king over them—the angel of the bottomless pit, whose name in Hebrew is "Abaddon," while in Greek he is called "Apollyon." The first woe is past; two other woes have still to come. 11 12

The sixth angel blew his trumpet; and I heard a voice speaking from the four horns of the golden altar which is in the presence of God. It said to the sixth angel—the angel who had the trumpet— 13 14

"Set at liberty the four angels who are prisoners near the great river Euphrates."

And the four angels who had been kept in readiness for that hour, day, month, and year, were set at liberty, so that they might kill a third part of mankind. The number of the squadrons of their cavalry was two hundred millions; I heard their number. 15 16

And this was the appearance of the horses and their riders as I saw them in my vision. The riders had breastplates which were red as fire, blue as jacinth, and yellow as sulfur; and the horses' heads were like those of lions, while from their mouths there came fire and smoke and sulfur. By these three plagues a third part of mankind was destroyed—by the fire and the smoke, and by the sulfur which came from their mouths. For the power of the horses is in their mouths and in their tails; their tails are like serpents: they have heads and it is with these that they do the damage. 17 18 19

But the rest of mankind, who were not killed by these plagues, did not even then repent and leave the things they had made, so as to cease worshiping the demons, and the idols of gold and silver, bronze, stone, and wood, which can neither see, nor hear, nor move. Nor did they repent of 20 21 their murders, their practice of magic, their fornication, or their thefts.

10 Then I saw another strong angel coming down from heaven. He was robed in a cloud, and over his head was the rainbow. His face was like the sun, and his feet resembled pillars of fire. In his hand he held a small scroll unrolled; and, planting his right foot on the sea and his left foot on the land, he cried out in a loud voice like the roar of a lion. And when he had cried out, each of the seven peals of thunder uttered its own message. And when the seven peals of thunder had spoken, I was about to write down what they had said; but I heard a voice from heaven saying, "Keep secret what the seven peals of thunder have spoken, do not write it."

Then the angel that I saw standing on the sea and on the land, lifted his right hand toward heaven. And in the name of Him who lives for ever and ever, the Creator of heaven and all that is in it, of the earth and all that is in it, and of the sea and all that is in it, he solemnly declared,

"There shall be no further delay; but in the days when the seventh angel blows his trumpet, when he begins to blow, then is the secret purpose of God fulfilled according to the message which He gave to His servants the prophets."

Then the voice which I had heard speaking from heaven once more addressed me, saying,

"Go and take the small scroll which lies open in the hand of the angel who is standing on the sea and on the land."

So I went to the angel and asked him to give me the small scroll.

"Take it," he said, "and eat the whole of it. It will give you great pain when you have eaten it, although in your mouth it will taste as sweet as honey."

So I took the scroll out of the angel's hand and ate the whole 10 of it; and in my mouth it was as sweet as honey, but when I had eaten it it gave me great pain. And a voice said to me, 11

"You must prophesy yet further concerning peoples, nations, languages, and many kings."

11 Then a reed was given me to serve as a measuring 1 rod; and a voice said,

"Rise, and measure God's sanctuary—and the altar—and count the worshipers who are in it. But as for the court which 2 is outside the sanctuary, pass it over. Do not measure it; for it has been given to the Gentiles, and for forty-two months they will trample the holy city under foot. And I will author- 3 ize My two witnesses to prophesy for one thousand two hundred and sixty days, clothed in sackcloth.

"These witnesses are the two olive-trees, and they are the 4 two lamps which stand in the presence of the Lord of the earth. And if any one seeks to injure them—fire comes 5 from their mouths and devours their enemies; and if any one shall seek to injure them, he will in this way certainly be killed. They have power given to them to seal up the sky, so 6 that no rain may fall so long as they continue to prophesy; and power over the waters to turn them into blood, and to smite the earth with various plagues whenever they choose to do so.

"And when they have fully delivered their testimony, the 7 Wild Beast which is to rise out of the bottomless pit will make war upon them and overcome them and kill them. And their 8 dead bodies are to lie in the broad street of the great city which is mystically called "Sodom" and "Egypt," where indeed their Lord was crucified. And men belonging to all peoples, 9 tribes, languages, and nations gaze at their dead bodies for three days and a half, and they refuse to let them be laid in a tomb. The inhabitants of the earth rejoice over them and are 10 glad and will send gifts to one another; for these two prophets had greatly troubled the inhabitants of the earth."

But at the end of the three days and a half the breath of life 11 from God entered into them, and they rose to their feet; and all who saw them were terrified. Then they heard a loud 12 voice calling to them out of heaven, "Come up here"; and they went up to heaven in the cloud, and their enemies saw them go. And just at that time there was a great earthquake, 13 and a tenth part of the city was overthrown. Seven thousand people were killed in the earthquake, and the rest were terrified and gave glory to the God of heaven. The second woe is 14 past; the third woe will soon be here.

The seventh angel blew his trumpet; and there followed 15 loud voices in heaven which said,

"The sovereignty of the world now belongs to our Lord and His Christ; and He will be King for ever and ever."

Then the twenty-four elders, who sit on thrones in the pres- 16 ence of God, fell on their faces and worshiped God, saying, 17

"We give thee thanks, O Lord God, the Ruler of all,
Who art and wast,
Because Thou hast exerted Thy power, Thy great power,
and hast become King.
The nations grew wrathful, 18
And Thy wrath has come,
And the time for the dead to be judged,
And the time for Thee to give their reward to Thy servants
the prophets and to Thy people,
And to those who fear Thee, the small and the great,
And to destroy those who destroy the earth."

Then the doors of God's sanctuary in heaven were opened, 19 and the ark, in which His covenant was, was seen in His sanctuary; and there came flashes of lightning, and voices, and peals of thunder, and an earthquake, and a storm of hail.

A Series of Marvels

12 And a great marvel was seen in heaven—a woman 1 who was robed with the sun and had the moon under her feet, and had also a crown of twelve stars round her head, was with child, and she was crying out in the pains 2 and agony of childbirth.

And another marvel was seen in heaven—a great fiery-red 3 dragon, with seven heads and ten horns; and on his heads were seven kingly crowns. His tail was drawing after it a third 4 part of the stars of heaven, and it dashed them to the ground. And in front of the woman who was about to become a mother, the dragon was standing in order to devour the child as soon as it was born. She gave birth to a son—a male child, 5 destined before long to rule all nations with an iron scepter. But her child was caught up to God and His throne, and the 6 woman fled into the desert, there to be cared for, for twelve hundred and sixty days, in a place which God had prepared for her.

And war broke out in heaven, Michael and his angels 7 engaging in battle with the dragon. The dragon fought and so did his angels; but they were defeated, and there was 8 no longer any room found for them in heaven. The great 9 dragon, the ancient serpent, he who is called "the Devil" and "Satan" and leads the whole earth astray, was hurled down: he was hurled down to the earth, and his angels were hurled down with him.

Then I heard a loud voice speaking in heaven. It said, 10
"Now is come the salvation and the power and the king-dom of our God, and the sovereignty of His Christ; for the accuser of our brethren has been hurled down—he who, day after day and night after night, was wont [accustomed] to accuse them in the presence of God. But they have gained 11 the victory over him because of the blood of the Lamb and of the testimony which they have borne, and because they held their lives cheap and did not shrink even from death. For this 12 reason be glad, O Heaven, and you who live therein! Alas for the earth and the sea! For the devil has gone down to you full of fierce anger, because he knows that his appointed time is short."

And when the dragon saw that he was hurled down to the 13 earth, he went in pursuit of the woman who had given birth to the male child. Then the two wings of a great eagle were 14 given to the woman to enable her to fly away into the desert to the place assigned her, there to be cared for, for a period of time, two periods of time, and half a period of time, be-yond the reach of the serpent. And the serpent poured water 15 from his mouth—a very river it seemed—after the woman, in the hope that she would be carried away by its flood. But 16 the earth came to the woman's help: it opened its mouth and drank up the river which the dragon had poured from his mouth. This made the dragon furiously angry with the 17 woman, and he went elsewhere to make war upon her other children—those who keep God's commandments and hold fast to the testimony of Jesus.

13 And he took up a position upon the sands of the 1 sea-shore.

Then I saw a Wild Beast coming up out of the sea, and he

had ten horns and seven heads. On his horns were ten kingly crowns, and inscribed on his heads were names full of blasphemy. The Wild Beast which I saw resembled a leopard, and 2 had feet like the feet of a bear, and his mouth was like the mouth of a lion; and it was to the dragon that he owed his power and his throne and his wide dominion.

I saw that one of his heads seemed to have been mortally 3 wounded; but his mortal wound was healed, and the whole world was amazed and followed him. And they offered wor- 4 ship to the dragon, because it was to him that the Wild Beast owed his dominion; and they also offered worship to the Wild Beast, and said,

"Who is there like him? And who is able to engage in battle with him?"

And there was given him a mouth full of boastful and blas- 5 phemous words; and liberty of action was granted him for forty-two months. And he opened his mouth to utter blas- 6 phemies against God, to speak evil of His name and of His dwelling-place—that is to say, of those who dwell in heaven. And permission was given him to make war upon God's 7 people and conquer them; and authority was given him over every tribe, people, language, and nation. And all the inhabit- 8 ants of the earth will be found to be worshiping him: every one whose name is not recorded in the Book of Life—the book of the Lamb offered in sacrifice from the creation of the world.

Let all who have ears give heed. If any one is eager to lead 9 others into captivity, he must himself go into captivity. If any 10 one is bent on killing with the sword, he must himself be killed by the sword. Here is an opportunity for endurance, and for the exercise of faith, on the part of the saints.

Then I saw another Wild Beast, coming up out of the earth. 11 He had two horns like those of a lamb, but he spoke like a dragon. And the authority of the first Wild Beast—the whole 12 of that authority—he exercises in his presence, and he causes the earth and its inhabitants to worship the first Wild Beast, whose mortal wound had been healed. He also works 13 great miracles, so as even to make fire come down from heaven to earth in the presence of human beings. And his 14 power of leading astray the inhabitants of the earth is due to the marvels which he has been permitted to work in the presence of the Wild Beast. And he told the inhabitants of the earth to erect a statue to the Wild Beast who had received the sword-stroke and yet had recovered. And power was 15 granted him to give breath to the statue of the Wild Beast, so that the statue of the Wild Beast could even speak and cause all who refuse to worship it to be put to death. And he causes 16 all, small and great, rich and poor, free men and slaves, to have stamped upon them a mark on their right hands or on their foreheads, in order that no one should be allowed to 17 buy or sell unless he had the mark—either the name of the Wild Beast or the number which his name represents.

Here is scope for ingenuity. Let people of shrewd intelli- 18 gence calculate the number of the Wild Beast; for it indicates a certain man, and his number is six hundred and sixty-six.

14 Then I looked and I saw the Lamb standing upon 1 Mount Zion, and with Him one hundred and forty-four thousand people, having His name and His Father's name written on their foreheads. And I heard music from 2 heaven which resembled the sound of many waters and the roar of loud thunder; and the music which I heard was like that of harpists playing upon their harps. And they were 3 singing what seemed to be a new song, in front of the throne and in the presence of the four living creatures and the elders; and no one was able to learn that song except the one hundred and forty-four thousand people who had been redeemed out of the world.

These are those who had not defiled themselves with 4 women: they are as pure as virgins. They follow the Lamb wherever He goes. They have been redeemed from among men, as firstfruits to God and to the Lamb. And no lie has 5 ever been found upon their lips: they are faultless.

Four Voices From Heaven

And I saw another angel flying across the sky, carrying 6 the eternal gospel to tell to every nation, tribe, language, and people among those who live on the earth. He said in a 7 loud voice,

"Fear God and give Him glory, because the time of His judgment has come; and worship Him who made heaven and earth, the sea and the water-springs."

And another, a second angel, followed, exclaiming, 8

"Fallen, fallen is Babylon the great—she who made all the nations drink the wine of the anger provoked by her fornication."

And another, a third angel, followed them, exclaiming in a 9 loud voice,

"If any one worships the Wild Beast and his statue, and receives a mark on his forehead or on his hand, he shall drink 10 the wine of God's wrath which stands ready, undiluted, in the cup of His anger, and he shall be tormented with fire and brimstone in the presence of the holy angels and of the Lamb. And 11 the smoke of their torment goes up for ever and ever; and the worshipers of the Wild Beast and of his statue have no rest day or night, nor has any one who receives the mark of his name. Here is an opportunity for endurance on the part of the saints 12 who carefully keep His commandments and the faith of Jesus!"

And I heard a voice speaking from heaven. It said, 13
"Write as follows:

"'Blessed are the dead who die in the Lord from this time onward. Yes, says the Spirit, let them rest from their labors; for what they have done goes with them.'"

Then I looked, and a white cloud appeared, and sitting on 14 the cloud was One resembling the Son of Man, having a crown of gold upon His head and in His hand a sharp sickle. And another angel came out of the sanctuary, calling in a 15 loud voice to Him who sat on the cloud, and saying,

"Thrust in your sickle and reap the harvest, for the hour for reaping it has come: the harvest of the earth is over-ripe."

Then He who sat on the cloud flung His sickle on the 16 earth, and the earth had its harvest reaped.

And another angel came out from the sanctuary in heaven, 17 and he too carried a sharp sickle. And another angel came 18 from the altar—he who has power over fire—and he spoke in a loud voice to him who had the sharp sickle, saying,

"Thrust in your sharp sickle, and gather the bunches from the vine of the earth, for its grapes are now quite ripe."

And the angel flung his sickle down to the earth, and 19 reaped the vine of the earth and threw the grapes into the great winepress of God's wrath. And the winepress was trod- 20 den outside the city, and out of it came blood reaching the horses' bridles for a distance of two hundred miles.

The Seven Plagues

15 Then I saw another marvel in heaven, great and 1 wonderful—there were seven angels bringing seven plagues. These are the last plagues, because in them the wrath of God has reached its climax.

And I saw what seemed to be a sea of glass mingled with 2
fire, and those who had gained the victory over the Wild
Beast and over his statue and the number of his name,
standing by the sea of glass with harps of God in their hands.
And they were singing the song of Moses, God's servant, and 3
the song of the Lamb. Their words were,

"Great and wonderful are Thy works,
O Lord God Omnipotent.
Righteous and true are Thy ways,
O King of the nations.
Who shall not be afraid, O Lord, and glorify Thy name? 4
For Thou alone art holy.
All nations shall come and shall worship Thee,
Because Thy righteous acts have been made manifest."

After this I looked and the sanctuary of the tent of witness 5
in heaven was thrown open; and there came out of the sanc- 6
tuary the seven angels with the seven plagues, clad in pure,
bright linen, and wearing girdles of gold across their breasts.
And one of the four living creatures gave the seven angels 7
seven bowls of gold, full of the wrath of God who lives for
ever and ever. And the sanctuary was filled with cloud from 8
the glory of God and from His power; and no one could enter
the sanctuary till the seven plagues brought by the seven
angels were at an end.

16 Then I heard a loud voice from the sanctuary say to 1
the seven angels,

"Go and pour on to the earth the seven bowls of the wrath
of God."

So the first angel went away and poured his bowl on to the 2
earth; and it brought noisome and grievous sores upon the

men who had on them the mark of the Wild Beast and worshiped his statue.

The second angel poured his bowl into the sea, and it became blood, like a dead man's blood, and every living creature in the sea died. 3

The third angel poured his bowl into the rivers and springs of water, and they became blood. And I heard the angel of the waters say, 4 5

"Righteous art Thou, who art and wast, the holy One, because Thou hast thus executed judgment. For they poured out the blood of Thy people and of the prophets, and in return Thou hast given them blood to drink. And this they deserved." 6

And I heard a voice from the altar say, 7

"Amen, O Lord God, the Ruler of all, true and righteous are Thy judgments."

Then the fourth angel poured his bowl on to the sun, and power was given to it to scorch men with fire. And the men were burned by a fierce heat; and yet they spoke evil of God who had power over the plagues, and they did not repent so as to give Him glory. 8 9

The fifth angel poured his bowl on to the throne of the Wild Beast; and his kingdom became darkened. People gnawed their tongues in anguish, and yet they spoke evil of the God in heaven because of their pains and their sores, and did not repent of their deeds. 10 11

The sixth angel poured his bowl into that great river, the Euphrates; and its stream was dried up in order to clear the way for the kings who are to come from the east. Then I saw three foul spirits, resembling frogs, issue from the mouth of the dragon, from the mouth of the Wild Beast, and from the mouth of the false Prophet. For they are the spirits of demons working miracles—spirits that go out to control the kings of the whole earth, to assemble them for the 12 13 14 battle which is to take place on the great day of God, the Ruler of all.

("I am coming like a thief. Blessed is the man who keeps 15 awake and guards his raiment for fear he walk about naked, and men see his shame.")

And assemble them they did at the place called in Hebrew 16 "Har-Magedon."

Then the seventh angel poured his bowl into the air; 17 and a loud voice came out of the sanctuary from the throne, saying,

"It is all accomplished."

Flashes of lightning followed, and loud blasts, and peals of 18 thunder, and an earthquake more dreadful than there had ever been since there was a man upon the earth—so terrible was it, and so great! The great city was split into three parts; 19 the cities of the nations fell; and great Babylon came into remembrance before God, for Him to make her drink from the wine-cup of His fierce anger. Every island fled away, and there 20 was not a mountain anywhere to be seen. And heavy hail, that 21 seemed to be a talent in weight, fell from the sky upon the people; and they spoke evil of God on account of the plague of the hail—because the plague of it was exceedingly severe.

The Great Harlot

17 Then one of the seven angels who were carrying the 1 seven bowls came and spoke to me.

"Come with me," he said, "and I will show you the doom of the great Harlot who sits upon many waters. The kings of the 2 earth have committed fornication with her, and the inhabitants of the earth have been made drunk with the wine of her fornication."

So he carried me away in the Spirit into a desert, and there 3
I saw a woman sitting on a scarlet-colored Wild Beast which
was covered with names of blasphemy and had seven heads
and ten horns. The woman was clothed in purple and scar- 4
let, and was brilliantly attired with gold and jewels and
pearls. She held in her hand a cup of gold, full of abominations and the impurities of her fornication. And on her fore- 5
head was a name written which is symbolical of

"Babylon, the great mother of the harlots and of the
abominations of the earth."

And I saw the woman drinking herself drunk with the blood 6
of the saints, and with the blood of the witnesses of Jesus. And
when I saw her I was filled with utter astonishment.

Then the angel said to me, 7

"Why are you so astonished? I will explain to you the
secret meaning of the woman and of the seven-headed, ten-
horned Wild Beast which carries her.

"The Wild Beast which you have seen was, and is not, and 8
yet is destined to re-ascend, before long, out of the bottomless pit and go his way into perdition. And the inhabitants of
the earth will be filled with amazement—all whose names
have not been inscribed in the Book of Life from the foundation of the world—when they see the Wild Beast: because he
was, and is not, and yet is to come. Here is scope for the exer- 9
cise of a mind that has wisdom! The seven heads are the
seven hills on which the woman sits. And they are seven 10
kings: five of them have fallen, and one is still reigning. The
seventh has not yet come, but when he comes he must continue for a short time. And the Wild Beast which once existed 11
but does not now exist—he is an eighth king and yet is one
of the seven, and he goes his way into perdition.

"And the ten horns which you have seen are ten kings who 12
have not yet come to the throne, but for a single hour they

are to receive authority as kings along with the Wild Beast. They have one common policy, and they are to give their 13 power and authority to the Wild Beast. They will make war 14 upon the Lamb, and the Lamb will triumph over them; for He is Lord of lords and King of kings. And those who accompany Him—called, as they are, and chosen, and faithful—shall share in the victory."

He also said to me, 15

"The waters which you have seen, on which the Harlot sits, are peoples and multitudes, nations and languages. And 16 the ten horns that you have seen—and the Wild Beast—these will hate the Harlot, and they will make her desolate and will strip her bare. They will eat her flesh, and burn her up with fire. For God has put it into their hearts to carry out 17 His purpose with one intent, and to give their kingdom to the Wild Beast until God's words have been fulfilled. And the 18 woman whom you have seen is the great city which reigns over the kings of the earth."

The Downfall of Babylon

18 After these things I saw another angel coming down 1 from heaven, armed with great authority. The earth was illumined with his splendor, and with a mighty voice he 2 cried out, saying,

"Fallen, fallen is Babylon the great,
She has become the haunt of demons
And the abode of every kind of foul spirit
And every kind of foul and hateful bird.
For all the nations have drunk of the wrath-provoking 3
wine of her fornication,

And the kings of the earth have committed fornication with her,

And the merchants of the earth have grown rich through her excessive wantonness."

Then I heard another voice from heaven, which said, 4

"Come out of her, My people,

That you may not become partakers in her sins,

Nor receive a share of her plagues.

For her sins are piled up to the sky, 5

And God has called her misdeeds to mind.

Give back to her as she has given; 6

Render unto her double for all her crimes;

In the bowl that she has mixed, mix twice as much for her.

As she has exulted and reveled in wantonness, 7

Pay back to her an equal measure of torment and woe.

For in her heart she boasts, saying, 'I sit enthroned as Queen:

No widow am I: I shall never know sorrow.'

For this reason calamities shall come thick upon her on a 8 single day—

Death and sorrow and famine—

And she shall be burned to the ground.

For strong is the Lord God who has judged her.

The kings of the earth who have committed fornication 9 and acted wantonly with her

Shall weep aloud and lament over her

When they see the smoke of her burning,

While they stand afar off because of their terror at 10 her doom,

And say, 'Alas, alas, thou great city, O Babylon, the mighty city!

For in one short hour thy doom has come!'

And the merchants of the earth weep aloud and lament 11 over her,

Because now there is no sale for their cargoes—
Cargoes of gold and silver, 12
Of jewels and pearls,
Of fine linen, purple, and silk, and of scarlet stuff;
All kinds of rare woods, and all kinds of ivory goods
And articles of costly wood,
Of bronze, steel, and marble.
Also cinnamon and balsam; 13
Odors to burn as incense or for perfume;
Frankincense, wine, oil;
Fine flour, wheat, cattle, and sheep;
Horses and carriages and slaves;
And the lives of men.
The dainties that thy soul longed for are gone from thee, 14
And all thine elegance and splendor have perished,
And never again shall they be found.
Those who traded in these things, who grew wealthy 15
through her,
Will stand afar off, through terror at her doom,
Weeping and wailing, and saying, 16
'Alas, alas, for this great city,
Which was brilliantly arrayed in fine linen, and purple and
scarlet stuff,
And richly adorned with gold, jewels, and pearls;
Because in one short hour all this great wealth has been 17
swept away!'
And every shipmaster and every passenger by sea
And the crews and all who ply their trade on the sea
Stood afar off, and cried aloud 18
When they saw the smoke of her burning. And they said,
'What city is like this great city?'
And they threw dust upon their heads, 19
And cried out, as they wept and wailed.

'Alas, alas,' they said, 'for this great city,
Where all shipowners made rich profit through her wealth;
Because in one short hour she has been laid waste!'
Rejoice over her, O heaven,   20
And you saints and apostles and prophets;
For God has taken vengeance upon her because of you."
Then a strong angel took a stone like a huge millstone, and 21
hurled it into the sea, saying,
"So shall Babylon, that great city, be violently hurled down
and never again be found.
No harp or song, no flute or trumpet, shall ever again be   22
heard in thee;
No craftsman of any kind shall ever again be found in thee;
Nor shall the grinding of the mill ever again be heard
in thee.
Never again shall the light of a lamp shine in thee,   23
And never again shall the voice of a bridegroom or of a
bride be heard in thee.
For thy merchants were the great men of the earth,
And with the magic of thy spells all nations were led astray.
And in her was found the blood of prophets and of   24
the saints
And of all who had been put to death on the earth."

19 After this I seemed to hear the far-echoing voices of a   1
great multitude in heaven, who said,
"Hallelujah!
Salvation and glory and power
Belong to our God.
True and just are His judgments,   2
Because He has judged the great Harlot who was corrupt-
ing the whole earth with her fornication,

And He has taken vengeance for the blood of His bond-servants which her hands have shed."

And a second time they said,   3

"Hallelujah!

For her smoke ascends for ever and ever."

And the twenty-four elders and the four living creatures   4 fell down and worshiped God who sits upon the throne.

"Amen," they said; "Hallelujah!"

And from the throne there came a voice which said,   5

"Praise our God, all you His bondservants—

You who fear Him, both small and great."

And I seemed to hear the voices of a great multitude and   6 the sound of many waters and of loud peals of thunder, which said,

"Hallelujah!

Because our God the Lord Omnipotent has begun His reign.

Let us rejoice and triumph   7

And give Him the glory;

For the marriage day of the Lamb has come,

And His Bride has made herself ready."

She has been allowed to robe herself in fine linen of daz-   8 zling purity—the fine linen being the righteous actions of the saints. And he said to me,   9

"Write as follows: 'Blessed are those who have been invited to the marriage banquet of the Lamb.'"

And he added, still addressing me,

"These are truly the words of God."

Then I fell at his feet to worship him. But he exclaimed,   10

"Do not do that. I am a fellow servant of yours, and a fellow servant of your brethren who hold fast the truth revealed by Jesus. Worship God."

For the truth revealed by Jesus is the inspiration of all prophecy.

Then I saw a door open in heaven, and a white horse 11 appeared. Its rider was named "Faithful and True"—One who in righteousness executes judgment and wages war. His 12 eyes were like a flame of fire, and on His head were many kingly crowns, and He has a name written upon Him which no one knows but He Himself. He is clad in raiment which 13 had been dipped in blood, and His name is THE WORD OF GOD. The armies in heaven followed Him—mounted on 14 white horses and clothed in fine linen, white and spotless. From His mouth there comes a sharp sword with which He 15 will smite the nations; and He will Himself be their shepherd, ruling them with a scepter of iron; and it is His work to tread the winepress of the fierce anger of God, the ruler of all. And on His raiment and on His thigh He has a name written, 16

KING OF KINGS AND LORD OF LORDS.

And I saw an angel standing in the sun, who cried in a loud 17 voice to all the birds that flew across the sky,

"Come and be present at God's great banquet, that you 18 may feast on the flesh of kings and the flesh of generals and the flesh of mighty men, on the flesh of horses and their riders, and on the flesh of all mankind, whether free men or slaves, great or small."

And I saw the Wild Beast, and the kings of the earth, and 19 their armies, all assembled to make war against the rider upon the horse and against His army. And the Wild Beast was 20 captured, and with him the false Prophet who had done the miracles in his presence with which he had led astray those who had received the mark of the Wild Beast, and worshiped his statue. Both of them were thrown alive into the lake of

fire that was all ablaze with sulfur. But the rest were killed 21
with the sword that came from the mouth of the rider on the
horse. And the birds all fed ravenously upon their flesh.

20 Then I saw an angel coming down from heaven with 1
the key of the bottomless pit, and in his hand a great
chain. He laid hold of the dragon—the ancient serpent— 2
who is the Devil and Satan, and bound him for a thousand
years, and hurled him into the bottomless pit. He shut it up 3
and sealed it over that he might not lead the nations astray
any more until the thousand years were at an end.
Afterwards he is to be set at liberty for a short time.

And I saw thrones, and men sat on them, to whom judicial 4
power was given. And I saw the souls of those who had been
beheaded on account of the testimony that they had borne
to Jesus and on account of the word of God, and also the
souls of those who had not worshiped the Wild Beast or his
statue, nor received his mark on their foreheads or their
hands; and they came to life and shared Christ's kingdom for
a thousand years.

The rest of the dead did not come to life until the thousand 5
years were at an end. This is the first resurrection. Blessed 6
and holy are those who share in the first resurrection. The
second death has no power over them, but they shall be
priests to God and to Christ, and shall reign with Him for the
thousand years.

But when the thousand years are at an end, Satan will be 7
released from his imprisonment, and will go out to lead 8
astray the nations in all the four corners of the earth, Gog
and Magog, and assemble them for war, in number like the
sand on the sea-shore. And they went up over the whole 9
breadth of the earth and surrounded the encampment of the

saints and the beloved city. But fire came down from heaven and consumed them; and the devil, who had been leading 10 them astray, was thrown into the lake of fire and sulfur where the Wild Beast and the false prophet were, and day and night they will suffer torture for ever and ever.

Then I saw a great white throne and One who was seated 11 on it, from whose presence earth and sky fled away, and no place was found for them. And I saw the dead, the great and 12 the small, standing in front of the throne. And books were opened; and so was another book—namely, the Book of Life; and the dead were judged by the record in the books according to their deeds. Then the sea yielded up its dead, Death 13 and Hades yielded up their dead, and each man was judged according to his deeds. Then Death and Hades were thrown 14 into the lake of fire: this is the second death—the lake of fire. And if any one's name was not found recorded in the Book of 15 Life he was thrown into the lake of fire.

The New Heaven and the New Earth

21 And I saw a new heaven and a new earth; for the first 1 heaven and the first earth had passed away, and the sea no longer existed. And I saw the holy city, the new 2 Jerusalem, coming down out of heaven from God and made ready like a bride attired to meet her husband. And I heard a 3 loud voice from the throne saying,

"Lo, God's dwelling place is among men
And He will dwell among them
And they shall be His peoples.
Yes, God Himself will be among them.
He will wipe every tear from their eyes. 4
Death shall be no more;

Nor sorrow, nor wail of woe, nor pain;
For the first things have passed away."
Then He who was seated on the throne said,   5
"See, I am making everything new."
And He added,
"Write down these words, for they are trustworthy and true."

He also said,   6
"They have now been fulfilled. I am the Alpha and the Omega, the beginning and the end. It is I who will give the thirsty man the right to drink of the fountain of the water of Life without cost. All this shall be the victor's   7 heritage, and I will be his God and he shall be a son to Me. But as for cowards and the unfaithful, and the polluted,   8 and murderers, fornicators, and those who practice magic or worship idols, and all liars—the portion allotted to them shall be in the lake which burns with fire and sulfur. This is the second death."

The Bride, the Heavenly Jerusalem

Then there came one of the seven angels who were carry-   9 ing the seven bowls full of the seven last plagues.

"Come with me," he said, "and I will show you the Bride, the Lamb's wife."

So in the Spirit he carried me to the top of a vast, lofty   10 mountain, and showed me the holy city, Jerusalem, coming down out of heaven from God, and bringing with it the glory   11 of God. It shone with a radiance like that of a very precious stone—such as a jasper, bright and transparent. It had a wall,   12 massive and high, with twelve large gates, and in charge of the gates were twelve angels. And overhead, above the gates, names were inscribed which are those of the twelve tribes of

the descendants of Israel. There were three gates on the east, 13
three on the north, three on the south, and three on the west.
The wall of the city had twelve foundation stones, and 14
engraved upon them were twelve names—the names of the
twelve apostles of the Lamb.

Now he who was speaking to me had a measuring-rod 15
of gold, with which to measure the city and its gates and
its walls. The plan of the city is a square, the length being the 16
same as the breadth; and he measured the city furlong by
furlong, with his measuring-rod—it is fifteen hundred miles
long, and the length and the breadth and the height of it are
equal. And he made the measure of the wall seventy-two 17
yards according to human, that is, angelic measurement.

The solid fabric of the wall was jasper; and the city itself 18
was made of gold, resembling transparent glass. The foun- 19
dation stones of the city wall were adorned with all kinds of
precious stones: the first was of jasper, the second of sap-
phire, the third of chalcedony, the fourth of emerald, the fifth 20
of sardonyx, the sixth of sardius, the seventh of chrysolite,
the eighth of beryl, the ninth of topaz, the tenth of chryso-
prase, the eleventh of jacinth, the twelfth of amethyst.

And the twelve gates were twelve pearls; each of them con- 21
sisting of a single pearl. And the main street of the city was
made of pure gold, resembling transparent glass.

I saw no temple in the city, for the Lord God, the Ruler of 22
all, is its temple, and so is the Lamb. Nor has the city any 23
need of the sun or of the moon, to give it light; for the glory
of God has illuminated it and its lamp is the Lamb. By its 24
light the nations will walk; and into it the kings of the earth
are to bring their glory. And in the daytime (for there will be 25
no night there) the gates will never be closed; and the glory 26
and honor of the nations shall be brought into it. And no 27
unclean thing shall ever enter it, nor any one who is guilty of

base conduct or tells lies, but only they whose names are registered in the Lamb's Book of Life.

22 Then he showed me the river of the water of Life, bright as crystal, issuing from the throne of God and of the Lamb. On either side of the river, midway between it and the main street of the city, was the tree of Life. It produced twelve kinds of fruit, yielding a fresh crop month by month, and the leaves of the tree served as medicine for the nations.

"Nothing accursed will be there." he said; "but the throne of God and of the Lamb will be in that city. And His servants will render Him holy service and will see His face, and His name will be on their foreheads. And there will be no night there; and they have no need of lamplight or sunlight, for the Lord God will illumine them, and they will be kings for ever and ever."

Conclusion

And he said to me,

"These words are trustworthy and true; and the Lord, the God of the spirits of the prophets, sent His angel to make known to His servants the things which must soon happen. 'I am coming quickly.' Blessed is he who is mindful of the prophecies contained in this book."

I John heard and saw these things; and when I had heard and seen them, I fell at the feet of the angel who was showing me them—to worship him. But he said to me,

"Do not do that. I am a fellow servant of yours, and a fellow servant of your brethren the prophets and of those who are mindful of the teachings of this book. Worship God."

"Make no secret," he added, "of the meaning of the prophecies contained in this book; for the time for their fulfillment is now close at hand. Let the dishonest man act 11 dishonestly still; let the filthy make himself filthy still; let the righteous practice righteousness still; and let the holy keep himself holy still."

"Lo, I am coming quickly; and My reward is with Me, that 12 I may requite [repay] every man according to his deeds. I am 13 the Alpha and the Omega, the First and the Last, the beginning and the end. Blessed are those who wash their robes 14 clean, that they may have a right to the tree of Life, and may enter the gates of the city. The unclean are shut out, and so 15 are all who practice magic, all fornicators, all murderers, and those who worship idols, and every one who loves falsehood and tells lies.

"I Jesus have sent My angel for him solemnly to declare 16 these things to you among the churches. I am the Root and the offspring of David, the bright Morning Star. The Spirit 17 and the Bride say, "Come"; and whoever hears, let him say, "Come"; and let those who are thirsty come. Whoever will, let him take the water of Life, without payment.

"I solemnly declare to every one who hears the words of 18 the prophecy contained in this book, that if any one adds to those words, God will add to him the plagues spoken of in this book; and that if any one takes away from the words of 19 the book of this prophecy, God will take from him his share in the tree of Life and in the holy city—the things described in this book.

"He who solemnly declares all this says, 20

"'Yes, I am coming quickly.'"

Amen. Come, Lord Jesus.

The grace of the Lord Jesus be with the saints. 21